WILLI MÜNZENBERG

Willi Münzenberg was a towering figure in the anti-fascist movement during the first half of the twentieth century. He was acquainted with many of the leading left wing activists and thinkers of his day including Lenin, Rosa Luxemburg, Karl Liebknecht, and Karl Radek. He also played a foundational role in several important transnational organisations such as the Socialist Youth International, the largest anti-war movement in opposition to the First World War, the International Workers' Relief organisation, and the League against Colonialism and for National Independence.

As a film distributor and promoter, he brought modern Soviet films to western Europe. As a publicist and manager, he built up the most influential left-wing media empire in the Weimar Republic and initiated the pioneering use of photography and photo montage. He was also a long-time member of the Reichstag. He was a pioneer in the use of a variety of media and the way he gained the support and collaboration of progressive politicians, artists and intellectuals ensured that he would become the leading, and most effective, opponent of Hitler's and Goebbels' propaganda machine, as he exposed the venality and brutality of the Nazis. Late in life, his turn against Stalinism almost certainly led to his mysterious death.

This is the first detailed biography in English to give coverage to the full range of Münzenberg's activism. There are valuable lessons to be learnt from the book about the best ways to counter fascism which are powerfully relevant to our contemporary political situation. It should be of great interest to activists, scholars and those studying the history of the radical left.

John Green is a journalist and author. He worked for two decades making television documentaries before devoting himself to writing. He has since written several biographies, including one on Friedrich Engels and this his second for Routledge. He lived in Germany for a number of years and has a keen interest in twentieth-century German political history and culture. He and his wife live and work in West London.

ROUTLEDGE STUDIES IN RADICAL HISTORY AND POLITICS

Series editors: **Thomas Linehan**, *Brunel University*, and **John Roberts**, *Brunel University*

The series *Routledge Studies in Radical History and Politics* has two areas of interest. Firstly, this series aims to publish books which focus on the history of movements of the radical left. 'Movement of the radical left' is here interpreted in its broadest sense as encompassing those past movements for radical change which operated in the mainstream political arena as with political parties, and past movements for change which operated more outside the mainstream as with millenarian movements, anarchist groups, utopian socialist communities, and trade unions. Secondly, this series aims to publish books which focus on more contemporary expressions of radical left-wing politics. Recent years have been witness to the emergence of a multitude of new radical movements adept at getting their voices in the public sphere. From those participating in the Arab Spring, the Occupy movement, community unionism, social media forums, independent media outlets, local voluntary organisations campaigning for progressive change, and so on, it seems to be the case that innovative networks of radicalism are being constructed in civil society that operate in different public forms.

The series very much welcomes titles with a British focus, but is not limited to any particular national context or region. The series will encourage scholars who contribute to it to draw on perspectives and insights from other disciplines.

For more information about this series, please visit: www.routledge.com/Routledge-Studies-in-Radical-History-and-Politics/book-series/RSRHP

Contemporary Left Wing Activism Vol 2
Democracy, Participation and Dissent in a Global Context
Edited by Joseph Ibrahim and John Michael Roberts

Cultural Protest in Journalism, Documentary Films and the Arts
Between Protest and Professionalization
Daniel H. Mutibwa

Left Radicalism and Populism in Europe
Edited by Giorgos Charalambous and Gregoris Ioannou

Orwell Reconsidered
Stephen Ingle

Willi Münzenberg
Fighter against Fascism and Stalinism
John Green

WILLI MÜNZENBERG

Fighter against Fascism and Stalinism

John Green

Routledge
Taylor & Francis Group

LONDON AND NEW YORK

First published 2020
by Routledge
2 Park Square, Milton Park, Abingdon, Oxon OX14 4RN

and by Routledge
52 Vanderbilt Avenue, New York, NY 10017

Routledge is an imprint of the Taylor & Francis Group, an informa business

British Library Cataloguing-in-Publication Data
A catalogue record for this book is available from the British Library

Library of Congress Cataloging-in-Publication Data
Names: Green, John (Biographer), author.
Title: Willi Münzenberg : fighter against fascism and Stalinism / John Green.
Description: 1 Edition. | New York : Routledge, 2020. | Series:
Routledge studies in radical history and politics | Includes
bibliographical references and index.
Identifiers: LCCN 2019036254 | ISBN 9780367344733 (hardcover) |
ISBN 9780367344726 (paperback) | ISBN 9780429326035 (ebook)
Subjects: LCSH: Münzenberg, Willi. | Communists--Germany--Biography. |
Youth movements--Germany--History. | Nazi propaganda--Germany--
History. | Propaganda, Communist--History. | Communism--
Germany--History--20th century. | Communism--Soviet Union--History.
Classification: LCC HX273 .G724 2020 | DDC 335.4092 [B]--dc23
LC record available at https://lccn.loc.gov/2019036254

ISBN: 978-0-367-34473-3 (hbk)
ISBN: 978-0-367-34472-6 (pbk)
ISBN: 978-0-429-32603-5 (ebk)

Typeset in Bembo
by Lumina Datamatics Limited

For Marla, Masha, Liliana, and Constanza

'Look in history not for the ashes but the fire'.

Lion Feuchtwanger

'Great individuals are meteors, that consume
themselves to enlighten the world'.

Napoleon

'You who will emerge from the flood in which we
drowned think when you talk of our weaknesses
also of the dark times that you have escaped'.

Bertolt Brecht

CONTENTS

LIST OF FIGURES

ACKNOWLEDGEMENTS

I would particularly like to thank the Gross family for giving me their permission to mine the rich seam of Babette Gross's biography of Willi Münzenberg, but particularly Catherine Gross who gave generously of her time to read the manuscript and pointed out a number of errors and solecisms, which I could correct in time. Any remaining errors or stylistic inconsistencies are, of course, my own.

I would also like to thank Uwe Sonnenberg at the Willi Münzenberg Forum, Berlin, Dr Kasper Braskén, and Jesper Jørgenson for permission to quote from the papers on Münzenberg which they gave to the first International Willi Münzenberg Congress held in Berlin in 2015. Dr Ursula Langkau-Alex for very kindly allowing me to use information based on her recent research concerning Willi Münzenberg's illegitimate son.

For their kind assistance, I am grateful to the staff at the Bundesarchiv Berlin, the Swiss Sozialarchiv, Zurich, the National Archives, Kew, and the British Library, as well as to Roland Bischoff – a close friend over many years and always a fount of wisdom, Ralph Gibson of Sputnik Images, William Tyrer, Anne Sudrow, Heimo Halbrainer, and Klaus Manzek.

I was also inspired by Hans Modrow, who has dedicated his own life to the struggle for Socialism in very similar ways to Willi Münzenberg. As always, I cannot thank my partner Bruni de la Motte enough for her constant support and for her critical skills, without which this project would not have come to fruition, also my daughters Galina and Franziska for their encouragement and always apposite critical comments. For their kind permission to quote from the publications mentioned. My thanks are also due to Aaron Agassi and other members of the Buber-Neumann family for permission to quote from Margarete Buber-Neumann's reminiscences, *Under Two Dictators: Prisoner of Stalin and Hitler*, with an introduction by Nikolaus Wachsmann (2009). Rowohlt Verlag for permission to quote from: *Die verratene Revolution* by Sebastian Haffner, Scherz Verlag Bern/München/Berlin, 1969.

Pluto Press (www.plutobooks.com) for permission to quote from Meyer-Leviné, Rosa, *Inside German Communism, Memoirs of Party Life in the Weimar Republic*, Pluto Press, London, 1977.

Der Funke publishing house for permission to quote from Willi Münzenberg's *Der Dritte Front*, Schriftenreihe AdV, Verein der Funke, Switzerland, 2015.

All translations from original German texts, including those from Babette Gross's book, are my own unless otherwise stated.

LIST OF ABBREVIATIONS

AIZ – *Arbeiter Illustrierte Zeitung* (Workers Illustrated Newspaper)

Comintern – The Communist International

IAH – Internationale Arbeiter Hilfe (International Workers' Relief organisation)

KAPD – Communist Workers' Party of Germany

KPD – The German Communist Party

SPD – The Social Democratic Party of Germany

TUC – British Trades Union Congress

USPD – The Independent Social Democratic Party of Germany

WEO – Western European Office of the Comintern

INTRODUCTION

FIGURE I.1 Willi-Müenzenberg portrait photo c. 1930

The few existing photographs of Willi Münzenberg show a man with rugged features, a mop of rather unkempt dark hair, and eyes that look at you unflinchingly. One can surmise that he was a man of determination, but the hint of a smile on his lips suggests that he enjoyed life too.

He was one of the most colourful and charismatic figures of the Communist and anti-Fascist movements during the first half of the twentieth century. His irrepressible energy and ability to inspire and galvanise others became legendary. Few in Europe who were involved in left-wing and Socialist organisations were unaware of who he was. He was so effective in campaigning on behalf of the Soviet Union and for international working-class solidarity, that, while he won widespread admiration, he also made implacable enemies, not only among Fascists and the powerful capitalist elite, but also within the leaderships of the Social Democratic parties who saw him merely as a tool of Moscow.

He became a popular figure in left-wing circles beyond the Communist Party, finding friends and supporters across party lines and socialising with ease. He was admired and respected by most of those who came in contact with him. Few, it appears, could resist being infected by his charm.

He was a visionary propagandist and in the words of the historian Walter Laqueur, 'a cultural impresario of genius'.[1] His influence resonated throughout Europe and beyond. His mysterious death, only nine months after the beginning of the Second World War, which would eventually see the defeat of Fascism – a cause to which he had devoted much of his life – was a tragic and ignominious coda to his stellar life. Since then his name and his exploits have been virtually airbrushed from history.

Münzenberg played a central organising role in the Social Democratic Youth International, turning it into a strong anti-war movement before the outbreak of and during the First World War. Virtually single-handedly, he took on the task of turning what, until then, had been a loose organisation of young Socialists and supporters of the Russian revolution into an effective campaigning force, the Young Workers' International. He became the Comintern's de facto head of propaganda for the Western world from the early days following the Bolshevik Revolution, up to the outbreak of the Second World War. He was also one of the founder members of the German Communist Party and the initiator and chief organiser of the Workers' International Relief organisation (*IAH – Internationale Arbeiter Hilfe*), that organised solidarity and aid to those in struggle – and out of which grew the colossal Münzenberg undertaking, with its many journals, book publishing ventures, factories, and film studios – known collectively as the 'Münzenberg Concern'. The *IAH* became the largest globally embracing solidarity movement during the inter-war years, and it inspired, motivated, and activated tens of thousands. As its founder, he was the forerunner of subsequent international solidarity organisations and, indeed, could be considered as the father of international solidarity.

In his capacity as head of Workers' International Relief, Münzenberg set up a whole number of other global campaign groups and convened international congresses to combat war, colonialism, imperialism, and Fascism, and in doing so, was able to bring on board numerous influential members of the left-inclined European intellectual elite during the inter-war years.

In the 1930s, with the rise of Fascism, he was one of the key organisers, even though very much behind the scenes, of the European-wide anti-Fascist movement.

Although he initiated the establishment of many campaigns and organisations, he ensured that they were then run by capable individuals, and once they were up and running, he let these individuals get on with things, while he remained in the background.

As Arthur Koestler writes, his role in ensuring that the Nazi show-trial of Georgi Dimitrov – who the Nazis had accused of being the instigator of the Reichstag fire – was turned into a debacle for the Nazi regime, and this was recognised by enemy and friend alike as largely down to the efforts of Willi Münzenberg.[2]

His friends and enemies called him variously a knight in shining armour, a pied piper, the red millionaire, and an éminence grise. His list of contacts and friends reads like a who's who of the European left-wing political and intellectual elite of that pre-Fascist period. But who knows Münzenberg's name today?

While there have been three previous biographies, they all have their short-comings. I became convinced that it was time to reignite interest in this fascinating and controversial figure and that a new biography was needed.

There have been no comprehensive biographical portraits or commentaries on his life written by friends or contemporaries apart from a detailed and highly informative portrayal by his partner, Babette Gross. His own quasi-autobiographical work, published under the title *Die Dritte Front* (The Third Front) and written in response to a request made in 1929 by the Communist Youth movement of the Soviet Union to document his role in the establishment of an international Socialist youth movement, covers only the 15 years in which he was active in creating and building that movement. It must also be seen in the light of its commission.

Babette Gross, wrote the first biography, *Willi Münzenberg – eine politische Biografie*, in 1967, to provide her own account of that turbulent period of history and to rescue Münzenberg from deliberate defamation and oblivion. Her work is undoubtedly the most accurate portrayal. After all, she had been his close companion from 1922 until his death in 1940. For her account, however, she has had to rely very much on her memory, as much of their correspondence and personal papers had been taken and presumably destroyed by the Nazis and other important documents were at that time held in Soviet or East German archives and not accessible.

Hers is, by its very nature, a firsthand account and, one can assume, not entirely unaffected by her intimate relationship with the subject, as well as by her own subsequent disillusion with the Communist movement as a whole, although these factors do not appear to have impacted in any significant way on her biography in terms of accuracy.

However renowned, revered, or despised a historical figure may be, we know that they were made of flesh and blood, subject to the same pressures and temptations, and just as idiosyncratic as everyone else. No one is wholly virtuous or wholly evil. The skill of any biographer will lie in revealing the complexities, the strengths and frailties of their subjects, and their ability to place them in a meaningful context. Münzenberg is no exception to this stricture, but two more recent biographers, the US authors, Stephen Koch and Sean McMeekin, paint him as a charlatan. Although McMeekin backs up his very one-dimensional view with copious and well-researched references, lending it a patina of academic rigorousness, he ignores the multiple evidence which contradicts his thesis. While Stephen Koch is even more fantastical in his allegations and is not averse to using novelistic speculation masquerading as truth.

Stephen Koch's *Double Lives: Stalin, Willi Münzenberg and the Seduction of the Intellectuals* (1996) and Sean McMeekin's *The Red Millionaire* (2003) serve more to entrench Cold War perceptions of Communists and Communism than to provide a more comprehensive and objective portrayal of Münzenberg.

Koch is primarily a novelist, and this is very apparent from his writing style. McMeekin is a historian specialising in early twentieth-century European history and adopts a more academic approach, but still very much ideologically motivated.

My differences with both Koch and McMeekin are that I feel the portrait of Münzenberg they have painted is one seen through the narrow lens of their own intellectual categories and moral standards, without due recognition of the unique historical circumstances, and with no attempt to provide a sympathetic understanding of that period and to comprehend those individuals who were active participants in it. Both writers portray Münzenberg as insincere and hypocritical, a willing tool of Bolshevik machinations and Stalin's loyal lieutenant until he eventually cuts himself loose from the latter's dictatorial regime.[3]

Whatever one's position on the significance of the Bolshevik Revolution and the global Communist movement, it must be recognised that millions of people were swept along by the ideas. At the end of the First World War, Europe was still characterised by autocratic regimes, crass inequality, and oppression. Ideas of justice, workers' liberation, and Socialism captured the imagination of peoples who were war-weary and thirsting for radical change. The fact that, as in any turbulent period of history, there will always be individuals who misuse the popular will, does not negate the fact that many others pursue the original aims of justice altruistically and selflessly. To characterise Münzenberg as one of those cynical manipulators, as the two authors do, is to seriously misread the times and the man himself.

A whole number of other writers make mention of Münzenberg in their works, but few go into much detail. The German writer, Peter Weiss, included an interesting mini-portrait of Münzenberg and his influence in his epic docu-novel, *Aesthetics of Resistance* (2005).[4]

Münzenberg even makes an unusual appearance in Antonio Muñoz Molina's novel, *Sepharad* (2003), about the Sephardic diaspora, and the author devotes a complete chapter to Münzenberg, in the form of a potted biography. However, he has based it almost verbatim on Koch's work, creating a fictional character, an incongruous conflation of the real and the imagined, but regurgitating Koch's Cold War narrative, and compounding the latter's inaccuracies.[5]

While Gross's work vividly captures the period, she also had a profound understanding of what motivated the numerous Communists and fellow travellers at the time to support the Bolshevik Revolution and the Soviet Union. And it is this context, I feel, that needs to be taken into account in order to do justice to a personality like Münzenberg.

Since these three biographies were written, there has been considerable research undertaken into that historical period in which Münzenberg played a significant role, as well as into Münzenberg's life and influence itself. The pioneering work carried out by the Willi Münzenberg Forum in Berlin and the work of scholars like Kasper Braskén, Bernhard Bayerlein, and Fredrik Petersson among others have helped increase our knowledge here considerably.

With this wealth of new research now available, as well as easier access to archives and vital documentation, I feel it is time a new biography is written.

In my own biography, I make full use of more recent research in so far as it provides fresh insights into Münzenberg's life. I have also been able to make use of Comintern and German Communist Party documents which include correspondence relating to Münzenberg and which have only relatively recently become accessible. Access to British Secret Intelligence Service and Labour Party archives that refer to Münzenberg are also sources that, as far as I am aware, previous writers have not considered.

I have attempted to write a biography that is not only factually based and, as far as is possible, free of any underlying ideological agenda, but one which is also easily digestible and hopefully of interest to a readership beyond academia. My approach has been to sift through as much as I can of the material relating to Münzenberg that is currently available, to help flesh out his life, while trying to comprehend it within the context of his times. Simultaneously, I have also tried to draw out the relevance of his life for us today.

I was determined to try and uncover the real Münzenberg beneath the layers of ideological fall out from the Bolshevik Revolution, the rise of Stalin, and the insidious influence of the Cold War. I wanted to re-evaluate what he actually achieved, the compromises he made, and how his late awakening to Stalin's corrupting and fatal influence on history came about. Of necessity, I have relied substantially on Babette Gross's work as being the most informed and accurate portrayal of Münzenberg's life, and I quote from her extensively in this biography. If I sometimes overstress the positive aspects of his life, it is in part out of an attempt to counter what I see as a jaundiced image of the man that has been accreted as a result of hasty judgemental attitudes and their repetition by those too indolent to question the shibboleths.

Not long after they first met, Münzenberg became one of Lenin's trusted friends and comrades and was entrusted by him with the task of promoting the Soviet Union and Communism in Western Europe. He set about the task with alacrity.

Münzenberg developed relationships at various levels in the Soviet Union with individual political leaders, different ministries, the party, and the Comintern. He had become friends with other leading Bolsheviks, too, and was given enormous scope by them to promote the revolution worldwide following its victory in 1917. He had met Trotsky already in 1914 and was introduced to Lenin in 1915 during their exile in Switzerland. Both recognised Münzenberg's commitment to Communism and the Bolshevik Revolution, as well as his talent as an intelligent and capable activist. Any documentation which exists about these relationships is distributed across various archives in Russia.

Despite his friendship with Lenin and his leading role in the worldwide Communist and anti-Fascist movements over several decades, he was airbrushed from official Soviet and Eastern European iconographies and histories, and has been almost totally ignored by Western historians, although he was the subject of continuous and detailed surveillance by Western secret services during his lifetime. While these secret service files offer some insight into the extent of their surveillance of Münzenberg, they cast little light on the personality of the man himself.

It is not easy to recreate an all round picture of someone who, although he was clearly larger than life and with an impressive track record, has left so few traces either in the form of his own reminiscences or in those written by others.

While I would argue that he was not as egotistical as many other high profile political leaders, he could not avoid becoming aware of his ability to influence others, to give rousing speeches, and to organise effectively. He knew his value and the widespread respect and admiration he encountered only cemented that realisation. He was elected time and again to leading positions in the organisations in which he was actively involved. Those who came in contact with him attest to his magnetism. However, he never seemed to covet top party political office, preferring to remain a semi-autonomous operator.

He remained throughout his life, almost to the very end, a supremely loyal member of the German Communist Party and supporter of the Soviet Union, but his ideas were at times contradictory, and changed during his lifetime.

Any would-be biographer should take Brecht's advice to heart and instrumentalise a 'Verfremdungseffekt': re-examine what is taken for granted and what we think we know and illuminate the subject from new angles.

Here, I have tried not to be judgemental or make claims of virtue or culpability on Münzenberg's behalf. I have attempted to stick closely to the facts of his life, based on the evidence available. Apart from Babette Gross, his other biographers have hardly taken readers on a voyage of discovery, but have charted a more or less ideologically predetermined course. In attempting to build up a more three-dimensional portrait, I have trawled through many autobiographies, biographies, and the writings of contemporaries who knew him in my search for a broader truth. My aim is also to reinstate Münzenberg once more in the prominent historical position he once occupied.

Some enjoy speculation, suggest psychological factors as keys to their subject's motivation and behaviour; and political actions are interpreted through authorial prisms. Here, I have tried to avoid such methodology and making judgements or claims without concrete evidence.

Münzenberg, like many another significant political figures in history, devoted himself to a cause, but his life took a path that in many ways veered in the opposite direction to the one for which he had striven. The names of historical figures like Mary Wollstonecraft, the Pankhursts, Tom Paine, Gandhi, Mandela, or Luther-King live on as paragons who brought about positive social change and who selflessly struggled for justice. They were men and women of courage, commitment, and dedication, and their lives have posthumously been incorporated into mainstream historical narratives. But individuals in the Communist movement like Münzenberg, who also devoted themselves to a cause they passionately believed would bring about social justice, throwing themselves wholeheartedly into the struggle for a Communist utopia, have been (excepting the founding fathers, Marx and Engels) largely forgotten or discredited because the process that was intended to usher in that change became corrupted and debased.

But why should the life of this man be of interest to us today? It is not only his unique relationships with some of the leading figures of early twentieth-century Socialism – Lenin, Rosa Luxemburg, Karl Liebknecht, Karl Radek, among others, which can give us intimate insights into their lives and political attitudes at the time, but his leading role in the European-wide anti-Fascist struggle and attempts to build a unity of all progressive forces can provide us with an instructive and inspiring example in the face of our own political and social challenges.

It is never easy to clearly distinguish between the contribution made to history by individuals and that made by the movements to which they belonged, but in Münzenberg's case this distinction is clearer cut. Without his intimate association with Lenin and the task the latter gave him as the Comintern's chief fundraiser and propagandist, he may have remained a minor historical figure, but it was as if he were destined for the role. He could have easily become just another apparatchik, but his creative drive prevented that from happening; he initiated campaigns, expanded the remit of his role, and successfully pursued the overall task with enormous panache during the tumultuous years of the Weimar Republic and the build up to the Second World War, revealing himself as a major politically creative figure on the world stage. He was, as we would say today, a 'mover and shaker'.

While he was dependent in his work on the consent of both the *KPD* and the Comintern, relevant documents in the archives in Moscow, Berlin, Amsterdam, and London reveal a man largely independent of such control. While he was a de facto employee of the Comintern and was obliged, nominally at least, to follow its instructions and orders, he nevertheless enjoyed an enormous amount of autonomy and, in his activities, was guided more by his own instincts, experience, and aims than by any bureaucratic demands. Koestler called him insightfully, 'a political realist in a time of awful realities'. He wrote that while Münzenberg 'was certainly no saint, nor was he a cynic – if one understands cynicism as a lack of principles'. He was someone 'who was devoted to three central principles: struggle against the war, exploitation and colonialism'.[6] He was a 'campaigns man' and contributed significantly to the development of techniques and methods of propaganda that raised the public profile of European left-wing radicalism during that era. Tragically, his ideas and methods of propaganda were also misappropriated by Goebbels and the Nazis for their own nefarious goals.

Münzenberg's life also throws light on the essential contradiction between an organisation, like the Russian Bolshevik Party – and imitated by other Communist parties elsewhere – geared to usher in a workers' utopia, but which was based on a centralised, quasi-military hierarchical structure of 'officers and foot soldiers', thus entrenching a serious democratic deficit on the left. That, of course, was hardly surprising in Russia, as the Bolsheviks inherited a country in which the masses were poorly educated, largely ignorant, and inured to centralised, authoritarian rule. Under Stalin's leadership, this weakness was exploited and led to an entrenchment of apparatchik mentality, in which subservience and mediocrity were rewarded, and where suspicion of intellectual, creative, and artistic individuals became a malignant cancer.

Notes

1 Laqueur, *Walter, Weimar, a Cultural History 1918–1933*, Phoenix Press, New York, 2002. p. 51. 'The only truly proletarian figure in these circles was Willi Münzenberg, not an intellectual himself but instrumental in establishing countless newspapers, magazines, film companies and cultural associations'.
2 Koestler, Arthur in the foreword to Babette Gross's, *Willi Münzenberg, a Biography* Forum Verlag, Leipzig, 1991. p. 7.
3 Cited below are several examples taken from Koch's and McMeekin's biographies, to give an indication of their approach and point out their repeated use of pejorative and ideologically loaded words and phrases. (Words highlighted in italic bold are this author's emphasis):

On Koch's book:

1. A key example of what I would argue is Koch's tendentious treatment of Münzenberg, is his repeated misquoting of the term 'Innocents Clubs', which has been taken up and repeated by many commentators since. He writes that, 'With a *light sneer*, Münzenberg dubbed this *vast horde* of radical devout "innocents". His own phrase for the fronts he created …' (p. 14). In Koch's own footnote he writes that the phrase is taken from Gross's biography, but the term actually used by Gross is 'harmless' – a subtle, but significant difference in meaning. Koch also, significantly, leaves out the context in which this phrase was purportedly used by Münzenberg.

   The source for these words Gross tells us in her biography, is a report published by the *Allgemeiner Deutsche Gewerkschaftsbund* (ADGB), the Confederation of German Trade Unions. This report [attacking Münzenberg and the *IAH*] Gross writes, 'illustrates, *even if perhaps not in every nuance authentically*, [this author's emphasis], but in an accurate way the arsenal and ingeniousness of the propagandist Münzenberg'.

   The quote is purportedly taken from an address made by Münzenberg to a closed meeting of *IAH* workers, presenting the context of the challenges facing the organisation. To give a fuller context, he is quoted as saying that 'recent events in America show that they are prepared to attack us politically. So we have to show even more agility in defending ourselves against that. Specifically at this time, we have to involve other names, other groups in order to make this persecution more difficult. Here, the question of Clubs for the New Russia is particularly important. For me personally, setting up these "Clubs of the Harmless" are of no particular interest. One shouldn't have any illusions about the significance of these clubs. It's a question of penetrating the broadest sections [of society], and winning over artists, professors, to use the theatre and cinema, and to announce everywhere that Russia is risking everything, Russia has humiliated itself, Russia is doing everything, in order to maintain a world of peace…' p. 133 in Marian Jackson's translation, p. 215 in the German original.
2. 'Lenin', Koch writes, 'made this dynamic man … the de facto director of the Soviet Union's covertly directed propaganda operations in the West'. Münzenberg's

activities were so 'covert' that anyone who was interested – and Western secret services certainly were – could easily determine for whom he was working and what he was doing (p. 5).

3. 'What Trotsky had spotted in the **cocky** 26 year-old German **hothead** was a talent for secret work', he writes (p. 5). This is typical of Koch's patronising descriptive style. How he divines that Trotsky spotted 'his talent for secret work' is difficult to imagine as Münzenberg hardly had any contact with Trotsky while he was working for the Comintern. The 'talent' that he did have and that was spotted immediately by Lenin, too, was an amazing organising ability, a flare for propaganda, and a passionate commitment to the Communist cause.

4. 'Beginning in his teens, Willi had been **promiscuously** supplying all kinds of revolutionary groups with freelance clandestine networks: undercover systems for transmitting information, **laundering money, forging passports** and beaming people across heavily-guarded borders as if by magic', Koch says.

   This, again, is wild exaggeration. In his teens, Münzenberg was an impecunious worker in a shoe factory in Erfurt and belonged to a tiny local group of Social Democratic workers. He only really began to become seriously involved in the Social Democratic movement after moving to Switzerland when he was 21 years old. Koch's description also fails to reflect the fact that many countries in Europe at this time were governed by authoritarian regimes and in which Social Democratic movements were illegal, so that travel between them was exceedingly difficult, especially for young radical activists. There is no evidence that Münzenberg himself forged passports and 'money laundering' has connotations of criminal activity rather than a means of ensuring that financial support from Moscow or elsewhere was not confiscated by the German authorities.

5. Koch writes that 'Münzenberg had managed, quite on his own to place an operative in the Vatican' and cites Gross (p. 47). This is in connection with the smuggling of illegal Socialist youth pamphlets and journals between the European countries, but Gross's words are: 'Even a Vatican courier allowed himself to be misused as a postman'. Hardly the same as Münzenberg placing an operative in the Vatican.

6. Koch states that Ruth (sic) Kuczynski (the Soviet agent 'Sonja') as being 'trained in Russia at a school for covert action founded hand in glove with Willi by the Comintern'. Again, this is conjured up out of nowhere. Ursula Kuczynski was trained in the Soviet military counter espionage school. There is no evidence whatsoever that Münzenberg had anything to do with this school or the training of Soviet secret agents – and it would be highly unusual for a foreigner to be involved; the Soviets were very particular on this score as any other nation would be. Koch goes on to say 'she worked in espionage first in China, under cover of Willi's illegal operations there'. Willi Münzenberg had no operations at all in China. It was a Comintern operation, but had nothing to do with Münzenberg.

   Further on, he talks of Sonja as 'spying against the British, hovering around Bletchley Park'. She had nothing at all to do with Bletchley Park where Britain's secret decoding of Germany's radio signals took place (p. 9).

On McMeekin's book:

McMeekin's approach is not dissimilar to Koch's and is signalled already in the disingenuous title: *The Red Millionaire*. While millions may have flowed through Münzenberg's hands, he owned no property, had no large bank accounts and, at his death, left no personal assets, so the title 'Millionaire' may be good publicity, but is hardly a true representation of the facts.

1. While Münzenberg is 'little remembered today', McMeekin writes in his introduction, 'the utterance of his name aroused **fear, loathing** and admiration amongst the world's political classes'. Those contemporary witnesses who refer

to Münzenberg talk of his charm and organisational flair, and he was certainly seen by Western secret services as a 'dangerous' man, but I have not come across anyone describing him in terms of 'fear and loathing'.

2. McMeekin goes on to write that, 'he demonstrated formidable talents in the *black arts* of propaganda'. He was certainly a supremely capable propagandist and pioneered many of the visual methods – use of photography and photomontage for instance – that are still in use today, but 'black arts'?

3. Münzenberg is also laconically characterised as a man of violence: 'If Münzenberg had merely been a sympathiser, as opposed to a *hard-core Communist devoted to the principle of violent revolution*, he never would have remained a trusted confidant in Moscow's ruling circles for two decades', McMeekin declares.

4. Despite the large body of evidence attesting to Münzenberg's business success, for McMeekin, 'Every business he touched ... haemorrhaged red ink' ... 'Münzenberg was the Comintern's junk bond king', he adds deprecatingly.

5. Again, a page or so later he writes: 'Those Western sympathizers who *churned through* Münzenberg's *propaganda thresher*, meanwhile often saw their careers mysteriously promoted or their lives suddenly ruined as they acquired notoriety and the enmity of their governments'. A wide-sweeping and questionable allegation (pp. 5/6).

6. He writes in conclusion: 'But risks to livelihood and limb did not lead all prospective Communists to shy away [from joining communist organisations]. The risks, Münzenberg rapidly learned, were part of the attraction. In fact *bloody rehearsals in class warfare* proved effective political advertising, nowhere more so than in Münzenberg's native Germany.

He accuses Münzenberg of abetting the 'Communist calls for an invasion of central Europe by the Red Army, to be accompanied by the *forcible expropriation of private property* and the *elimination of millions of class enemies*' ... '[and] from his seat in the cockpit of a global propaganda empire, Willi Münzenberg planned to lead Germany, and with her all of Europe, into the cataclysmic class war that would destroy capitalism for ever'[and in this way] 'helped to rally mass support for extremist right-wing extremist parties who vowed to exterminate Communists before they could exterminate everyone one else, then all the better'.

Such allegations are the product, I would argue, more of a vivid imagination than based on factual evidence. Munzenberg demonstrably spent most of his life struggling to prevent war and bloodshed, and no one could, in all fairness, accuse him of approving 'bloody rehearsals' or advocating the 'elimination of millions of class enemies' or of promoting 'a Red Army invasion of western Europe'. (p. 4) In his final paragraph, McMeekin places the blame on Münzenberg for the 'Bolshevik invasion of the European Left'.

4 Peter Weiss: *The Aesthetics of Resistance, Volume 1: A Novel*, Duke University Press, 2005.
5 Muñoz Molina, Antonio, *Sepharad*, Harcourt Books, 2001.
6 Koestler Arthur, in his foreword to Babette Gross's book, *Willi Münzenberg*, Forum Verlag, Leipzig, 1991. p. 11.

1

EARLY LIFE

Born in Germany, in 1889, the same year as Adolf Hitler, Wilhelm 'Willi' Münzenberg first saw the light of day on 14 August in Erfurt, the regional capital of Thuringia. This picturesque town is situated on the Via Regia, a medieval trade and pilgrim route. Its university was founded in 1379, the first to be established within the geographic area that constitutes modern-day Germany, and it is where Martin Luther was a theological student from 1501. Still today, it is one of the most intact of Germany's medieval towns and was largely spared the devastation of the Second World War. Its medieval core and unique Krämer bridge, with its half-timbered shops and houses, have hardly changed in over 500 years.

FIGURE 1.1 Willi Münzenberg c. 1917 (Courtesy of das Schweizerische Sozialarchiv, Zürich, Switzerland.)

The Industrial Revolution reached Erfurt during the 1840s, and a railway was built connecting Berlin and Frankfurt. During the following years, many factories were established there. One of the biggest was the Royal Gun Factory of Prussia that was built in 1862. After the unification of Germany in 1871, Erfurt found itself transported from what had been the southern border of Prussia to the centre of Germany, and its old fortifications were no longer needed. The demolition of those fortifications in 1873 led to a construction boom, because it now became possible to build in the area formerly occupied by the city walls and beyond. Many public and private buildings emerged and the infrastructure (such as tramways, hospitals, schools) improved rapidly. The number of inhabitants grew from 40,000 around 1870 to 130,000 in 1914.

Among socialists, the name Erfurt is most likely to be associated with 'The Erfurt Programme', a more specifically Marxist one, adopted by the Social Democratic Party (*SPD*) of Germany during its congress there in 1891. It was largely formulated by Eduard Bernstein, August Bebel, and Karl Kautsky, and it superseded the Gotha Programme, which Karl Marx had strongly criticised in his *Critique of the Gotha Programme* (1875). The programme announced the imminent demise of capitalism and the necessity of the social ownership of the means of production. However, the party intended to pursue these goals by participation in the established political processes and structures, rather than by armed revolution. Kautsky argued that because capitalism, by its very nature, would inevitably collapse, the immediate task for socialists was to work for the gradual improvement of workers' lives rather than for revolution. Münzenberg could hardly have been born in a city more closely associated with the early socialist movement in Germany.

His parents ran a small bakery on Augustiner street, above which he was born, and where today there is a plaque commemorating his birth. His father, Friedrich, was a choleric and tyrannical man who regularly beat his wife and children. Also, largely because of his alcoholism and gambling, to whatever he turned his hand, he never achieved success, with the result that the family was continually on the move from place to place in search of an elusive stability.

In his autobiographical reminiscences, Münzenberg wrote that because the family was always moving around, he attended school sporadically in eight different places, usually small villages. As a result, his education was continually disrupted and minimal. After his mother, Wilhelmine, died in 1893, when he was only 4 years old, the family moved to the village of Friemar, near Gotha, where his father, who remarried, took over a small inn. His second wife would also die not long after this latest move.

Willi was the youngest of four siblings, but his two older brothers had left home shortly after he was born. Only his sister, Emmy, who was expected to fill the role of her deceased mother, remained at home to begin with. These two children were expected to pull more than their weight in helping to run the inn, and when their father was drunk, they would manage it by themselves.

Young Willi tried his best to evade his father's choleric outbursts and the endless chores he had to undertake, and as a result, he was often the butt of his father's uncontrollable anger. Willi was a scrawny, rather sensitive boy, with a stubborn streak that infuriated his father. Unlike his brothers, who went off heroically to fight in the First World War, he was a big disappointment to his father. We have a laconic, but graphic portrait of his childhood years in the form of the autobiographical sketches he wrote while imprisoned in Zurich in 1917/1918.

He attended primary school in Friemar and Eberstadt, among others, where he was subjected to an education that was less than basic and was dominated by religious indoctrination; he wrote of 'learning by rote excerpts from the Bible and hymnals'. Mathematics consisted of memorising the times tables, geography covered the grand dukedom of Gotha, and history consisted of the Grand Duke's family history. The schools had 'eight classes', but all pupils sat in one classroom and were taught simultaneously by one teacher. He found school a torture and struggled, even into later life, with writing and grammar. Its rote learning certainly didn't satisfy his curiosity and thirst for genuine knowledge, so he played truant as often as he could, using the time to sit in a quiet corner somewhere and read books from the library, and, in this way, he developed into a keen reader and, for a few snatched hours, was able to escape claustrophobic reality, even if only in his mind.

Most of his 'free' time, though, he had to devote to helping his father with the running of the pub. In the course of this work, he became well known to the regular customers and, if a partner was lacking in a group of card players, he would be invited to join the group, soon becoming quite an expert player. His alertness, curiosity, and easy banter endeared him to the peasants and farmworkers who frequented the hostelry, and it was also through them that he gained his first introduction to politics.

His childhood view of the world, strictly circumscribed as it was, would have been formed against the background of the 'scramble for Africa' in the wake of the Berlin Conference of 1884, which regulated European colonisation and trade in Africa. As a consequence of the political and economic rivalries among the European empires towards the end of the nineteenth century, the partitioning of Africa was how the Europeans had avoided warring amongst themselves over the continent. Germany had been unified under Prussian rule only since 1871, in the wake of the Prussian defeat of the Austrians in 1866 at the Battle of Königgrätz and the defeat of France in 1870. However, in 1890, Kaiser Wilhelm II adopted a foreign policy of *Weltpolitik*, with the aim of transforming Germany into a global power through assertive diplomacy, the acquisition of overseas colonies, and the development of a powerful navy. Germany very soon became a rapidly rising industrial power.

At the beginning of the 1880s, the *Deutscher Kolonialverein* (German Colonial Association) was established and from 1884 published its own magazine, the *Kolonialzeitung*. During the 1890s, Wilhelm II unleashed an aggressive policy of colonisation and colonial expansion. Germany soon became the third largest colonial power in Africa. Nearly all of its empire of 2.6 million square kilometres and 14 million colonial subjects in 1914 was found in its African possessions of Southwest Africa (today's Namibia), Togoland, the Cameroons, and Tanganyika (Tanzania today). This general atmosphere of assertive nationalism and imperial ambition would have a considerable impact on many a young German of Münzenberg's generation.

He was 10 years old when the Boer War (1899–1902) began and, like many of his peers, followed its progress with fervour, hoping the hated British would lose. He would have seen the Boer War as a battle between a proud people fighting a bullying and powerful imperial power. Only 11 years old, he even formulated and attempted to carry out a plan to run away and join the Boer army, but his father was able to catch him and haul him back before he managed to get too far. He was desperate to escape the purgatory of life with his abusive father.

On top of the wasted hours at school, he hated the daily drudgery of cleaning the pub and polishing the furniture. One day, when he thought he had successfully escaped the task of polishing the brass petroleum lamps, his father, who was drunk at the time – a not infrequent state – set about him with a stick, but in his blind stupor, hit and smashed one of the lamps. Now, even more incensed, he threw a rope at Willi and told him to go hang himself – a terrible augury of what was to come. But such an extreme confrontation was not the norm, and the two, being interdependent, managed to achieve a fragile modus vivendi for much of the time.

Willi's schooling provided no antidote to the total lack of intellectual stimulus in the home, where there were no books and not the slightest wider cultural stimulus. What he did learn from an early age, though, was that he had to take responsibility for his own existence. It strengthened his sense of independence, coupled with a determination to make things happen. He revealed early organising skills when, as a 12 year old, 'with no instructions or orders', he arranged a celebration in his village on Germany's national day, to which half the villagers came and all the youngsters. He also delivered impromptu 'sermons' to his fellow school pupils and was active in 'setting up theatre and football clubs' well before he would become involved in any political activity.

Despite managing the pub, his father never had any money, and his alcoholism and gambling didn't help improve the family's dire financial situation. Willi was obliged to go to school in second-hand, patched, hand-me-down clothing and had to fight to assert himself against his better-off fellow pupils who mocked his dress.

Years later, in a police cell in Zurich, he wrote of his childhood, 'If today, during the quiet and long nights [...] I let my early childhood memories run past me, then I become increasingly conscious of the fact that the roots of my being, my passion, my sympathies and antipathies, impact on me still today'. His deep aversion to alcohol, violence, militarism, and petit bourgeois attitudes represented by his father would remain formative aspects of his character. He only fully realised, in Zurich, he says, how he and hundreds of thousands like him had been deprived of a proper childhood and youth.

At the age of 14, in 1904, like many other working-class and poorer children, he was forced by economic necessity to leave school and learn a trade. His father had determined that he would become a hairdresser, and a relative of the family was enlisted to secure him an apprenticeship with the local barber, but the latter turned out to be as authoritarian and violent as Willi's own father, and anyway, such work was not what he had envisaged as a lifetime occupation. He had to work from 6.00 a.m. to 8.30 p.m. every day during the week and Saturday and Sunday mornings. That same year, to compound his troubles, his father accidently shot himself dead while cleaning his hunting rifle while in a drunken stupor. Willi used the opportunity to abandon his apprenticeship and, to begin with, moved to Gotha to live with his sister Emmy who had, in the meantime, married and left home.

After a short time with his sister, he returned to Erfurt that same year, and, only 15 years old, began work as a 'cobbler boy', an unskilled labourer, in the Lingel shoe factory, which was at the time Germany's second largest, with over 1,000 workers. He lived, as he himself described it, in a 'twilight state', leaving for work before dawn and returning home in the darkness of late evening, tired out. 'I was without feeling and sensation just like the machines, that whirr and pound in the factory. My world is my workplace', he wrote.

While at the factory one day, Willi and a colleague were offered free tickets for a performance at the local theatre. It would be the first time in his life that he had been inside a theatre. The play they were to see was *Iphigenia in Tauris* by Goethe. Inside the theatre, their excitement was soon dissipated, though. They were unable to understand anything of what was happening on stage, and his mate summed up the experience with the laconic comment, 'That was silly. They gave long speeches, waved their swords in the air and in the end didn't even come to blows!'

In the factory, harassment and bullying continued. His task was to deliver the cut leather pieces to the skilled workers who sewed them together, but he would be continually chided and cuffed by the older employees. The wages of the apprentices were minimal, and even if they didn't starve, they were always hungry and tired. In his reminiscences he wrote movingly how, 'We never saw how the trees burst into leaf and the flowers blossomed, we didn't see the beauty of nature and the countryside, that the better-off youngsters celebrated in poetry and song. We were constantly dreaming about food. In a group of four, we would meet every Sunday in a smoke-filled pub to play cards; the resulting winnings went into a collective pot and when we had enough we would have a large sausage-eating binge'.[1] His experience in the factory mirrored that of thousands of other working-class youngsters with little education and class consciousness, and it reinforced his later commitment to campaigning for better conditions and training for apprentices. One of the oldest extant photos of him, taken several years later, shows him marching on May Day in 1912 as a representative of the *Jungburschenverein Zurich III* (Zurich III young men's association) in front of a banner which reads: 'Down with the exploitation of apprentices'.

In 1906, at the age of 17, he experienced a significant political awakening. One of the workers at the shoe factory to whom he had to bring the shoe parts was a much older man, nicknamed 'codfish' because he wore a pinz-nez. He was a member of the Social Democratic Party and encouraged Willi to join the local social democratic discussion group, the so-called Propaganda Club.

The Propaganda Club was the local Social Democratic Party's educational and cultural club, and its members met every Wednesday in *Die Forelle*, an inn on the *Grafengasse* in Erfurt. There, members would discuss politics, take delivery of illegal leaflets, and circulate banned journals. On his first tentative attempt to visit the club with a friend from work, neither of them dared mount the stairs to the meeting room, not knowing anything about what was involved, only that its members were 'socialists' who undertook educational work. They didn't even know what the word 'propaganda' meant.[2] They imagined the club to be a sort of Freemasonry organisation, and that they would have to undergo various arcane rituals and take an oath. Although the word 'propaganda' frightened him, he later overcame his inhibitions and, desperate for a wider comradeship, took the plunge and joined the club. Münzenberg wrote that 'I was completely unaware at the time of what a decisive role this club would play in my life. Today, I know that I was then at a critical phase in my life and that it determined, completely unconsciously, as these things often do, the trajectory of my life'. Here, for the first time, he was able to ask questions of the older members and learn about trade unionism, socialism, and class struggle. On their free days, these young socialists went for rambles together in the Thuringian countryside, to Weimar, or into the hills around Gotha.

At this club he would meet the toolmaker, Georg Schumann, who was 4 years older than he was and someone who would have a significant impact on his political development. Georg was a committed Social Democrat and, until 1907, the chairman of the 'Propaganda Club'. It was here that Willi's political education really began, and it was Schumann who opened his eyes to socialism and gave him his first lessons in politics and trade union organisation, explaining to him the role played by class conflict in society.

Schumann would, in 1918, become one of the founding members of the *KPD* (Communist Party of Germany), a leading official and editor of the *Rote Fahne* (Red Flag, the official organ of the *KPD*). He would be executed by the Nazis in 1945.

When Schumann left Erfurt in 1907, Willi took on his role as chairman of the club. In the meantime, he had already persuaded a number of his fellow workers at the shoe factory to join. He would transform this small group into the core of the Erfurt young socialists organisation.

Despite a hard-working day at the factory, Willi still found the energy to visit the municipal library on a regular basis in the evenings and read widely on all sorts of subjects. When he first asked the librarian for a book by Ferdinand Lassalle – up to then, he'd only read cowboy and Indian stories by Karl May – the librarian looked condescendingly at him and said, 'that's not suitable for you', but he wasn't to be put off. He began devouring socialist literature, keen to overcome his lack of knowledge. In a very short time, he had read all the socialist classics he could lay his hands on: Engels, Kautsky, Bebel, moving on to read even more widely, but with no systematic plan, books by Haeckel and Darwin, as well as poetry by Freiligrath, Herwegh, and Heine.

In this way, his wider cultural education began. The few evening hours were, though, not sufficient to still his reading hunger, so he called in sick at the factory and began reading 'world history' for several weeks in his room. He understood little, he said, and only later did the interconnectedness of things become apparent to him. He still attended youth club meetings, and he and his comrades went rambling in the countryside on weekends when they would 'carry on debating for hours at a time'.

In his own autobiographical sketch, *Die Dritte Front* (The Third Front), Münzenberg provides vivid descriptions of his early days establishing a socialist youth group in Erfurt and, subsequently in Zurich, sowing the seeds of what would become an international socialist youth movement. While he didn't achieve this single-handedly – he does give due credit to his comrades – he was certainly at its centre and very much its leader.

He wrote euphorically that, 'Life had suddenly been given a different and new content. My wages were still the same, I was just as hungry, but life seemed to become richer, more sunny. Every book was an experience, every new piece of knowledge awakened in me an up-till-then unknown feeling of strength, my existence was no longer a hopeless one; we felt that there must be a release from the daily drudge and greyness of this dull factory life'.[3]

He was gripped by the 'propaganda fever' that never left him throughout his life. This club would also form the core of opposition to the rather staid official social democratic politics in Erfurt, and many of its members would later go on to join the Communist Party when it was founded in 1918. When Willi joined the club in 1906, he was the youngest member.

The discovery, in 1904, of the badly beaten body of a young engineering apprentice who had been thrashed to death by his employer caused national outrage. It provoked the renowned Social Democratic Party leader, Eduard Bernstein, to write an article for the *SPD's* monthly journal attacking the appalling treatment experienced by most apprentices in Germany, where it was still legal for employers to mete out physical punishment on their apprentices. In the wake of this, a whole number of proletarian youth organisations mushroomed throughout the country. The Social Democratic Party's national youth section was founded in 1903, and only 2 years later, the 1905 revolution in Russia would have a considerable impact on it.

The headquarters of these new radical youth groups in the south was based in Mannheim. In 1904, the *SPD* politician Ludwig Frank established the *Verband*

Junger Arbeiter (Association of Young Workers). He took his inspiration from the Belgian 'Young Guard', which focussed on explaining to young people the roots of war and militarism. It began publishing its paper, *Die Junge Garde* (The Young Guard). 'We felt really happy', Münzenberg writes, to sell this paper which the Prussians had banned, largely because of its strong anti-militaristic stance'. He soon persuaded his group to collaborate on Frank's southern German section; they could not formally affiliate, though, because the organisation and its paper were banned under Prussia's draconian anti-socialist legislation.

All such 'political' clubs were, in fact, banned under Prussian laws of association, but this no doubt made it all the more exciting to challenge the restrictions. It certainly motivated Münzenberg to sell the paper in the shoe factory, and he very soon managed to double its circulation there. His role in establishing what had now become a militant group also brought him irrevocably into conflict with the local conservatively minded *SPD* leadership.

When he first joined the club, there were around 15 to 20 members of between 18 and 28 years old, most of whom were 'bright and spirited socialists, dissatisfied with official party politics, demanding more radical tactics'. He threw himself wholeheartedly into its activities and began playing a key role. As a result, the club took on a more revolutionary character and began to attract other young workers.

Another group, the *Verband junger Arbeiter Deutschlands* (Association of the Working Youth of Germany) was established by Max Peters in Berlin in 1906, and Münzenberg affiliated his Erfurt group to it, with the aim of being able to function legally under its aegis. So, out of a workers' educational and cultural club, a fully fledged semi-autonomous political youth organisation emerged – newly named the *Freie Jugend Erfurt* (The Free Youth of Erfurt), the city's only 'proletarian youth organisation'. By 1907, only a year since he had joined the original club, he was elected its secretary and became its de facto leader.

The older members of the Social Democratic Party and trade unions felt it beneath them to give talks at the club; the young members were seen as an irrelevance. This attitude only played into the hands of the youngsters who responded by preparing and delivering their own lectures. Every month, one of them would be selected to give a lecture to the others, and in this way, they were obliged to do their own research and talk freely in front of an audience. In a very short time, they all gained in confidence and became more relaxed about talking and debating in public. In this way, it provided all of them with a valuable education, honed their rhetorical skills, and stimulated the discussion of ideas.

In the spring of 1907, the group began holding public meetings for apprentices in the city in the hope of bringing more of them into the Free Youth movement. They printed their own leaflets advertising the meetings and distributed them among the young workers, but Münzenberg was arrested for doing this. It was the first time in his life he had been arrested. The following day, his case was covered in the local newspaper, the *Erfurter Allgemeine Zeitung*, and he felt very proud to see his name in the paper, but he was soon brought down to earth again with a thud, when the shoe factory told him if he did anything like that again, it would mean the immediate sack.

The group's first meeting went ahead as advertised, but this time the police showed a keen interest. It was held in a small room in a pub frequented by working men. Despite the big leafleting action, only about 20 young workers turned up, but their numbers were unexpectedly boosted by an officer from the criminal police, two security guards, and two heavily armed regional gendarmes. From then on, the police would take a keen interest in the group's activities.

While he remained financially poor, and his wage at the shoe factory was barely enough for survival, Willi's inner life had, as he says, become much richer. At the same time, he had become very much aware of how young workers had no means of representation at their disposal and were forbidden from organising politically even by the trade unions and the *SPD* leadership.

On a national level, the government was beginning to take the burgeoning youth movement seriously, fearing its radical and anti-military stance. It wanted to prevent German youth from being 'corrupted' by socialist ideas before they underwent their military service. With this aim, the law restricting political associations was reinforced in 1908 with a new amendment that forbade young people under 18 years old from joining political organisations or even attending political gatherings.

Instead of opposing such draconian legislation, the Social Democratic and trade union leaderships utilised it gladly to achieve their aim of dissolving and ridding themselves of their own radical youth sections. Only militant leaders like Karl Liebknecht spoke out against this policy. The Social Democratic establishment feared the revolutionary ideas of the party's younger members and also strongly disapproved of their firmly held anti-militarist views. This attitude was also reflected in the Social Democratic-led national trade union body. At its 1908 Hamburg congress, it agreed on a motion to dissolve its youth sections. This policy was vehemently opposed by the many youth sections throughout the country, and in Erfurt, the group was even more determined to maintain its autonomy and radical approach. Münzenberg wrote that, 'The Erfurt party bureaucrats were a special mixture of shamelessness, stupidity and nastiness. We had to struggle against this group to maintain our independence. In this way I learned right at the beginning of my work in the working class movement what it meant to fight against a pompous bureaucracy'.[4]

The efforts of the Social Democratic establishment to suppress its uppity youth failed miserably. By 1907, the independent youth groups in the country had grown from strength to strength, boosted also by the influence of the 1905 Russian Revolution.

In September 1908, Münzenberg undertook his first journey outside the region, to Berlin, as a delegate from the Erfurt youth group, one of five other delegates from Thuringia, to the national conference of young socialists that had been called by the north German association in response to the anti-youth policy adopted by the Hamburg trade union congress. Georg Schumann, from the shoe factory, was also a delegate. Münzenberg managed to obtain time off work by inventing an aunt who had just died. It was the delegates' first visit to a large city and their excitement was palpable. They took a 4th class carriage in the train, in which 'we spent the whole night discussing with the other passengers about the need for proletarian class struggle', Münzenberg said.

Two umbrella organisations for young workers had been established in the country – north and south. However, only two weeks later, at its national conference, the *SPD* leadership made the decision to close down its political youth wing and incorporate it fully into the party structure. This was a reflection not only of the always ever-present generational differences, but also of the sharpening battle between reformism and revolutionary militancy – the leadership feared the radicalism of these young socialists. With the onset of the First World War, this conflict would lead to a split in the social democratic movement, with the reformists taking full control of the *SPD* apparatus and the radicals forming themselves into the *USPD* (Independent Social Democratic Party) and the Spartacists.

In Erfurt, Münzenberg and his close comrades did not take the dissolution of the national youth organisations lying down, and even without the former links to other groups, without publicity or even their own newspaper, they began, step by step rebuilding an autonomous movement in the city.

Despite the steadily increasing electoral gains of the *SPD* nationally, Münzenberg was chafing at the bit and becoming even more frustrated with the domination within the Social Democratic Party of a cautious, ageing generation represented by its leaders August Bebel and Karl Kautsky. Many of the party's officials he encountered were very conservative in their views. 'Soon in the daily political work [...] the great goal of public ownership of the means of production became forgotten. Masses of middle-class elements flooded into the party, hoping to gain office and influence as the party increasingly won political clout. The ground for revisionism was prepared and, around the turn of the century, its propaganda became more vocal. Momentary success is everything, belief in a proletarian revolution a romantic fantasy, that was the motto', was how he characterised this period.[5] He and his comrades were not prepared to go down that road. Their models were Karl Liebknecht and Rosa Luxemburg with their more radical politics.

Their hopes were raised by the call made by Rosa Luxemburg in 1909, for a general strike to get rid of the Prussian 'three class' suffrage system, which was quite complicated and based on income tax paid by citizens, thus discriminating against the less affluent. But while the mass strike did not take place, the widespread and animated discussions, demonstrations (despite a ban), and mass meetings around the campaign to abolish these outdated suffrage laws encouraged increased political involvement throughout the country. The three class suffrage system would, though, only be abolished at the end of the war with the fall of the monarchy.

During this campaign, Münzenberg delivered his first big public speech at a rally called by a coalition of concerned citizens in which he demanded the right to vote for 20-year-olds. According to his own description, he told his audience that 'A crown prince is mature enough to reign at 18, while working class youth are still not deemed mature enough at 20 to be granted the vote'.[6] He was strongly applauded and felt very proud. His élan could not be dented even by the next day's report in the *Erfurter Allgemeine Zeitung* stating that 'the one who really took the biscuit at the meeting was the 17-year-old Willi Münzenberg'. But the real repercussion came the following day when his boss at the factory called him in and gave him his cards on the spot.

The trade union in the factory was still weak, so he obtained little help from that quarter. He traipsed around other workplaces in the city desperately seeking work, but all jobs 'were taken' or there was nothing available 'at that moment'. He realised that for him, there were indeed no jobs available. His only option was to become a 'wanderer', tramping around the country and looking elsewhere in the hope of finding work.

Before the outbreak of the First World War, tens of thousands of German workers were forced to take to the roads in their search for work. 'On a lovely late summer morning in 1909 we set out fresh and happy, with light packs and a still lighter purse', he wrote.[7] He and another workmate set out with eight Marks between them. Their aim was to walk through the Thuringian forest, over the French border, and look for jobs there. They managed to reach Offenbach, by which time their little money was almost gone, and they were extremely hungry. His companion was overcome with homesickness and a desire for 'Erfurter dumplings'. Münzenberg, though, refused to give up and continued alone. Very soon he met another young job-seeker who agreed to share a room with him as this would save them both money. When Willi awoke the next morning, though, he discovered with dismay that his companion had disappeared in the night and taken his only set of clothes! Managing to borrow an old pair of trousers from the landlord, he was obliged to register with the police in Heidelberg as a homeless person. There, no doubt as a result of the strain and lack of food, he began spitting blood and was verbally abused by the police officer as a 'filthy pig'. Dejected and defeated, he, too, set out for home and arrived back in Erfurt a week later and had to spend several weeks in hospital there recovering from his ordeal.

Once recovered, he now did manage to find a job in a local factory, where they had apparently forgotten or were unaware of his past. That winter, he spent his free time working actively for the trade union and the Social Democratic Party, listening to lectures and reading and saving money as best he could.

The local party leaders, however, were very much opposed to his views and activities; the conflict between him and the old guard was making it impossible for him to work politically in an effective way. So in the spring of 1910, for the second time, he decided to take to the road, but this time with slightly more resources, and he was eventually able to make his way over the Swiss border to Zurich.

Notes

1 Münzenberg, Willi, *Die Dritte Front*, Verein der Funke, 2015, p. 34.
2 At the turn of the nineteenth-twentieth century, propaganda did not have the negative connotations with which we often associate the word today. It comes from the
   Latin propagare, to distribute or promote; today, particularly in the Western world,
   it is more often associated with misinformation and deceit.
3 Münzenberg, Willi, *Die Dritte Front*. p. 37.
4 Ibid. p. 49.
5 Ibid.
6 Ibid.
7 Ibid.

2

AN ÉMIGRÉ IN SWITZERLAND

Münzenberg's decision to leave Erfurt and head for Switzerland was undoubtedly influenced by his having heard from his Social Democratic compatriots about the wider freedoms afforded Socialists in that country. This was certainly underlined by the welcome he received in Zurich which couldn't have been more different to the way he had been treated in Erfurt.

The Swiss Socialist Youth Organisation was among the oldest of such organisations anywhere, as it was already established during the mid-1890s. On arrival, Münzenberg immediately sought out the local Social Democratic organisation in the city. Max Bock, the chair of the Swiss Young Socialists, also a German, immediately took him under his wing, and they soon became good friends. Bock found him accommodations with Dr Fritz Brupbacher, an anarchist politically, a practising psychologist and 'doctor to the poor'. Bock had also hoped to find paid work for Münzenberg in the city, but this was not so straightforward as he had hoped. With his resources used up and the prospect of a job still looking doubtful, Münzenberg decided to continue his journey to Marseilles in France, and then perhaps go overseas, rather than hang around in Zurich.

On his way towards Marseilles, Münzenberg spent a short sojourn in Berne, where he managed to find temporary work in a hotel bar, but the hours were long and the pay poor. When he wrote about his situation to his comrades in Zurich, they told him to return immediately, as Bock had, in the meantime, been able to find him a job. It was a paid one with a Social Democratic sympathiser who ran a small chemist shop in the town. The owner was a Polish émigré who, although he hated Germans and German nationalism, was prepared not only to offer Münzenberg a job, but to give him every encouragement to take part in Socialist activities. His friends, keen to sing his praises, had informed the chemist that Münzenberg knew Latin and understood all about drugs. Despite the chemist realising very quickly that this was blatantly not the case, he still took Münzenberg on as his assistant.

Once settled in a steady job, Münzenberg joined Brupbacher's circle of friends and found the discussions enormously stimulating. Brupbacher became an important mentor for him at this time and was one of his chief supporters. In this circle, he also began to better understand his own personality and his relationship with the world around him.

He began to be very much influenced by Brupbacher, and the anarchist ideas of Kropotkin and Bakunin, which found fertile ground in the mind of such a fiery and adventurous young man who had not yet developed a fundamental ideological outlook.

Brupbacher, frustrated by the lethargy and obstructionism of the old guard of the Social Democratic Party, had set up his own educational group for young Socialists called the Schwänli Club after the inn where they held their meetings. This club attained a certain renown, attracting a number of leading writers like Leonhard Frank and Erich Mühsam and artists like Max Oppenheimer to its meetings. Brupbacher invited Münzenberg and several of his young Socialist colleagues to join them.

The context in which Münzenberg began to mature, during the early years of the twentieth century, was one in which young adults in Germany faced legal discrimination, oppression, and marginalisation by the establishment. This had ignited in him a determination to fight for better and fairer social conditions in a double sense: as a member of the working class and as a young person. He rejected old hierarchies and ossified ways of thinking and operating. While he was more than happy to belong to a political party, he was certainly not prepared to collaborate in the organising of young people under any party's domination. So he was very receptive to anarchist ideas at this time.

The Swiss youth movement itself was still heavily influenced by anarchist and syndicalist ideas. Its newspaper, *Der Skorpion* (The Scorpion), celebrated individual terror as a means of achieving working-class freedom, and it put little emphasis on developing mass organisations and mass action. During his time there and under the strong influence of these ideas, the youth organisation in Zurich decided to do away with executive committees and chairs, as it was considered 'unworthy for free individuals to have to be kept in order by a chair'. This immediately had serious and debilitating consequences for the organisation, Münzenberg noted retrospectively, as everyone just spoke willy-nilly and concerted action became impossible. But he certainly sympathised with the 'anti-authoritarian and anti-militarist attitudes of the anarchists after his bitter experience with the party big wigs in Erfurt'.

This short period, though, represented an important learning process for him and other like-minded members who began to realise that this was not the best way forward. By the autumn of 1910, a small group of them, at least, had overcome their anarchist tendencies and began a lively debate with the others in the organisation about how to take the movement in a new direction.

Although he was already familiar with a range of Socialist literature, it was here that he 'learned for the first time to understand historical processes

FIGURE 2.1 Münznberg relaxing on Lake Zurich with fellow delegates to the Young Socialists' conference in 1916 (Courtesy of das Schweizerische Sozialarchiv, Zürich, Switzerland.)

FIGURE 2.2 In the Socialist Youth office in Zurich (Courtesy of das Schweizerische Sozialarchiv, Zürich, Switzerland.)

independently, look at them critically and evaluate them'. He was just 20 years old, but it was here that he would experience those unforgettable younger years as part of a circle of, in his own words, 'the best comrades and as leader of a militant group, eager for action'.

His working hours at the chemist's shop, the *Josef Apotheke*, were reasonable, and the work was relatively light. He found he had more free time than he'd ever had. Bock, his friend and comrade, soon entrusted him with the job of editing the Social Democratic Youth Organisation's journal, *Die Freie Jugend* (Free Youth), and his flat became the editorial office and the contact address for the organisation.

During these early years in Switzerland he also experienced, as he put it, 'a romantic phase'. Alongside his daily work in the chemist's shop and on top of his political work, he began writing plays, poems, and short stories, several about the violent relationship between a father and son, no doubt reflecting his own childhood conflicts, but nothing much came of these early literary attempts.

In the foreword to Münzenberg's reminiscences about his time in the youth movement, *Die Dritte Front* (The Third Front), his friend Fritz Brupbacher wrote:

> Pre-war Zurich was a scintillating chaos. Against a background of around 200,000 citizens and bourgeoisified workers a thousand souls from all over the world could be found cavorting there. Russian Bolsheviks and Mensheviks, revolutionary syndicalists and anarchists from Italy, Poland, Germany, Russia, Austria. Marx-, Bakunin-, Kropotkin- and Stirner-microbes were swarming around in the air. Everything that was in ferment in Europe, sent a representative to the *Roter Völkerbund* (Red People's League) in Zurich. And into this whole atmosphere Willi Münzenberg breezed in and began to ferment alongside the others and to mature ...[1]

James Joyce was one of those exiles living in the city during most of the war years, and it was there that he completed his novel *Ulysses*. The German novelist Leonhard Frank also found refuge in the city and, as an occasional visitor to Brupbacher's Schwänli Club, must have come across Münzenberg, but doesn't mention such an encounter in his semi-autobiographical novel, *Links wo das Herz ist* (Left where the Heart is).

Another small, but significant, group which settled there were the Dadaists, joining the growing colony of central and east European opponents of the war. The Dadaist movement took shape in Zurich, where a number of its leading exponents sought refuge from 'an increasingly unbearable' Germany. Hugo Ball, Tristan Tzara, and Richard Huelsenbeck gave the movement its distinctive name. The Cabaret Voltaire they ran in Zurich was located on the same street on which Lenin lived. Both of them were friends of Fritz Brupbacher, who was also close to Kropotkin. It was through Brupbacher that Ball seems to have made contact with Münzenberg and wrote for the latter's *Jugendgarde* (Young Guard) newspaper.[2]

Ball, Huelsenbeck, and Tzara would write poems each evening, rejecting any lines that made any sense, and the next day recite them simultaneously in three languages to a handful of curious visitors in the cabaret.

Scandal was in essence Dadaism's only uniting principle of cohesion, and it certainly succeeded in scandalising the staid art world of the time. As Hobsbawm notes, cultural and artistic change invariably precedes and predicts political and social change, and Dadaism certainly prefigured the chaos and 'times out of joint' that characterised Europe during those first decades of the twentieth century.[3]

Another young man who would gain prominence during a later conflict was the Socialist journalist, Julio Alvarez del Vayo, who was also active in the Zurich Young Socialist movement. He would become foreign minister in the Spanish Republican government and work closely with Münzenberg and his close collaborator Otto Katz during the Republic's short life.

In the spring of 1911, Münzenberg and a group of his young Socialist comrades made a trip over the Alps to Italy to meet their counterparts in various cities there, and he became particularly impressed with the Italians' strong anti-war stance. He wrote that, 'the Italian socialist youth organisations belonged among the best revolutionary, militant anti-military organisations, which were active in the socialist youth international before the war, and maintained that position even during the war'.[4] In Florence, he was surprised to witness even soldiers in uniform marching alongside civilians, waving red flags, and singing the *Internationale*.

Always alert to the beauties of nature, he was also enraptured by the Italian scenery and the atmospheric redolence of the small villages. His enjoyment and indeed his life were almost cut short, though, by an incident in Genoa. When he and his comrades arrived in the city, they decided to go for a swim in the enticing sea, but he lost his footing and was almost drowned, because when he began shouting for help, everyone thought he was just play acting. In land-locked Erfurt, he'd had no opportunity to learn to swim properly, but his friends didn't know that.

Once back in Zurich and enthused by their Italian experience, he and his comrades began the task of re-building the local youth organisation. They were now firmly moving away from their flirtation with anarchism and began concentrating on educational work, organising economic struggles, and carrying out anti-military propaganda.

The first yearbook edited by Münzenberg in May 1913 and published by the Swiss Socialist Youth Organisation under the title *Frührot (Red Dawn)* included a full calendar of forthcoming educational activities.

Their group held meetings every week, and among the 36 lectures they organised were ones on the question of alcohol, on the March revolution of 1848 and the Paris Commune of 1871, on the poetry of Heinrich Heine, protection for apprentices, and on other equally varied subjects. Alongside its educational tasks, the group also began taking economic struggles much more seriously, particularly those of apprentices and young workers.

In July 1911, the youth movement collaborated in the organisation of a large anti-military rally organised by the Social Democratic Party and held in Zurich's Velodrome at which Karl Liebknecht spoke. Münzenberg had, though, already met Liebknecht beforehand at a meeting on the Bodensee, and the great German anti-war leader undoubtedly helped cement his own already firmly held anti-war sentiments and also helped steer him away from anarchism and towards Marxism.

Münzenberg's organising talents and broad knowledge had become increasingly recognised by his fellow young Socialists and, not long after his return from Italy, they elected him as leader of the Zurich Young Socialists. One of his early pioneering decisions made after his election was to set up a girls' section, which, unsurprisingly, hadn't existed until then; only boys had been eligible for membership. After this decision was taken, one of the first group lectures was titled, intriguingly, 'Who should the working girl marry?'

He wrote that they were able to bring together young people whose lives became inseparable from the organisation itself and 'the work in the socialist youth movement became a lifetime task. Every day, every free hour belonged to the youth organisation. We were filled with youthful idealism and wanted to lift the world off its hinges'. However, the group's avid organising of lectures and meetings soon drew the ire of the adult section of the Social Democratic Party, which viewed it as challenging their own authority.

Clearly the youth organisation at this time still contained residues of anarchist ideology, as expressed in several youthful pranks its members carried out. The main Zurich daily newspaper, the *Bürgerzeitung* (Citizens' Newspaper), was vehement in its opposition to the working-class movement, Münzenberg says, and particularly its Socialist youth wing. So a small group of members gathered one night at its publishing offices, unscrewed the marble name plate, and took it to the flat of one of the editors of the Social Democratic newspaper, who was not at all pleased with being implicated in their prank. As if this was not enough, several days later a group of them returned to the building housing the *Bürgerzeitung* and threw stones through the windows.

Just before Christmas, at the end of 1911, ten members of the youth group created a minor furore by gathering on the first public holiday and, using an old hand cart, erected a sad-looking Christmas tree, which they had decorated provocatively. On its branches, instead of tinsel and baubles, they had hung legal indictments, empty pay packets, eviction notices, and similar documents representing, as they saw it, state oppression. At around midday, they towed it through the centre of Zurich while its staid citizens were on their way home from church. To accompany their little procession, they also sang carol tunes, but to their own politicised lyrics. The outraged citizenry shouted abuse at them and tried to involve the police, but at the sight of this wild bunch of young men, obviously carrying out a prank, the officers of the law chose to look the other way.

Although political activity took up much of their time, the group still managed to organise outings to the lakes in the mountains around Zurich or to the Graubündener Alps, which no doubt helped them maintain a fitness of body as well as mind.

A section of the youth group specialised in literary studies and Münzenberg joined them. They worked their way steadily through the classics of Russian literature, the works of Ibsen and Strindberg, and then French literature. But their study of Strindberg almost led to Münzenberg's expulsion from the *Arbeiter Union* (Workers' Union) for 'offending those members who held strong religious views'.

Towards the winter of 1911/1912, the group's members were beginning to feel frustrated as the movement was not progressing at a pace that they felt it should. 'We became sceptics', Münzenberg writes, 'made cheap jokes and the whole world seemed to us to be stale and empty. Some even had thoughts of suicide because their lives seemed aimless'. But in the spring of 1912, the core leadership managed to put the group on a new organisational and broader basis. However, the ongoing conflict with both the Social Democratic and trade union leaderships remained until eventually a compromise agreement could be reached.

In his book of reminiscences, *Die Dritte Front*, Münzenberg also notes proudly that already at this early stage in its development the movement showed concern about colonial oppression and gave full support to the Indian independence movement, as well as publishing articles on such issues. In October 1913, his own youth group organised a successful public protest against British imperialism and in that same year set up an aid association for political prisoners in Russia. Münzenberg himself spoke at a number of meetings and rallies on behalf of the aid association. As a result of his activism, during this time, he met and got to know a number of Russian Menshevik leaders, like Salomon Dolidse.

In the autumn of 1912, the group began showing films of an 'educational' nature, i.e., not escapist entertainment, but non-fictional, informative ones. The first of these screenings was an outstanding success with over 1,000 attending. This was long before the Bolshevik revolution and access to Soviet films. Those films that were available were invariably about non-political cultural matters or nature. For this activity, they came under vehement attack from the more religiously minded Social Democrats who viewed this relatively new form of entertainment as corrupting and called for the closure of all cinemas. Partially as a result of this conflict, the group went on to organise a number of debates with evangelical and Catholic youth groups that fuelled a lively exchange between Christian and Marxist ideas. Such events encouraged more and more young members to join the Socialist movement.

In 1912, the group became actively involved in the organising of a general strike in the city of Zurich. The government responded by occupying the *Volkshaus* (People's House – a cultural and meeting place for ordinary citizens) and arrested some of the strike leaders, including Münzenberg's comrade and secretary of the workers union, Max Bock, who would be expelled from Zurich. Bock had also been the editor of its newspaper, *Die Freie Jugend* (Free Youth), which sold around 2,000 copies each month. As Münzenberg had already worked on the paper, and with Bock now out of action, he was asked to become its interim editor, although he confessed he did so with trepidation because it was an onerous task and he had, as yet, little journalistic experience.

After discussing it with colleagues, he decided to make the paper much more of a campaigning instrument, but without neglecting the educational aspect and the communicating of political and trade union ideas. It took until 1915 before the editors were able to fully implement this new approach, but, as Münzenberg wrote later, 'thanks to the excellent circle of collaborators, later augmented by Lenin, Trotsky, Zinoviev, Liebknecht, Bronski, Balabanoff and many others, the newspaper from 1915 onwards became an exemplary youth paper, as even Lenin confirmed'.[5] The first issue edited by Münzenberg and published on 1 August 1912 was dedicated to the general strike and to Max Bock, the second was devoted to anti-military propaganda, and a further issue also took an adamantly anti-war stance.

In November 1912, Münzenberg attended the Extraordinary Ninth Congress of the Second (Socialist) International, held in Basle Minster. Everyone who was anyone in the European Socialist movement was there, including Clara Zetkin, Lev Kamenev representing the Bolsheviks, Julius Martov from the Mensheviks, Trotsky, Mussolini – at this time still a leading Socialist – Filippo Turati, Victor Adler, and Jean Jaurès among them. It was at this congress that all the European Socialist leaders agreed on the historic resolution to oppose a new war in Europe.

Two weeks beforehand, Münzenberg had organised a publicity conference to which he had invited Liebknecht and Luxemburg, but such independent initiatives made the elders of the Social Democratic Party livid, as they saw it as their responsibility to organise such events and not some upstart.

At this time, small numbers of interested members of the youth group began looking more closely at literature as a means of promoting the organisation, and they published a small brochure 'Workers' literature' around Christmas time in 1932 with the title *Christmas Bells*. It was a collection of poems and short stories by worker writers, including their own literary efforts. Because it sold so well, they saw this as a key to success and that 'as proletarian writers they could awake the masses'.

Münzenberg himself had begun writing plays intended for workers' theatres. His first effort focussed on the suffering of apprentices, and although 'it was no enrichment to proletarian literature it did serve to help improve the group's financial situation', he wrote. His next one was a polemic against the physical punishment meted out to young workers. He admitted that the success of his first play had led him to a poetic effusion and to even publish his versifying. He went on to write another play about the Paris Commune which was also a surprising success. Mesmerised by this unexpected response, he suggested to Brupbacher that he do a reading at the latter's literary circle. After reading only a few pages of his play to the group he became aware of an ominous silence in the room and stopped reading. In the following discussion, Brupbacher tore his play to shreds, and the others in the circle grinned as they witnessed this demolition job. After that, Münzenberg commented humbly, 'I gave up trying to write literature'.

In September 1913, the Zurich Young Socialists would turn out in large numbers to pay their respects to the greatly admired German Socialist leader, August Bebel, who had died that month in a Swiss sanatorium. His funeral cortege through Zurich was accompanied by thousands of workers. He had been one of their heroes and his books, particularly *Woman and Socialism*, had been enormously influential in the Socialist movement worldwide.

In January 1914, a referendum was held among all members of the Swiss Socialist youth groups and a decision made to set up an autonomous national organisation with its own secretariat and full-time secretary. Münzenberg and his close comrades Ede Meyer, Willi Trostel, and Guilio Mimiola had fought long and hard for this decision. The 25-year-old Münzenberg was elected by the central committee as its first secretary. As a result, he gave up his day job at the chemist's and from then on became a full-time and paid political activist.

To begin with, his small flat was his office. His comrade, Ede Meyer, also had a flat in the same building, and from there, over the following six years, the two carried out their political work. Very soon new sections of the organisation sprang up in a number of other towns and villages throughout the country; membership rose from 763 in the previous year to 1,342, among them 200 female members. In the organisation's yearbook for 1915, it was noted that 'the success of our organisation over recent years, particularly the development of the newspaper, has been largely as a result of the efforts of the Secretariat'. There is no doubt that under Münzenberg's leadership, it had expanded rapidly and the circulation of its paper, the *Freie Jugend* (Free Youth), had risen to around 5,000. Building on this success, the organisation began publishing a second newspaper, the *Jugend International* (Youth International), and then added a children's paper, *Junge Saat* (Young Seedcorn), to the stable.

He appeared to be indefatigable in his role as secretary, and during 1914 alone, he is said to have organised 336 meetings and events. But that fateful year also saw the opposition of European Socialist Parties to war collapse like a punctured balloon. Münzenberg was shattered by the declaration of war and the spectacle of European countries now confronting each other with all the good sense and rationality of posturing peacocks high on testosterone. He saw their capitulation as a complete betrayal of Socialist principles.

Even as a young man, he was, unusually for the period, also passionately anti-military and anti-war. Prussian authoritarianism was anathema to him. He was devastated when the Social Democratic leaders in Germany and Austria capitulated so readily as the clouds of war gathered in early 1914, gleefully jumping onto the militarist and jingoist bandwagon, despite earlier pledges of international working-class solidarity and adamant opposition to war.

After the assassination of Archduke Franz Ferdinand of Austria, the situation in Europe deteriorated rapidly, and nationalist fervour gripped the masses in virtually all European states apart from Italy, where the response was more muted and reluctant. Münzenberg and his few stalwarts found themselves fighting a losing battle, but that didn't deter them from continuing to oppose the war with all their might.

Although, to begin with, even in Germany there was no immediate gung-ho war fervour and, particularly in Social Democratic circles at the grassroots level, there were still strong anti-war sentiments. In July 1914, the German Social Democratic Party (*SPD*) leadership had even called on German citizens to demonstrate for peace and there was a large turnout, but already by August, once the parliamentary leadership had capitulated and voted to support the war, the mood in the country began to change. These developments provided Münzenberg with a strong motivation to press on with setting up an autonomous international youth organisation.

Already in the early autumn of 1913, the Zurich Youth Group had suggested holding an international gathering in Stuttgart, at Whitsun the following year. The suggestion was taken up with alacrity by their comrades in Stuttgart. The Swiss youngsters who travelled there that Whitsun in 1914 managed to smuggle 50 copies of Hervés *Das Vaterland der Reichen* (The Fatherland of the Wealthy) and 100 copies of Liebknecht's *Militarismus und Antimilitarismus* (Militarism and Anti-militarism) into Germany, although these were strictly banned, and they went like hot cakes among the delegates.

Münzenberg delivered a rousing speech at the conclusion of the rally in Stuttgart, replete with Biblical references and florid imagery, intended to send off the delegates with élan and a determination to 'fight the good fight' more steadfastly than ever. The Stuttgart event was the last such cross border anti-militarist gathering of any size in Europe before war broke out later that year.

From Stuttgart, he travelled to Erfurt, Leipzig, and Dresden to address other gatherings of young Socialists. Because his speech in Leipzig was deemed 'political' by the local police commissar, the organisers were fined 100 Marks. Only a few weeks after he returned via Munich to Zurich, the First World War had shattered hopes and would plunge Europe into more than four years of bloody mayhem.

In Germany, even before the declaration of war, the majority of the population had become fed up with the seemingly eternal state of political and economic uncertainty, so it was not surprising that there was no great clamour to seek a peaceful solution to the Austrian-Serbian conflict, but instead a rise in nationalist fervour. Shortly before war was declared by Germany, Kaiser Wilhelm made his infamous statement from the balcony of the palace in Berlin, in which he declared, 'If it comes to war, there will cease to be parties, we will all be Germans only'.

The nineteenth century didn't really come to an end on 31st December 1899, but on that fateful day 4 August 1914, when a wanton Kaiser in his resplendent uniform fired the first shot. The masses rallied to his call with alacrity and a tsunami of rabid nationalism swept the country; only very few remained immune to this epidemic, but Münzenberg was one who did.

That fateful year, with the imminent outbreak of hostilities in Europe, Zurich became a veritable beehive. Leonhard describes it as teeming 'with spies from the belligerent countries, a pack of diverse adventurers, rich people who had brought their fortunes to a safe haven, currency speculators from every European country, followed by gold-digging girls … and increasingly, from France and Germany, opponents of the war, who believed they could work more effectively against the war from a base in Switzerland'.[6] It was also a melting pot of political and artistic refugees from a whole number of countries, including, as is well known, a number of Russians. There was an atmosphere of vibrant creativity and political debate. Münzenberg's conversations with many of those who made up this heady mix of foreign activists, helped internationalise his outlook and increase the breadth of his knowledge and political and cultural understanding.

The European elites felt that a war could also play a key internal political function. Tsarist Russia had been shaken by the 1905 revolution, but the enormous gap between rich and poor and the old semi-feudal system of government continued. In the face of social unrest, it was felt in both Germany and Russia that a successful war would serve to consolidate the established, but wobbly, systems.

In the German national elections held in1912, the *SPD* had become the strongest faction in the Reichstag, but the party was still viewed in conservative circles as a gang of 'renegades with no sense of fatherland'. The war provided the *SPD* leadership with the opportunity of demonstrating its patriotism and love of nation, and as a result, it found a grudging acceptance in those same conservative circles. The Second International, despite its firm declarations of international solidarity, broke up like a rotten ship on the reef of war.

The declaration of war transformed millions of normally rational and peace-loving individuals into gung-ho nationalists and belligerent warriors. In Zurich, noisy crowds paraded through the town centre, waving the imperial German black-white-red flags and singing patriotic songs. The young Socialists were livid and called a counter-demonstration, but their numbers were tiny compared with the pro-war adherents. Even in the ranks of the Socialist youth, despite the organisation's track record of anti-militarism, war hysteria would infect it too, and many of its members willingly donned uniforms, although the leadership around Münzenberg remained steadfast opponents of the war.

He continued to campaign ceaselessly, writing articles, pamphlets, and editorials in the organisation's newspaper. His arguments were clear, unequivocal, and even prophetic in terms of the Second World War: 'Whatever the outcome of this massive war, it will make no difference to the workers in the battling countries. Their interests are not part of the game; the war is raging solely to promote the interests of the capitalists. No clever rhetoric can hide that. Earlier such economic struggles were clothed in the mantle of religious justification, later in a nationalistic one, but because neither of these has pulling power anymore, an attempt is being made to characterise it as a "racial struggle". German culture is being threatened by the Slavs, scream the German capitalists … new colonies and thus new exploitable territories will be the victors' trophies once the war is over'.[7]

The young Socialists who remained true to their anti-war principles felt badly let down by Europe's Social Democratic leaders who, only weeks beforehand, had been vociferous opponents of the rising militarism and war hysteria, but who now beat the drums of war as heartily as their erstwhile opponents in the right-wing parties.

In Germany, only Karl Liebknecht, Rosa Luxemburg, and a few others in the leadership of the Social Democratic Party continued to oppose the war. In Switzerland, what remained of the Socialist Youth Group rallied around a number of progressive religious figures like the Socialist theologian, Professor Leonhard Ragaz. Speeches by Ragaz were reproduced in the pages of the Socialist youth newspaper. His leader in the second edition of *Freie Jugend* was titled: 'Why has Social Democracy failed?' However, the largely anti-religious young Socialists soon broke away from this collaborative work, particularly once they began receiving solidarity messages and promises of support from a number of friendly left-wing political groups in other countries. They also felt boosted by the new influx to Switzerland of anti-war refugees from Germany, France, Russia, and other countries, including individuals like Lenin, Trotsky, Grigory Zinoviev, Georgi Plekhanov, and Karl Radek. After arriving in Switzerland shortly after war was declared, Lenin settled in Berne, before moving to Zurich in February 1916.

Despite the communication difficulties now caused by the war, Münzenberg continued to correspond with Socialist youth organisations in the other European countries, particularly in Italy, Norway, Denmark, and Sweden. In agreement with these organisations, he wrote to the secretary of the international youth office in Vienna requesting that it convene an international conference of youth organisations by Whitsun 1915 at the latest. Unsurprisingly, given the precarious situation and logistical problems, his request was rejected. Not satisfied with this response, he decided to go ahead and organise a conference in Berne off his own bat. He was ashamed and disgusted by the way the German Socialist youth movement had so easily reneged on its principles. This change in attitude was poignantly reflected in a leading article in the southern German *Arbeiter Jugend* (The Young Worker) newspaper. The young Social Democrat, Ludwig Frank, who had immediately volunteered once war was declared, had fallen after only a few days at the front. His death was commemorated in the paper as a heroic one and as an example to millions of other young German workers. Münzenberg characterised this as revealing the whole mendacity of the Social Democratic hierarchy which, 'considered proletarian youth mature enough for seventeen-year-olds to shed their blood on the killing fields but not mature enough to debate the question of the rationale of war'.

The Berne conference took place at Easter 1915, despite the German section's refusal to take part and of reservations on the part of the French. It was a very modest affair, with only 14 delegates attending, from Poland, Holland, Italy, Norway, Sweden, Denmark, Switzerland, Bulgaria, Germany, and Russia, but he received many 'letters and telegrams of support from numerous youth groups in Germany'. At the conference, representatives from Poland and Russia took part for the first time. Although Lenin was himself unable to take part in the sessions, his close companion and comrade, Inessa Armand,[8] and Alexander Yegorov did, and Inessa spoke about the current situation in Russia.

Lenin, Münzenberg notes, 'followed the debate with great interest and had a decisive influence on it', and he would not only continue his criticism of the policies of the Socialist youth movement in personal discussions, but also publicly in the Russian language press. This criticism was viewed by Münzenberg and his comrades in the spirit it was meant, as helpful and constructive. Lenin became affectionately known to them all as 'The Old Man'.

How much was due to Lenin's advice and criticism cannot be ascertained, but Münzenberg and his close comrades certainly made good use of their experience gathered in Zurich and from their ongoing discussions with the small group of Bolshevik emigrés gathered there.

Meeting Lenin

Münzenberg's first encounter with Lenin, he says, was while travelling from Zurich to Lucerne, although Gross says he first met him in Berne during the spring of 1915. At this time, he had already read Lenin's book *The War and the Second International*, as well as Zinoviev and Lenin's co-authored work, *Socialism and War*, both of which he studied avidly and which 'rapidly cured me of the last traces of social religious sermons', he noted.

In the spring of that same year, at the Socialist conference against the war held in Berne, he would encounter Lenin once more, together with Georgi Plekhanov. At that conference, Lenin called for the turning of, what he rightly called, an imperialist war into a civil war, i.e., a class war.

Münzenberg had already met and conversed with Trotsky, as the latter had been an irregular participant in the leadership of the Workers' Education Association in Switzerland. At the same time, he also became close friends with the Polish-born revolutionary and leading Bolshevik, Karl Radek. The Bolsheviks in Zurich met regularly for discussions and, on learning about their discussion club, Münzenberg soon joined them.

Lenin's charisma and powers of persuasion had considerable impact on many young Socialists who came in contact with him, and Münzenberg was one of them. But Lenin, too, was enthused by the vigour and competence of such young and committed Socialists like Münzenberg, who he felt sure would play key roles in any future Europe, and devoted much effort in helping to develop their political thinking. At this time, Lenin was 45 and Münzenberg only 29 years old. Lenin, he remarked, was always keenly interested in the current thinking of all the Socialist Party leaders and would pump him and any visiting comrades for information.

A conference, held in Zimmerwald, Switzerland from 5 to 8 September 1915, became a key moment for the anti-war forces and is now termed the Zimmerwald Conference by historians. It was the first of three international Socialist conferences convened by anti-militarist forces from within the mainstream Socialist parties. Among those attending were Oddino Morgari and Angelica Balabanoff from the Italian Socialist Party, Adolf Warski from Poland, Grigory Zinoviev and Pavel Axelrod from Russia, together with Lenin, Trotsky, and Radek, who were conveniently in exile at the time in Switzerland. Münzenberg immediately joined and became active in what is now known as the Zimmerwald anti-war movement.

Lenin had been busy preparing for the conference for several months, in an attempt to rally the more radical, left-wing delegates, by drafting preparatory documents. However, Lenin's own draft declaration was eventually rejected by the left-wing caucus in favour of Radek's, and the conference itself failed to adopt a final resolution at all, but it did establish an International Socialist Commission or Committee with a mandate to set up a temporary secretariat in Berne, who would act as an intermediary between the different groups and would publish a *Bulletin* containing the manifesto and proceedings of the conference.

Faced with the stolidity and intransigence of the old guard in the *SPD* leadership, Münzenberg became increasingly frustrated and, in response, called for the setting up of an autonomous youth section of the Socialist International in order to generate some new ideas and momentum. The resultant Socialist youth organisation that he founded would become the largest and most effective anti-war grouping to exist during the First World War.

The Young Communist International, founded in Berlin in 1919, grew directly out of this Socialist youth organisation. By 1920, 49 separate youth organisations would become affiliated to it, representing 800,000 members, including some from outside Europe. This global dimension of the organisation, which would be built very much on Münzenberg's initiative, is often forgotten – because it was these youth groups which, in most cases, created the basis on which the Comintern would later build and out of which a number of national communist parties would emerge.

With fairly regular contact, his friendship with Lenin deepened over the years 1915–1917, until Lenin left Switzerland. Münzenberg would often visit him in his tiny flat on the Spiegelgasse in Zurich, where he lived with his wife Krupskaya, or Lenin would drop into the youth office or join the young comrades at a local café. He also gave lectures for them and wrote articles for the *Jugend Internationale* newspaper, as well as giving Münzenberg regular 'valuable advice on editorial matters'. At this time, Münzenberg noted, Lenin was particularly interested in the agricultural situation in the Western countries – it being a key factor in a country like Russia with its dependence on a large agricultural sector with a huge workforce.

In a letter from the Bolshevik Party, signed by Lenin and addressed to Swiss workers, which was published by Münzenberg in the *Jugend Internationale* newspaper, he specifically thanks the 'Swiss revolutionary Social Democrats and … the courageous young vanguard of the "Free Youth" who supported the anti-war movement and their struggle'. It was written shortly before his final departure for Russia.

The anti-war movement in Switzerland gathers strength

In the aftermath of the 1915 Berne conference, the influence of those opposing the war had gained in strength, as the early pro-war hysteria began to wane in the face of the rising losses at the front and with the prospect of a long drawn-out conflict. Out of that conference, an international Socialist youth organisation had been founded and a secretariat elected, with Münzenberg as its first secretary, alongside his fellow members of the secretariat, Ansgar Olaussen from Norway, Christian Christiansen from Denmark, Dietrich Notz from Germany, and Amadeo Catanesi from Italy.

Out of that conference came the call to celebrate Swiss Youth Day at Whitsun 1915. On the Whit Sunday, thousands of young people and over a thousand workers came together in an impressive rally and demonstration opposing the war. When the marchers streamed past the local barracks, singing the *Internationale*, 'they were given a hearty welcome by the recruits and soldiers'. The demonstrators took over the centre of Zurich and stopped the traffic, but one irate tram driver decided to ignore the demand to stop and drove his vehicle towards the demonstrators. Münzenberg threw himself in front of the tram, which hit him and threw him to the ground, but did then come to a halt. Münzenberg was immediately arrested, but later freed after a large group of demonstrators gathered in front of the police station demanding his release. The right-wing press reacted to this incident with an incendiary call for all foreigners to be expelled from the country.

FIGURE 2.3 Anti-war march in Zurich c. 1915 (Courtesy of das Schweizerische Sozialarchiv, Zürich, Switzerland.)

Although Switzerland had been spared direct involvement in the war, the belligerent states' economic warfare and insufficient preparations for a protracted European-wide conflict resulted in tremendous economic and social impact in the country.

As the war dragged on, the repercussions on the civilian population grew progressively worse: food shortages, price rises, and cuts in wages. Imports of vital foodstuffs and fuel collapsed, especially during the second half of the war. During the final two years, imported cereals declined by 68 per cent and the import of coal dropped by more than a third from 1915 to 1918. These factors boosted wartime inflation and made basic consumer goods very expensive for ordinary people. The price of bread doubled and that of sugar even trebled between March 1914 and December 1918. Overall inflation from 1914 to 1918 reached 195.8 per cent. Strikes and go-slows were widespread, and after the publication of the Zimmerwald anti-war manifesto, Socialist anti-war demonstrations took place in 60 Swiss towns during October 1915 alone. From the summer of 1916 onwards, market riots broke out in a number of cities.

The mood among the working population had become steadily more angry and demands for better conditions were also fuelled by the small groups of radical émigrés who functioned like 'yeast in a dough' within the Swiss working-class movement. But it was the small group of Bolshevik émigrés that had a particularly strong influence, especially on the young Socialists. They helped ensure that anti-military motions were tabled at many of the cantonal and national party meetings and the *Freie Jugend* paper continued to carry anti-military articles.

Münzenberg recalled that the renewed political life of the Socialist youth organisation brought over other non-Socialist youngsters, including whole groups to its side, among them Catholic and Evangelical ones. It was working with such disparate groups and individuals that undoubtedly gave Münzenberg a foretaste of how to build a popular front movement.

Between 1906 and 1918 Socialist youth groups in Switzerland had grown from a mere 3 to 164 and from 180 members to 5,500. Quite an achievement under the difficult circumstances, and much of this success was due to the hard work put in by Münzenberg and his comrades.

On the communication and publicity front, too, the national organisation was still publishing a monthly newspaper with sections on working-class art and education and also produced separate pamphlets as part of its 'Socialist Youth Library'. It also established its own bookshop in Zurich.

In 1916, their dogged campaigning for better conditions for young workers was rewarded with the introduction by the government of national legislation to protect apprentices.

On 1 August 1916, in response to a call by his comrade Willi Trostel, an anti-war demonstration was to be held in Zurich. This time, though, the authorities were determined to prevent it happening, and the forces of law and order turned out in strength. Without warning, they fell upon the demonstration with brute force, including the use of truncheons and swords, managing to drive the demonstrators apart. The organised working-class movement, however, threw its weight behind the young demonstrators and, two days later, called a sympathy demonstration at which, according to Münzenberg, more than 20,000 workers and 2,000 youngsters took part. According to the local press, 12,000 workers took part and 60–80,000 citizens formed protective barriers for them.

Switzerland after the Bolsheviks' departure

In Russia, the first of the two 1917 revolutions erupted, the so-called February Revolution (11 March in the Gregorian calendar), centred on Petrograd, and it took almost everyone by surprise, even those who had worked most diligently for it. It led to the Tsar's abdication and the forming of a Provisional Government under Kerensky. Immediately on hearing the news, a central evacuation committee was formed by leading Russian exiles in Zurich. Lenin was itching to return and wrote to his comrade Yakov Hanecki in Stockholm that 'you can imagine what a torture it is for all of us, having to sit here in such a situation'. We must get to Russia 'at all costs', he said. He thought through all possible ways of reaching Russia, but none appeared to be feasible.

In desperation, Lenin asked Münzenberg to act as intermediary for him and to try and arrange passage through Germany somehow. However, it was Fritz Platten, a Swiss Social Democrat, who eventually managed to make the breakthrough and persuade the German authorities to allow a small group of Bolshevik leaders travel unmolested through Germany, on their way to Russia. For purely opportunistic reasons, the German government agreed to grant Lenin and his entourage safe passage, hoping Lenin's presence in Russia would further weaken the Russian government's resolve to pursue the war.

A few months before they had received news of the revolution, Münzenberg had had a discussion with Lenin in the café of Zurich's Hotel Astoria, where Lenin had tried to convince him that there would shortly be a revolutionary uprising in Russia, and that this would be the prelude to a proletarian revolution on a global scale. Münzenberg remained sceptical, as he had been deeply affected by the arrest of Liebknecht in Germany and the general passivity of the majority of the working class there; he was in a pessimistic mood and not easy to convince.

On 9 April, the day of their departure, the 29 who would be travelling to Russia, including Krupskaya and Armand, plus Fritz Platten, met together for a last midday meal on Swiss soil, in the *Zähringer Hof* restaurant in Zurich. At 3.30 p.m. the train pulled out of the station to begin its historic journey.

There have been questions raised about whether Lenin actually did travel through Germany in a 'sealed carriage', but that term was used metaphorically. The agreement reached with Germany for his safe transport from Switzerland merely specified that the carriages were to be treated as 'foreign territory', i.e., not to be entered or checked.

Münzenberg describes the elation that accompanied the departing Bolsheviks on 9 April 1917 and the sense of high optimism everyone felt. Just before the group's departure, he says, Radek told him: 'We'll either be hanged in three months or we'll have taken power'.

Although Münzenberg had earlier been rejected by the German authorities for military service on medical grounds, he had several times since then been sent his call-up papers, but had simply ignored them. This meant he couldn't risk joining his Russian comrades on their return to Russia, as he could have been arrested. He felt obliged to remain behind in Zurich, throwing himself with renewed vigour into his work in the Youth International. However, later that same year, he was, to his surprise, given permission by the German government to travel by train through Germany to Sweden for the founding conference of the Swedish Left Socialist Party, which the Germans understandably assumed would also help promote the anti-war movement and, as they saw it, further weaken the allies' resolve to pursue the war. There, he again met Radek and other Bolsheviks at the conference. Radek suggested that he should accompany them back to Russia, but he declined. Perhaps he realised that as a non-Russian speaker, he would be like a fish out of water there, or he had other more personal reasons for wishing to return to Switzerland.

On his journey back to Switzerland, on 20 May, he made a short stop-over in Copenhagen and, in his capacity as the secretary of the International Federation of Socialist Young People's Organisations, also known as the Youth International, he spoke at a large anti-war meeting organised by the Copenhagen Young Socialists. His opening words were as follows:

> I would like to thank you for your enthusiastic reception and hope that it was not meant for me personally, but for the ideas for which we are all fighting. I will convey your greetings onwards. Copenhagen is a city of great significance for social democracy. It was here that the 1910 international congress and the congress of the Youth International was held. That was at a time when we all believed in social democracy and the power and strength of the International. Even when the storm was imminent, in the last days before the war, we hoped that we were still in a position to be able to prevent war. Our hearts glowed with joy when we heard that 50,000 workers had marched through the streets of Berlin in solid opposition to the war, and when we heard that the German social democrats had sent a representative to France. But our disappointment was therefore all the greater once the armies marched to confront each other, once proletarians began to shoot other proletarians.[9]

This short extract gives a flavour of his passionate anti-war stance and his rhetorical skills. The young Socialists in Copenhagen were indeed excited by his speech. According to their journal, *Fremad* (Forward), the evening with Münzenberg was enthralling and unforgettable. The audience 'glowed with enthusiasm and solidarity, and the "red songs" were sung with vigour as never before'.

As Jesper Jørgensen writes: 'In other words, Münzenberg poured petrol on a revolutionary fire that was already well underway under war and revolution. And there is no doubt that he was a key player in promoting radical solidarity among the young socialists during the First World War – a process which would eventually tear the international socialist movement apart. Like many other socialist youth organisations, in 1919 the Danish Social Democratic Youth League followed Münzenberg, into the Communist movement, although historically its political position was that of a free and independent youth movement'.[10]

FIGURE 2.4   Lenin addressing a meeting of workers (Courtesy of Sputnik Images.)

FIGURE 2.5   Grigory Zinoviev (Courtesy of Sputnik Images.)

FIGURE 2.6 Trotsky addressing a meeting shortly after the 1917 revolution (Courtesy of Sputnik images.)

FIGURE 2.7 Karl Radek (Courtesy of Sputnik images.)

Back in Switzerland he had to laugh after he read in the mainstream press, particularly in the French-speaking part of Switzerland, that the Bolsheviks were responsible for the mayhem in the country and accusing Radek and Lenin alongside Münzenberg himself of being paid agents of the Germans, helping to undermine the war effort. This accusation is not entirely surprising when we take into account how close to a revolutionary uprising Switzerland itself appeared to be.

The success of the Bolshevik-led November Revolution in Russia had sent shock waves around the world. That same year, 1917, things were coming to a head in Switzerland itself. A revolutionary situation appeared to be unfolding there too, with widespread strikes and even barricades erected; it was certainly a highly volatile situation. The country also witnessed a peak in conscientious objection mainly by Socialists. The protest movements first climaxed in the autumn when, on 15 November, several hundred people in Zurich, including many members of the Socialist youth movement, celebrated the Russian Revolution. They then joined a demonstration led by the radical pacifist Max Dätwyler, which forced the closure of two munitions factories. This demonstration was followed by riots lasting over two days in which four protesters were killed by the military. Although Münzenberg supported the demonstrations, he did not take part.

Feeling elated by the news of the successful Bolshevik Revolution and their own successful demonstrations at the munitions factories, the Dätwyler group and its young Socialist supporters were convinced that their actions forcing the closure of the armaments factories would, in a few weeks, bring the war to a close for lack of ammunition. Very much wishful thinking, of course.

After the demonstrations, its leaders would meet at Münzenberg's flat where lively debates ensued on the way forward. He argued strongly with them that their action was simply an isolated act of rebellion and would not of itself lead to a genuine revolution unless they were able to win over the majority of working people.

On 17 November, the government decided to crack down on the increasingly volatile demonstrations and the determination of the participants to keep the armaments factories closed. A bloody confrontation took place in which hundreds were injured, 28 of them badly, and four were killed – three workers and one policeman. There had been no confrontation like this in Switzerland in living memory, and it caused consternation throughout the country. The mainstream press, Münzenberg wrote, published extra issues and aimed all their vitriol at the Socialist youth movement, and the federal authorities despatched more troops to Zurich. The leaders, Willi Trostel and Ernst Martin, were arrested as was Münzenberg a day later, on 19 November 1917.

The Swiss authorities had for some time been keeping Münzenberg under close surveillance, but now they felt he had overstepped the mark, even though he had not been a direct participant in the demonstrations. They knew he was one of the key figures behind the protests. In the eyes of the Swiss authorities, he was a gadfly and dangerous agitator.

In his book, *Die Dritte Front* (The Third Front), Münzenberg describes his arrest amusingly, almost as if the police officer were inviting him to a dinner party rather than arresting him: in a polite fashion – 'gemütlich' or laid-back – the way the Swiss do things! Very different from the way he would have been treated in Germany.

Two days after his arrest, the ruling Swiss Federal Council issued instructions for deportation procedures against Münzenberg to be implemented forthwith. It didn't even await a police report about whether Münzenberg had actually taken part in the demonstrations, been one of the organisers, or not. They simply jumped at the opportunity of at last being able to get rid of this uppity foreigner who, in their eyes, had been such a corrupting influence on Swiss youth.

While under arrest, his flat was searched by the police and documents, including letters from Lenin, Liebknecht, and other friends were confiscated.

For the first weeks he was held in the Zurich police barracks, an old building with primitive cells, even though security itself was quite lax and his cell was not uncomfortable, those few days were a torture for him as he received no letters, could not deal with organisational matters, and was not allowed to communicate with his comrades outside; he was unaccustomed to such enforced inactivity. At night, though, he was able to establish communication through the walls with his fellow prisoners, the pacifists Rotter and Dätwyler.

FIGURE 2.8 Münzenberg with his girlfriend and fellow young Socialist Adele Kluser in Switzerland (Courtesy of das Schweizerische Sozialarchiv, Zürich, Switzerland.)

Over the past years, the daily hectic and urgent demands had kept him preoccupied 24 hours a day, now he had nothing to do but stare at the ceiling. All his links were severed and thoughts circled in his head like hurtling planets. How could he make use of this situation? What could he do? This impotence tormented him.

It wasn't too long before the police barracks became inundated with hundreds of angry letters demanding his release. This expression of international solidarity was followed up in the winter of 1917–1918 with demonstrations in Zurich and other Swiss cities, as well as smaller ones in other European countries, declaring their solidarity with the arrested German Socialist leader and demanding his release.

One of those imprisoned with him, Friedrich Bartel, managed to escape after his fiancée smuggled a file into the prison. This incident unfortunately led to a security clampdown for those left behind, and shortly thereafter, they were all transferred to a regional prison, a new building with more secure cells. There, Münzenberg would spend five months in custody while his case was scrutinised by the officials. According to the Swiss legal system, it was not a simple matter to deport foreigners who had been granted residency, without due process, and this took time.

There was also the pressure exerted from the outside world by his supporters, although it took time to organise and mobilise, as three of his closest comrades in the leadership, Alfred Bucher, Ernst Marti, and Willi Trostel, had also been arrested with him. However, his comrade Fritz Platten, who was still at liberty, set about turning the arrests into an international cause célèbre.

During this time, a whole number of demonstrations and rallies were organised by the young Socialist organisation in Switzerland calling for his release, and he received thousands of postcards of solidarity from young Socialists around the world. Even the Soviet government called on the Swiss authorities to release him.

While he was still in prison, on 15 December 1917, the Soviet Union and Germany signed a truce, which must have pleased him greatly, as it brought an end to the war that much closer.

In the meantime, Willi Trostel, who had been released from prison early, took over the leadership of the youth organisation and became instrumental in organising an ongoing campaign in support of Münzenberg's release. As part of that campaign, he was also able to assemble six years' worth of Münzenberg's writings and publish them in a booklet titled *What did Münzenberg Want?*

Trostel would become a founder member of the Swiss Socialist Party and, from 1923, he was a long time member of the Canton Council of Zurich; he became editor of the Swiss Socialist newspaper, *Kämpfer* (Fighter), and the director of the Swiss Red Aid organisation. Later, with the rise of fascism, he would play a key role in providing support and accommodation for Italian and German refugees.

The Swiss federal government was now in somewhat of a bind, as Münzenberg had to be considered as a 'military refugee', and deporting him to Germany would not only irritate the Entente allies, but could mean his immediate arrest in Germany for desertion.

Although there were strong voices in Switzerland itself calling for his deportation, the country's strict adherence to the legal rules meant that it would not be legal to deport someone into almost certain military detention, who, as in his case, had refused to be conscripted. Thus, in the meantime, he would have to be detained in Switzerland until a neutral country could be found that would accept him.

After several weeks in prison, his health began to deteriorate, and this also helped increase the pressure for his release. The last thing the Swiss authorities wanted was to have a martyr on their hands.

In March 1918, after five months, he was conditionally released after his friend Gustav Nüssli posted the bail money of five thousand Swiss Francs. His bail conditions, though, meant that he was not allowed to partake in any further political activities. In his case, of course, this was a bit like asking a starving man to refrain from eating.

He was not to enjoy much time in freedom, though, as the mainstream press continued its campaign of hounding the youth organisation and clamouring for 'the dangerous agitator' Münzenberg to be either immediately deported or re-interned.

When he couldn't resist giving a short speech to a small gathering of young Socialists in Birsfelden, near Basle, the authorities pounced, and on 31 May, he was re-arrested for breaking his bail conditions. This time they decided to send him far from his urban stronghold to the isolated prison fortress of Witzwil, in the canton of Berne and the largest such institution in the country, where it was more difficult for comrades from Zurich to visit him regularly. This new situation would bring him close to despair.

Before he left to serve his time, Münzenberg's friends organised a farewell dinner for him at the *Ristorante Cooperativa* in Zurich. Over a meal of roast goose, washed down with excellent Italian wine, he enjoyed his last hours of freedom: there were speeches, poetry readings, and lusty songs. The next morning, his comrades gave him a colourful send-off from the station platform in Zurich, showering him with bunches of flowers, as if he hadn't enough to carry with his large case full of books, essential to keep him occupied during his indefinite incarceration.

The criminal police officer who accompanied him to Witzwil appeared at the gate of the prison administration office looking more like a florist, with his arms full of flowers, and accompanied by a young man with an unruly mane of hair, wearing a black velvet jacket, and hauling a heavy case full of books. The governor was discombobulated by this sight, and the first thing he did was to order a haircut for his new charge and made him change into the standard, striped prison uniform, like those seen in US comedy films of the period. He put Münzenberg in an unlighted cell for the next six hours, where he could kick his heels until the governor decided what to do with him.

Despite his protests that he was no murderer or thief and was merely being interned on a civil charge, he was still obliged to follow regulations. Like all the other inmates, he was also forced to undertake agricultural labour: prisoners were woken at half past four and taken out to the fields where they were expected to work, even in the hot sun, until 8.00 in the evening or later. However, even this brutal introduction to prison life in Witzwil couldn't dampen Münzenberg's spirits for long.

After protesting strongly about being treated like a common criminal, he was given lighter garden work. Later, he was able to hold long discussions with the prison governor and his sons about their plans for prison reform, but they were of the opinion that taking the prisoners out of their cells and giving them fieldwork to do was a sufficiently reforming accomplishment.

Münzenberg had plenty of experience in dealing with people of all sorts, friend and foe alike, and the prison governor was no match for his persuasive personality. In only a short time, he had persuaded the governor to give him a certain privileged status, and instead of going out to work in the fields at dawn every morning, he was now allowed to wander off into the woods, enclosed by the huge moat around the prison, where he could pick Elderberry and camomile blossoms. The food in the prison here, he said later, was also certainly better than what he would receive in German prisons.

Several months into his internment, another comrade who had refused to carry out military service was also brought in, and the two were allowed to have cells next to each other and could communicate through the bars. He was also now allowed to receive visitors, and one day, the 60-year-old Social Democrat leader Karl Moor appeared at the gate, sent by the Bolsheviks to find out how he was surviving his internment.[11] So, all-in-all, this three month period of internment turned out not to be as bad as it could have been.

A letter Münzenberg had written to Fritz Platten from Witzwil in the summer of that year, in which he described his dream of escaping and joining the Bolsheviks in Russia, had been intercepted by the authorities. As a result, they decided, on 28 August, to move him to the district prison of Meilen on Lake Zurich, where they could question him further and draw up the final indictment against him, as well as others of his comrades. Out of the blue, one morning, he was told to pack his bags.

He had, though, been treated decently by the authorities in Witzwil and had been able to follow in the newspapers the final unfolding events of the war. He had gathered that the Bolsheviks had surrendered to Germany at Brest-Litovsk in order to extricate themselves from the debilitating 'imperialist war'.

On the train journey back to Zurich, he was accompanied by one lone police officer in civilian clothes. Münzenberg was able to persuade this officer to let him visit his girlfriend 'who he hadn't seen in ages', he told him. The good man agreed to wait in the pub while he visited her. The policeman appeared to be so perfectly happy sitting in peace with his tipple that, after Münzenberg had given him more money to keep his thirst quenched, he was even allowed to pay a visit to the office of the Youth Secretariat as well. Münzenberg returned to the pub in the early evening so that the officer could deliver him safely to the state prosecutor's office, as planned!

From this point on, Münzenberg would be held in Meilen, where he was given the 'Herrenstübl' or gentleman's room, which was a largish cell with a window overlooking Lake Zurich. There were 16 prisoners in total in this facility, among them other political prisoners, including Fritz Platten.

As the original prison governor had died some time before his arrival, it was being run by his liberal-minded widow. Here, Münzenberg was granted even more privileges than he had had in Witzwil: he was allowed to have visitors in his 'Herrenstübl', and his cell door remained unlocked during the day. This gave the mainstream press a great opportunity for lurid exaggeration and to give full vent to their outrage at the 'luxury' he was enjoying in prison.

Every afternoon, the state prosecutor, von Brunner, would send a boat across the lake to bring Münzenberg to his house on the other side for questioning. The result of these interrogations was that the final report compiled by the prosecutor was a surprisingly favourable one for Münzenberg. von Brunner provided a succinct analysis of the development of the Swiss working-class movement, the influences and changes that had been wrought on it, on the one hand, through Lenin's influence and, on the other, by the impact of the war on workers' living standards. Babette Gross wrote that, the lawyer's analysis 'was marked by an unusual objectivity and political understanding'. And the way he characterised Münzenberg betrayed his undoubted sympathies:

> What made him [Münzenberg] stand out from the mass of his like-minded associates was his varied and literary talent, his continued effort to overcome the gaps in his education and thereby be able to better help his fellows, his unbridled need for action, a prodigious work ethic and energy in the imaginative and reckless pursuance of his goals, aspects that one would hardly expect in such a sensitive, still very youthful and gentle-looking man.... [12]

His opponents would later accuse Münzenberg of shamelessly 'cosying up to Brunner, the "class enemy"'. Münzenberg, however, described the situation as one where he had been able to successfully convince the state prosecutor, who was not politically well versed on the question of socialism, and to 'dialectically pull the wool over his eyes,' an explanation Gross felt was hardly credible given the lawyer's own shrewd intelligence and analytic ability.

What Münzenberg omits from his own reminiscences of this period is anything about his personal relationships. According to Rosa Meyer-Leviné, he had two 'fiancées', Adele and Fanny, and that they were both allowed to visit him in prison. According to Meyer-Leviné, Adele 'was a sweet, blonde, rather domestic-oriented girl', while Fanny, she suggests, was more his intellectual equal and with whom he undertook long walks in the mountains.

The young bookbinder, Adele Kluser, came from the French-speaking part of Switzerland, and joined the Young Socialists when she first arrived in Zurich. She was, according to Gross, 'petite, raven-haired, full of temperament and had a good political sense'. Not long after arriving in the city, she became Münzenberg's girlfriend and remained so until the mid-twenties, despite the turbulence of his life. 'She looked after him and developed all the attributes of a good housewife', as Gross puts it. It was a relationship based less on passion than on close friendship and mutual attraction. But not long after he got to know Adele, he met Fanny Ehrensperger from Winterthur, who was the local delegate to the Zurich central committee. After meetings finished in Zurich, Münzenberg would often travel out to Winterthur just to spend a few hours with Fanny. She gave him a golden engagement ring – 'the only piece of jewellery' he ever possessed, Gross says. She seems to have been the real love of his life.

Despite the fact that on questions of personal relationships and love affairs, Münzenberg was exceedingly reticent, he spoke often about Fanny, Gross says, even years later, and could even describe the clothes and hats she had worn on their rambles in the mountains or when they went to the theatre. They parted for good when Münzenberg returned to Germany in 1918.

Not even his colleagues in the youth movement knew about his love relationships, he kept them very low key and anyway did not believe in mixing the personal with the political.

During all this time, Adele kept tactfully in the background, she did not complain or make difficulties, was always even tempered, and in a happy mood. She continued to work tirelessly for the Youth Secretariat and was a well-know figure among visiting delegates to Zurich. Adele would follow him to Germany and continue working for him. She would die in 1936 in Berlin. Fanny remained in Switzerland and their relationship appears to have ended once Münzenberg left Switzerland.

With the collusion of the governor, both women were allowed to visit him while he was held in the prison of Meilen, but at different times so that they wouldn't meet. In the end, according to Meyer-Leviné's recollections, Adèle won the day because Fanny, 'fed up with his broken promises, walked out on him', but that assertion is at variance with Gross's.[13]

His relationship with Adele Kluser is reliably documented, and there is an endearing photographic portrait of them both together in the Swiss *Sozialarchiv* and several taken of Adele separately, captioned as 'Münzenberg's girlfriend'.[14] Sean McMeekin takes up Meyer-Leviné's anecdote, but names 'Fanny' as Fanny Awensparger, but there is no record of anyone with this name associated with Münzenberg or the youth movement. McMeekin says that she was from the village of Winterthur, but he gives no source for this information. There are, though, in the *Schweizerisches Sozialarchiv* (Swiss social archives) a number of references to a young activist, Fanny Ehrensperger, who is from Winterthur, and she can be seen in several photographs of the Social Democratic Youth Group in Zurich, together with Münzenberg. This is almost certainly the 'other girlfriend' referred to, and is corroborated by Gross. McMeekin uses the tenuous story of these 'two fiancées' to underline his allegation of duplicity on Münzenberg's part.

Münzenberg was certainly not bored anymore in prison and continued his lively correspondence with comrades around the world, received visits from friends daily, and began making notes for his planned book of reminiscences, published later as, 'The Third Front', about his work in the youth movement. He would have been aware by now that it couldn't be long before he too was released.

That autumn, there began a rapid turn of events; offers of ceasefires were being discussed to bring the war to an end, and news of increasing unrest in Germany was filtering through, including that of a mutiny by sailors in Kiel.

In the autumn of 1918, the deterioration of living conditions for Swiss workers reached its nadir, and the people's anger erupted. On 6 November, in the face of increasing pressure from the working people, the Oltener Action Committee, set up by the Swiss trade unions to review the situation, held an emergency meeting and called a 24 hour strike for the 9th of that month. On the same day, the Federal Council expelled the Soviet ambassador from Switzerland, no doubt out of concern that he could play an unwelcome role in Swiss affairs. The military in Zurich were well prepared and had already occupied all important public buildings in preparation for the strike.

On 10 November, a rally on the Fraumünster Platz of between 15,000 and 20,000 workers had gathered and military units, clearly nervous, shot blindly into the demonstrators. This caused the trade union leaders to call an all-out general strike, the first ever to take place in Switzerland. It was an unmitigated success with over 400,000 workers downing tools. In the face of such determination, the military were at a loss as to what to do, so they limited themselves to carrying out arrests of individuals in the towns.

On 14 November, the last day of the strike, there were again bloody clashes and three workers were killed by the military. If the leaders of the strike had remained steadfast at this time, they could probably have squeezed considerable concessions from the government, but the Social Democratic faction and the Oltener Committee hesitated, not knowing how to take advantage of their victory. In the night between the 13 and 14 November, without consulting the strikers, the Social Democratic leadership called off the strike, capitulating unconditionally to the government. The announcement of the capitulation had a predictably demoralising impact on the strikers.

The Federal Council, in response to the demands by the Oltener Committee for Münzenberg's release, was only too ready to get him off their doorstep. In Germany the monarchy had collapsed, the Kaiser had abdicated, the war was over, so it was now no longer problematic to expel him from the country.

The state prosecutor thus decided to close his case, rather than carry out a drawn out prosecution with all the potential for creating a martyr, unleashing more protest, and giving him a platform to express his revolutionary views. So, within days, on 11 November, before the strike had reached its pinnacle, he was taken by car from his Meilen internment to the German border near Stein am Rhein and, although it was already pitch dark, deposited unceremoniously on the German side and left to make his own way onward.

He proceeded to walk towards lights of the nearby small town of Singen, which he could see in the distance. On the way, though, he stumbled into a ditch full of water, but after managing to crawl out, he found himself confronted by a German soldier, his rifle at his shoulder, ready to fire. The soldier yelled, 'Who's there?' Münzenberg was not able to provide a plausible answer, so the soldier ordered him to stand still and announced that he was under arrest.

His expectations that things would have changed in Germany in the intervening years were sorely dashed. Despite all the explaining on his part and appeal to reason, the arresting soldier refused to be moved, kept him under arrest, and took him the next morning to local headquarters. In the end, Münzenberg was able to persuade the arresting officers to contact the German military attaché in Berne, who luckily knew his name from the newspapers and who nullified the arrest order. He was eventually released the day following his arrival. He had hoped, he says, that with the end of the war, Prussian-military authoritarianism would have collapsed and that 'red flags would have been flying from all the houses and jubilant citizens filling the streets'. A more sober reality faced him.

His fiancée Adele joined him in Singen, and, on his release, the two immediately took the train to Stuttgart, but not before he was able to alert comrades there of his impending arrival. He was met on the station by his old comrades from the youth movement there, Edwin Hörnle and Max Barthel.

Adele, probably realising very quickly that he would, from now on, have even less time for her, returned to Switzerland a few days later.

After his expulsion from Switzerland, his secretarial and editorial roles in Zurich were taken on by Willi Trostel and later Emil Arnold, who went on to become editor of the Communist Party paper in Basle.

Notes

1 Münzenberg, Willi, *Die Dritte Front*, Verein der Funke, 2015. p. 25.
2 John Willett, *The New Sobriety: Art and Politics in the Weimar Period 1917–1933*. p. 26.
3 Hobsbawm, Eric, *The Age of Catastrophe*. p. 179.
4 Münzenberg, Willi, *Die Dritte Front*. opus cit.
5 Ibid.
6 Frank, Leonhard, *Links wo das herz ist*, Aufbau Taschenbuch Verlag, 2003. p. 95.
7 Münzenberg, Willi, *Die Dritte Front*. opus cit.
8 Inessa Armand, born in Paris to theatrical parents, was sent to Russia as a young girl and there later married into a wealthy textile manufacturing family. As a young woman she became increasingly interested in left-wing politics and, after having five children, took herself off to join Lenin and the Bolsheviks in exile. Alongside, Krupskaya, Lenin's wife, she became his closest companion and comrade, playing a key role not only in promoting his ideas, but making her own significant contribution.
9 Jesper Jørgensen, 'Radicalising Solidarity: The Danish Social Democratic Youth League and International Federation of Socialist Young People's Organisation, 1914–1919' (paper given to the Willi Münzenberg Forum's first international congress held in 2015 in Berlin). p. 99.
10 Ibid.
11 Karl Moor was a wealthy Swiss Social Democrat who gave financial support to the Bolsheviks in Switzerland. He was the illegitimate son of a Swiss mother, Mary Moor, and the Swiss aristocrat Ernest de Stoeklin. Moor studied at universities in

both Switzerland and Germany. In the 1870s, his interest in the ideas of socialism led him to join the German *SPD*. As a result of his political activities, he was expelled from Bavaria and moved to Basle. There he became a leading figure in the Swiss Social Democratic movement. From 1889, he lived in Bern, where he edited the social-democratic newspaper *Berner Tagwacht*. Münzenberg intimated to Gross that he also played a key role in preparing Lenin's departure from Switzerland to Russia in 1917.

12 Babette Gross, *Willi Münzenberg: Eine politische Biografie*, Forum Verlag Leipzig, 1991, pp. 121–122.

13 In Meyer-Leviné – *Inside German Communism, Memoirs of Party Life in the Weimar Republic*, Pluto Press 1977.

Meyer-Leviné wrote:

'For quite a time I was Münzenberg's confidante'. 'He would often come just to pour out his heart. He would hardly mention Adele, but spoke in raptures of Fanny, describe their wanderings in the mountains, and the great harmony of their souls. He could not leave Adele, he explained; she would not survive it. I found out later that his choice was not such a noble sacrifice. He preferred the cosiness, care, all the little things that usually make a marriage work, and particularly the excellent food.' Of the two women, she wrote, 'He himself favoured the blonde Adele'.

One has, though, to question Meyer-Leviné's recall here in terms of dates and whether she confused the two women. In the *Schwiezerische Sozialarchiv*, there are a number of photographs of Adèle Kluser, who does not appear to be blond at all and was also clearly an active member of the young women's group of the Socialist Youth Organisation, appearing on several of the group photos. So she was hardly someone concerned only with domestic affairs. Fanny came from Winterthur, a town close to Zurich, which was hit hard in the Great Depression in the 1930s. 60% of the total employees in town worked in the machine industry. And, certainly by 1922, he was already deeply involved in full-time work for the Internationale Arbeiter Hilfe (*IAH*) and living in Berlin. I know of no evidence that he remained in close contact with either of the two women much after his arrival in Germany after being expelled from Switzerland.

14 Research carried out by Ursula Langkau-Alex, and revealed in the paper she gave to the first International Willi Münzenberg Congress: 'Die Frau im Hintergrund. Babette Gross und die anderen in Münzenbergs Netzwerken der 1930er Jahre' (The woman in the background. Babette Gross and the others in Münzenberg's networks of the 1930 years), has revealed for the first time that Willi Münzenberg had an illegitimate son in Switzerland, called Uli. And one of Uli's daughters was still alive and spoke to the author of the paper. Ursula Langkau-Alex came across a photo of Uli. The original, as a postcard, was found among the 1938 letters of Babette Gross in the IISH Fritz Brupbacher Papers, file 147. On the back Babette has written: 'This is Willi's sprig. Many thanks for all! Yours Babett'.

At the time of writing, it had not been ascertained who Uli's mother was, but it seems highly likely that it was Fanny.

https://www.muenzenbergforum.de/wp-content/uploads/2018/07/IWMF_V15.pdf

3

GERMANY IN TURMOIL

Well before Münzenberg's enforced repatriation to Germany in November 1918, the country had already been in turmoil for months. The years of war had transformed the mood in the country completely. The population was weary of the seemingly unending conflict with receding hope of victory. The majority of young men had been in the army constantly during the last four years, and many of the families they had left behind were now starving and penniless. Shop windows were empty, many closed and boarded-up, and poorly clad children roamed the streets scavenging. Two million German soldiers had died on the battlefields and up to 900,000 civilians had perished on the 'home front'.

Already during 1917 and 1918 there had been outbreaks of strikes by workers – many of them women – in the munitions factories, and the anti-war sentiment that had been growing now erupted into an uncontrolled anger.

On 22 January, the Spartacus Group in Berlin, inspired by the Bolshevik Revolution in Russia, had begun distributing leaflets calling for a mass strike to begin on the 28 January. The strike leaflet was titled, 'All out for the mass strike; all out to take up the struggle!' No time limit was given for the duration of the strike, and it was aimed primarily at realising Spartacus's minimal demands as a necessary prerequisite for revolution to overturn the old order, the launching of the battle for power. It called for an immediate ceasefire, the lifting of the state of siege, abolition of censorship and all restrictions on the rights of assembly and trade union activity, as well as the release of all political prisoners. The Berlin strike call was taken up in other parts of the country, and there followed mass strikes in Kiel on 25 January and in Dortmund and Düsseldorf on 26 January, as well as in other cities.

In Berlin, in response to this call from Spartacus and the USPD (Independent Social Democratic Party), over a million workers, mostly employed in the armaments industry, downed tools, and in other parts of the country too, there

FIGURE 3.1 Workers patrolling a street in Dortmund 1918 (Images taken from the book Deutschland Deutschland über Alles by Kurt Tucholsky, published by Universum Bücherei, Berlin, Germany.)

were increasingly shrill demands for peace with no annexations or indemnities. This wave of strikes became known as the January Uprising and lasted from 5 until 12 January.

To begin with, in the face of such a massive working-class response to the strike call, the German Social Democratic Party (*SPD*) under Friedrich Ebert, its leader, and future president of the Weimar Republic, expressed sympathy with the strikers – the party leaders had little option if they wished to maintain face – but they refused to provide proper leadership and were more intent on dampening down the militancy.

Ebert made every effort to persuade the strikers to return to work. He was a believer in reform from the top not revolution from below and was intent on preventing working people taking revolutionary action. With this goal, he was prepared to collaborate with conservative political forces in order to defeat the militants. As far as he was concerned, they posed the greatest danger to the German state.

In response to the strikes, the police were ordered to occupy trade union meeting halls to prevent large gatherings of disgruntled workers, but they were aware of how explosive the situation already was, so they were cautious enough to allow the offices to continue functioning.

The government of the time, under Chancellor Georg von Hertling, refused to negotiate with the Berlin workers' action committee and went on to ban meetings of the strikers, arresting the leaders, and even banning the *SPD*'s newspaper, *Vorwärts* for three days. He placed factories under military control and ordered the strikers to return to work. While some were arrested, several thousand were also drafted into the army, where they would play a key role later in the formation of Soldiers' Councils in the November uprising in that same year. From January onwards, there were strikes intermittently all over the country until the November Revolution erupted.

On 3 March 1918, the German and Soviet governments signed the Brest-Litovsk Treaty, which brought the war on the Eastern front to a close. Throughout June and September, strikes were still breaking out sporadically all over Germany, demonstrating the people's anger and urgent demand for an end to the war.

On 29 September 1918, General Erich Ludendorff, the most powerful man in the German armed forces, told the Kaiser that only by immediately signing a ceasefire could the total collapse of Germany be prevented. He also told him that a new parliament and government should be established immediately – something the military had previously vehemently opposed – and this new government should include opposition parties, including the *SPD*. By implementing this proposal, the ceasefire would then be officially concluded by the new government and thus, in the eyes of the public, Germany's defeat could be laid at its door, rather than at the military's. This then took place and, despite heated discussions in the *SPD*, Friedrich Ebert, the party's chairman, was able to force through his policy of collaboration.

On 7 October, the Spartacus Group held a clandestine conference in Berlin, and on 26/27 October, the militant Socialist youth organisation in the city held a national conference. From mid-October to the end of the month, there were continued demonstrations, rallies, and strikes in Berlin, Hamburg, Leipzig, and other big cities. The country was becoming ungovernable and the traditional conservative establishment no longer appeared capable of imposing its will.

By the autumn of 1918, the whole country was seething with unrest. The end of the war was now palpably close, working people were hungry; at the front, the soldiers and sailors were facing an increasingly hopeless situation. On the coast, in Kiel, the situation reached a boiling point.

Towards the end of October, some naval crews in Wilhelmshaven refused to obey orders to set sail to confront British battleships – a pointless and suicidal attempt to prolong the conflict – the sailors had had enough of war, and they mutinied. This, though, was not a spontaneous mutiny, as it has sometimes been portrayed, but the result of careful and lengthy preparation by those sailors who had a background in the trade union and Social Democratic organisations. Around 600 of the mutineers were subsequently arrested and imprisoned.

But by 3 November, the mutiny had spread to Kiel, where large numbers of sailors and soldiers, also led by left-wing *SPD* members in their ranks, joined it, marking the opening shot in the so-called November Revolution. Within 24 hours rebellions erupted in Hamburg, Lübeck, Neumünster, Bremen, Wilhelmshaven Bremerhaven, and other northern cities, before sweeping the country.

From Kiel, delegations of sailors travelled to most of the major German cities, encouraging others to join the revolt, and by 7 November, the revolution had seized all large coastal towns, as well as Hanover, Brunswick, Frankfurt am Main, and Munich, where Workers', Soldiers', and Sailors' Councils, modelled on the Russian soviets, were established in place of the old administrative structures. These councils were made up almost entirely of *SPD* and *USPD* members. Their basic programme was for democracy, full suffrage for men and women, and peace and anti-militarism. Already by 16 December 1918, Workers', Soldiers', and Sailors' Councils had been established in all the big cities. The revolutionary upsurge took place in two stages, the first between 29 October and 9 November 1918, and the second, lasting until August the following year. The movement was led by sailors and workers with solid political and trade union experience.

On 7 November, the Workers', Soldiers', and Peasants' Council in Munich announced the establishment of a Bavarian Soviet Republic, under the leadership of Kurt Eisner. The next day, Workers' and Soldiers' Councils were set up in the industrial Ruhr.

The revolutionary tsunami had already reached Berlin by the time Karl Liebknecht returned home from the front at the end of October. After his release, in early November, he returned to Berlin to re-found the Spartacist League. There, together with two other Spartacus members, Wilhelm Pieck and Ernst Meyer, he would provide leadership to the revolutionary shop stewards' movement.

On 9 November, the Reichstag had the feel of a huge army barracks, with soldiers and workers marching in and out, many still shouldering their weapons. The *SPD* leader, Friedrich Ebert made his way through the throng and the Chancellor, Prince Max von Baden, who had already announced the abdication of Kaiser Wilhelm, handed over his post to Ebert, asking him to form a Social Democratic provisional government. It was clear that only Ebert could prevent 'the catastrophe of a Bolshevik takeover'.

Although there was now, de facto, a new government, to begin with, the old secretaries of state remained in office, including the recently appointed Phillipp Scheidemann. At the Reichstag, the masses were demanding a statement by the *SPD* leaders, but Ebert refused to speak and let *SPD* deputy chairman Scheidemann do so instead.

Having been told that Liebknecht intended announcing a Soviet Republic, Scheidemann decided to pre-empt him and announced a German Republic with the words, 'The old is rotten, the monarchy has collapsed. The new may live. Long live the German Republic!' This proclamation was made against Ebert's expressed will, and only a few hours later, the Berlin newspapers reported that in Berlin's Lustgarten – in the afternoon of that same day – Liebknecht had declared a Socialist Republic from the balcony of the Kaiser's vacated palace: 'The day of freedom has arrived. Never again will a Hohenzollern set foot here … I announce the free, socialist republic of Germany', he told the amassed audience of sailors and workers.[1]

Ebert was livid – in his eyes this was not constitutional. He had been holding secret talks with the old guard about preserving the monarchy in some form. He simply told the assembled masses to return to their homes quietly and orderly. But by the next day, Berlin, like many other cities, was in the hands of the newly formed Workers and Soldiers Councils; administrative offices and public buildings were handed- or taken-over by the Workers and Soldiers Councils.

Desperate to remain master of the situation, on the afternoon of that fateful day on 9 November, following the Kaiser's abdication, Friedrich Ebert demanded the German chancellorship for himself. However, the news of the abdication came too late to influence the demonstrators and defuse the situation on the ground. Nobody heeded the public appeals. More and more demonstrators came out onto the streets of Berlin and were demanding the total abolition of the monarchy. Kaiser Wilhelm fled to the Netherlands. Events were happening at an alarming pace, and the country, it appeared, was threatened with a descent into anarchy. Ebert was forced to recognise that he and his party were no longer able to stem the tide; he even offered Liebknecht a cabinet post in his government in an attempt to incorporate and disarm the revolutionaries.

The radical demands made by the sailors and workers in Kiel, Hamburg, Bremen, and Lübeck were inspiring the whole country and were demonstrating, even to sections of the peasantry, that things could be run in a different way, and that there was a road out of the misery of war and capitalist exploitation.

As a result of the war, the country and the powerful *SPD* itself had become strongly polarised politically, with the right-wing party leadership fighting for its life against the more militant, revolutionary wing which was pushing forcefully for a genuine revolutionary transformation of the country. Events were moving at an alarming rate. The old, conservative elite which realised it could no longer govern in the same way, sought collaboration with the right-wing leadership of the *SPD* in its attempt to survive and stave off a Socialist revolution. The *SPD* was at this time clearly the strongest organised political force in the country and certainly could not be ignored.[2]

The leadership of the *SPD* was seriously alarmed by the grassroots earthquake shaking the country and was determined to return the country to stability at all costs, and that meant undertaking every effort to prevent the Workers' and Soldiers' Councils from consolidating their power; at the same time, it sought to water down their revolutionary demands.

Although the young Soviet Union in 1918 was facing not only the terrible aftermath of the war, international boycotts, civil war, and invading foreign forces, as soon as the Soviet government heard about the revolution breaking out in Germany, it immediately pledged to send 50,000 pud (c. 820 tons) of wheat to help feed the German people who had been, until very recently, their implacable enemy.

The old is dying, but the new is reluctant to be born

The ruling elites realised that the old order was collapsing around them with Germany's defeat in the war. The beacon of the Russian Revolution was spreading its flames and threatening to engulf Germany too. They had to move quickly if they were to head off full-blooded revolution and establish a coalition government which could stabilise the situation.

The Council of People's Deputies (the provisional government in place from November 1918–February 1919) was completely satisfied with the establishment of a solid, democratic, and republican base, which would, it was argued, prepare the road for future social transformation. The radical left, represented by the Spartacists under Liebknecht and Luxemburg, were an unwelcome and threatening element that needed to be eradicated. The latter was committed to a continuation of the revolution to a higher stage and the establishment of a Socialist Republic.

In response to the revolutionary demands echoing around the country, the Ebert-Scheidemann government that had taken power after the abdication of the Kaiser, paid lip service to the widespread calls for a 'Socialist Republic', but only in order to hinder a fundamental Socialist transformation, true to the Bernstein formula that 'the goal is nothing, the movement is everything'.

There is no question that while the radical left, under the leadership of Liebknecht and Luxemburg, was prepared to confront the entrenched powers, the ruling class in its turn was preparing to resist revolution with all the forces at its disposal.

The German 1918 Revolution has been invariably characterised by historians as a 'Communist' and/or 'Bolshevik' attempt to overthrow German democracy. As Stefan Bollinger notes, however, it is a myth that the 1918 revolution was a Communist-inspired 'Bolshevik' revolution. 'This legend was invented by the social democrats and supported, willingly or not, by the communists', he says.[3] There was, in fact, no Communist Party at the time, and the revolution was instigated and led by members of the Social Democratic Party.

Although the demands put forward by many of the Soldiers' and Workers' Councils were often similar to the demands being made by the Spartacists and, not coincidentally, had taken their inspiration from the Russian Revolution, that in itself hardly made it a Soviet-instigated movement. What had taken place in Russia, though, did provide the model for this and other proletarian revolutions.

Both Luxemburg and Liebknecht were fully aware of what the Russians had achieved, and while Rosa Luxemburg had early on expressed serious disquiet about the way the Bolshevik Revolution was unfolding and criticised the increasing domination of the process by one party, the over centralisation, and the resulting serious democratic deficit, she still paid homage to the achievements of the Bolsheviks.

Luxemburg had only been released from prison on 10 November, but was immediately caught up in the rapidly escalating fervour. While Liebknecht was calling for all power to be devolved to the Workers' and Soldiers' Councils, as the basis for the creation of a Soviet Republic, Luxemburg felt the time was not ripe for such a radical development. She viewed the priority for the Spartacists as awakening a deeper Socialist and class consciousness among the workers.[4]

Despite the strong reservations she still held about developments in the Soviet Union, she emphasised that 'Lenin and Trotsky with their friends were the first to lead the world proletariat with their example and are still the only ones who can cry out with Ulrich von Hutten: I have dared! That's the essential and lasting policy of the Bolsheviks'. … 'The Bolsheviks have demonstrated that they have done everything that a real revolutionary party is capable of doing within the constraints of the historical circumstances'.[5] However, she did not feel Germany could or should imitate their example.

Münzenberg did not share Luxemburg's doubts about the direction the Bolshevik Revolution was taking. Babette Gross writes that his reaction to the October and November events in Russia was one of 'a huge sigh of relief'. On the left in general there was a basic trust in the Bolsheviks under the leadership of Lenin and Trotsky. Many workers viewed the increasingly rabid anti-Russian stance in the German media as defamatory.

By late 1918, anti-Bolshevik propaganda had reached fever pitch, both from the *SPD* and from conservative forces. An Anti-Bolshevik League was established to help focus the opposition.

At a large anti-Socialist gathering, the wealthy industrialist Hugo Stinnes – probably Germany's most influential capitalist, who had made a fortune from the war – announced that, 'If the German industry, trade and banking worlds are not prepared and able to put up an insurance sum of 500 million Marks, then they cannot be dignified with the term German economy'. As a result, large sums were raised to unleash a wave of propaganda and to support the activities of the *Freikorps* and other secret right-wing organisations. The league rallied not only industrialists, political parties, and military figures, but also *SPD* leaders.

Even before the founding conference of the *KPD* (Communist Party of Germany) on 30/31 December 1918, the *SPD* Party newspaper, *Vorwärts*, did not spare in its rhetoric against what it saw as the 'Bolshevik danger' in Germany. In its edition of 29th December, it devoted a whole page to telling its readers how German soldiers returning from Russia were bringing stories of horrendous events that were happening there. It wrote floridly that, 'Russia lies before us today like a mass grave of moral and economic values, human hopes and desires. In Germany, too, the Bolsheviks are raising their heads ever more brazenly. Soldiers, Workers, citizens, the wellbeing of all of us, the future of our fatherland is in mortal danger. Stay on guard everywhere and at every hour!... Germany protect your house! The Russian plague is at your door!'[6]

The widely respected liberal journalist Sebastian Haffner wrote perceptively much later that he was incensed by the way the *SPD* had missed the opportunity offered by the 1918 November Revolution.

'By not utilising

> the revolution, but suppressing it instead, they "betrayed" it, as I say bitterly in my text. And it has to take responsibility for the consequences. Because the chance did not really come again – never. Instead Hitler came, the Second World War, the second defeat, [and the country's] division. That is what makes the 1918 German revolution and its suppression by the appointed leaders still so bitterly topical: that they prevented what was the best, and with historical hindsight, really the only opportunity, of averting all that …'

Haffner clearly recognised that the conservative forces in the country were obliged to cosy up to the formerly hated Social Democrats if they were to escape complete political and economic annihilation:

> In the face of apparent defeat in 1918, the doorkeepers of the Kaiser's empire themselves opened the long-closed doors to the Social Democratic leadership and, not without ulterior motives, of their own accord, allowed them into the ante-chamber of power; and now the Social Democratic masses, storming in from outside, overwhelming their leaders and pulling them with the current, through the last doors to central power.
>
> In November 1918, after a century of waiting, it seemed that German social democracy had achieved its goal at last, and then the unbelievable happened. The Social Democratic leadership, reluctantly placed on the empty throne by the Social Democratic masses, immediately mobilised the old leaderless palace guards and allowed their own supporters to be driven out. A year later they found themselves outside the door – for eternity.
>
> The German Revolution of 1918 was a Social Democratic revolution, which was suppressed by the Social Democratic leadership: a process that has no parallel in world history.[7]

Haffner argued emphatically that the revolution was no Russian import, but was entirely a German affair.

Münzenberg back in Germany

On arrival in Germany that November in 1918, Münzenberg found a country in the throes of transformation. The abdication of the Kaiser and the declaration of a German Republic had been announced only two days earlier, on 9 November, and the armistice, ending the war, was signed on the 11th. Certainly in the larger cities many administrative structures had ceased to function, and among the working classes, as well as in the armed forces, there was an increasing revolutionary fervour, even though it was patchy.

Münzenberg and Barthel, with a group of sailors from Kiel, their uniforms adorned with red ribbons, took a car to the regional administrative offices in Stuttgart where a meeting of the Soldiers' Council was taking place. But even here, he was disappointed. There were calls for 'law, order and discipline', but little demand for revolutionary action. Workers' and Soldiers' Councils had been established and, even before Scheidemann had declared Germany a republic on 9 November, the Stuttgart Workers' and Soldiers' Council began publishing a radical new newspaper, *Die Rote Fahne* (The Red Flag). The large armament and vehicle-making factories in and around Stuttgart employed tens of thousands of workers and many of them supported revolutionary change. The new newspaper would be addressed to them.

The left group around Clara Zetkin represented a strong oppositional force within the Social Democratic Party and already during the war had moved to join the *USPD*, and among the latter, many were Spartacus sympathisers. They were also represented in the newly formed Swabian regional government and held several cabinet seats.

To begin with, Münzenberg remained in Stuttgart, where he joined Clara Zetkin, who took him under her wing, giving him invaluable advice and support. In a matter of days he had joined the Spartacus Group under the leadership of Karl Liebknecht and Rosa Luxemburg. He threw himself into political work, and made his first task the rebuilding of the Socialist youth organisation in the region.

Every day he spoke at well-attended meetings in the city, and on 18 November, with Fritz Rück, he spoke at a large gathering of young Socialists in the main hall of the city's art gallery. This meeting agreed to the reorganisation of the Stuttgart youth section, and on that same evening they gained 100 new members. From there they went on to re-establish the regional Württemburg movement.

Immediately, on 18 November, they published an appeal in the *Rote Fahne* newspaper, the organ of the Workers' Council in Stuttgart, calling on the young workers of Württemburg to organise themselves now that the old anti-association laws were no longer in force. Münzenberg managed to procure a room in the regional government building where he could set up a new office for the Youth International. Since his internment in Switzerland, he'd lost contact with most of his comrades in other countries; those links also had to be re-established. Münzenberg was certainly making up for the years lost during the war, and he worked at a frenetic pace to re-establish the youth movement organisation.

Already by 30 November, he and his comrades in the leadership of the German Socialist Youth International published the first issue of a new paper specifically for young Socialists, *Jugend Internationale* (Youth International),

FIGURE 3.2 Willi Münzenberg addressing a meeting (place and date unknown) (Courtesy of German Federal Archives, Koblenz, Germany.)

FIGURE 3.3 Willi Münzenberg addressing a large election rally for the Communist Party (With permission of the Bundesarchiv.)

but its political line would be sharply criticised by ultra-leftist forces in the country as being too conventional and tentative. Münzenberg responded by calling a regional conference of Socialist youth, which declared itself whole-heartedly behind the programme formulated by the Spartacists. 'Although the Social Democratic Party leadership nationally was moving daily to the right', he wrote, 'more and more *SPD* members began supporting the Spartacus programme'.

His attempt to arrange an international gathering of leading comrades from the youth movement had to be postponed because the Swiss authorities had intercepted invitations sent to his comrades there, leading to their arrest. So he hastily rearranged the meeting for Berlin on 7 December, where many potential delegates would be convening anyway for the first national Congress of the Workers' and Soldiers' Councils.

Tensions were still high in Berlin and, in contrast to Swabia, the situation had unfolded with more vehemence. While Scheidemann was announcing that the country had become a republic, Liebknecht was raising the red flag on Berlin's palace and proclaiming Germany a free Socialist Republic and calling for power to be handed over to the Workers' and Soldiers' Councils. There was an atmosphere of dangerous tension in the capital.

On his arrival there, Münzenberg immediately made his way to the office of the Spartacus League and there met Rosa Luxemburg and her comrade and partner Leo Jogiches – this would be the first and last time that they would see each other.

He marched alongside Liebknecht in the largest demonstration Berlin had witnessed up to then, with around 250,000 participants. They had joined the march to the state parliament, where the Workers' and Soldiers' Council was meeting, in order to urge the council to support the revolutionary Spartacus programme. He also spoke with Liebknecht at other large gatherings in the city. On 18 December in Neukölln, they both addressed a gathering of around 2,000 and were greeted with stormy applause.

The young Socialists' conference itself, though, was only poorly attended, he noted, as transport within the country was still in a chaotic state, and people found it difficult to travel. It was, however, agreed at that conference to relocate the secretariat from Zurich to Stuttgart and for Münzenberg to continue in his role as secretary. It was further agreed to continue publishing the 'Youth International' and to organise a new conference as soon as possible.

To Münzenberg's great disappointment, the meeting of the Workers' and Soldiers' Council in Berlin, instead of grasping the power they had, took the decision to hand it over to a national assembly, and in several other centres the scenario was similar. He was forced to recognise that the battle to establish a Socialist Republic in Germany would not be straightforward. The fundamental differences between those arguing for a reformist or parliamentary road and those demanding a revolutionary one would increasingly become the defining characteristic of German politics for years to come.

While there were strong revolutionary forces at work in the *USPD* – demanding a soviet (council) system, dictatorship of the proletariat, a complete dissolution of the army and a separation of church and state, for the judiciary to be elected by the people, for a progressive welfare system, and a Socialist economy – they were still in a minority.

Münzenberg was asked in mid–December 1918 by the Spartacus leadership in Berlin to return to Stuttgart and continue organising and carrying out vital agitational work there. He had planned to return to Berlin two weeks later for the founding conference of the *KPD*, but on his train journey back to Stuttgart he had fallen ill with pneumonia and was forced to spend the following weeks confined to bed.

The intention of founding a *KPD* was opposed at the time by Luxemburg and her partner, Leo Jogiches, among others, because they feared it would lead to an irrevocable split in the Socialist movement, and they deemed such a move to be premature. They argued that it was better for the Spartacists to remain part of the *USPD*, which was already a mass party in its own right. Even within the ranks of the Spartacists, there were still unresolved questions about whether to support parliamentarianism and take part in elections or not.

The ideological differences between Liebknecht and Luxemburg had widened during the months of November and December 1918, and these would be expressed openly at the founding conference.

The conference was held between 30 December 1918 and 1 January 1919 in Berlin's city hall, '*das Rote Rathaus*'. There, Luxemburg clarified her position and made a passionate appeal for direct action by the masses on the one hand and for a programme of political abstinence on the other, i.e., a policy of non-interference in the politics of the new republic and for taking part in elections to a new national assembly only as a form of propaganda. In her speech, she also revealed the close co-operation that had been taking place between Ebert and the German military high command, accusing the *SPD* government of being counter-revolutionary. She adamantly rejected any idea of a compromise with it, but just as forcefully rejected any attempt to forcibly overthrow it.[8] She argued that socialism could only be created by mass action, in each factory, and by each worker against the employer.

Karl Radek, the official representative of the Soviet government to Germany, had been refused entry to the country, but managed to enter illegally and was able to take part in the discussions leading to the foundation of the *KPD*. Radek and Luxemburg had frosty relations going back to their days together in the Polish Social Democratic movement, and here too, they tiptoed warily around each other. Paul Levi supported Luxemburg's position about taking part in the elections to the national assembly; others opposed it on the basis that it granted legitimacy to the assembly. A majority eventually voted not to take part.

There was also a vibrant discussion held on the attitude to the trade unions (at the time firmly dominated by the *SPD*): should trade unions be abolished or could they be drawn into the revolutionary movement?

Radek had brought a message from Lenin to the leadership of the young *KPD* asking it to collaborate in the convening of a congress to establish a new International, the third, as quickly as possible. Rumours had come to Moscow's ears that the Social Democrats were planning to resuscitate the Second International and the British Labour Party had been making preparations for a conference in Berne to implement this policy. They wanted to pip the communists to the post and unite the Left-wing parties, but excluding the communists, under their banner.

In his speech to the conference, Radek drew parallels between the Kerensky government and the Ebert-Scheidemann one in Germany and explained to his German comrades how the Russians had waged the class struggle, but he also warned that, 'The fear of Bolshevism will grow. They will organise everything against you'. He told the delegates that they would be labelled as imitators of the Russian Revolution, as agents of Soviet Russia, but in terms of imitating, he said, it was the Russians who had in fact learned from the German working class. He concluded on an optimistic note and expressed his conviction that Germany was on the verge of following in the Bolsheviks' footsteps. He did, though, also strongly criticise the confrontational policy pursued by many of those advocating the establishment of a Communist Party and told them to 'put a brake on this pointless battle', but neither the *USPD* nor the Spartacists themselves had enough influence to change the course of events.

Although not present at this founding conference, Münzenberg was a firm supporter of the new party and immediately following his recovery began writing for its newspaper, *The Red Flag*.

The counter revolution gathers strength

The 1918 November Revolution and its aftershocks would not reverberate with any strength beyond January 1919. The events on the 6th and between 23 and 25 December had dealt lessons to both the left and the right.

On 6 December, counter-revolutionary forces had made a concerted attempt to destroy the power of the Workers' and Soldiers' Councils. Following the Kaiser's abdication, loyal troops were brought into the city centre to guard the chancellery, and Friedrich Ebert was made president of the country. Simultaneously, troops attempted to arrest the coordinating council of the Workers' and Soldiers' Councils and temporarily occupied the offices of *The Red Flag* newspaper. This putsch attempt met vehement opposition, and a bloody confrontation took place in which government troops opened fire on unarmed workers, leaving 14 dead and 50 wounded lying on the streets of Berlin.

Only a fortnight later, a second attempt was made to end the power of the councils. The sailors of the People's Marine Division, known for their militancy, were a thorn in the side of the government and military hierarchy, and although they were involved on the government side in the putsch attempt on 6 December, they had, in the meantime, become very angry at the non-payment of their wages and so changed sides. On Christmas Eve, a delegation was sent to the chancellery demanding payment. The sailors proceeded to take the government and commander of the city's garrison hostage in order to reinforce their demands. Ebert and Noske managed to bring in outside troops loyal to the government, and artillery was used in an attempt to dislodge them. Alarmed by this attack, and alerted by the factory sirens, thousands of workers came to the aid of the embattled sailors. In the ensuing confrontation, 11 sailors died, as well as numerous government troops, and there were many wounded on this 'Bloody Christmas'.

In the face of such determined resistance by the sailors and thousands of angry workers, the troops loyal to the government were forced to retreat. The sailors were paid their wages and made no further demands. Those fiascos led to a more systematic organisation of forces calling for 'law and order', and the counter revolution gathered momentum, while the rabid anti-Spartacist propaganda reached its zenith. Although the Spartacists could still mobilise hundreds of thousands on the streets, the consolidated *SPD* leadership and its right-wing military allies now sought a suitable opportunity to strike the mortal blow.

FIGURE 3.4 General Ludendorf, the most prominent of the right-wing military leaders in Germany (Images taken from Deutschland Deutschland über Alles by Kurt Tucholsky, published by Universum Bücherei, Berlin, Germany.)

The regular armed forces were war-weary, but enflamed with revolutionary ideas, very much through the influence of the Workers' and Soldiers' Councils; the ordinary soldiers were taking no notice of their officers anymore. The authorities were forced to look elsewhere for support.

Provided with political backing by the new Social-Democratic-led government and by Gustav Noske, the man given responsibility by the People's Representative Council, new military groups, *Freikorps* and citizens' militias were systematically created for the purpose of smashing the revolution. With the return of the troops from the front, the offensive against the Workers' and Soldiers' Councils and against Spartacus and the radical left began in earnest. A series of provocative bloody clashes ensued and were intended to make it clear that the Ebert-led government was now firmly in the saddle. This process would be concluded on 29 December with the resignation of the USPD members in the government.

Shortly before the founding conference of the KPD, on 25 December 1918, the SPD newspaper *Vorwärts* had again been occupied by 500 dissident party members in protest of the Ebert government's right-wing policies. As a majority of SPD members in Berlin had already left Ebert's party, and the paper's offices had been paid for out of members' subscriptions, they felt it was their right to take over what they considered was theirs anyway and were supported by large sections of the workers. To maintain his status as leader, Ebert wanted to despatch troops to retake the building, but the police president, Emil Eichhorn, a member of the USPD, was determined to solve the issue peacefully. However, the military were only too ready to grasp such an opportunity of teaching the revolutionaries a harsh lesson.

Because of his refusal to use strong-arm tactics to retake the *Vorwärts* building, Eichhorn was sacked by Ebert, triggering the resignation of other USPD members in the government, and thus polarising even further the left- and right-wing forces in the SPD. As a result, Ebert's reformist government became increasingly more belligerent towards the left, in an attempt to strangle any remaining revolutionary potential.

In the first days of January 1919, the recently elected central committee of the KPD (Spartacus League) discussed the critical situation. Liebknecht argued for the creation of a united revolutionary force, made up of the People's Marine Division, the revolutionary shop stewards, the USPD, and Spartacus League; Luxemburg and Jogiches argued against this and called for the removal of Liebknecht as the representative of the shop stewards.

The Berlin shop stewards movement was one of the most radical and organised core of the revolutionary movement and had more power in its hands than the Workers' and Soldiers' Councils. It would organise the most effective opposition to a restoration of a Kaiser's regime in Germany. It demanded of the Ebert government that Eichhorn be reinstated as police president and that the military be disarmed, along with a number of other radical demands for social reform.

On Sunday, 5 January, hundreds of thousands of workers and war veterans poured into the centre of Berlin, many of them armed. In the afternoon, they occupied train stations and that quarter of the city where the offices of the bourgeois newspapers were located. Some of these papers had, over previous days, called not only for the recruitment of more *Freikorps* troops (right-wing paramilitary units of demobilised soldiers), but also openly for the murder of the Spartacists.

On 6 January, there was a new demonstration in support of Eichhorn that surpassed all expectations: hundreds of thousands of workers marched through central Berlin. Liebknecht and Pieck explained to the shop stewards' executive committee that the Eichhorn issue could be the factor to bring the counter revolution to a halt. The executive committee then voted to maintain the occupation of the *Vorwärts* building and to call for a general strike. The situation was confused and unclear; Ebert was unable to immediately bring in sufficient military forces to suppress the rebellion. The fall of the Ebert government would have sent the flames of revolution shooting all over Germany, but this did not take place. In the meantime, the troops of General Lüttwitz had been quickly assembled from around Berlin. On 8 January, the leaders of the *SPD* government announced that they would answer 'the violence of the Spartacists' with counter force. This was the signal for the Potsdam regiment to march into central Berlin. It met no opposition, but the troops were met by citizens carrying placards and banners that proclaimed, 'Brothers, don't shoot!'. Government troops began occupying strategic positions, watched with hatred by the citizens. Flame-throwers and canons were put in place, and the first objective was to retake the *Vorwärts* building.

The provisional government, under Ebert, the *SPD* leader, and now president of Germany, had declared open war on Spartacus in an attempt to stem the revolutionary tide, and the counteroffensive had now began in earnest.

On 9 January 1919, only a week after the conclusion of the founding conference of the *KPD*, the *USPD* and Spartacus League in an extra supplement of the *Rote Fahne* called for a general strike and the taking up of arms, but the call came too late. By 12 January, the notorious, anti-republican *Freikorps*, which had been formed more or less as death squads since the beginning of December, moved into Berlin. The force had been established by the most conservative and reactionary forces in Germany with the express aim of suppressing the working-class struggle. Ebert was more than happy to give the green light to the *Freikorps*, who began ruthlessly clearing several occupied buildings and executing the occupiers on the spot. Others surrendered, but were still shot. In the overcrowded quarters of the city and its narrow streets, the effects were devastating. The January revolt in Berlin would eventually claim 156 lives. This action spelt the beginning of the end for revolution in Berlin.

Those occupying the *Vorwärts* building surrendered and where whipped, beaten with truncheons, and then shot. Street battles flickered here and there, but the well-drilled government troops had the upper hand. Groups of workers were hunted through the streets, and barbed wire was used to seal off the central areas of the city. Many working-class leaders were arrested.

Gustav Noske, who had become the People's Representative for Army and Navy, took command of these troops and was relaxed about their use of brutal force. On 15 January, Luxemburg and Liebknecht were arrested by *Freikorps* officers. That same night both prisoners were beaten unconscious with rifle butts and then shot in the head. Rosa Luxemburg's body was thrown into the *Landwehr Kanal* that runs through Berlin and was only found on 1 July. Karl Liebknecht's unidentified body was delivered to a morgue. The deaths of Luxemburg and Liebknecht, together with the defeat of the revolutionary shop stewards' movement in Berlin, marked the end of the first phase of German Communism. Luxemburg who had vociferously opposed the use of terror as a weapon in the struggle had been murdered by terrorists. The killing of a Socialist leader, a defenceless woman, with the full collaboration of the state was something new in Germany and set a precedent. It sent a clear message to all those who desired a more egalitarian state that revolutionary action would be answered in the most ruthless fashion.

While the Weimar government had moved irrevocably to the right, the nominally banned *Freikorps* was being given secret support. General von Seeckt, commander in chief of the German Army, carried out a systematic reorganisation of it beginning with the entrenchment of groups of right-wing officers and non-commissioned officers who made up the core of the *Freikorps* (Free regiments).[9] The new army he created would provide the backbone for Hitler's *Wehrmacht* eight years later.[10]

There were not only clashes in Berlin. Already by January 1919, many coal mines in the industrial Ruhr area of Germany had gone on strike and a Workers' and Soldiers' Council was set up in Essen, including representatives from the *SPD, USPD,* and the *KPD.* The miners were demanding nationalisation of the pits.

In Stuttgart, too, where Münzenberg was at this time in prison, a big demonstration had been organised for 9 January, and he, in the meantime recovered from his pneumonia, took part and spoke. Here, the main challenge facing most people was straightforward economic survival. There was already widespread unemployment in the area, but with the end of the war, many thousands of workers, particularly those in the armaments industries, saw their very existence now under threat and demanded urgent action to save their jobs.

While the provisional regional government was in session, the streets around were seething with angry and demonstrating citizens demanding action. A group of workers took over the *Stuttgarter Tageblatt* (one of the main newspapers in the city) and intended to turn it into a 'mouthpiece of the revolution'. Münzenberg and his close comrade Hoernle were made editors. They deliberated over what to call the new paper; the name *Rote Fahne,* they felt had been overused, so they decided on the title, *Die Rote Flut* (The Red Flood).

They had only just begun to lay out the first pages when there was a call by the 40-strong workers' security unit to switch off the lights and to 'man the barricades'. In front of the building, several hundred right-wing officers and non-commissioned officers with machine guns had taken up position. They yelled anti-Spartacist abuse and threatened to storm the building, but eventually retreated and everyone returned to work.

The roads outside were then filled with masses of demonstrating workers, chanting pro-Spartacus slogans. However, only a short time after they'd passed, a different group of soldiers and officers made an impromptu attempt to free the *Tageblatt* from the 'Red Flood', but Münzenberg, Barthel, and Hoernle negotiated with them on the staircase of the building. Their back-up troops outside melted away, and they too were forced to retreat. Then, just as the new paper was being printed, a few minutes before midnight, a larger force of government troops returned and once again surrounded the building.

According to Babette Gross's account, Münzenberg, who had not fully recovered from his recent bout of pneumonia, developed a high temperature and collapsed as a result of the sudden strain and burden of work. Two comrades decided to take him home, but, once on the street, they were surrounded by a belligerent group of officers. At this moment, 'a brutish young man, his face twisted with hatred', grabbed Münzenberg, yelling 'That's him!' But at that moment, another well-built officer, and a secret Münzenberg sympathiser, intervened and, putting on an authoritarian voice, shouted at Münzenberg that he was under arrest. He marched Münzenberg off, but, once outside the encircling forces and out of view, he released him. An hour later government forces stormed the building and retook it. Only a few of the freshly printed newspapers had been smuggled out beforehand.

By 11 January, government forces had taken control of the city from the insurgents once more and despatched a victory telegram to Berlin, boasting of their 'defeat of the Spartacist uprising'.

Münzenberg and his comrades did not reckon on the government taking further action against them, and so continued to hold public meetings and remain living in their flats. But they had seriously underestimated the government's intentions. Two days later, at five in the morning, several military officers with revolvers cocked, hammered on his door and, on entering, placed him under arrest. While he and his two comrades were getting dressed, the officers meticulously searched the flat and found several revolvers and rifles, 'a veritable armoury!', one of the officers remarked.

It was still dark outside and the streets were completely empty, so there was no possibility of drawing attention to their arrest. They imagined they would be summarily shot at the next street corner, but instead they – Münzenberg, Max Barthel, and Albert Schreiner – were taken first to government headquarters that was temporarily housed in the new railway station, from where they were then transported to the prison fortress in Ulm.

Midway on the journey to Ulm, their own vehicle made an unexpected stop, and the prisoners were ordered to get out. However, one of the officers in an accompanying vehicle, a certain Karl Albrecht – a secret supporter of the Spartacists – also got out and approached them with his revolver drawn and commanded them to stay in their vehicle. They then continued their journey without incident. Albrecht was convinced that he had prevented a bloodbath.

Not long after being taken to their cells, someone spoke to Münzenberg through the spy hole in his cell door, 'Willi don't you recognise me?' He couldn't see anything through the tiny opening, so answered in the negative. But the sentry identified himself as a former member of the St. Gallen Socialist youth group in Switzerland. He offered Münzenberg his help and obtained ink and paper for him. A day or so later, to many readers' surprise, a long article appeared in the local Stuttgart *USPD* newspaper giving details of the arrest and their adventurous journey, which the regional government was trying to keep secret.

The Ulm prison was located in an old fortress with walls over a metre thick, and as Münzenberg noted in his reminiscences, food was insufficient and of bad quality. In addition, he was still suffering from the lingering effects of his pneumonia.

It was a few days into their incarceration when he heard a tormented cry and his comrade in a neighbouring cell, Fritz Rück, yelling that Karl Liebknecht had been murdered. They were loth to believe it at first, but it would soon be confirmed as was the death of Rosa Luxemburg immediately afterwards. It was a terrible blow to their morale. Neither Münzenberg nor his comrades could have envisaged with what brutality the Social Democratic-led government would suppress the revolution, and that it would be complicit in the murders of Liebknecht and Luxemburg. The dreams of following the Soviet example and creating a revolutionary Socialist government in Germany appeared to have been irrevocably smashed.[11]

Münzenberg and his comrades would be kept in Ulm for two months. In the meantime, the Social Democratic state government, led by Wilhelm Blos, brought charges of high treason and rebellion against those arrested. However, it filtered through to them that many of the soldiers in the Ulm barracks were sympathisers with the Spartacists, and a group was working on a plan to set them free. But before any such plan could be put into operation, the prisoners were moved again. In the middle of the night, they were awoken and then transported in a convoy of cars to Rothenburg prison on the river Neckar.

Alongside the security unit of military officers were several sailors accompanying them, who 'were known as police spies of the worst kind', Münzenberg said. 'We learned later from one of those involved, that they had planned to finish us off with a couple of hand grenades during the journey'. 'Happy coincidents', he writes, without divulging any details, 'frustrated their plan'. In Rothenburg, after weeks of protesting, they eventually managed to obtain better conditions for all political prisoners. For the *SPD*, the Spartacist-led revolution had come to an end with elections to the National Assembly on 19 January 1919. This also spelt the end of the Workers' and Soldiers' Councils as effective new structures of administration and government.

A cabinet was formed under Philipp Scheidemann bringing together the *SPD*, several centrist parties, and the German Democratic Party. While the new central government was prepared to conduct negotiations with the revolutionary councils, it was simultaneously preparing military action to smash them once and for all. On 12 February, the infamous *Freikorps* 'Death Blow' was unleashed by Defence Minister Gustav Noske to suppress the last remnants of Workers' and Soldiers' Councils, in a wave of brutality and bloodletting.

Over 180,000 miners in the Ruhr region were still on strike, but facing overwhelmingly superior armed forces, they retreated. Only three days later, as a response, a general strike erupted in central Germany, which involved not only the miners, but those in the chemical and allied industries too.

On the 21st of that month, the leader of the Munich Workers' Peasants' and Soldiers' Council, Kurt Eisner, was murdered by a right-wing army officer. By March, rumours were being deliberately circulated alleging that the Spartacists had murdered 60 military officers. This allegation was repeated in the main newspapers, including in *Vorwärts*, the *SPD*'s national newspaper. As expected, this 'news' infuriated the *Freikorps*, whose forces went on the rampage, encouraged by defence minister and *SPD* leader, Gustav Noske, who gave them free rein. Many workers were arrested and summarily executed, but as in the past, no one was ever held to account for these murders. On 10 March, Rosa Luxemburg's partner, Leo Jogiches, was also murdered 'while attempting to flee'. He had been investigating the circumstances surrounding the earlier murders of Liebknecht and Luxemburg.

Despite the brutality of the military, the strike wave developed a dynamic and force of its own that brought Berlin and Germany as a whole to a virtual standstill. In the Ruhr a 'Red Army of the Ruhr' was formed and was prepared to defend the Socialist Republic with arms.

The mass disillusionment that was still felt in the country as a result of the ravages of the war and Germany's defeat, widespread unemployment, and desperate hunger compounded the continued uncertainty and strikes continued unabated. In Württemburg, a general strike lasting several days took place, the demonstrators demanding the release of Münzenberg and the other political prisoners. Given the fluidity and uncertainty of the situation, the governor, Münzenberg relates, realised that there was a possibility that his prisoners could one day be members of a new government, so treated them accordingly, and they began to enjoy considerable privilege.

During his three months in Rothenburg prison, Münzenberg was able to complete his book about the Socialist youth organisation before and during the war (*Die Dritte Front*) and wrote a pamphlet for the Communist Party, titled ironically, 'Down with Spartacus'. Hundreds of thousands of copies of this pamphlet were distributed. He also penned a second one, 'From Revolt to Revolution', a polemic against Kautsky.

His comrades Edwin Hoernle – who would later become a regular contributor to Münzenberg's Worker Photographer journal – and Max Barthel wrote copious poems; so the whole group was able to use its time productively. All of them helped in the editing of the *Jugend Internationale* newspaper and maintained a lively correspondence with youth organisations in other countries. In between, they were brought to a number of interviews and interrogations in Stuttgart, before it was finally time for their case to be heard. During their imprisonment, there had also been a massive nationwide campaign unleashed by young Socialists to obtain their release.

They'd been over five months in custody awaiting trial, but conditions outside the prison had changed dramatically in the meantime. The short-lived Munich Soviet Republic, announced on 7 April 1919, had been bloodily suppressed,[12] other revolutionary Workers' and Soldiers' Councils had been dissolved, Liebknecht and Luxemburg had been murdered, the Weimar National Assembly installed, and Germany firmly established as a republic.

The jury of 12 members at the trial was made up of a mixture of small tradesmen, middleclass citizens, and peasant farmers. It lasted eight days. Each day the public chamber was crammed full and, according to Münzenberg, they defended themselves with passion and conviction, arguing persuasively that they had been organising a peaceful demonstration, and that it was the government that had first used armed force against them. Münzenberg said that it was the provisional government under Wilhelm Blos that had broken the constitution and committed high treason. He argued further that his group had merely wanted to hold the government to its promises and heed the demand of the workers, 'not a single demonstrator on 9 January had the aim of bringing down the government or mounting a putsch', he stated brazenly.

Although not of such international significance, his eloquent and effective defence could be compared with that to be made by Dimitrov at his Nazi show trial in Leipzig, over a decade later, in 1933.

Münzenberg so impressed members of the jury, that in the end, they unanimously declared the accused not guilty, and the chair of the jury made a statement apologising for the fact that it was not in the jury's power to offer compensation to the accused. Released from prison, they were welcomed by hundreds of demonstrating workers; one factory had donated a big barrel of potato salad and meat, and women presented them with bouquets of flowers.

The trial had been given widespread publicity and provided a significant impetus to the Württemburg Spartacus League, which had now become part of the Communist Party.

Immediately after their release, Münzenberg and his fellow ex-prisoners went on a lecture tour of Württemburg, gathering support for the new party, of which he had just been elected regional chair, but in addition was still responsible for the Youth International.

The first congress of the Third International had been convened in March 1919 in Moscow; to which 39 organisations had been invited. Münzenberg was selected as a delegate representing the Youth International, but was unable to go as he was still in custody in Ulm and then in Rothenburg at the time.

In a fiery speech at that founding congress, Lenin declared this International to be the real successor of the First and Second Internationals. The Comintern was born, and Grigori Zinoviev became its first president.

Notes

1 Fischer, Ruth, *Stalin und der deutsche Kommunismus*, Dietz Verlag, 1991.
2 It should be remembered that by the turn of the nineteenth-twentieth century, the German Social Democratic Party was the largest in the world. Under the leadership of influential figures like August Bebel, Karl Kautsky, and Wilhelm Liebknecht, it had become a formidable political force. Until the formation of the Communist Party, it was the party which represented and united all German workers and trade unions under its banner and was characterised by a strict, hierarchical discipline. This unity was fractured, though, shortly before the outbreak of the First World War, when the leadership endorsed the government's military budget in the Reichstag, thus reneging on the party's promise to oppose war in Europe and maintain an internationalist position. First the USPD broke away in 1917, together with the Spartacus Group, which then went on to form the Communist Party in 1918, later to be joined by the USPD.
3 Bollinger, Stefan, *November '18 – als die revolution nach Deutschland kam*, edition ost, 2018.
4 Fischer, Ruth, opus cit. p. 105.
5 *Sämtliche Schriften über die Russische Revolution*, Musaicum Books, OK Publishing, 2017.
6 *Vorwärts* of 29.12.1918.
7 Haffner, Sebastian, *Die verratene Revolution, Deutschland 1918/1919*, Berne, Munich, and Vienna, 1969.
8 Fischer, Ruth, opus cit. p. 106.
9 The 'Freikorps' were volunteer units that had existed from the eighteenth century onwards. They were in essence a mercenary army. They were sometimes in company strength, but could be in formations of up to several thousand strong. In the aftermath of the First World War and during the November Revolution of 1918–1919, the *Freikorps* consisted largely of war veterans that were brought together as paramilitary units ostensibly on behalf of the government to fight against the revolutionary forces attempting to set up a Socialist republic.
10 von Seeckt laid the foundation for the doctrine, tactics, organisation, and training of the German army. By the time he resigned in 1926, the *Reichswehr* had a clear, standardized operational doctrine, as well as a precise theory on future methods of combat, which greatly influenced the military campaigns fought by the *Wehrmacht* during the first half of the Second World War.
   von Seeckt served as a member of parliament from 1930 to 1932 and from 1933 to 1935 was repeatedly in China as a military consultant to Chiang Kai-shek in his war against the Communist-led Chinese Liberation Army.
11 Ruth Fischer, in her book, *Stalin und der deutsche Kommunismus*, Vol. 2, writes that after the Kapp Putsch in 1920 and the Kronstadt rebellion in Russia in March 1921, 'Münzenberg withdrew from Party activity and began his real life's work'... 'At the third world congress (of the Comintern) it was agreed to appeal to sympathisers outside Russia', to help counter the famine. 'A month later, on 12 September, Münzenberg founded the International Workers' Aid, the first communist organisation that penetrated deep into non-communist workers' and intellectual circles – the model for a thousand later organisations of this sort.' pp. 275–81.
12 By 7/8 November, revolution had broken out in Munich, King Ludwig III was deposed, and Kurt Eisner (USPD) declared a republic in the Bavarian Free State of

workers, peasants, and soldiers. 17 April, German Defence Minister Noske sends government troops to Munich. The *Freikorps* broke through the Munich defenses on 1 May, leading to bitter street fighting that involved flamethrowers, heavy artillery, armoured vehicles, and even aircraft. It became a bloodbath, with at least 800 workers and 'red army' members killed at the Munich slaughterhouse. Leviné was condemned to death for treason and shot by a firing squad. The fighting continued for over a week without the German central government taking any measures to stop it.

Lt. General Oven declared the city to have been secured on 6 May, finally ending the reign of the Bavarian Soviet Republic. The Hoffman government was restored, but then ousted a year later by the right-wing military.

By 2/3 May, government troops, together with Freikorps, have retaken the city and bloodily suppressed the revolutionary government. One of its leaders, Eugen Leviné, is executed on 3 May.

4

REBUILDING THE SOCIALIST YOUTH MOVEMENT

After his release from prison, Münzenberg once again returned to his main task of establishing a well-functioning International Youth movement. At this time, under the influence of the Bolshevik Revolution, he, like many of his comrades, was convinced that the parliamentary system was simply a bourgeois construct to hoodwink the working classes with its façade of democracy and was a hindrance to their taking power; it had to be swept aside if socialism were to be triumphant. With the country still gripped by revolutionary agitation, radical Socialists in Germany were still convinced that a genuine revolution was imminent, despite the setbacks of the previous year. With his strongly held anti-parliamentary views, Münzenberg was firmly in the ultra-left camp within the Communist Party at this time.

FIGURE 4.1   Willi Münzenberg

The recently formed Communist Party had been banned by the government in early 1919, in the wake of mass strikes and armed rebellion. In October, shortly after the defeat of the Hungarian Revolution in September, the second illegal congress of the recently established German Communist Party was held secretly in Heidelberg. It was convened at a time when the country was still in chaos, travel was difficult, many members were on the run, or had been arrested. It was certainly not a propitious time for undertaking an in-depth discussion in a democratic manner. The main points of discussion at the congress, in the wake of the failure of the November Revolution the previous year, were the liquidation of 'national Bolshevism' (a putative alliance between the insurgent Communist movement and dissident nationalist groups which rejected the Versailles Treaty), the 'trade union question', and the issue of 'parliamentarianism'. At this congress, Münzenberg was one of those who spoke in opposition to the party taking part in parliamentary elections, adopting a sectarian and ultra-leftist position.

His views were opposed by leading figures in the party, with more experience, from the older generation, such as Paul Levi, Clara Zetkin, and Albert Schreiner. These comrades argued that the party should not, in principle, reject any political means that would contribute in some way to preparing for the main struggle. The upcoming elections to the National Assembly should be seen, they argued, as such a preparatory means, but subordinated to the revolutionary struggle itself. This latter position was carried at the congress, but by a very slim majority, leaving the left faction, which included Münzenberg at this time, still with a strong influence in the country at large.

As a result of his stance, Münzenberg and those comrades of the same persuasion were not elected onto the central committee. Despite the leadership's arguments, the Münzenberg group felt that the decisions taken were tantamount to abandoning the revolutionary road.

Although the Heidelberg congress had delivered a slim majority in favour of participation in parliamentary elections and for working with the (German Social Democratic Party [SPD]-dominated) trade unions, the left opposition within the party remained very strong. The theses approved at Heidelberg, according to Hugo Eberlein,[1] generated strong opposition when they were made known in local Party branches, which were largely in opposition to this policy. In Berlin, a stronghold of those opposing parliamentarianism, many members left the party and joined the far-left KAPD (Communist Workers' Party of Germany) over this issue, but Münzenberg decided to remain in the Communist Party of Germany (KPD). The KAPD would continue to exist as a Party until 1922 before collapsing in sectarian disagreement.

Despite the decision taken to participate in parliamentary elections, the congress had revealed a deep split in the party between its so-called right and the left wings. The parliamentarians held a majority in the leadership, but almost certainly not among the members, as Eberlein noted above. Differences were certainly not resolved at Heidelberg, and the debate on parliamentarianism versus revolution would remain a subject of heated debate within the party for some time to come.

At that congress, Ruth Fischer[2] writes in her reminiscences, 'The left opposition, this time led by Willi Münzenberg, argued for abstaining in the elections to the *Nationalversammlung* (National Assembly) – a demonstrative gesture that was to make it clear to the working class that a parliament elected in the midst of war would have no claim to democratic legality'.[3] Münzenberg had argued vociferously against a parliamentary road to socialism, saying that, 'Our joining this bankrupt institution [parliament] would only give the workers new hope in that institution … a critique of parliamentarianism is much more successful from outside than inside. The masses who are following us today do so out of a sense of disappointment with the other parties, particularly the *USP[D)*, which also maintains that it is participating in the parliamentary system only as "dynamite"'.[4]

As a corollary to the party's position on parliamentarianism, in the summer of 1919, the *KPD* dissolved its organisation within the army – the League of Red Soldiers – which had become a gathering point of the opposition. But many combat organisations continued their activities even after being officially dissolved. Eberlein wrote that the majority of those in the armed groups were later incorporated into the *KAPD*.[5]

During this period, Münzenberg had been largely pre-occupied with picking up the threads of his comrades in the Socialist Youth International and had begun organising for an international congress to be held in Vienna in August 1919. Attendance here would be much better than at the improvised 1918 conference in Berlin. For the first time, the newly founded Austrian Young Communists as well as a representative of the Soviet Union's Communist Youth Group would be present at such an international congress. As there were so many key issues to discuss and agree upon, the conference decided to hold a second session in the autumn in Berlin.

Like many of the other delegates at the Vienna congress, Münzenberg was still without proper ID papers and had entered the country illegally. There, he says, he felt safe because, despite their Socialist friends giving wide publicity to their attendance at the conference, they experienced no immediate repercussions from the Austrian state. That feeling, however, was to be short lived. Only a day or two later, a whole number of congress delegates were arrested. After holding them for a whole day in police custody, and then taking them to holding cells in the police presidium building, where they were held for several days, they were summarily expelled from the country and banned from re-entering Austria for life.

Back in Stuttgart, he and his comrades began preparing for the Berlin congress, but then because of discussions at the Heidelberg Communist Party congress, to which he was delegated by the Württemburg Party group, he was forced momentarily to shelve his youth work.

On his return journey from Heidelberg to Stuttgart by train, he happened to read in a Stuttgart newspaper that the police were undertaking a round-up of the party leadership in the city, and that a new warrant had been issued for his arrest.

The Stuttgart state prosecutor was intent on revenge after Münzenberg's earlier acquittal and had opened a new case of high treason against him. He certainly did not relish facing more months in custody, so a few stops before the train was due to arrive in Stuttgart, he got off and went underground, making his way to Berlin where it would be easier for him to stay undercover. His comrades collected his papers from the apartment in Stuttgart and forwarded them to him.

In the autumn of 1919, there was a resurgence of strike action by Berlin's workers opposing the policies of the Ebert-led government. The militant electricity workers in the city even cut off the city's electricity supply in protest. They also demanded that the trade unions be given a legitimate role in the new republic. In the new year, there were stormy protest demonstrations outside the Reichstag against what the organised workers saw as their exclusion from the decision-making process and several demonstrators were killed and others wounded.

That year brought yet further defeats for the revolutionary movement in Germany and elsewhere. The Workers' and Soldiers' Councils in all the big cities had been crushed and closed down; the short-lived soviet government in Hungary had also been suppressed – it lasted from March until August 1919 – while the Soviet Union itself was also facing a powerful counter-revolution, supported by the big capitalist nations. The Social Democratic parties affiliated to the Second International now also threw in their lot with their own national ruling élites to oppose the Soviet Union.

The founding of the Communist International [abbreviated as Comintern] in Moscow in March 1919 reflected the final worldwide rupture between the reformist Social Democrats and the Communists. Although the new German Communist Party attended this founding conference, it abstained in the final vote on its constitution.

The Berlin Socialist Youth International congress took place on 20 November of that year and delegates from 14 countries took part, representing over 200,000 members. At this congress, it was decided to rename the organisation the Communist Youth International, in response to the establishment of the Comintern itself.

Only two months beforehand, on 7 September, Socialist youth groups in a number of cities had organised mass demonstrations in celebration of International Youth Day. In many cases, these had ended in bloody clashes with the police and military. In Berlin, Noske's military forces had even set up machine guns and fired into the demonstrators – there was one death and many injured.

Münzenberg delivered the main speech to the youth congress delegates gathered in Berlin, and amongst other things, stressed 'the high value that should be placed on the ethical education of young workers, how, through early training, they would learn to take independent action within their own organisations; there was a need to awaken a sense of responsibility, to develop self-confidence, to be courageous, pioneering and, where the opportunity arose, to demonstrate solidarity, idealism and determination'. He also reported that the youth organisation could be proud that in a number of countries former members now made up significant numbers of the leaders in their socialist parties and trade unions.

Following the congress, he saw his main task thereafter as creating an effective secretariat and a functioning organisational apparatus. This was not easy, as it all had to be done in the utmost secrecy because the authorities were desperately trying to find out where the organisation's offices were; 'Wanted' posters adorned Berlin's hoardings. Despite this, the Berlin police failed to locate the leaders and, Münzenberg writes, 'we were able to continue working almost undisturbed for more than a year'. It was only in the spring of 1921 that the police had success, but after raiding their offices found them deserted, as the occupants had been able to move out and take with them the most important documents before the raid took place.

The most difficult part of the work, he found, was to maintain contacts with the youth organisations in other countries and receive foreign delegates while himself obliged to live and operate under cover. He and his close comrades still had no legal papers or passports, so they found it almost impossible to travel outside the country, although they did manage to organise some safe crossing points over the German-Swiss, German-Austrian, and German-Lithuanian borders.

While Münzenberg and his comrades were risking long prison sentences if they were caught, those in a number of other countries faced more dire consequences. In 1927, their comrade Viktor Greiffenberger in Lithuania would fall into police hands and be shot the same evening after an impromptu court martial.

Despite having to operate clandestinely and dodge police surveillance, Münzenberg was able to set up country-based secretariats in Stockholm responsible for Scandinavia, in Switzerland for the surrounding Western countries, in Moscow for the east, and in Vienna for southeastern Europe. In this way, international links were strengthened and the groups managed to carry out effective political work despite the suppression.

The first large international conference after the one in Berlin was planned for Stockholm in December 1919. This was undertaken partly to counter an attempt by the Social Democrats to organise their own youth conference in Denmark with the aim of distancing themselves from what they felt was being transformed into a Communist Youth organisation. The Social Democrats at this time undertook strenuous efforts in a number of European countries to establish their own separate Socialist Youth organisations and to distance themselves from Münzenberg's outfit.

Münzenberg and his two comrades had to travel to Stockholm for the conference illegally of course. After staying in a seaport in northern Germany for a few days, they managed to find a boat owner willing to take them across the Baltic Sea to Denmark. But as storms were predicted before they were due to sail, the boatsman got cold feet, and it took considerable persuasion to get him to change his mind.

'We'd hardly left the port when the storm broke', Münzenberg wrote in his reminiscences, 'the boat tossed about like a nutshell on the heaving waves'. Then suddenly the boatsman shouted at them to hide in the chain hold as a patrol boat was approaching. There, 'pressed together like sardines', they had to squat for two hours before the danger had passed, but they still had to face the continuing storm and a very irate captain.

In the end, they managed to reach Stockholm and, at last, felt able to move about freely. But this sense of freedom was illusory and short-lived; they had, unwittingly, already attracted police attention. The flat of the Swedish comrade with whom they were staying was soon raided, and the police demanded to see their papers, which the Germans did not have. They were taken to police headquarters to establish their identities. The investigating officer had photos showing Münzenberg on German 'wanted' posters, but he denied that he was the same man.

He would spend three weeks in custody. The Swedish prison was a modern-built building, but conditions were strict; however, the weekly church service gave him much cause for amusement: every prisoner had to sit next to the half-open door of his cell and listen to the priest, in the corridor below, intoning in a language none of those who didn't speak Swedish could comprehend.

After three weeks, Münzenberg was told he would be deported, but he was given three days to remain in Sweden before the deadline. The Swedish police then brought him to the ferry and made sure he left the country.

He knew, that in Sassnitz, the arrival port in Germany, the police would be waiting for him with an arrest warrant for high treason. He was desperate to devise a way of avoiding almost certain arrest and so befriended a young sailor in the hope that he might be able to help. Shortly before they reached the coast, he discovered a livestock transport wagon with a large air vent, and while his young sailor friend stood guard, he managed to climb into it, and found that it was fortunately filled only with wooden crates and not livestock.

After the wagons were unloaded in Sassnitz, he remained hidden until darkness, but he soon heard the voices of customs officials who were opening the wagon doors. He took his chance and clambered back out through the air vent and made his escape without being detected.

There were no more trains to Berlin at that time of night, so he began walking in the direction of the small town of Bergen. Beforehand, he made a stop at a small roadside inn, but had hardly sat down before he was horrified to hear galloping horses and to see a coach with four border guards arriving. This is it, he thought, but they paid him no attention at all, and he soon gathered that they had other things on their minds, as they were on their way to a big military ball being held in Bergen. Münzenberg pretended to be a war veteran and asked if they would give him a lift. For a round of cognacs, they were prepared to do so. From Bergen, via Stralsund, he then managed to make his way safely back to Berlin.

Despite this hair-raising adventure, he and several other comrades would undertake yet another illegal journey to Vienna in May 1920, where an international conference had been convened of what had, in the meantime, become the Communist Youth International. All went well on this trip, until shortly before Salzburg an official asked to see their papers, but as they had none, they were all arrested once again.

At police headquarters, the officer in charge felt he needed to obtain instructions from the ministry in Vienna, so let the group wander off to have breakfast, but made them leave their cases behind as security. They were more than ready to do this, as their cases contained only a few items of clothing, They made off postehaste for the border and what would be a strenuous six-hour march across the mountains to arrive safely, but exhausted in Berchtesgarden, where they separated. Münzenberg took a train north the next morning, and while he 'chatted to a staid Bavarian family about the state of the spring sowing, we had to smile as we watched several police officers looking for two young people on their own. Unchallenged, we continued our journey', as he noted in his reminiscences.

In the summer of 1920, the first meeting of the executive of the Communist Youth International took place in Berlin. This meeting was controversial because the international leadership was very unhappy about the direct interference in their affairs by the Comintern through its Western European Office and its representative James or 'Jakob' Reich, alias 'comrade Thomas'.

The chair of the Comintern, Grigori Zinoviev, had communicated directly with the individual national youth sections, inviting them to the second congress of the Comintern to be held in Moscow without informing the Youth International's leadership in Berlin, although such a move had been expressly vetoed by the Berlin office.

Münzenberg was livid about this interference and felt the Western European Office of the Comintern was deliberately undermining his work. The Western European Office accused the Berlin-based youth leadership of being ultra-left with 'semi-anarchist tendencies'. On top of this slight, all correspondence between Moscow and Berlin now had to go through comrade Thomas's office, but Münzenberg very much resented having to send and receive letters from or to Lenin via Thomas.

Twenty representatives from 14 organisations came together for the meeting of the Communist Youth International in the summer of 1920, mostly travelling illegally and then having to meet clandestinely in various working-class pubs and in the old tower of the Ruinenberg near Sanssouci in Potsdam. At this meeting, three delegates, including Münzenberg, were elected to go to the second congress of the Communist International which was to meet in July in Moscow, where he hoped to raise the issue of Comintern interference directly.

He still had no passport and the warrant for his arrest was still valid, so travelling to Russia confronted him with another tricky problem. Up until then he had been able to dodge arrest through ingenuity and serendipity, but the day before he was due to travel to Moscow his luck ran out, not, as he emphasised, due to police astuteness, but as a result of denunciation by a spy in the youth organisation's office.

He was sitting in a café with friends. And, 'Not far from their table two men were seated who were obviously plain-clothed policemen', he recalled. Before the policemen had time to call for support, Münzenberg emptied his pockets and gave any incriminating material to one of his friends and headed for the door, where four men jumped on him and told him he was under arrest. He was too high profile an operator to escape the authority's notice forever.

He was taken to the Berlin police headquarters and was told he had been arrested in the first instance on the basis of a warrant issued in 1917 for desertion and only secondly as a result of the outstanding Stuttgart warrant for high treason. He was arraigned the next day, with 'around forty others who had been taken into custody on the Sunday – "petty thieves and pimps," – and hauled before an investigating lawyer, a man no longer young, but of jovial disposition. The lawyer flicked through the files in front of him, and when he came to Münzenberg's, he saw only that he had been arrested on the basis of a warrant issued in 1917. He burst into an angry tirade against the incompetent police officers who had arrested him on a charge that had been amnestied long ago. He slammed the file closed without examining any further documents in it and ordered Münzenberg's release. The latter made off posthaste to the Polish border en route for Moscow before the mistake was discovered and he could be re-arrested'.

A day later, his comrade Leo Flieg, also travelling to Moscow, was arrested at the border in Stettin (today Szczecin in Poland) in the hope that he could be persuaded to divulge Münzenberg's whereabouts. He put the police off the trail by telling them that Münzenberg had left for Frankfurt am Main.

In the meantime, Münzenberg had in fact also arrived in Stettin, but had donned the field-grey uniform of a Russian prisoner of war and with the help of sympathising sailors, managed to board a boat taking several hundred Russian ex-prisoners of war back to Russia. Together with him on the boat was the Communist leader, Ernst Meyer (who would later marry Eugen Leviné's widow Rosa), as well as several other comrades. After several days of a pleasant and uneventful journey, they arrived in Narva, Estonia.

A tourist in the Soviet Union

Once in Petrograd, in late July 1920, he contacted his old comrades from his Swiss exile years, like Grigori Zinoviev, and spent his first evening reminiscing with him about old times, the party, and about the coming congress, but also, of course, about the Comintern's role concerning the Youth International.

In the Soviet Union on this occasion he was there as a guest of the Soviet Communist Youth organisation and was taken from one meeting to another to talk to young workers, 'who competed with each other to show me and the other delegates the achievements of the revolution': the new factories and working people's clubs, schools, and children's homes. He was particularly impressed to visit a former Tsarist village which had been converted into a children's village, run for and by the children themselves. In the Tsar's former palaces the children of Petrograd's workers and soldiers were given pride of place. The children clamoured to show them everything they had been doing, their wall newspaper, handicrafts, and paintings.

In the German ambassador's former palace in Moscow, he had an informal meeting with Karl Radek, who had become secretary of the Communist International. He also spoke with many other comrades he knew from his time in Switzerland.

Lenin welcomed him with the words: 'How are the youth doing?', and then questioned him closely about other members and friends from the Zimmerwald Group and the Swiss youth movement. 'I know no other leader of the working class movement, like Lenin', Münzenberg said, 'who at the same time as carrying enormous responsibility on the world stage, and occupying a similar position, would be so comradely and behave in such a decent fashion towards the comrades. He asked about every worker, even those who he may have seen before only once or twice in the "Schwänliklub" [where the leftists would meet in Zurich] and would continue to probe: Where is he? What is he doing? Is he with us? Is he working in the party? and so on'.[6]

Lenin, he said, ensured him his full support in building the youth movement which, he emphasised, was the most important and urgent task. 'Just let them call you a "youth careerist", he said to Münzenberg. Without the youth we will be unable to build a Communist Party!'

Lenin, despite all his other responsibilities, always maintained links with young people, attending their conferences, corresponding, and helping write policies. 'Apart from Karl Liebknecht, I knew no other working class leader who devoted so much time and showed real interest as Lenin did', Münzenberg noted.

'After hours of discussion, when we were about to say our goodbyes, Lenin looked at me with his curious, crafty smile and said: "Who was right about the bet we made in the "Astoria" in Zurich?"'[7] This bet was made shortly before Lenin left Switzerland to return to Russia, and he had predicted a revolution there very soon and with it the beginnings of a Socialist revolution on a world scale. Münzenberg had been extremely sceptical. But history has shown that Lenin was right in the short term, even though very wrong in the long term!

This Second Congress of the Communist International was a particularly significant one because it laid down the conditions and clarified the character of the Comintern itself; it also formulated policies on colonialism, the trade union movement, and the chief aims of its own organisation. The youth question was also on the agenda, but it had to be referred back to the Executive Committee because of lack of time, despite the strong protest of many youth delegates.

At this congress, Münzenberg alongside British delegate Willie Gallacher and from Italy Amadeo Bordiga took an uncompromisingly ultra-left position and defended their anti-parliamentary stance, which he had elaborated at the Heidelberg congress. And, in another example of sectarian intolerance, Münzenberg also spoke vehemently against allowing the German delegation from the *USPD* (Independent Social Democratic Party) to join the Comintern, even though it had sent delegates. Lenin told him, jokingly that he'd almost certainly end his life as an ultra leftist.

Münzenberg's stance clearly irritated the Comintern leadership which called on the Youth International to cease its 'revolutionary offensive' and concentrate on building Communist Party organisations.

At the congress, he felt frustrated and irritated with what he felt were the entrenched and often intransigent attitudes on the part of a number of leading comrades. Afterwards, he was cheered up considerably by having the opportunity of travelling around the vast country for a fortnight as a member of a congress delegation. While he had experienced warm hospitality at the congress and had not been aware of any material shortages, he was horrified by the level of devastation that had been left by the war and by the poverty and the ramshackle state of industry and agriculture he later witnessed in the country at large.

The Soviet Union was in the grip of a bitter civil war and was not only facing internal chaos in the wake of the revolution, but unprecedented outside intervention on a massive scale.

Once Russia had withdrawn from the war, the Allied powers gave full military backing to the anti-Communist 'White' forces in Russia. The Czechoslovak Legion was already occupying most of the Trans-Siberian Railway and major cities in Siberia. For their own Russian incursion, the Italians created the special *Corpo di Spedizione* with Alpini troops and ex-POWs from the former Austro-Hungarian army who were recruited into the Italian *Legione Redenta*. Finnish volunteers joined the Estonians to fight the Red Army in the northwest of the country, and Romania, Greece, Poland, China, and Serbia also sent contingents in support of the intervention.

In July 1918, against the advice of the United States (US) Department of War, Woodrow Wilson agreed to the participation of 5,000 US troops, which were sent to Arkhangelsk (Archangel), followed by another 8,000 soldiers, organised as the American Expeditionary Force. That same month, the Canadian government agreed to a British request to provide most of the soldiers for a combined British Empire force, which also included Australian and Indian troops.

A Royal Navy squadron was sent to the Baltic, consisting of modern cruisers and destroyers. In December 1918, it sailed into Estonian and Latvian ports, sending in troops and supplies and, as Rear Admiral Edwyn Alexander-Sinclair declared at the time, promising to attack the Bolsheviks 'as far as my guns can reach'. The Japanese, though, sent the largest military force numbering about 70,000. They sought to establish a buffer state in Siberia. The effectiveness of these interventions, however, would be undermined by not only war-weariness among allied troops, but also hostility within the armed forces, and at home, to fighting this new Socialist 'workers' state'.

The Allied powers were eventually forced to withdraw from northern Russia and Siberia in 1920, although Japanese forces continued to occupy parts of Siberia until 1922 and the northern half of Sakhalin until 1925.

The situation for the inexperienced Bolshevik government looked grim, and it was under these circumstances that the congress delegates began their journey through the Soviet Union.

In many places workers were occupied solely with clearing the rubble left by the war and only in very few towns was there any new construction taking place. On several of the big stations the delegation encountered trains transporting the many injured from the battlefronts.

For much of their journey, they were obliged to travel in a special train with armoured carriages in front and rear and manned by 100 marines. In addition, each of the delegates was given a rifle and a revolver to be used in emergencies. Such were the times.

In Odessa, they saw firsthand what the Red Army was up against: only a few months before, the city had been in the hands of the rebels and gangs of bandits. A delegation of rebels had tried negotiating a truce with the Red Army on the basis of dividing the city up between the warring groups, but this was rejected out of hand and the rebels shot.

When Münzenberg and his delegation arrived in the city, it was firmly in the hands of the Red Army, but other parts of the country were far from safe. While travelling through the Ukraine hinterland, the delegation was followed for some time by the Cossack anarchist rebel Nestor Machno, who commanded over a thousand horsemen and was a thorn in the side of the Red Army. He tried to kill them all on several occasions, including by blowing up a bridge and tearing up the railway tracks in front of their train.

In Odessa, a captain Georges Sadoul joined the delegation for its journey through the Ukraine, where they again witnessed firsthand the devastation left by the war: whole towns and villages razed to the ground, fields untended, extreme deprivation, and squalor. Sadoul, a conscripted soldier in the French armed forces during the wars of intervention, had defected to the Russians in Odessa; in later years, back in France, he would become a well-known journalist, author, and renowned authority on cinema. From Odessa, the delegation could see French warships still blockading the port, which had also been mined to prevent Russian ships leaving or entering.

For the Soviet government, their delegation was a valuable demonstration to the Russian people of Western interest in and support for the revolution. At many of the places en route where they made temporary halts, delegates would be asked to talk to the local people and give impromptu speeches.

After this tour, which took several weeks, the delegates returned to Moscow to begin their often tortuous journeys back to their home countries, through what were, for Communists at least, hostile territories. Several of his fellow delegates set out from the Siberian port of Murmansk in order to avoid an overland journey, but three French comrades died on this route when their small motorboat capsized.

Münzenberg was able to join a large group of German soldiers being repatriated to Germany. During the celebrations at the port of Stettin to welcome the soldiers home, he managed to slip away with all the documents he was carrying and reach Berlin without being stopped and searched.

The problems Münzenberg was now facing, trying to consolidate and build the youth organisation on a truly international scale, were no less daunting than the ones he encountered during the war; the atmosphere was just as hostile, if not more so. 'On several fronts the persecution of our organisations was even more acute and more brutal than during the war', he wrote in his reminiscences. In the east, the Whites were waging a war of terror against the young Soviet Union, particularly in Lithuania, Hungary, Finland, and what is today Belarus and Ukraine, as well as surveillance and harassment carried out in Western countries.

During the war, many young Socialists in these east European countries had been given long prison sentences for participating in 'banned organisations', but now hundreds were being summarily executed for promoting Communism. Even in those countries with Socialists in coalition governments, Communist organisations were often banned along with their publications. This was certainly the case in Germany, so the Communist Youth International was forced to organise under conditions of illegality. Surprisingly, despite having to work clandestinely, Münzenberg was still able to do so effectively and gain widespread support. There is little doubt that the still widespread unemployment, particularly among the young, and general dissatisfaction with the new Weimar government were helpful factors here.

In October of that same year, 1920, Communist youth groups in Germany organised numerous political demonstrations and instigated a broad international campaign to aid the victims of the White Terror sweeping Hungary. This would be the first such relief operation undertaken by Münzenberg, which undoubtedly helped him gain valuable experience that would become useful later in creating what would become the biggest solidarity and aid programme ever undertaken on a worldwide scale.

In Hungary, in the wake of the collapse of the Soviet Republic in August 1919, over 30,000 working-class men and women, as well as children, had been imprisoned for their political allegiances and desperately needed food and clothing. In support of this campaign, Münzenberg managed to bring on board writers like Romain Rolland from France, Upton Sinclair from the USA, and the Flemish artist Frans Masereel among other leading figures from the cultural world. In Germany alone, they collected around 30,000 Marks in cash, as well as shoes, clothing, and food donations. But even bigger than the material aid was the political success. In hundreds of meetings, and through the columns of the *Jugend Internationale* newspaper and pamphlets, people were made aware of the repression and suffering in Hungary as a result of the White Terror.

The Youth International was also active in other campaigns and solidarity actions in Germany itself, such as the blockade of Poland, in response to its invasion of the Soviet Union, to prevent the delivery of weaponry to the Poles.

On 1 November 1920, only a year after the establishment of the Communist Youth International, Münzenberg travelled, once again illegally – he still had no valid identity documents – to Czechoslovakia in an attempt to win over the youth movement there to affiliate to the International. In Paris, the French youth organisation had already voted overwhelmingly to join. In all, there were now affiliated Socialist or Communist youth organisations in 49 different countries around the world, with around 800,000 members. Not all of this success was down to his efforts alone, of course, but he certainly played a leading role in building such a network. It had grown to become an international organisation in more than just name, in a relatively short time and under extremely difficult circumstances.

Münzenberg was also behind the expansion of the organisation's publishing and publicity work. He had realised very early on what a key role the print media can play in reaching out to people and promoting Socialist ideas. This experience would come in very useful later once his publishing and propaganda work really took off.

The youth organisation's newspaper, *Jugend International*, came out regularly every month, supplemented by the *Internationale Jugendkorrespondenz* (International youth correspondence) every 10 days, and later a special magazine for the very young, *Der Junge Genosse* (The young comrade), would be published alongside many leaflets and pamphlets. In Stuttgart they even established a dedicated International Youth publishing house. Similar publishing activity was replicated in other countries where effective youth organisations existed.

Even under extremely harsh and repressive conditions during the years 1920 and 1921, they managed to maintain a functioning and effective movement. In early 1921, they began preparing for the second congress of the Communist Youth International to be held in Germany in the spring. This was at the height of the suppression of revolutionary groups by the Social Democratic Weimar government and its draconian Minister of Defence Noske, who was all too willing to use the army and the paramilitary *Freikorps* to suppress any Communist-led rebellions and attempts at taking power.

On 20 January 1920, the Treaty of Versailles came into force, restricting the German army to 100,000 men or less. In February 1920, Noske, following orders from the *Allied Military Commission*, which controlled Germany's compliance with the Treaty, ordered the dissolution of several *Freikorps* units, but the highest ranking general of the *Reichswehr*, von Lüttwitz, refused to carry out the order, culminating in what became known as the Kapp Putsch on 13 March 1920.[8]

With the defeat of the revolutionary workers' organisations and the weakness of central government, right-wing forces in the army grasped the opportunity of restoring the monarchy. Their aim was to undo the German Revolution, overthrow the Weimar Republic, and establish a right-wing autocratic government in its place. The putsch was supported by sections of the military establishment together with other conservative, nationalist, and monarchist factions.

To restore order, Noske asked the regular army to put down the putsch. Its generals refused to do so, and the government was forced to flee Berlin. At this moment of extreme danger to Ebert's government, he realised that the military upon whom he had relied to defeat the revolutionaries, was now determined to get rid of his government too. Ebert used the only real option open to him if he wished to defeat the putschists and cling onto power: he called a general strike and relied on the support of the trade unions. This would be the first complete political general strike to take place in a modern industrial country, and it brought the country to a complete standstill.

The strike, combined with a refusal by the bureaucracy to accept the new chancellor, Wolfgang Kapp, resulted in a quick collapse of the coup. However, as one of the conditions for ending their general strike, the unions demanded Noske's resignation, which came about on 22 March.

At the time of the Kapp Putsch, Münzenberg was living in Lichtenberg, a working-class district of Berlin, and there the comrades held Party meetings every evening, but they had to be prepared to flee at any moment because their venue could be raided at any time. Every comrade was very much aware of the dangers they faced. Nevertheless, the Kapp Putsch took Münzenberg and his comrades very much by surprise.

While living in Lichtenberg, for the first time in his life, and instructed by a comrade, he learned to use a rifle. With the outbreak of the general strike in response to the putsch, the comrades felt that armed clashes between workers and the military would be unavoidable. They brought out any weapons they could procure or had hidden in cellars and cupboards. However, after three days of effective strike action, the putschists threw in the towel, so Münzenberg was spared having to use his gun.

Once the Kapp Putsch had been defeated, the SPD-led government had no qualms about deploying the very same *Freikorps* units that had been behind the putsch against the 'Red Army of the Ruhr', which had played a key role in defeating the putschists and to suppress the remaining Workers' and Soldiers' Councils there. This successfully snuffed out what had survived of the German November Revolution. Under Freiherr von Watter, troops marched into the Ruhr area on 2 April 1920 and bloodily suppressed the uprising. Extrajudicial shootings by the *Freikorps* troops resulted in more than a thousand dead.

In elections to the Reichstag on 6 June 1920, the people gave its verdict on the SPD's betrayal of the revolution: its vote dropped by 10%, which went instead to the much more militant USPD, and throughout the continued existence of the Weimar Republic, the party would never recover its previous high vote.

In October 1920, the left-wing USPD held its Party congress to discuss, among other things, whether to join the Comintern or not. Zinoviev, who had been invited, gave a long speech to try and convince the party to join and in the end won them over. From 4 to 7 December 1920, at a joint Party congress, the USPD (with 349 delegates representing 300,000 members) and the KPD (with 146 delegates, representing 70,000 members) agreed to join forces to become the *Vereinigte Kommunistische Partei Deutschlands* or *VKPD* (The United Communist Party of Germany), and at this moment, it also became a true mass

Party. It further agreed to join the Comintern and to accept as its goal the 'dictatorship of the proletariat' and the establishment of a Soviet or council Republic (*Räterepublik*) in Germany.

Moscow takes control

It was not only the young *KPD* that was riven by factional infighting and indecision. Münzenberg and the youth movement he led were also now faced with a crucial dilemma: hand over the reins to Moscow or be ostracised.

In view of the Comintern's political line of imposing centralised control, it is hardly surprising that its leaders also began putting pressure on Münzenberg, viewing his independent way of thinking, and taking action not conducive to the adoption of a unified policy. Although its leaders were very much aware of the youth movement's strength and potential, they also knew that Münzenberg was the key to winning the organisation over to its policy position.

Moscow made it clear to Münzenberg that the agreement made at the second congress of the Comintern, to recognise the youth section's autonomy, had only been a tactical one, and they demanded that the next youth congress be held in Moscow. Münzenberg rejected both demands vehemently and wrote to Zinoviev in no uncertain terms that the Comintern had no right and no reason to unilaterally change the venue for the congress planned for Berlin. He received no response.

Most of the national youth groups agreed with Münzenberg on the need to maintain a wide degree of autonomy for the Youth International. He continued to argue strongly for holding the next congress in a Western country, to demonstrate that the organisation was not simply a 'tool of Moscow'.

In March 1921, while he was busy preparing for the congress, others had been busy persuading the German Communist Party leadership that the time had arrived to take decisive action because the country was now deemed to be in a pre-revolutionary situation.

That same month, emergency measures were imposed by the government on central Germany, and armed police units were deployed, in an attempt to suppress the increasingly militant strike movement. This, the *KPD* viewed as a provocation, and the Central Committee, supported by the Comintern, called on the workers to take up the armed struggle, which would lead to what became known as the 'March Uprising'.

Following weeks of brutal and bloody battles, the uprising was successfully suppressed by government forces and a reign of terror unleashed against the Communists, accompanied by a full state of emergency which was declared throughout the area.

This defeat led to a profound crisis within the *KPD* and brought into question the role of the Comintern in this defeat and its hegemonic relationship with the German Party. Despite the fact that the country was indeed in a dire situation politically and economically, with mass unemployment, hunger, and widespread anger, the majority of the workers were clearly not prepared to mount the barricades and put their lives on the line yet again for what seemed like an impossible dream.

Gross, in her Münzenberg biography, describes how ten years later she and he were attending a commemoration of the March Uprising, organised by the regional Communist Party in Halle-Merseburg. They went from village to village, from one working-class suburb to another on lorries, accompanied by a brass band, and in every locality they passed through they came across the graves of the victims from that uprising.

It was during those turbulent March days that the first delegates to the congress of the Socialist Youth International began arriving in Jena, in southeast Germany, most of them having to enter the country illegally. Münzenberg had defied the Comintern's demand for the congress to be held in Moscow.

Even before the congress was to begin that March 1921, Münzenberg had already spoken out against the proposal for an uprising in an article written for the journal, *Internationale Jugend Korrespondenz* (International Youth Correspondence). His earlier fervent support for using Bolshevik tactics in Germany had ebbed, and he now took a more cautious approach. He rejected the idea of taking the offensive at this time, as he felt that it was too early for a conclusive battle. He argued, rightly, that counter-revolutionary forces were still far too strong. This viewpoint was supported by a majority of the German and Scandinavian delegates to the congress, but the Italians, Austrians, and Swiss took an opposing position. At the congress, his opponents would attack him for his 'opportunism and anti-Moscow attitude'. The position he took on this issue was also not at all to the liking of the Comintern leaders in Moscow.

Although the congress was well attended, it was noteworthy that there was no Soviet delegation. The reason they gave for this was that attending would place their delegation in unnecessary danger, but it was almost certainly to send a message to Münzenberg expressing the Comintern's clear disapproval of what they viewed as his 'autonomous behaviour' in holding the congress in Germany and in opposing the March Uprising.

On the second day of the congress, several Polish delegates were unexpectedly arrested by the police, but after strong protests were released again. However, these arrests alerted the authorities to the fact that a congress of revolutionaries was taking place under their noses. The organisers therefore decided to move the remaining sessions to Berlin, but continued the day's business until 6.00 in the evening, and then surreptitiously each delegation made its own separate way to Berlin so as not to alert the authorities by having a single mass exodus.

Punctually at 10.00 a.m. the next day, the session continued in the teachers' union building, right next door to the police headquarters in Berlin. However, after three days of deliberations and under the hourly threat of another police raid, the executive decided to postpone further business and reconvene in Moscow at the close of the third congress of the Communist International (Comintern), to take place in the summer of that year. Münzenberg, however, in the meantime, would continue to fight for the Youth International's autonomy from the Comintern and would emphasise this in no uncertain terms in an article he wrote for the May issue of *Die Jugend Internationale.*

Exhausted by the end of the interrupted Berlin congress, he took a few days off to go walking in his beloved Thuringian Forest. This gave him time to reflect on the dilemma he was facing. There, in the footsteps of Goethe, soaking up the bracing, resinous air, the quiet broken only by birdsong and the sound of his own footsteps, he could let his thoughts soar and take stock. He had fought determinedly to keep control of the Youth International, but he was realistic enough to know that he couldn't hold out any longer against Moscow's insistence on taking over the reins.

In June 1921, Münzenberg again travelled to Moscow as a delegate to the third congress of the Comintern and to take part in the youth congress that had been interrupted in Jena and Berlin.

On arrival, he first had a long meeting with Radek, whom he told that he was feeling quite frustrated and angry about what he felt was the sluggishness and inflexibility of many in the party and Comintern leadership, despite the enormous challenges both countries were facing.

The Soviet Union he encountered was also undergoing serious difficulties on many fronts. There were peasant uprisings and strikes, industry was collapsing, and people were starving. At its 10th Party congress, the Bolsheviks had taken the decision to abandon the policy of 'war Communism' and introduced the New Economic Plan which involved taking a step backwards by re-introducing a certain amount of capitalist leverage.

Then, on 28 February, a large group of Kronstadt sailors rebelled against what they saw as an increasing centralisation of decision-making, bureaucratisation, and a betrayal of the revolution, and they were soon joined by the Kronstadt Soviets.

Kronstadt had been one of the key centres of Bolshevik action at the very beginning of the 1917 revolution, so this rebellion was symbolic of a deep-lying malaise in the country. It would be suppressed in a bloody and brutal attack by government forces. The Bolshevik Revolution was facing the very real danger of collapse.

On this visit Lenin took Münzenberg under his wing, offering protection from the resentment and animosity of some of the old guard. In defending him to others, Lenin emphasised that it was, 'Münzenberg who gave me a newspaper and a platform when during the war we had no other means of broadcasting our views', and Lenin was determined to ensure that he would be given a responsibility commensurate with his abilities. He managed to convince Münzenberg that he should abandon his aspirations for an autonomous Youth International. He bowed to the inevitable – it was a lost battle.

It was Lenin, more than anyone, though, who recognised the unique genius of this hyperactive man. He realised also that his political élan, his ability to think and act independently would not necessarily be to the liking of other Comintern executive members, but these were particularly invaluable attributes during this difficult period and should not be left underutilised. Rather than see him marginalised, Lenin looked to find him a task and role that he wouldn't view as a demotion.

As planned, at the close of this congress, the Youth International then continued its own interrupted congress. It would be addressed by Kalinin as representative of the Soviet government and by Trotsky representing the Comintern. Discussions focussed on the specific role of youth in the Communist movement, but there still remained considerable differences in approach between the various sections, and on a number of issues agreement was difficult to reach. There was strong opposition among a number of delegations to the idea of the Youth International's headquarters now being located in the Soviet Union, but in the end the Soviet delegation succeeded in getting its way. A new international executive committee was elected and as secretary, the Russian Lazar Shatzkin took over – a bitter blow for Münzenberg.

The main Soviet argument was that with the extreme animosity in the West and the draconian measures taken in a number of countries, including Germany, against Communists, it would be more effective to have the leadership in a safe place, and where better than in the Soviet Union? Münzenberg, in a private letter, later claimed that his ousting from the Youth International's leadership was down to Zinoviev's personal animosity towards him.[9]

Although saddened and demoralised by the decision, while he was seated in the meeting hall, surrounded by the atmosphere of jubilation and dedication, he reflected with satisfaction on the stages the movement had gone through to reach this position, from the small meetings of only a dozen young Erfurter workers in the *Forelle* pub in 1906, to the modest group established in the *Pocken Hüsli* in Zurich, to the thousands of members worldwide that the organisation could now count on. The task they now faced was building the organisation into an even more effective force outside Russia, and he had looked forward to taking up the baton again, but that was not to be.

In terms of 'converting the communist organisations from small propaganda groups into a revolutionary mass party, this third Comintern congress had been of great significance', Münzenberg noted. However, his élan was seriously dented. The defeat of revolutionary forces in Germany, the Kronstadt rebellion, and all the other seemingly intractable problems he encountered in the Soviet Union, made Münzenberg acutely aware that building a Socialist state was fraught with unforeseen difficulties. From this time onwards, he would also take a back seat within the German Party and remain largely uninvolved in the internal debates and factional infighting.

Famine threatens the revolution

In spring and summer of 1921, in the Russian 'breadbasket' of the Ukraine not a drop of rain had fallen, creating the worst drought to hit the country since 1891. *Pravda* reported that 25 million people were facing imminent starvation. On top of that, the administrative structures, transport and distribution, in most regions had been crippled during the difficult years of 'war Communism'. Now tens of thousands of people were leaving the drought areas to seek food elsewhere, but there was no administrative structure in place to regulate this movement or to feed those fleeing.

Maxim Gorki, on behalf of the Soviet government, appealed to Western intellectuals to exert pressure on their governments to provide emergency aid. He did so, on 14 July 1921, by writing a personal and highly emotional letter to the great German dramatist Gerhart Hauptmann, requesting help for 'this land of Mendeleev, Pavlov, Mussorgsky, Glinka and other world famous men'.[10]

The American Relief Administration run by Herbert Hoover offered to help, but only if the Soviet government accepted their conditions for delivering aid. They wanted to ensure the aid really did go to the starving, and that it was made clear who was giving the aid. Once the Soviet government agreed – it had little choice – the Americans began distributing food in the famine areas.

An International Committee of Aid to Russia was also set up by a number of charities in the West, but Western governments themselves were reluctant to offer meaningful aid, as they feared this would serve only to bolster the Bolshevik government.

Lenin also appealed to workers' organisations throughout the world, stressing how the terrible years of war, then revolution, followed by armed foreign intervention had taken an enormous toll on the country, and this was now compounded by the famine. Many trade unions reacted to this call and sent substantial support, and the Soviet government set up its own All Russian Aid Committee, which was given the green light to set up branches abroad.

During the weeks he spent in the Soviet Union at this time, Münzenberg experienced his own personal crisis. He had been taken aback by the sudden turn of events. He had been hoping to return to Berlin and continue his work consolidating the Communist Youth International to which he had devoted 15 years of his life. He had built up what had, in the meantime, become a powerful and effective international organisation. Understandably, he felt it was his baby, and he wanted to keep it under his control, but it was being taken away from him. He was also depressed by the generally demoralising situation and the seemingly insurmountable problems the Soviet Union was facing. Gross, in her biography, says that it was in these summer days of 1921 that Münzenberg first began to see the Bolshevik leadership with a certain disenchantment, and he realised that he could never feel comfortable living and working in Moscow.

He talked often with Karl Radek and pleaded with him to find him a suitable task now that his work with the Youth International had come to an end. He also badgered Lenin with the same request.

Then, towards the close of the congress, he received a call from Lenin which would give him new hope. Lenin briefed him extensively on the famine and made clear to him its implications for the very survival of the revolution.

Lenin had little hope that the capitalist countries would come to the country's aid, given their open hostility to the Bolsheviks. His only hope, he told Münzenberg, was to ask the international proletariat for help. Lenin's plan was to ask the Comintern to organise a massive aid campaign and for Münzenberg himself to lead it. Up until then, the various aid efforts had been poorly co-ordinated and Lenin wanted Münzenberg to bring them all under one umbrella and co-ordinate the work.

With his organising ability, it was a task ideally suited to him and would also remove him from the political frontline, where he was subject to attacks by elements within the Moscow Comintern apparatus, as well as the danger of his being made a scapegoat for factional in-fighting within the German Communist Party. It would also give him a real sense that he was being usefully employed promoting the Communist cause.

Lenin's offer represented on the one hand a great honour for him and, on the other, such a campaign would fit in with his own international vision and what he recognised as the vital need for the first workers' state to survive this serious setback.

Karl Radek and Willi Münzenberg were nominated as those responsible for the rather cumbersomely titled 'Foreign Committee for the Organisation of Workers relief for the Starving in Soviet Russia'. In practice, though, Radek would be in charge of the Russian side of things and Münzenberg for the campaign in the capitalist world. The Comintern and the all-Russian central Aid Committee, led by Kamenev, gave them complete control of the campaign. With this new and enormous responsibility, Münzenberg would no longer play a key role in the youth movement. And although he would be nominally carrying out all forthcoming tasks on behalf of the Comintern, he would be allowed wide scope to operate relatively autonomously.

Notes

1   Hugo Eberlein (1887–1941) was a founder member of the German Communist Party and went on to hold top positions in the party. He fled the Nazis to the Soviet Union, where he became a victim of Stalin's purges. He was imprisoned and then shot in 1941.
2   Ruth Fischer was the leader of the Left opposition within the Communist Party.
3   Fischer, Ruth, *Stalin und die Deutsche Kommunismus* (2 volumes), Berlin: Dietz Verlag, 1991.
4   Gross, Babette, *Willi Münzenberg: Eine Politische B*, Leipzig: Forum Verlag, 1991.
5   https://www.marxists.org/subject/germany-1918-23/dauve-authier/ch10.htm#h2.
6   Münzenberg, Willi, *Der Dritte Front*, Schriftenreihe AdV, Verein der Funke, 2015.
7   Opus cit.
8   The Kapp Putsch, named after one of its leaders Wolfgang Kapp, was an attempted coup on 13 March 1920, aiming to reverse the German Revolution of 1918–1919,

overthrow the Weimar Republic and establish a right-wing autocratic government instead. It was supported by sections of the *Reichswehr* (German military) and other conservative, nationalist, and monarchist factions.

9 Münzenberg letter to Ulbricht, Pieck, and Dimitrov (15 November 1937), SAPMO-BArch, NY 4036/515, 135.

10 https://digital.staatsbibliothek-berlin.de/werkansicht?PPN=PPN771074980&PHYSID=PHYS_0001&DMDID=DMDLOG_0001.

5

THE COMINTERN'S EMISSARY IN WESTERN EUROPE

Smuggling Russian diamonds

Münzenberg saw his new job as only temporary and may have felt a mixture of deep disappointment at being ousted from his old one, but also elation in the face of this new challenge. His new role, though, would represent the real moment when his career took off and allowed his inchoate talents to unfold.

He returned to Berlin from Russia in early August 1921 with solid funding, including diamonds sewn into his shirt cuffs to evade customs and which he would later convert into hard cash. A number of reliable comrades were also given funds in this way, presumably 'expropriated' from the estates of those affluent citizens who had fled the revolutionary chaos at the end of the war.

Already, in 1920, the editor of the *Daily Herald* and later Labour Party leader, George Lansbury, who would become a key Münzenberg supporter, also received Soviet support in the form of diamonds for his struggling newspaper. They were given to Francis Meynell, the *Herald*'s youngest director, by Maxim Litvinov, and were sent to London hidden in a box of chocolates. However, Lansbury rejected this form of support, not the least because the story got out, and he was mercilessly attacked over it by mainstream conservative papers.

Hardly had Münzenberg's feet hit the ground in Berlin, when he stormed into action. In only a few days he had published his first appeal from the newly founded 'Foreign Committee for the Organisation of Workers' International Relief for the Starving of Russia' – a cumbersome title, but also a daunting task, which only someone of Münzenberg's stamina and imagination could turn into the success it would become.

Before he left Moscow, he fired off a letter to Zinoviev, head of the Comintern:

Moscow 2 July 1921

'Dear Comrade Zinoviev

I understand my task thus: carrying out the most urgent work for the famine campaign in the West as swiftly as possible, so that we can guarantee full success, and immediate return to Moscow. I will carry out the job with this in mind. ... for the most urgent work in Berlin I need urgently (reporting facilities and initial contact with the Communist Party centre and other organisations ... 'to bring on board other literary forces like Wilhelm Herzog and Barthel etc. Communications with a whole number of leading personalities etc. having influence in the Communist press, despatch of people to the individual countries, organisation of special newspaper editions, etc ...two big lectures [to be held] in Berlin, obtaining passports etc. – at least a week. Then two days to and in Prague, two to Vienna, three to Rome, and 5 days for the return journey, several days in Berlin, and then back. I will hardly manage all this in a fortnight. I'll do my best to speed things along. I will limit myself to the absolutely necessary in terms of the organisation of the famine campaign and involve proficient comrades, like Wilhelm Koenen etc. But if I should still need several more days, so don't get angry with me. You can be certain that it won't be down to any lack of willingness on my part, but blame will lie solely on the simple technical impossibilities.

signed Your Willi Münzenberg'[1]

He certainly was not wasting any time and was already full of ideas. He first had to gather around him a group of trusted activists who could be depended upon to take some of the responsibility, and so, to begin with, he sought out those comrades he knew well from the youth movement. At first his small team operated out of 'an office' in a comrade's apartment. Working night and day, they began tackling this new challenge.

The organisation soon began to expand at such a fast rate that there arose an urgent need for proper office space. So Münzenberg arranged to rent rooms in the Berlin City Council building and was thus able to appropriate this address for his letterhead, lending gravitas to his appeals.

By 21 August, he and his comrades had already managed to despatch the first boat with food supplies from Stockholm to Petrograd. Within just a few months, the aid to Russia campaign had become a worldwide one. His work on the campaign was, though, interrupted by the Communist Party of Germany (KPD) congress held in Jena towards the end of August of that same year, and which he attended as a delegate. At that congress, the Party agreed to give his campaign its full support, thus lending it official backing.

At this time, Germany itself was in the throes of rampant inflation, and the economic conditions for working people were becoming harsher by the day.

A sheet of writing paper cost a lot more than a thousand Mark banknote, beggars had their pockets stuffed with notes, gamblers went to the betting shops pushing wheelbarrows of money, and even girls from middle-class families, who had become impoverished overnight, walked the streets looking for customers. But even during this inauspicious time of economic chaos, Münzenberg's organisation still managed to raise considerable sums.

The less clumsily titled, *Internationale Arbeiterhilfe* (*IAH* or International Workers' Relief, later to be popularly characterised as 'The Münzenberg Trust') was founded in September 1921. From October onwards, as a result of campaigning by the *IAH*, boats were now setting sail from Scandinavia, South Africa, Australia, Argentina, and the USA with aid. The US Friends of Russia Group alone sent around five million dollars worth of aid. The campaign had gained momentum.

In the autumn of 1921, the German writer Franz Jung visited the famine areas along the banks of the Volga, on behalf of the *IAH*, and in his reports, which were used to help raise awareness of the dire situation, he painted a shattering picture.

On the banks of the river, many thousands of people had set up temporary camps and were waiting patiently in the hope of finding a boat to take them out of the famine area. Typhus had broken out and thousands were dying.

Jung and his companions travelled through some of the German villages (there were many, known as Volga Germans, who had settled there during the eighteenth century, encouraged by Peter the Great) and found cottage upon cottage boarded up, and on breaking down a door to one of them, he found a whole family still seated around a table with an open Bible in front of them, all dead of starvation. There could be no doubt about the country's desperate need. Such graphic reports could not fail but to shake people's consciences.

The main causes of the terrible famine were a combination of the devastation caused by the war, compounded by a serious drought, resulting in poor harvests. In April 1922, the League of Nations' High Commissioner for Refugees, the polar explorer, Fridtjof Nansen, calculated that the number of starving in Russia and Ukraine was between 35 and 40 million. Once the worst of the famine was over, towards the close of 1922, it was estimated that around five million people had starved to death.[2]

Even one of Münzenberg's harshest critics, Ruth Fischer, the fiery ultra-left Communist leader, confirmed that, 'under Münzenberg's direction the *IAH* became an enormous success. Workers at a Berlin car factory sent a lorry; a Chemnitz company sent 14 knitting machines; a Stuttgart factory sent five milk centrifuges; the workers of a Leipzig factory sent medicines; other groups donated fridges for hospitals, machine tools and technical instruments. In 1921, twenty one shipments of goods were despatched to Russia. In 1922, 78 shipments. In 1926, the *IAH* collected, according to Münzenberg's estimate goods to the value of 25 million gold Marks. All in all, between 1921 and 1922, material to the value of 2 million (US) dollars was collected'.[3]

Even if the actual impact of such generosity was limited, the propaganda effect of these collections was invaluable, 'everyone who gave even a little felt a bond with the fatherland of the workers', Fischer wrote.[4]

Although the International Red Cross and other aid organisations were giving considerable charitable help to Russia at this time, Münzenberg's campaign was more focussed on strengthening the young Soviet Union.

He devised all sorts of ingenious strategies to win support for the aid campaign, such as asking workers to 'donate a day's wages in solidarity' rather than just appealing to them to give money as if to a charity. He utilised every opportunity not just to raise money, but also awareness: street collections, concerts and art exhibitions were organised, everything possible was offered for sale, and special awards of badges, medals, pictures of life in the Soviet Union, and busts of Lenin and Marx were given to those raising significant sums of money. He would later replicate this very effective form of solidarity when setting up similar relief organisations for China and Spain.

Before he began his own campaign, there had already been a number of smaller, more or less effective organisations in a number of countries sending aid to Russia, but he had to try and bring these disparate groups under one umbrella and co-ordinate their action. He knew he could not achieve all that seated at his desk in the tiny, provisional offices in Berlin, so he travelled first to France in October, where he launched an 'Action Week' on behalf of Russia. Following that, he returned to Germany where he organised large celebratory events around the anniversary of the Revolution, persuading the artist Käthe Kollwitz to design posters for it – her most famous drawing of a starving mother with the child in her lap only a small skeleton, accompanied by the one word, 'Hunger' became an iconic poster image – and he was also able to make use of a whole cache of unseen photos from Russia, many of which he published in his magazine, *Soviet Russia in Pictures*.

Within a short space of time, Münzenberg was able to demonstrate that he was capable of organising on a broad scale, and that he could mobilise support worldwide. He would accomplish this very much by marshalling all the means at his disposal for communication and advertising, but often in innovative ways, using picture postcards, posters, illustrated magazines, films, and pamphlets. With little previous experience, he would become what we would today call a top 'publicity manager' with innovative verve. His methods, in turn, would be adopted by the *KPD* in its own publicity and educational campaigns.

As a result of his many contacts in the Socialist youth movement and sheer hard work, Münzenberg quickly won the support of a number of leading European and US intellectuals to his cause, people like Albert Einstein, George Bernard Shaw, Anatole France, Henri Barbusse, Heinrich Mann, Arthur Koestler, John Dos Passos, Romain Rolland, Clara Zetkin, Maxim Gorky, Leonard Frank, the Danish writer Martin Andersen Nexø, and dozens of lesser-known Communist, Socialist or sympathising writers, photographers, and visual artists. Even the Italian writer, D'Annunzio, before he fully embraced a Fascist ideology, publicly accused the governments of the world of complicity in the mass murder of the Russian peasantry by not giving aid. All of these individuals signed up as founder members of his organisation and helped give the campaign a respectable profile.

In mid-August 1921, in Berlin, he met for the first time the charismatic General Secretary of the International Federation of Trade Unions, the Dutchman Edo Fimmen, who would not only become an indispensable ally in his relief work, but also a lifelong friend. Fimmen was certainly not someone one would automatically associate with the radical Communist Münzenberg. He was from a middle-class background, but became an ardent trade unionist. His trade union and philanthropic work were very much nurtured by his religious convictions; his wife was active in the Salvation Army and also had a significant influence on his outlook.

In 1918, in the aftermath of the First World War, Edo Fimmen had gained valuable experience co-ordinating aid to Austria, which had been suffering severe food shortages after losing Czechoslovakia and Hungary, two of its main suppliers of agricultural products. He would later go on to found the International Transport Workers' Federation and become its general secretary.

FIGURE 5.1 Willi Münzenberg with Dutch trade union leader Edo Fimmen (Courtesy of German Federal Archives, Koblenz, Germany.)

Münzenberg was more than happy to work with anyone who supported his solidarity work. Defying the left sectarians within the *KPD*, he attempted to bring on board both the Second (Socialist), together with the Third (Communist) Internationals, appealing to the British Labour leader Ramsay MacDonald, who was at the time still secretary of the Second International, to join him in organising joint action between the Social Democrats and Münzenberg's own aid committee. But MacDonald declared that any aid they managed to collect would be sent through the International Federation of Trade Unions in Amsterdam. However, James O'Grady of the Independent Labour Party (ILP), and general secretary of the British National Federation of General Workers, managed to collect a substantial sum of money in aid in his own initiative and travelled to the famine areas in Russia to help distribute it.

Münzenberg laid great emphasis on winning over sympathetic personalities and middle class intellectuals of whatever political colour, persuading many of them to visit the Soviet Union, and following that up by encouraging them to write reports of their experiences and publishing what they wrote. In doing so, he had to ensure that their visits went smoothly, and that they could travel in and out of the Soviet Union without becoming entangled in red tape. He did not want their experiences and meetings with ordinary Russians to be tarnished by unnecessary bureaucracy.

Although the aid campaign had been conceived originally as a means of drumming up financial support globally to alleviate the famine in a Russia devastated by war and torn apart by civil strife, it was Münzenberg's imagination and verve that made it possible to put in place an effective propaganda campaign not only to raise funds, but to expand that role by giving publicity to the Soviet Union and its achievements. For Münzenberg, it was clear that mounting a strong defence of the Soviet Union was essential if working people in other countries were to attain a position from which they themselves could also take power.

The young Soviet Union embodied all his own hopes and aspirations of a Socialist society based on workers' power. By organising his aid campaign and at the same time publicising the achievements of the revolution, he was giving expression to his own firmly held commitment. To accomplish his aim of broadcasting Soviet achievements as widely as possible, he was fully aware that he had to reach people from all walks of life and political persuasion. Despite the entrenched sectarianism on the left within the German Communist Party at the time – and he himself was by no means free of it in the early years – he was able to reach out across the political ring-fence.

In the concluding paragraph of an article he wrote for the Comintern paper, *International Press Correspondence* (23 December 1921), with the headline, 'From Famine Relief to Aid for Soviet Russia', he made an appeal in response to the positive stand taken at the December conference 'of the English Labor Party (sic) and its parliamentary group'. He quoted a statement issued by the Foreign Committee for the Organization of Workers' Relief for the Famine-stricken in Soviet Russia, based in Berlin: 'There is no doubt that a unified move in all parliaments on the part of the working-class parties, supported by the entire economic and political power of the working-class, will in no small degree hasten the slowly developing understanding between the Western states and Russia. We hope in the interest of 20,000,000 starving Russian workers and peasants, and in the interests of the entire working-class, suffering under the decay of the world's economic life, that our appeal will be heard and followed by all working-class parties'.

'The communist parties', he concluded, 'can support this move by immediately communicating with the other workers' parties and organizations in their countries and calling upon them to act in concert in the Parliaments. There is no doubt that the last few weeks and months have considerably hastened the recognition of the necessity of economic relations with Soviet Russia even in the circles of the bourgeoisie and that a determined and concerted action of the working-class can speedily bring about the necessary agreement'.[5]

Münzenberg was 29 years old when he returned to Germany in 1918 from his early exile in Switzerland. From being a relatively small-time political activist, working on shoestring budgets, he now found himself head of a transnational organisation with considerable financial resources at his disposal.

His consciousness had been transformed by his short stay in Switzerland; it had turned him into a full-time professional revolutionary travelling throughout Europe. That itinerant life style continued after his return to Germany, often in hiding, in flight from the police, or in prison. Once he took on the job of Comintern representative for Western Europe, his life changed dramatically, and he began to move in different circles, but it was still marked by frenetic activity and much travelling. Wherever he was, he lived in temporary accommodations. In Berlin, he took lodgings in a furnished room with a worker's family in the central borough of Pankow, whose address very few knew. There, he could withdraw for very short spells if he needed quiet.

His increasingly high profile role as the representative of the Comintern in Germany brought with it further obligatory changes to his lifestyle; he would very soon become a widely known businessman as well as organiser.

Now based firmly in Berlin, he began renting a modest flat in a lower middle-class area, located between the Tiergarten and the river Spree, from Prof. Hirschfeld, who was a Social Democrat, but sympathetic to the Communists, and who ran his renowned Institute for Sexual Theory from the annexe to his house.

The corridors and walls of the passageways in his large house were hung with sexual artefacts culled from 'primitive' communities, as well as sexually explicit photographic material. Münzenberg's visitors were often shocked and/or amused that he had chosen to live in such an exotic (erotic?) place. Among others who lodged in the Hirschfeld complex during this period were Walter Benjamin, Ernst Bloch, and the British writer Christopher Isherwood.

In Comintern circles, this abode achieved a certain renown, not simply for its erotic attractions, but as a very suitable place for clandestine meetings with foreign visitors. There was a permanent coming and going of leading figures like Georgi Dimitrov, who met there with representatives of the revolutionary movements in the Balkan countries.

Münzenberg was taken care of by a matronly lady, called Frau Krüger, recommended by Hirschfeld, and she would remain very loyal to Münzenberg. When, much later, in 1933, in the wake of the Nazi takeover and the Reichstag fire, the police would raid the house and show her photos of people who they alleged had visited Münzenberg, she denied knowing any of them. She was completely apolitical, but clearly fell under Münzenberg's spell, calling him 'a noble gentleman'.

While in Berlin, he lived modestly, but went to the theatre or opera when he could. However, the little time he was able to steal for himself was invariably spent with books. His great love, though, and where he could really unwind, was the countryside. On those rare occasions when he could take more than a few hours, he would return to his beloved Thuringia for a few days to walk in the woods and mountains.

Business manager

Münzenberg worked around the clock, pulling activists together and sending out appeals in all directions. Well before the idea of Popular Front politics became the official line, he was already putting such policies into practice. Over the coming years, he would virtually single-handedly turn what began as a small famine relief operation into a massive media and business empire. He could only do this by drawing on forces beyond the Communist Party.

In one of the rare private letters that exist, in which Münzenberg writes to a close comrade, he reveals how he felt about the burden of work he had taken on:

> Since August 1921, I have been working continuously, almost all day and all night, dragging heavy loads with practically no support of any kind. I was in Moscow alone four times and, despite this absence of several months, I conducted the entire business in Berlin, organised three conferences, etc. I am so tired I could fall down. But the certainty that my work is saving thousands of people and providing real practical help to Russia in a very small way keeps me on my feet and allows me to persevere, despite fatigue and illness.[6]

For Münzenberg, as for many Communists, giving vital support to the struggling Soviet Union to help ensure its survival was seen as the only way of achieving the eventual liberation of workers worldwide. And he was fully aware that this could only be achieved with the support of Social Democratic parties and sections of the bourgeoisie. It is also very clear from his words here that his concern for the starving of Russia was no cynical ploy, but a genuine humanitarian concern.

He was carrying out vital propaganda for the struggling Soviet Union in ways that were not possible for the country's own leaders, due to its isolation

FIGURE 5.2 Willi Münzenberg with delegates to an IAH conference in Berlin October 1931, on his right, Maria Reese, and left, Margarete Buber-Neumann (Otto Storch. Courtesy of German Federal Archives.)

and pariah status. Faced with the enormous task of winning widespread support for the Communist cause, Münzenberg could not afford to take the sectarian approach adopted by many of his comrades if he were to be successful.

If those with similar views to Münzenberg had prevailed at the time and a genuine collaboration between Communists and Social Democrats in Europe had been firmly established early on, subsequent history may well have turned out very differently.

On the negative side, the small splinter Communist Workers' Party, which still had a dedicated following in Germany on the extreme left, vehemently attacked the *IAH* as a 'social democratic and opportunistic' undertaking, arguing that it would serve merely to promote petit-bourgeois attitudes among the proletariat. Only a genuine proletarian revolution in the capitalist world could solve the problems of working people, it argued. This echoed the criticisms of Münzenberg made by Fischer and Maslow in the *KPD*.

On 1 November 1921, the *IAH* published the first issue of its innovative journal dedicated to a working-class readership, the *Illustrierte Arbeiter Zeitung* (Illustrated Workers' Newspaper), with the motto: Soviet Russia in Word and Picture. Out of this paper grew the *Arbeiter Illustrierte Zeitung* (Workers' Illustrated Newspaper), which by the beginning of the 1930s, had achieved a circulation of around 420,000 and, despite not being an official Party journal, became the Communists' main vehicle of propaganda. In its pages, Münzenberg would also provide a platform for some of Germany's leading artists and writers, like Kurt Tucholsky, John Heartfield, Käthe Kollwitz, and George Gross (see Chapter 7 Entrepreneur and Propagandist).

His close comrade Max Barthel provided valuable support in bringing such artists on board, as he was directly responsible in the Party for propaganda work among artists and intellectuals. But there is no doubt that it was Münzenberg's reputation that helped draw in many who were sympathetic to the Soviet Union, but were not members of the Communist Party.

On the heels of the *IAH* came a plan to form a specific international committee of intellectuals interested in strengthening relations with the new Russia. The Berlin-based theatre director Erwin Piscator became secretary of the *Künstlerhilfe* (Artists' Aid), founded in January 1922 and, with the support of the Berlin-based painter Otto Nagel, appealed to artists to support Russian relief. A number of Bauhaus artists would also contribute works to be sold by the organisation at exhibitions.

With his new role, Münzenberg occupied a unique position within the Comintern hierarchy. Although nominally a paid emissary of the Comintern, in effect, he was given the opportunity of building up a parallel political organisation based in Germany, outside the constraints of formal party structures, and relatively free of interference from the Party's leaders. This role would bring him renown, but also make him enemies.

He was not a politician as usually understood by the term or a theoretician, but an activist, organiser, and effective propagandist. He took little part in the factional battles of the Party or the Comintern, largely no doubt because he had no ambition for political power or position within those organisations.

From the outset, the *IAH* was set up specifically to counter the effects of the famine in Russia, only later was its propaganda role given increased emphasis. Münzenberg was not satisfied with simply raising money, he was deeply interested in forging stronger links between Germany and the Soviet Union and was aware of the role cultural activities could play.

Lenin asks Münzenberg to help re-invigorate industry

By the end of 1922, Lenin and most of the Comintern executive were extremely pleased with what Münzenberg had been able to achieve in such an incredibly short space of time. On the basis of this success, they felt he could perhaps also be useful in the Soviet Union itself by bringing in a much needed sense of urgency, and Western methodology to tackle their own still serious economic problems.

Münzenberg had been able to demonstrate that he was able to set up an administrative structure, even within a country that vast, to distribute the collected food supplies and other materials effectively. He had also realised that skilled workers needed to be given priority in the distribution of food, as it was essential to get the wheels of industry turning again if the country was not to collapse totally.

In the wake of the 1917 Revolution, Soviet industry had found itself in a state of catastrophic decline; every branch required an emergency blood transfusion of new equipment and skilled workers. There was a lack of machine tools, of raw materials, and money. Although Lenin's New Economic Plan would help overcome this bottleneck to some degree by granting concessions to foreign companies, and by importing modern equipment including machine tools, and $250,000 had been donated by US trade unions, this in itself was not enough. So, from being simply a distributive organisation, the *IAH* in Russia now had to be transformed into an entrepreneurial one.

Throughout this huge country, the *IAH* was given responsibility for factories, large and small, setting up trade schools, repair and renovation workshops, and in several locations it set up skills training centres. *IAH* repair teams rebuilt or renovated ruined buildings, built houses, and attempted to bring industrial plants up to modern standards, all to help revive the moribund economic infrastructure, raise standards, and bring some order to the chaos.

The government had already placed buildings in Moscow at the Münzenberg organisation's disposal to facilitate the distribution of aid. And soon, a whole number of concessions would be handed over to his organisation, which it was hoped would help run things more efficiently, even though the *IAH* was, at this time, still only a skeletal, understaffed operation, with few specialists at its disposal.

In Tsaritsyn (later Stalingrad and today Volgograd), the *IAH* took on the management of a large fishery, but the 18,000 workers there were so malnourished that they first had to be properly fed before they could begin working again. Once it was up and running, the Tsaritsyn fishery would be handed back to the Soviet government, but the *IAH* would then go on to manage another fishing and processing plant on the Caspian Sea. Here, new fishing vessels were procured, warehouses built, and it would become one of the Soviet Union's largest fisheries; under *IAH* management, almost four million kilograms of fish were caught in 1923 alone.

Near Kazan, the *IAH* took on a number of large farms, and in Moscow, a shoe factory and a health clinic. From the Ukraine to the Urals, more than 100 children's homes were also placed under its aegis, and between 1922 and 1923, it organised over four million kilograms of food exports to Russia for 'Children's Aid'.

The massive expansion of the *IAH*'s role and its support for the struggling Soviet Union infuriated its enemies because they would have preferred to see the country under its Soviet government collapse.

In 1924, the Social Democratic Party of Germany (*SPD*)-dominated Confederation of German Trade Unions issued a polemical brochure titled, *The Third Column of Communist Policy – IAH*, which utilised leaked internal information to accuse the *IAH* of financial mismanagement.

In the Russian sector of the organisation, there had indeed been cases of corruption, misuse of funds, and a total lack of bookkeeping. This was underlined by Trotsky's sister, Olga Kameneva, who was a long-time co-worker at the Russian *IAH* headquarters in Moscow and who confirmed that, 'An accounting system in the Russian business arm does not exist'.

The *SPD* critique focussed on the role played by the controversial journalist and economist, Franz Jung, who had developed utopian plans for a gigantic agricultural centre in the Urals and, through the *IAH*, had ordered 400 tractors and dreamed of building a modern town constructed of concrete – an innovative material for Russia at that time. There had been no viability assessment, and the whole project foundered.

Although Münzenberg rejected many of the accusations contained in the *SPD* brochure, he had to admit that there were serious bookkeeping problems with the Russian arm of the organisation and tried to address these. Such serious problems were symptomatic of those early years during the implementation of the New Economic Plan, and the *IAH* office merely mirrored what was happening elsewhere in the country.

As Gross put it, 'it had become a playground for dilettantes and adventurers'. She goes on to say that Münzenberg, as a perfectionist, was not at all happy with this situation, but he could only work with the human material at his disposal. In the face of such problems, the fact that he did not speak Russian and did not know the country's customs or their multiple cultures, it is quite extraordinary that he was able to get as much done as he did and on such a broad front.

Many of those recruited to work for the *IAH* in the Soviet Union were motivated by idealism, but did not necessarily possess the skills or expertise to deal with the daily realities of Russian life. There were undoubtedly many examples of incompetence, of mistakes being made, and a wastage of resources, but these were perhaps not unexpected given the challenges. However, the work of the *IAH* in Russia demonstrated solidarity in practice and gave inspiration to those involved, and this was not a small achievement.

When in the spring of 1922 his old Danish friend Ernst Christiansen arrived and told him that a large delivery of dried milk from Denmark had been 'mislaid' somewhere, he was surprised at how Münzenberg was able to sort things out with the Soviet bureaucracy in a very short space of time.

At its third world congress, held in Berlin, the *IAH* took the innovative decision to launch an international workers' loan scheme. The idea had surfaced earlier, and the Comintern had welcomed it, and Zinoviev had pledged his support. It was given the clumsy title of *Industrie- und Handels-Aktien-Gesellschaft: Internationale Arbeiterhilfe für Sowjet-Russland* (Industry and Trade Stockholding Company: International Workers' Relief for Soviet Russia). The *IAH* became the official distributor of the bonds. Incoming funds would be used to invest in the active reconstruction of the Soviet economy, and thus help oil the wheels of trade between the Soviet Union and the West.

Although it was a shareholding company, set up in accordance with the decision taken by the executive committee of the *IAH* together with the Council of Ministers in the USSR, all shareholders, management, and supervisory board members forewent any right to material reward from any profits the company might make. This restriction applied to all companies set up by Münzenberg or the Communist Party.

In August, the issuing of bonds, the so-called 'international workers' credit' issue, went ahead. Ten-year bonds were issued of up to one million dollars with a guaranteed interest of 5%. In this way, the Soviet Union would be enabled to access hard currency, which was desperately needed to boost its industry and economy. Alongside this bond issue, a Guarantee and Credit Bank was established in Berlin, as a branch of the Soviet State Bank, to facilitate financial dealings. With this initiative, Münzenberg also hoped to be able to persuade working-class organisations elsewhere – trade unions, co-operatives, and other public bodies – to buy the bonds and thus invest in the Soviet Union.

In this initiative, Münzenberg was given enormous support by the Swede Olof Aschberg, a Jewish banker and businessman, with strong leftist sympathies who he had met previously in Stockholm. Aschberg helped finance the Bolsheviks in the early years after the revolution. In gratitude, the Bolshevik government allowed Aschberg to do business with the Soviet Union during the 1920s. In 1922, he founded Roskombank, the first Soviet international bank.[7]

Shortly after the establishment of the workers' bond issue, in the autumn of 1922, Babette Gross, Münzenberg's future partner, took a job in the office of the *IAH* in Berlin. Henry Meyer, a manager there, was desperately looking for an assistant who would 'help bring a little order to the chaos'.

Initially, she was given the ask of writing letters to the foreign branches of the *IAH* and sorting bond applications according to which hard currency they referred to. Münzenberg was absent at the time, in Moscow.

She provides a vivid description of the *IAH* offices at the time:

'The office was located in an old building on Berlin's famous *Unter den Linden*, on a floor that originally belonged to the Russian Red Cross and then the Russian embassy. It was a hive of activity, an uninterrupted flow of foreign visitors traipsed through the rooms. In one room was the editorial of the illustrated magazine *Sichel und Hammer*, in another, a young woman from Leipzig ran the department of Aid for Russian Children. In what had been the conservatory, a secretary was typing a script written by an expressionist dramatist, a Russian woman was translating the correspondence as well as picture captions and articles for various publications. In several rooms, there were piles of unsorted files with thousands of photos taken of the revolution, in the famine areas and of the civil war in Russia. From there, thousands of postcards were despatched around the world.

Shortly after my provisional start, Münzenberg returned from his Moscow trip. His imminent arrival provoked widespread nervousness and clearly impacted on the work zeal. Tired, unshaven and wordless, he wandered through the rooms, back and forth, greeting and scrutinising each member of staff. Next to my desk he stopped and I was introduced to him by Henry Meyer, but Münzenberg remained absent-minded and worried, because the workers' bond issue had apparently brought still more complications with it'.[8]

Employees of the *IAH* were apparently paid in US dollars – this was the time of rampant inflation in Germany, when the currency would become worthless overnight – and these dollars could be exchanged daily at the current rate.

'The Russian embassy was next door and the *IAH* co-operated closely with it. Everyone – all the embassy personnel, including the ambassador, and their families, as well as all *IAH* staff – came together for their midday meal in the embassy canteen. It was basic traditional Russian food, but for the Germans, who had been used to American aid kitchens and any scraps they could find, the meals seemed luxurious', Gross wrote.[9]

With the increasing visibility of the work carried out by the *IAH* in the Soviet Union, the name Münzenberg would become a household name there. A number of children's homes and a boat on the Volga were named after him, and a militia battalion in Petrograd gave Münzenberg, as head of the *IAH,* the rank of honorary commander; he was also made an honorary member of the Petrograd Soviet. This popularisation of the *IAH* throughout the Soviet Union was also due to the personal interest taken by Lenin in its valuable contribution to the work of reconstruction.

No one, least of all Münzenberg, had envisaged the organisation playing such a key role as the one it had now taken on. It was hardly equipped to do so, as it began with only a few full-time employees and even fewer who were skilled or trained in the necessary fields.

With time, Münzenberg's storming of the heavens style idealism had to give way to a more rational approach, suffused with a strong dose of realism. But during this period, Münzenberg had been able to gather around him a small core of capable individuals, who knew their onions. One of those was the journalist Max Wagner who Münzenberg had known from his Socialist Youth International days. Wagner had the experience of working in a shipping company and was able to give valuable advice on how to despatch goods safely and reliably by train, ship, and road.

Towards the end of 1923, he accompanied Münzenberg and several other *IAH* workers to the Party congress of the *KPD* in Leipzig, and recorded that he was quite surprised that on arrival Münzenberg went straight to the biggest hotel in the centre of the city and booked rooms for himself and his colleagues. Wagner thought this was not exactly 'proletarian behaviour' and compared Münzenberg to 'one of those powerful US businessmen, through whose hands millions of dollars flowed'. In this comment, we can detect the sort of disapproval of the lifestyle Münzenberg had adopted since becoming head of the *IAH* and which would give his enemies the ammunition they needed to attack him.

Attempts to forge an alliance with the Social Democrats

In October 1920, at the Independent Social Democratic Party (*USPD*) congress in Halle, attended by Zinoviev as the Comintern representative, the Party split in two. At this congress, Ernst Thälmann – then a *USPD* member – took a prominent place on the political stage for the first time when he adopted the Comintern line, arguing for joining together with the Spartacus League to form a United German Communist Party.

The split in the USPD resulted in the left majority joining the KPD to form the United Communist Party of Germany and thus the Comintern in December of that year. But although the two parties were now united, ideological differences between the KPD and former USPD members remained unresolved. While the former Spartacus leaders were pleased with the long-desired opportunity of being able to help build a mass party which could compete with the Social Democrats, the former USPD members wanted exactly the opposite: the creation of a vanguard party, capable of waging an effective revolutionary struggle.

In the heavily industrialised sector of central Germany, the KPD had by the Spring of 1921 become a strong force since its merger with the USPD, and membership was around 67,000. Also, because of the militancy demonstrated time and again in the area, it was decided to launch the insurgency there at the end of March 1921. It was hoped that this would lead, at least, to the toppling of the government as a first step to power. The slogan for the uprising was to be: 'For an alliance with Soviet Russia and the removal of the government'.

The then Communist Party leader Paul Levi had, though, already been calling for closer contact at government level between the Weimar Republic and the Soviet Union. This urging was given extra emphasis when, in 1922, the Soviet Union itself began making serious efforts to break out of the isolation imposed upon it.

At the same, on behalf of the Soviet government, Radek had been holding talks with General von Seeckt, the German military chief of staff, to promote co-operation between the Red Army and the German armed forces. Germany had little option at this time but to co-operate with the Soviet Union, if it were to circumvent the stringent restrictions on military development laid down by the Treaty of Versailles.

This closer co-operation between the Soviet Union and Germany at government level was also reflected in an about-turn in Comintern policy. It began pushing the KPD towards closer co-operation with the SPD, in order to create a 'united front', and wanted it to play a more prominent role in the political life of the country. To this aim, Comintern leaders held a meeting with representatives of both the Socialist Internationals shortly before the European-wide conference to be held in Genoa in 1922.[10] The Soviet government was keen for the two Socialist Internationals to come out in favour of giving support to the Soviet Union in its post-war negotiations with the Western powers.

As a result of Radek's urging, Fritz Adler, the Austrian Social Democrat, called a conference of the three Internationals to be held in Berlin.[11] A nine-person committee was elected to take matters forward, but it would remain inactive.

The Russians had put forward the idea of holding another joint conference to discuss outstanding issues, but this was rejected by the Social Democrats, who demanded that the Soviets withdraw their forces from Georgia before further discussions could take place (The Red Army had invaded Georgia in February 1921, in a military campaign to overthrow the Menshevik government of the Democratic Republic of Georgia.).

Co-operation between the Social Democrats and the Comintern was, in any case, dead in the water once the trial of a group of Russian Social revolutionaries began in June 1922. They were given long prison sentences, and the Comintern opened its punitive campaign against 'Social traitors'. As a result, the united front campaign collapsed. Radek, however, continued his own campaign for such an international united front.

Despite these setbacks, and as a result of the conference, the Social Democrats did eventually agree to issue a joint declaration 'For the Russian Revolution and the establishment of political and economic relations of all states with Soviet Russia' and 'for the establishment of a proletarian united front in each country and in the Internationals'. This new, seemingly pro-Russian atmosphere among Social Democrats would be of great assistance to Münzenberg in his own efforts to gain wider support and raise funds.

As a result of Münzenberg's efforts and preparedness to work with the Social Democrats, he became a figure of hate for the leaders of the *SPD* in Germany. As his organisation grew in strength and influence, it came under increasing attack and was condemned as simply an arm of the Communist Party and the Comintern. In the Social Democratic press, he was vilified as a diabolical seducer, a people catcher par excellence. One leading Social Democratic journalist characterised him as a callous wheeler-dealer and dubious boss of a financial imperium. His effective propaganda in promoting a humanitarian face of the Soviet Union and Communism enraged the *SPD* leadership.

While it is true that he was an agent employed by the Comintern, to circumscribe his role in this way would be an oversimplification. It is not easy to establish who was actually responsible for Münzenberg's various activities. Even though he was nominally carrying out Comintern work, he had considerable autonomy.

From the start, there was a multi-track approach as far as the *IAH* was concerned, which began with the relatively autonomous mandate Lenin gave him, but this became enmeshed with the subsequent demands made by the Soviet government as well as those of the Comintern – not always the same thing. Once the *IAH* became involved in the Soviet Union itself, the trade unions were given a key role in terms of guiding the work of the *IAH* and collaborating with it. This rather ad-hoc arrangement of joint responsibility and involvement still left Münzenberg with considerable freedom to act independently. If criticised or attacked by one group, he could always find cover in the other.

There were those in the German Communist Party who looked askance at his work and called him scathingly a 'factory boss'. Although he was called 'The Red Millionaire' and 'Propaganda Tsar' among other similar epithets, he himself never viewed making money or acquiring status as his aim; he was always concerned primarily with the propaganda potential of any undertaking and how it would further the aims of the working-class movement and the Communist Party. This 'Red Millionaire' had no private capital, and any money he was able to provide to support various initiatives was, nominally at least, subject to Comintern and *KPD* strictures.

McMeekin in his Münzenberg biography describes him in 1921 as being 'far too wrapped up in the Russian operations of the IAH to pay close attention to political developments in Germany'. While he wasn't in the central committee of the German Communist Party at this time, he was still an important and leading member, and his work was very much intertwined with Communist Party activity, so to suggest he did not pay close attention to German politics is hardly credible.[12]

On 16 April 1922, government representatives of Russia and Germany came together at Rapallo and sealed their post-war rapprochement with a treaty (The Treaty of Rapallo) under which each renounced all territorial and financial claims on the other following the Treaty of Brest-Litovsk. This created a better climate for Münzenberg to expand his activities. With his skill as an organiser and talent as a propagandist, he now had free rein to recruit and win support for the Soviet Union within the circles of the *SPD* and the German middle class.

By the latter half of 1922, the Communist Party had gained significant influence and membership to give it greater political clout in the country. In the third quarter of 1922, it could boast over 200,000 members; and in elections, it was winning from 20 to 40 times more votes than it had members.[13] This helped boost confidence within the Party and also strengthened Münzenberg's hand in negotiations.

In that same year, when the Social Democrats and Communists met in Berlin to explore ways of normalising relations with the Soviet Union, Münzenberg was very much aware of how important this was for his own work. In a report beforehand to the *IAH* and in an attempt to stifle disruptive sectarian attitudes, he told his employees that delegates to the conference, alongside the Norwegian diplomat and Nobel prize winner, Fridtjof Nansen, would include German and English Quakers, possibly Red Cross organisations, with around 80 representatives from German industry – engineers, business owners, scientists – as well as cultural figures, writers, journalists, and trade unionists, all interested in developing better relations with the Soviet Union. He wanted it to be a success.

He was very keen for such sympathisers to be brought on board and not be frightened off by unnecessarily divisive political debates. He hoped the conference would conclude by adopting a resolution expressing a preparedness to help with reconstruction in the Soviet Union. The last thing he wanted was for any sectarians to disrupt things or for delegates to feel they were being 'manipulated by communist forces'. He wanted them to return home and feel empowered and willing to promote public awareness of what was being built in the Soviet Union.

Sometime after the conference, at an internal *IAH* meeting, he told his colleagues, 'The reason we exist is essentially to carry out extensive propaganda work for Soviet Russia. In all countries where the revolutionary political struggle has less significance, as in America, the *IAH* has a role to play', and he stressed that 'the *IAH* can play a role that political parties cannot'.

At the IV Comintern world congress held in Moscow and Petrograd in November/December 1922, an attempt was made to clarify policy on the united front issue. As a result, the congress did not rule out attempts to collaborate with the Social Democrats – this was well before Stalin's disastrous concept of 'Social Fascism' was formulated in 1928. At the congress, Radek argued that Germany faced two choices: militarism and nationalism or a Germany of the trade unions, and he hoped that some form of unity between the two big working-class parties would be possible.[14] His concept of a worker-led government coming to power in Germany as a result of a broad alliance marked the end of attempts to implement Bolshevik policies in the country, at least until a policy about-turn shortly before the Hamburg putsch attempt in 1923.

Münzenberg attended the congress as an advisory delegate. It was being held at a time marked by the onset of Lenin's arteriosclerosis which seriously affected his energy levels and ability to partake in congress work. This illness would eventually lead to his death in 1924.

Münzenberg presented an evaluation report on behalf of the *IAH*, in which he said that as the repercussions of the famine had now been largely overcome, it was time to tackle something new, i.e., support for the reconstruction of Russian industry and the economy.

As a result of the campaign to raise funds to help overcome the Russian famine, the *IAH* now had branches in many countries around the globe. These would now be involved in other solidarity campaigns. Münzenberg emphasised that it was the presence and effectiveness of the *IAH* in both Japan and the USA that had helped promote the Communist cause. By doing so, he was countering those within the movement who had criticised the role played by the *IAH* in its fundraising work. Ernst Meyer, a leading member of the German Communist Party's Central Committee, was one of those he was targeting.

Meyer had argued that because the *IAH* focussed too much on the starving masses in the Soviet Union, it 'brought the revolution into discredit'. Of course, such critics were not entirely wrong, as the famine was indeed being used by the enemies of the Soviet Union to cast the revolution as a catastrophe and argue that revolution can only lead to poverty, death, and downfall. But it was hardly a fair criticism of an organisation that had been able to transform the famine relief appeal into a high profile international working-class solidarity campaign and, in the process, promote Communist ideas. It had also emphasised the fact that the famine was largely as a result of the extreme drought, the civil war, and armed Western intervention in the Soviet Union and not directly the result of Socialist maladministration.

Despite Meyer's critique of Münzenberg and the *IAH*, at the *KPD* conference that same year, it was reported that the Party was now attempting to broaden its radius of activity. It wanted to move away from a purely proletarian focus, by setting up special sections responsible for local communities, co-operatives, women's youth and children's groups, for schooling and leisure activities, and work in rural communities, among others. The Party now had its own press agency, published 34 daily newspapers, as well as a range of specialist journals and leaflets printed in editions of millions; it also published the first translations of Russian authors in special editions. It was clear that the Party had now deserted an insurrectionist Bolshevik course and was trying to establish itself as a mainstream Party with wider appeal.

Towards the end of 1922, the Soviet government had indeed succeeded in largely overcoming the effects of the famine and was able to return the country to some sense of normality. This was underlined in a graphic description given by Rosa Meyer-Leviné, a friend and contemporary of Münzenberg and, as Ernst Meyer's wife, someone who travelled to the Soviet Union often at the same time as he did. She writes that:

> The revolution released unimaginable energies, awakening initiative and the joy of experimentation. The Party and the state apparatus gained new life through the influx of talented, energetic men and women, recruited from among ordinary working people, who were brought on board to undertake administrative and government tasks. The revolution didn't come to an end, it presented new tasks, and its leaders wore themselves out in fulfilling those superhuman efforts they were called upon to make.[15]

She also argued that the new challenges the leaders faced internally made it impossible to provide the leadership required to direct revolutionary activities abroad in an effective way. She highlighted this as an explanation for the apparent abandonment of the Soviet Union's earlier policy of actively promoting world revolution.

That year, 1922, when she spent time in Moscow with Ernst Meyer, there was, she noted, an increasing xenophobia and the first purges were taking place, to free the Party of 'foreign elements'. As fear spread, so did moral cowardice and opportunism, but she was still impressed with the way the police and the militia dealt with small infringements of the law, with leniency rather than with draconian action. She didn't know another country with such energy and stamina, she wrote.

She compared the observations she made about the Soviet Union in 1925 with those she made in 1922:

> [It was] '... the happiest time in Soviet history and I felt I had been transported into another world. It was no longer the world of a harsh life, the grim struggle of survival that I'd seen in 1922 ... the train [I was on] was packed: clean, well-fed citizens, simply, but adequately clothed, deeply

immersed in their evening newspapers. They didn't read the gossip or sports pages; that was easy to see because Russian newspapers have their political reports on the front page. We had the same interests, we read the same newspapers, it was as if we all belonged to one big family. This feeling was reinforced from minute to minute....

On the day celebrating the 200th anniversary of the Russian Academy of Science, hundreds of men and women marched to the station with red flags to welcome the arrival of foreign scientists ... The backward Russian worker honours the scientists! Where else could such a demonstration take place? The words "we", "our", "ours" could be heard everywhere – "our bus", "have you seen our new houses?" "our gardens", "our kindergartens" – not many, not enough by far, but "ours".[16]

Perhaps her descriptions are rose tinted, but her observations of a genuine change for the better and the existence of new hope at that time were based on her own first-hand observation.

Notes

1 Comintern archive Moscow RGASPI 324/1/554.
2 See: Regine Heubaum, Das Volkskommissariat für Außenhandel und seine Nachfolgeorganisationen 1920–1930, Diss. Humboldt-Universität Berlin 2001. p. 85.
3 Fischer, Ruth, *Stalin und der deutsche Kommunismus*, dietz berlin, 1991 (2 volumes), in English: *Stalin and German Communism: A Study in the Origins of the State Party* (Social Science Classics), Routledge, 2017.
4 Ruth Fischer, leader of the left opposition within the German Communist Party leadership at the time became a vehement opponent of Münzenberg and his work. See: Fischer, Ruth, opus cit.
5 https://ia902806.us.archive.org/30/items/211223InprecorrV01n19/211223-inprecorr-v01n19_text.pdf.
6 Braskén, Kasper, *The International Workers' Relief, Communism, and Transnational Solidarity. Willi Münzenberg in Weimar Germany*, Palgrave Macmillan, 2015. p. 65 (The letter can be found in the Comintern archive: RGASPI 538/2/9, 39ob.).
7 Aschberg was already a successful banker and businessman when he first met Münzenberg, who was visiting Stockholm for a Socialist Youth congress in 1917. Later, during the Bolsheviks attempts to rebuild the Russian economy, it was Münzenberg's task to expand their modest pool of capital by floating a so-called 'workers' loan' using his *IAH*. Established in Berlin in the 1920s, Aschberg's Guarantee and Credit Bank for the East was charged with repaying the IAH workers' loan. Aschberg had already gained the confidence of the Soviet leaders by being one of the main financial supporters in the early years after 1917, helping the young Soviet government evade the international boycott on Soviet gold, which he offered on the Stockholm market after melting down the bullion and giving it new markings.
8 Gross, Babette, *Willi Münzenberg: eine Politische Biografie*, Forum Verlag, 1991. p. 209.
9 Ibid. p. 210.
10 The Genoa Economic and Financial Conference was a formal international conclave of 34 nations held in Genoa, Italy from 10 April to 19 May 1922. It was convened to plan the restoration of Europe following the economic cataclysm resulting from the First World War. The conference was particularly interested in developing a

strategy to rebuild Central and Eastern Europe and negotiate a relationship between European capitalist economies and the new Soviet regime in Russia. The event was of great importance to the Soviet Union, as it heralded a de facto recognition of the Soviet government and represented a breakthrough in the lifting of the economic blockade of the country.

11 The international alliance made up of Fritz Adler's Austrian Socialists and the British Independent Labour Party was dubbed the Two-and-a-Half International by Lenin. Thus, the meeting brought together the (Communist) First International, the Social Democratic Second International, and the so-called 'Two-and-a-half' one.

12 McMeekin, Sean, *The Red Millionaire*, p. 144.

13 Fischer, Ruth. opus cit. p. 281.

14 Fischer, Ruth. opus cit. p. 273.

15 Meyer-Leviné, Rosa. *Im Innereren Kreis: Errinnerungen einer Kommunistin in Deutschland 1920–1933* (published in English translation as *Inside German Communism: Memoirs of Party Life in the Weimar Republic*, Pluto Press, 1977). p. 46.

16 Ibid. p. 119.

6

THE COMMUNIST PARTY
AND CIVIL WAR IN GERMANY

While in the Soviet Union the economic and political situation was becoming more stable, in Germany, uncertainty and instability remained. Since the chaos unleashed by the 1918 November Revolution and its bloody repression by government forces, there had been hope that the country would from then on enjoy a period of relative stability, but that did not happen: there was continued and widespread unrest, strikes, demonstrations, and armed confrontations, a situation that would be compounded in 1921 by the hyper-inflation that hit the country.

The young Weimar Republic was assailed from all sides: from the right by disgruntled monarchists and nationalists, supported by the conservative military elite, the semi-autonomous and paramilitary *Freikorps* and on the left from the Communists, who were still determined to bring about a radical Socialist revolution, and on top of that, by the victors of the First World War, with their impossible reparation demands.

This state of affairs would continue until the end of 1923, and it was in that context that Münzenberg had to operate. He had thrown himself into rebuilding the Socialist youth movement and into the newly founded Communist Party, as well as into the International Workers Relief organisation (*IAH*). He managed, though, to pursue his aims and to build effective organisations without becoming completely embroiled in insurrectionary adventurism or the infighting within the German Communist Party.

Paul Levi, who became the chair of the Communist Party after the murder in 1919 of Luxemburg and Liebknecht, had begun leading it away from a policy that anticipated every rebellion as a sign of imminent revolution and removed a number of extreme leftists from the Party leadership. Levi, Clara Zetkin, and other more moderate figures in the central committee would make serious efforts to win over supporters from the Social Democratic Party and the more radical Independent Social Democratic Party in order to forge a stronger working-class movement.

Although developments in the country since 9 November had fully exposed the bankruptcy of reform Socialism as practised by the Social Democratic Party (*SPD*) – its policies had helped heave the ruling class back into the saddle, while crippling the working-class movement – that did not mean that revolution was imminent. Up until Levi became leader, the Communist Party itself had largely neglected the development of Socialist theory and taken the road of adventurism and putschist action, fomented by powerful factional groups who thought they could bring about revolution in this way. Such policies had led to further splits and terrible defeats. Levi attempted to draw lessons from those defeats and to analyse the causes, but he would be ousted by the extreme left-wing faction within the Party before he was able to act on them.

In February 1921, Paul Levi was forced to resign his leadership position, largely due to Comintern pressure, and a more radical leadership under Heinrich Brandler took over. The Comintern felt Levi was too much of a conciliator and looked towards cooperation with the Social Democrats rather than promoting revolution. Brandler adopted a more left-wing position within the Party, but the even more radical faction led by Ruth Fischer and her partner-to-be Arkadi Maslow enjoyed backing from Radek in Moscow, who had been warning the Party about the 'dangers of opportunism', which was a critique of the more conciliatory position taken by Levi.

The fiery and extreme-leftist Ruth Fischer had by then become a rising star in the German Communist Party. She and Arkadi Maslow came to represent the so-called left opposition within the Party; they opposed any attempts to cooperate with the *SPD*. From 1921 onwards, she and Maslow would lead the strong Berlin Party organisation and were, in effect, the de facto leaders of the left opposition within the Communist Party of Germany (*KPD*) central committee after Levi's resignation and his replacement as Party chairman by Heinrich Brandler.

Fischer was convinced the time had now arrived for an armed uprising of workers in Germany with the aim of at last wresting power from the Social Democrats. The radicals took the successful Bolshevik Revolution as their template. Pressure from the Soviet Union on this policy issue was decisive, as the Party leaders there were also convinced that Germany was ripe for revolution and would follow their example and thus spark further revolutions worldwide.

At the urging of the Comintern, the German Party leadership, now dominated by its left wing, accepted that the time was ripe once more for an armed uprising. It began in the Ruhr region in March, spreading to other areas of the country, and became known as the 'March Action'. But in the end, it was easily crushed by government forces.

Although Münzenberg had earlier been an anti-parliamentarian advocating Bolshevik tactics to take power, and had belonged to the Party's left faction, in the meantime, he had moderated his position and now supported the idea of broad alliances. Over time, his former allies Fischer and Maslow would become entrenched critics of both him and his work, seeing it as a reformist undertaking, detracting from the central task of making revolution. Fischer would also label him scathingly a 'robber baron'.[1]

Following the disastrous 'March Action' in 1921, Paul Levi wrote the pamphlet *Unser Weg: Wider den Putschismus* (Our Path: against Putschism). In it, he criticised the Comintern – particularly the leaders Béla Kun, Radek, and Zinoviev who had encouraged such adventurism – and the *KPD* itself for the many premature attempts to take state power in Germany. As a result, Levi was expelled from the Party for having 'failed to grasp' what his opponents maintained was a revolutionary opportunity and for publicly criticising Party policies in his journal *Unser Weg* (Our Way). Although Lenin and Trotsky largely agreed with Levi's criticisms, and Lenin argued for his reinstatement in the Party, he went on to join the Independent Social Democratic Party. After Levi's departure, the Fischer-Maslow faction gained even more influence.

A number of other leading comrades who had supported Levi's position also left the Party – the second large haemorrhaging for the young *KPD* in a very short space of time. However, Münzenberg stayed.

FIGURE 6.1 A relaxed Willi Münzenberg (Courtesy of Bundesarchiv.)

Parallel with what was happening in the *KPD*, Moscow was still secretly maintaining relations with the small breakaway ultra-leftist Communist Workers' Party, which had been expelled from the Comintern. In the run-up to the March uprising in Germany, Moscow secretly held talks with its leaders in the hope that they could be persuaded to launch military action and thus spark a wider uprising.

Although Brandler, as the new *KPD* chair, adopted a more radical left-wing position than Levi within the Party, it was the even more extreme Fischer-Maslow faction that enjoyed full backing from Radek in Moscow.

Despite the defeats of 1921, which demonstrated the wrong-headedness of the insurrectionist position, Ruth Fischer would remain an influential figure and reach the zenith of her influence in the Party during the autumn of 1923.

In the wake of the March Action, around 6,000 Communists had been arrested, of these, 4,500 were put on trial and 4,000 given sentences of 3,000 years in total. All of these individuals and their families had to be offered legal and financial support, which they received from the 'Red Aid' (*Rote Hilfe*) organisation set up specifically by the German Communist Party for this purpose. It had branches in numerous places and in 1922 would raise almost 310 million Marks.[2]

In January 1922, a little-known Austrian-born nationalist called Adolf Hitler was also put on trial and sentenced to nine months in prison for violently disrupting a political meeting in Munich. He was incarcerated in June, thus turning him into a minor hero for the right. But right-wing forces elsewhere in Germany were becoming evermore confident. Demonstrators took to the streets yelling slogans of hate such as: *Knallt ab den Walther Rathenau! Die Gott-verfluchte Judensau!* [Shoot Walther Rathenau/The Goddamned Jewish pig!].

This duly happened. On 24 June 1922, only two months after he had signed the Treaty of Rapallo, Walther Rathenau, the German foreign minister, who was Jewish, was gunned down in a Berlin street by fanatical *Freikorps* officers. It was an ominous sign of the lengths to which right-wing extremists and the disaffected officer caste were prepared to go to undermine the Weimar Republic, and it reflected their rising confidence.

Such actions caused extreme alarm on the left and many Communists began taking action to defend themselves against a possible right-wing coup. Even at Münzenberg's *IAH* headquarters in Berlin, in the wake of Rathenau's murder, young Communist employees began bringing rifles into work and keeping them within easy reach on top of the filing cabinets.

Throughout the rest of the year and countrywide, younger Party comrades were divided up into groups of five members, under strict conspiratorial rules, so that only one member of the group would have contact with anyone else from a different group. Young Communists went secretly into the countryside north of Berlin to undertake shooting practice. The Party was clearly preparing for being forced underground and facing what it feared would be a bitter struggle.

Waves of strikes and 'hunger marches' continued unabated around the country, Party members became increasingly agitated and anxious. Everyone felt the situation was about to explode. Although there was, objectively, no question of revolution, there was a considerable amount of revolutionary romanticism, even though most Party members hoped that a successful general strike would be sufficient to bring the Party to power without bloodshed. After all, a general strike had brought down the putschist Kapp regime in 1920.

Towards the end of the year, tensions were reaching breaking point. Already in September 1922, the Reichstag had declared a state of emergency in order to try and bring matters under control. In other parts of Europe, too, tensions were increasing. Mussolini's march on Rome on 27 October and his proclamation of a Fascist state in Italy gave the right wing in Germany new hope.

Chemnitz had one of the strongest Communist Party organisations, but during the Kapp Putsch, it had been cut off from the central committee in Berlin. Brandler, the Chemnitz Party leader at the time, began setting up Workers Councils, and all those who were suspected of being Kapp supporters were disarmed and arrested. The Workers Council took over the city hall and began to prepare a defence of the city. In nearby Falkenstein, the maverick Communist Max Hoelz set up his own guerrilla units. This virtual civil war situation would continue to exist, flaring up and then dying down throughout the country for several years to come.

The continued pressure by the Western allies on Germany, insisting on full payment of reparations, as stipulated in the Versailles Treaty, only served to bring Germany and the Soviet Union – also deemed a debtor country[3] – closer together. By using its leverage as an industrial nation, Germany could, by secretly collaborating with the Russians, overcome the restrictions on its military developments imposed at Versailles.

When Germany fell behind on its payments, in January 1923, French and Belgian troops moved in and occupied the Ruhr industrial region, which only made the situation in the country worse. Massive inflation was already having a devastating effect on living standards in Germany, and the occupation only compounded matters. Hundreds of thousands of miners and steel workers in the Ruhr region were already jobless, and the little financial support they received from the government was eroded daily by inflation. When the German government began printing money to offset the damage done by the French occupation, this only made matters worse.

In response to the occupation, the German government, under Chancellor Wilhelm Cuno, called for nationwide passive resistance, and the *KPD* was the only faction in the Reichstag to vote against the policy, arguing that it would be ineffective. His call was also ridiculed by the right wing and nationalist forces, led by General Ludendorff, who were calling for armed resistance to the French and Belgian occupation.

As a result of the Chancellor's appeal, but also the Communists' counter call for a general strike, telephone wires were cut and the whole of industry along the Rhine and Ruhr came to a complete standstill. In Berlin, too, the trade unions called for a national strike in support of those in the occupied territory.

On 7 April 1923, Albert Schlageter, a member of the *Freikorps*, was arrested in Düsseldorf by the French army because he had been involved in bomb attacks on railway lines. Sentenced to death by a military court, he was executed on May 26. The nationalist, right wing immediately turned him into a martyr. The French occupation had provided the German right wing with the impetus it had lacked.

The increasing popularity of the nationalists in Germany was causing some rethinking in the Comintern. Radek at a meeting of the executive committee in

June, proposed that the *KPD* could win over workers and elements of the middle class, which had been seduced by the Fascists, if they joined this campaign and reclaimed nationalism from the Fascists. Radek had pointed out earlier that the nationalist-inclined masses were undoubtedly more in sympathy with the Socialists than with the capitalists.

'The petty-bourgeois masses, the intellectuals and technicians who will play a big role in the revolution are in a position of national antagonism to capitalism, which is declassing them', Radek announced. 'If we want to be a workers' party that is able to undertake the struggle for power, we have to find a way that can bring us near to these masses, and we shall find it not in shirking our responsibilities, but in stating that the working class alone can save the nation'. At the meeting, he also praised Schlageter's action in carrying out acts of sabotage against the French occupation.

McMeekin in his Münzenberg biography interprets Radek's position rather differently. He describes Radek as 'flirting with Fascism'.[4] Apart from the fact that Radek was Jewish, this appears to be a wilful misinterpretation, as he is hardly suggesting that the Communists should get into bed with the Fascists. He also distorts 'Münzenberg's commentary on the Ruhr occupation', saying that it 'vividly illustrates the convergence between Communist and Nazi responses to the crisis'.[5]

The so-called Schlageter line (i.e. supporting nationalist sentiment) was then taken up by the Communist Party newspaper, '*The Red Flag*', and it created a great deal of confusion in Communist ranks, which up till then had resisted nationalist pressures. The Schlageter-campaign also provided ammunition for the anti-Communist propaganda campaign of the *SPD* and made it very difficult for the French Communist Party to argue for solidarity amongst French soldiers for the German workers.

Münzenberg himself, perhaps rather surprisingly also adopted a pro-nationalist position on the French occupation of the Ruhr region. Already on 17 March 1923, in Frankfurt am Main, where an international 'Conference for a United Front against Fascism' was held, Münzenberg spoke and appealed to the foreign delegates to take a stand on the occupation of the Ruhr region. This, though, again placed the attending French Communists in a difficult position.

In Berlin, he also addressed a meeting with the provocative title: 'The Battle on the Ruhr. Who are the traitors to the nation?' This was dangerous terrain and seemed to indicate that the Party no longer viewed the battle against rising poverty and unemployment as the only way to radicalise the masses. It appeared to be saying: Why not join the nationalist front against France?

The following September, the French Communist leader Jules Humbert-Droz wrote a letter to Zinoviev, the chair of the Comintern, in which he criticised what he saw as the increasingly nationalist line taken by the German Party and told him that it was making the work of the French Party very difficult and undermining French workers' solidarity with and support for the German revolution.

Bavaria in particular, with its large rural areas, developed into a stronghold of the extreme right. After the bloody oppression of the Munich Soviet Republic in 1919, the state had become a hotbed for nationalistic, fascistic, and paramilitary organisations.

As Gross notes in her Münzenberg biography, another man, with the name of Hitler, had also realised this and why, 'early on, he gave his nationalist movement a socialist mantle'. The leading Nazi and close friend of Hitler, Gregor Strasser, called national Socialism 'the great anti-capitalist yearning of the masses'.[6] The Nazis knew that if they were ever to become a mass party, they had to win over large sections of the working-class Socialists then in the Social Democratic and Communist parties.

It was true that neither at this time nor later did the German middle classes show much sympathy for Communist ideas. But in Berlin and other big cities during 1923, there was a strange, all-pervasive atmosphere, as if many people were just waiting for the Communists to bring a radical solution to the increasingly intolerable conditions. It was extremely unlikely that large numbers of the middle classes would have welcomed a Socialist revolution, although they were certainly prepared to follow the siren call of the National Socialists.

In response to the increasing use of violence by right-wing military forces, the KPD had begun to establish security units of its own, which to begin with, were intended to offer protection to Communist meetings and demonstrations. But in the event of the party itself being banned, they were also designed to form the kernel of an effective resistance movement. The formation of armed workers' groups was undertaken particularly rigorously in the Rhineland and Ruhr regions, where the army, commanded by General Freiherr von Watter, had been working closely with extreme right-wing *Freikorps* units.

The establishment of these armed worker battalions was supported not only by the Communists, but also by Social Democratic and Catholic workers who were determined to rid the region of *Freikorps* troops and, in March 1920, had been prepared to march on Berlin to remove the Kapp putschists. This loosely formed 'Red Army', a quasi-guerrilla force, chose its own officers and at its height comprised around 50,000 men. Similar armed groups were set up in Thuringia, in southern Germany, and in the provinces bordering the North and Baltic Seas.

In the year 1923, the *Freikorps* attacked a large meeting in Essen of workers, arrested dozens, beating them up before shooting them in the street. Such incidents were etched in the memory of the local people. After the Kapp Putsch, they had expected the government to take decisive action against the *Freikorps*, but this had not happened. It had become clear to many Communists that any collaboration between the KPD and the Social Democratic government was unlikely to materialise. The latter apparently preferred to collaborate with the conservative and right-wing military forces to defeat the Communists.

Fischer, as the leader of the radical left faction within the Communist Party, attacked 'Communist reformism', as she termed the leadership's central policy, and said that it had lost any appeal for the members at this time; many of the party's provincial organisations clearly agreed with Fischer's assessment and followed the radical line. Many party members now put their energy into the organisation of military units, so-called 'Hundertschaften' (para-military groups of 'proletarian self-defence units' of around 100 men each, with a national membership in total of around 50,000–60,000, made up mainly of communists, but with many Social Democrats as well. These armed units, although set up by Communists, also welcomed those from outside party ranks.

Fischer was the *KPD*'s representative in the Rhineland and the Ruhr areas in the spring of 1923. She said that the central party leadership had, up to this time, been satisfied with hanging onto the government's coat-tails and its passive resistance policy, but the left wing, under her leadership was calling for decisive action against the government.[7] She wrote that plans formulated in 1920 were rekindled with increasing calls for the establishment of a workers' republic in Rhineland and the Ruhr.

Fischer and Maslow were key organisers of a conference, held on 25 March 1923, of trade unionists in Essen in the Ruhr region called to discuss taking revolutionary action and to develop a programme for the takeover of factories and government offices. This followed secret meetings held by local branches. At that conference, Fischer called on workers to seize factories and mines and take political power to establish a workers' republic in the region. Such action, they hoped, would trigger insurrection in other parts of Germany. It was an attempt to repeat the so-called 'March Action' of 1921, which had, though, been brutally suppressed by government forces.

The party leadership, now with the backing of Karl Radek and the Comintern, which had done a policy U-turn, sent Clara Zetkin to the Ruhr region to warn local party organisations about repeating the adventurist mistakes of the past. They hoped to prevent Fisher and Maslow's incendiary advice taking hold. Zetkin told them that the Comintern would not support such action and other regional party organisations would be told not to join in. This may have dampened the ardour of some, but sporadic armed action continued, nevertheless.

The Ruhr crisis would come to a head during spring and early summer of 1923. With the economy cracking under the weight of rampant inflation, small businesses being badly hit, but the peasantry was affected too, farmers could no longer sell their products profitably and food became evermore scarce.

On 20 March 1923, the party's '*Red Flag*' newspaper had already carried the provocative headline, 'Solidarity', and announced the delivery of flour and bread from Russian trade unions for the 'struggling Ruhr workers'. This was a response to the aid given by German workers to the Soviet Union during the great famine. The distribution of the Russian supplies was organised by Münzenberg's *IAH*, together with a government committee comprised of shop stewards and consumer groups.

The Soviet Union, though, was sending not only food aid, but also military experts to give advice and support to the *KPD,* as it felt that a revolution could erupt at any time. However, neither the Comintern nor the *KPD* could decide whether the time was now really ripe for a revolutionary uprising, and while they dithered, the right wing struck first.

The national government and the local authorities in the Ruhr region were not at all happy about the Russian aid once they realised that the deliveries were accompanied by representatives of the Soviet trade unions who gave 'inflammatory' speeches while helping to distribute the food. The authorities raged about this attempt at the 'Bolshevisation' of German workers and the situation escalated into a diplomatic contretemps.

In June, the 'Red Flag' contained even more provocative content. There was a prominent article on civil war tactics, explanations of guerrilla warfare, and firsthand reports on the revolution and civil war in Russia. The readership was left in no doubt by this that armed conflict now appeared to be unavoidable. The Soviet leadership, however, soon began urging caution and warned against taking isolated action.

By the end of July, the Cuno government was facing implosion. Its call for passive resistance to the French occupation was having little impact in terms of solving the impasse, and the political crisis continued unabated. On 10 August, the Communists in the Reichstag introduced a vote of no confidence in the Cuno government, and on August 1923, the SPD withdrew its support, calling for the formation of a grand coalition.

A general strike called in Berlin caught on in the rest of the country like wildfire. In many towns there was open rebellion, and on 11 August, 35 workers were shot dead and a hundred or more wounded by government forces; this was followed by more deaths and injuries the next day. Chancellor Wilhelm Cuno, who was politically independent, resigned on 12 August to be replaced by Gustav Stresemann.

The German currency had tipped into the abyss: by late summer 1923, a single dollar was valued at between 200 and 300 million Marks. The situation was deteriorating rapidly and strikes and confrontations multiplied in the Ruhr region as a response to the extreme scarcity of food supplies, and in the face of galloping inflation; riots and strikes flared up again elsewhere in the country.

In that summer of 1923, Münzenberg, together with Valerie Marcu, the Berlin-based Romanian poet, writer, and historian, had published a series of bulletins that attempted to analyse the new phenomenon of rising Fascism and argued that it was due to mistakes made by the two big working-class Socialist parties, both in Italy and Germany, that had allowed the Fascists to jump in and fill the political vacuum; this analysis, as history has shown, was not wrong, and the prognosis was a dark one, but one that nobody in the KPD leadership at the time wished to hear. Münzenberg was severely criticised by the party leadership for taking such a stance and was forced to distance himself from Marcu.

Münzenberg's views on whether or not there was a revolutionary situation in Germany in the autumn of 1923 were ignored by the hard-left group within the KPD who interpreted Comintern advice as a call to the barricades.

In any case, already by September, Münzenberg's attentions had become diverted elsewhere. He travelled to the Soviet Union to meet leaders of the Soviet trade unions to discuss possible aid to Japanese workers. On 1 September, in Japan, there had been a horrendous earthquake, and the Japanese trade unions had appealed to the *IAH* for help. Together with the Soviet trade unions, he was able to collect a considerable amount of material and send shiploads of supplies to Japan.

There the authorities at first refused to let the ships unload because they were convinced they were laden not with flour, as the bill of lading described, but with weapons and Communist propaganda material. Only with the assistance of the Prefect of Hokkaido was it made possible to unload some of the ships at a port on the island. But of more concern than getting aid to the Japanese, was the logistical problem of making aid deliveries to the Social Democrat and Communist coalition governments that in the meantime had been established in Saxony and Thuringia if, as was then planned for and expected, the revolution in Germany would break out and spread from there.

Münzenberg returned from the Soviet Union to Germany to oversee the unloading of deliveries of Soviet wheat in Dresden and to hold negotiations with the government of Saxony about delivering machinery to the Soviet Union.

During October, a number of further shipments from the Soviet Union had arrived on freight trains, but German customs officers alleged that on searching the trains they found hidden weapons. Several transport officials were arrested and the offices of the *IAH* in Berlin were searched, but no further action was taken by the authorities. This was before the two regional governments in Saxony and Thuringia had been toppled.

The French had responded to resistance by the Ruhr population by imposing large fines and arresting the mayors of many towns. In August, they expropriated the coal mines in order to ensure the continued delivery of coal to France as part of the reparations commitment.

There were huge demonstrations by the population demanding price controls, and there were increased clashes with French forces. Many workers were also demanding the nationalisation of their industries and were increasingly frustrated by the ineffectiveness of the central government's policy of passive resistance.

It was, though, not only in the Ruhr that things were bad, but throughout the country. In Hamburg, tensions were such that the police did not dare intervene when grocery stores were plundered by hungry crowds. In such crisis situations rumours take on a new and often dangerous force. And two of those circulating were that the Kaiser was about to return from Holland and that Bavaria and Rhineland were about to leave the German empire.

The trade unions feared they were losing control of the situation as separatist movements in the Rhineland, Ruhr, and in Bavaria were given a new boost by the crisis and central government's inability to solve it. And, in those early summer months of 1923, for the first time, Hitler's name began to resonate beyond his Munich headquarters.

Following Cuno's resignation and the appointment of Stresemann to the German chancellorship on 26 September, the situation was transformed, and the Comintern changed its own approach from one of advocating collaboration with other left forces to one advocating insurrection.

By late August 1923, with Stresemann now in power, the Soviet Party and Comintern leaderships had undertaken a re-assessment of the situation in Germany and had become convinced that a new revolution was on the cards. Together with the leaders of the *KPD*, they planned the launch of a 'German October', a replication of the successful Bolshevik Revolution in Russia, on German soil.

As the newly appointed chancellor, Stresemann announced the end of passive resistance. He argued that there was no other way to get hyperinflation under control. This provoked an outraged reaction by the extreme right.

On that same day, the Bavarian government declared a state of emergency and installed a dictatorship led by Ritter von Kahr. Von Kahr collaborated with Hitler's Nazis and, imitating Mussolini's march on Rome, planned his own march on Berlin to install a dictatorship at the national level. Kahr was supported by the commander of the Reichswehr units positioned in Bavaria.

The Berlin government responded by setting up its own form of dictatorship. The entire executive power was transferred to the minister of defence, who delegated it to General Hans von Seeckt, commander in chief of the Reichswehr. But Seeckt sympathised with the extreme right and refused to discipline the rebellious Bavarian commanders.

On 13 October, the Reichstag, after several days of discussion, passed an empowerment act, authorising the government to abolish the social achievements of the November Revolution, including the eight-hour day. The *SPD* voted in favour of the empowerment act, further infuriating the trade unions and those on the left.

During this time, communists and Social Democrats in Saxony and Thuringia had begun discussing the formation of coalition governments as a way out of the seemingly intractable situation. When the opportunity for this arose in these two regions, the Communist Party leadership was, to begin with, equivocal about whether the party should participate – many, particularly those on the far left, felt this would only serve to defuse what they considered to be a revolutionary moment.

The group around the party's Chair Heinrich Brandler was in favour of setting up 'peoples governments', but the attempts to form such regional coalition governments in Thuringia and Saxony had been vehemently attacked by the leftists in the party led by Fischer and Maslow. They considered that Germany was ripe for revolution and labelled such collaboration and Brandler's policies 'reformist passivity'. In the end, the party leadership, with Radek's agreement, agreed to support the policy of collaborating with the *SPD* where possible, and the two coalition governments went ahead.

The fact that Communists were now installed in two regional governments, gave the new Stresemann-led national government sufficient reason to use force to remove them. It was particularly alarmed because in these two regions the paramilitary 'Hundertschaften' had been firmly established. Elsewhere in Germany the Communist Party had been appointing military leaders, and for the centre of Berlin, an employee of Münzenberg's *IAH* became one of them.

On 26 September, faced with a situation in the country rapidly slipping out of control, Stresemann, following his call for an end to passive resistance in the Ruhr region, brought in martial law, which would last until February 1924. By simultaneously introducing his financial reforms to combat the hyper-inflation and by taking such decisive action against the Social Democrat-Communist regional governments, he was able to nip any inchoate revolution in the bud. He also set up a state-owned *Rentenbank* (pension bank) and announced that a new currency, the so-called *Rentenmark* (pension Mark) would be introduced, intended to bring an end to the inflationary spiral. As a consequence, on 1 October, a planned general strike in the country was called off, and the situation in the Ruhr began to stabilise.

With no end in sight to the increasingly polarised situation, the Communist Party took the initiative in October of organising a special conference of industrial shop stewards in Chemnitz to address this seemingly intractable situation. It was called ostensibly to popularise the recent Russian food deliveries to Saxony which Münzenberg had organised, but in fact it was convened to put forward a plan for revolution, which would support a general strike and armed resistance to the military. The Comintern gave the green light to commence preparations for a nationwide uprising.

The conference was attended by Communists, but also Social Democrats. The Social Democratic Party sent only a few delegates as its party officials were not keen to lend legitimacy to the conference. The Communist Party, though, hoped that the Chemnitz conference would issue a call to arms throughout the country to topple the central government. It had prepared couriers from each region to take the news back to their areas as soon as the decision was taken, so that an immediate and co-ordinated insurrection could take place. The delegates were, though, taken by surprise when the party chair, Heinrich Brandler apparently got cold feet and removed the resolution calling for immediate armed insurrection from the agenda. This resolution would, in any case, have been made null and void because the government was already taking preventative military action. In response, the party leadership dropped its plans not only for Saxony, but for the rest of the country.

The couriers would now have to return and tell their comrades that the uprising was off. The courier responsible for Hamburg had, though, left the conference before this decision had been taken and informed his comrades there that they should begin the uprising immediately.

The successful establishment of joint Communist and Social Democratic regional governments in Saxony and Thuringia had not only infuriated the conservative forces in the country, but also the central Social Democratic government. Ebert and Stresemann were not prepared to tolerate Communists even in regional governments. So between 21 and 27 October, after already demanding the immediate resignation of Erich Zeigner's left-wing coalition government in Saxony and its counterpart in Weimar, Ebert ordered the military to move in.

On 23 October, only two days after the beginning of the Chemnitz conference, General Müller marched into Dresden without incident, although he did meet armed resistance in Meissen, Zwickau, and Pirna. In Freiburg, too, there were clashes.

The resulting confrontations left several dozen dead and many injured, but the army had soon occupied all the administrative buildings, banned Communist publications, and arrested hundreds of party members. The proletarian 'Hundertschaften' were disbanded and Communist ministers removed from office or they resigned. The Communist Party was then banned throughout Saxony. The government also sent General Hasse to Thuringia to carry out a similar operation.

The toppling of the coalition governments in both Saxony and Thuringia demonstrated very clearly that there was little possibility of Communist and Social Democratic collaboration on a national level, if it was not possible on a regional one. It also put a large spike in the wheel of those like party chair Brandler who had been arguing for collaboration and at the same time it strengthened the hand of the far-leftists around Fischer and Maslow.

The Hamburg uprising

On 23 October, the final day of the Chemnitz conference, the courier, Hermann Remmele, who had left the conference early, arrived back in Hamburg to give the orders for the uprising to begin. Once the party's city leader, Ernst Thälmann, received it, he immediately mobilised his forces. The pre-planned action began at 4.15 in the morning on 23 October, when around 300 armed men attacked 17 police stations and occupied public buildings. The rebels felled trees and used vehicles to form barricades. There was little opposition to the rebellion expressed by working-class communities in the city, and the rebels found themselves confronted by only a few police units. Thälmann's men were poorly armed and began attacking police stations in the hope of procuring more weapons. He and his comrades were completely unaware that they were on their own, believing that co-ordinated uprisings were taking place throughout the country. The uprising lasted until 25 October.

Once the news that the party had called off the uprising and that Hamburg was on its own reached Thälmann, he did not have the heart to relay this to his fighting comrades and so the battles continued for two days. On the second day, the leaders of the red 'Hundertschaften' had been ordered by the party leadership in Berlin to pull back. In the end, within those few days, the police were easily able to suppress the rebellion, but it left 24 Communists and 17 policemen dead.

The events in Hamburg, Germany's second largest city, could have had repercussions for the whole country had its lead been followed, rather than that of the

Chemnitz conference. The failure of the planned revolution and the debacle in Hamburg now created a real headache for the Communist Party.

The background to the renewed revolutionary upsurge in Germany and the Hamburg uprising had been the rapidly deteriorating economic situation, the mass unemployment, and the associated hyper-inflation in the country. As a result, the *KPD* had been rapidly gaining members and supporters. This surge in support had given the pro-insurrectionary forces additional impetus. However, even the Soviet military representative in Germany, General Vladimir Efimovich Gorev, made it very clear to the German Party leadership at the time that he felt an attempted uprising would be suicidal because there were not enough weapons available to arm the workers. In the end, Comintern representatives in Germany came to the same conclusion, but somewhat belatedly.

The ineffectiveness of central government in opposing the allied occupation of the Ruhr valley and the continued instability throughout the country had also provided the extreme right-wing forces, centred around Hitler in Munich, the excuse to attempt their own putsch.

Hitler, then known in Munich circles as the 'German Mussolini' and inspired by Mussolini's 'March on Rome', prepared his own 'March on Berlin' for 9 November, – for the right-wing nationalists, a day of national shame (it was the day on which the German Soviet-style Revolution of 1918 took place). This became known as the so-called 'Beer Hall Putsch'. However, the march of several thousand, led by Hitler and with the support of Generals Ludendorff and von Lossow, was met by a large force of police at the *Feldherrnhalle* in Munich. There were scuffles and fights in which 14 demonstrators and police were killed. Hitler fled the scene, but was arrested a few days later.

While the group around Ruth Fischer and Arkadi Maslow in the Communist Party leadership were still convinced that the year 1923 was a suitable year for revolutionary action, Münzenberg did not share their view. He was very sceptical about the situation, and he was not at all convinced that the *SPD* would join the Communists if it came to an attempted counter-revolutionary coup by the right-wing military. He was convinced the *SPD* would rather join General von Seeckt and the Minister of Defence Gessler than the Communists.

On 23 November 1923, following the toppling of the left-wing coalition governments in Saxony and Thuringia and the Hitler putsch, the German chief of staff and minister of defence, General von Seeckt, declared a state of emergency and had posters displayed throughout the country with the words, 'I am banning the Communist Party of Germany and all its organisations' (this ban included the Communist Party's press). He took no action against the Fascist putschists with whom he sympathised. Not aware of the full details, Münzenberg must have been devastated by the dangerously adventurist action taken by the leadership in Hamburg. All his hard work in attempting to build broad alliances was put in jeopardy.

Surprisingly, the listed organisations von Seeckt banned did not include the *IAH*, and while the forces of law and order hunted down leading Communists and closed the party's offices, the *IAH* was left unmolested. This probably had a number of reasons, but one would have been an unwillingness to attack what was widely perceived as a humanitarian effort by the *IAH* in Germany itself. Münzenberg had just begun to organise soup kitchens and bread distribution points everywhere and to refocus his organisation on helping destitute German workers who had been particularly hard hit by the economic crisis and rampant inflation.

In 246 large and smaller towns, food centres were set up for the unemployed; in Berlin alone, there were 58 street kitchens handing out 7,000 plates of food daily. Communists and Social Democrats joined together to staff the kitchens and hand out the food. In the wake of the banning of the *KPD*, the *IAH* would become increasingly important as a presence and a voice of the left. It was able to publish and distribute written material widely and information to the party's officials and thus help it get around the banning order.

There is little doubt that the national government's decision to leave the *IAH* off the list of banned organisations was a sensible calculation in the face of the *IAH*'s charitable work. In addition, Münzenberg was still seen very much as Moscow's trusted representative in Germany, and the government was reticent about antagonising the Soviet Union when good relations between the two countries were mutually useful. Germany was, more than ever, interested in military and trade relations with the Soviet Union in view of the draconian stipulations, still in force, of the Versailles Treaty.

Because the *IAH* itself, surprisingly, had been left, temporarily at least, unaffected by the ban imposed on the Communist Party, he could go ahead with the planned *IAH* international congress in Berlin. His organisation would, though, soon come under attack from European-wide Social Democratic forces and be stigmatised as a 'Communist front'.

On 9 December, Münzenberg organised the large international *IAH* conference in Berlin which was attended by leading European Social Democrats, like Edo Fimmen. The Committee for Food Aid to Germany could count on a whole number of intellectuals in support of this cause.

Münzenberg and his like-minded comrades hoped that the *IAH* would still be able to ride out the crisis and through its network of contacts and good relations with the trade unions continue work that the banned Communist Party was now unable to undertake.

As early as 1922, Ruth Fischer, one of the German Communist Party's leading representatives on the Comintern executive committee – later in life to become a vehement critic of the worldwide Communist project – had written to Stalin complaining about Münzenberg's 'alienation from the Party and alleging that he had ceased his close involvement in Communist Party work to become a law unto himself'. He had, she continued, 'since 1921 withdrawn from party activity; he no longer took part in factional struggles and was already standing with one foot outside the Party'. She was not the only one to take such a sharply critical position towards Münzenberg.[8] However, the justification for Fischer's attack is rejected by Gross, who argued that the new leaders, Ernst Meyer and his successor, Heinrich Brandler, had given Münzenberg free rein to take his own course. Fischer's complaint about his seeming freedom to operate outside party control was a critique that would not have worried Münzenberg unduly.

Münzenberg's sober assessment of the situation in Germany in 1923 was at odds with the far-left leadership of the party under Ruth Fischer, Arkadi Maslow, and Ernst Thälmann. Fischer had hoped that Münzenberg would come on board and rejoin her faction, but he now had little sympathy with her group's radicalism. This attitude probably only helped cement the views of many on the extreme left in the party that the *IAH* was simply a version of the Salvation Army.

Despite the continued critique of Münzenberg by the *KPD*'s hard-left faction, at the party's Leipzig congress in March 1923, he was elected onto the Central Committee, and he used this opportunity, for a short time, to become more involved in day-to-day policy-making discussions, including how the Party should react to the recent occupation and de facto annexation of the industrial Ruhr by France. Now, as a member of the party's central committee, Münzenberg began a closer involvement in the party's political work and spoke at a number of public meetings on political issues of the day.

From 7 to 10 April 1924, the illegal and thus secret IX congress of the still banned German Communist Party took place in Frankfurt am Main. At this congress, Ruth Fischer,[9] one of Münzenberg's harshest critics, rose to become the leading figure in the party. After Paul Levi's expulsion, his successor Heinrich Brandler was blamed for the disastrous failure of the 1923 uprising, and Fischer and her partner Arkadi Maslow came to dominate the German Communist Party. Fischer also led the German section of the Comintern, the largest representation alongside that of the Soviet Union.

At this time, the German Party found itself in the deepest crisis since its founding, and this was characterised by deep ideological divisions. At its core, the ideological split was about the reasons for the catastrophic defeat of the October 1923 insurrection. Was it because the party leadership had misread a genuinely revolutionary situation and failed to provide leadership, thus betraying the revolution, or was it the result of an adventurist attempt by hot heads in the party to bring about revolution at an unsuitable time when defeat was certain? Fischer, along with Maslow and Thälmann of the left opposition, were of the opinion that the party should have fought, but did not do so because 'the opportunist leadership was paralysed'.

Although Münzenberg had been one of those who had opposed the launching of revolutionary uprisings in 1923 on the basis that the situation in the country was, in his view, not a truly revolutionary one, he was still proposed as a *KPD* candidate to the *Reichstag* for the constituency of Hessen-Nassau at the IX congress of the party.

Despite the banning of the Communist Party and the serious internal divisions, it had been gaining new members in the country as a whole during this turbulent period. However, it was not only the Communist Party that had been gaining strength. The Nazi Party had also been profiting from the developing crisis and was now attracting more working-class adherents. By 1923, its membership had grown rapidly to 55,000 and, particularly in its Bavarian stronghold, it had become a significant force.

With the increasing success of the Nazis in attracting working-class adherents, the still banned Communist Party was not averse to utilising non-party media to regain influence and was now more than happy to have Münzenberg's publications quasi at their disposal. This helped silence many of his critics for some time to come.

By May 1924, the nationwide ban on the Communist Party in Germany was lifted, and the party was able to take part in that month's national elections. Münzenberg was elected and would remain a member of the *Reichstag* until the end of the Weimar Republic.

In the aftermath of the 1923 debacle for the Communist Party, the Soviet Union had begun hedging its bets and, behind the scenes, decided to give modest support to a new party, the Republican Party, founded by the journalist Karl Vetter and Carl von Ossietsky, the peace campaigner and Nobel Peace Prize winner. In the *Reichstag* elections of 1924, this party hoped to attract left-wing voters who were not committed to either the Communists or the Social Democrats.

In her biography of Münzenberg, Babette Gross relates that on one occasion during this time when she met him as he left the Soviet Embassy, he showed her a large wad of dollars that he was to give to Karl Vetter for the 'Republic'. A rare indiscretion on his part, she says. However, despite this assistance, the Republican Party made no headway at all and not long afterwards disappeared into political oblivion.

The elections gave the Communists a great boost, and the party won 62 seats out of the 472 total. However, most of those elected belonged to the hard-left faction within the Communist Party and were still opposed to what they saw as 'sham' parliamentary democracy, as Münzenberg himself had been in 1918 and 1919. On the day the new Reichstag opened, many of the Communist representatives wore black shirts and red ties and blew toy trumpets to drown out the president's opening speech, which Münzenberg considered rather childish.

In June 1924, he once again travelled to Moscow for the fifth World Congress of the Comintern, which he attended as an advisory delegate. In the foyer of the Kremlin where it was being held, the *IAH* put on an exhibition highlighting its many achievements. At the congress, the main subject of debate was again the failure of the German Revolution in 1923. There, Stalin, Zinoviev, and Kamenev would, once more, utilise the German events to attack Trotsky and his supporters, including Radek, for misreading the situation.

After the death of the Social Democratic German President Friedrich Ebert on 28 February 1925, the process to elect a new one began. The Communist Party nominated its chairman, Ernst Thälmann, as its candidate for the post, but in the first round none of the candidates obtained a clear majority. In the obligatory second round, it would have made sense for the two largest left-wing parties to have agreed on a common candidate who would then have stood a good chance of defeating the right. However, the Social Democrats and Communists could not agree on a single candidate. The dominant hard-left wing in the Communist Party leadership made it impossible to reach a compromise on the issue and lend the party's support to a Social Democratic candidate.

If the Communists and Social Democrats had united behind a single candidate in the second round the right could have been defeated, but as they did not, the door was left wide open for Hindenburg, the right-wing candidate, to become the new president.

Münzenberg, who had advocated voting for a compromise candidate, was devastated that the *KPD* had insisted on standing its own man again in the second round, even though he had no chance of winning, and thus fatally split the opposition vote. His angry and perceptive comment at the time was: 'We're helping put the reactionaries in the saddle, a monarchist as Reich's President!'.[10] His anger was directed at the dominating hard-left Fischer-Maslow faction in the party leadership. However, despite the uncompromising attitudes expressed by the hard-left, the party as a whole adopted more of a wait and see strategy and a preparedness to work with others on the left.

The increase in membership of the legally registered and 'non-partisan', but Communist-led, *Rotfrontkämpferbund* (Alliance of Red Front Fighters), established in July 1924, demonstrated that it was possible to bring together workers who were not organised in any political party. Such paramilitary organisations would become an increasingly common phenomenon on the German political scene and reflected the fact that violent confrontation and the possibility of armed struggle had not disappeared.

With the Communist and Social Democratic parties unable to agree on a common candidate in the May 1925 German presidential elections, they handed Paul von Hindenburg, the right wing candidate, victory on a plate. With Hindenburg's accession to the presidency, the years of open civil war in Germany came to a close. Münzenberg was dismayed by the consequences of this lack of unity on the left.

Once it was realised that the more Germany was impoverished, the more disgruntled the population became as a result, increasing the probability of revolution and of Germany moving ever closer to the Soviet Union – its only option for emerging from the mess it was in. The Allied Reparations Commission, urged into action by Britain and the United States, had asked the US banker, general, and diplomat, Charles Dawes to come up with a solution to Germany's economic crisis. This resulted in the setting up of the Dawes committee which elaborated a rescue plan.

As a result of the implementation of this plan in August 1924, the German economy began to rebound from the mid-1920s onwards – now funded by a large scale influx of American capital. This capital, now made available to German industry, functionally transferred the burdens of Germany's war reparations from the German government and industry to American bond investors. The Dawes Plan was also the beginning of close ties between German industry and American investment banks.

Hindenburg was able to capitalise on the recent upturn in Germany's economic situation, defuse the dangerous situation that had arisen following the French and Belgian occupation of the Ruhr, and to increase the chances of Germany being able to resume the reparation payments.

As a result of his critique of party policy, it became clear to Münzenberg that his views no longer concurred with those of the majority in the German Communist Party leadership. However, because he was still a semi-autonomous operator he could, through his good connections with the Comintern, counter his critics by asserting that his ultimate responsibility was to the Comintern and not the *KPD*. He was also at this time, according to Gross, becoming increasingly cynical as far as party politics were concerned and decided to concentrate instead on turning the *IAH* into an efficient propaganda machine for the Soviet Union and for Communist ideas as such.

In a speech he gave to *IAH* colleagues at the beginning of 1924, he said that he believed that the revolutionary period in Germany was over for the time being. In the short term, he told them, no revolutionary developments could be expected, so comrades would have to draw the correct conclusions and devote themselves patiently to day-to-day work in order to gain influence and win over the non-Communist masses. This work had to be carried out in the spirit of a united front in which the *IAH* could play a key role, one that had now been denied to the political parties. Even in those other countries where Communists were being persecuted, the *IAH* could play a positive role and work with other groups that enjoyed legal protection.

During this period, Münzenberg was also divesting himself of his responsibilities in the Soviet Union and handing back *IAH*-run undertakings to their respective local administrations there. He held on, though, to several that he considered important in terms of continuing propaganda for the Soviet Union abroad, such as film production and distribution. He saw clearly the potential of film in terms of propaganda and education, and his influence in this field would be a pioneering one.

Notes

1 At the party congress in the spring of 1924, Fischer became the leading figure in the party. Alongside Maslow, she led the German section of the Comintern, the largest next to that of the Soviet Union. At this time the party found itself in the deepest crisis since its founding and was characterised by deep ideological divisions.

At its core, the ideological split was about the reasons for the October 1923 defeat: was it because the party leadership had misread a genuinely revolutionary situation and failed to provide leadership, thus betraying the revolution, or was it the result of an adventurist attempt by hot heads in the party to bring about revolution at an unsuitable time when defeat was certain? Fischer, along with Maslow and Thälmann, was of the opinion that the party should have fought, but did not do so because 'the opportunist leadership was paralysed'. Stalin, Zinoviev, and Kamenev utilised the German events to attack Trotsky and his supporters, including Radek, in the Comintern.

In her book, *Stalin and German Communism*, Ruth Fischer combines a general and informative history of the period 1923–1944, with her own reminiscences as an active participant in the process described. She provides detailed descriptions of the development of the German Communist Party from its establishment, through the fractious infighting of the 1920s to become the largest Communist Party outside the Soviet Union, to its virtual destruction by Hitler, and its battles to survive during the late 1930s and early 1940s in the face of Hitler's success and Stalin's dictatorial control. Although strongly coloured by her own ideological position, it is nevertheless highly informative. She also throws light on the workings of the all-powerful Comintern.

She wrote the book during the early years of the Cold War, when she was living in exile in the USA and had become a vehement opponent not only of Stalin, but of the world Communist movement as a whole. It is very much stamped by that context.

The Left opposition attacked the majority united front policies pursued by Heinrich Brandler and was able to hinder its implementation largely through its dominance in the Berlin section and in Hamburg. Maslow became the theoretician of this radical opposition, Fischer the passionate propagandist. Brandler (1881–1967) was chairman of the *KPD* during the party's ill-fated 'March Action' of 1921 and the aborted uprising of 1923, for which he was held responsible by the Comintern. He was expelled from the party in December 1928.

The leitmotif of the 5th World Congress of the Comintern in 1924 and its call for the 'Bolshevisation' of the sections of the Comintern was taken up by Fischer and Maslow and utilised in their battles against the 'right'. Fischer felt no qualms about jumping on the anti-Trotsky bandwagon at this time and in attacking the policies of Rosa Luxemburg, which she described 'as a means of schooling the revolutionary elements to negate the role of the party'. (Quote from: Arkadi Maslow: *Die Zwei Russischen Revolutionen des Jahres 1917*, Berlin 1925, p. XV). And against those who tried to use Luxemburg's ideas to combat Brandler as 'trying to cure a victim of gonorrhoea by administering syphilis bacteria'.[1]

During the year 1925, in terms of determining the general course of the *KPD*, the inner-party struggles intensified. The formerly united leftist opposition split and there was increased opposition within the party as a whole to the Fischer line. These struggles were also, in part, a reflection of the struggles taking place in the Soviet Party too. The weakening of Zinoviev's position within the Comintern undoubtedly also undermined that of Fischer and Maslow. Fischer lost her position on the Comintern executive and in 1926, and she and Maslow were expelled from the party.

2 Fischer, Ruth. opus cit. p. 279.

3 France, particularly, was insisting that the Soviet Union recognise the debts incurred by the former Tsarist government.

4 McMeekin, Sean, *The Red Millionaire: A Political Biography of Willi Münzenberg, Moscow's Secret Propaganda Tsar in the West, 1917–1940*. New Haven, CT: Yale University Press, 2003.

5 Ibid. p. 145.

6 The brothers Otto and Gregor Strasser were popular figures in the Nazi Party and represented the Socialist faction. They were seen as a challenge to Hitler, and his cohorts and would be murdered in the 'Night of the Long Knives' at the end of June 1935.

7 Fischer, Ruth. opus cit. p. 321.

8 Gross, Babette, *Willi Münzenberg, eine politische Biografie* Forum Verlag Leipzig, 1991. p. 211.

9 Ruth Fischer, *Stalin and German Communism*.

10 Gross, Babette, *Willi Münzenberg*, Forum 1991. p. 243.

7

ENTREPRENEUR AND PROPAGANDIST SUPREMO

Münzenberg's business undertakings and solidarity campaigns were becoming more global and increasingly complex during the mid- to late 1920s. As his profile and influence grew, he would also be unwittingly caught in the cross-fire of the ideological battles taking place inside both the Soviet and German Communist parties.

The meeting of the Executive Committee of the Comintern in January 1924 was largely devoted to dissecting the 1923 German debacle and the failure of a German revolution to materialise. In his report, Zinoviev blamed the Social Democrats as 'the fascist wing of the working class movement', and the German Communist Party was criticised for letting a revolutionary situation slip through its fingers by inaction – this was an attempt by Zinoviev to get himself off the hook. His labelling of the Social Democrats as Fascists would resurface later in their demonisation as 'Social Fascists' under Stalin in the 1930s.

In his turn, Stalin used the Comintern debate to attack Zinoviev (as chairman of the Comintern and nominally responsible for what happened in Germany), but also Trotsky and his supporters. Radek, who had been a Trotsky supporter, remained convinced that the situation in Germany in 1923 had been a revolutionary one and that the German Communist Party together with the Comintern had failed to take advantage of it.

Vladimir Lenin's death on 21 January 1924 threw the executive's deliberations into disarray and ignited a battle within the Soviet Party leadership for a new leader to step into his shoes. It was this event that set the tone for the debates.

In the background, even before Lenin's death, but palpable for all those on the Comintern Executive Committee and in the Soviet Party leadership, was the emerging infighting over Lenin's legacy which was played out in coded form on the conference floor and behind the scenes.

Münzenberg returned to Berlin from this executive meeting and the commemorations surrounding Lenin's death quite depressed. Not only was he very conscious of the fact that he had lost a close friend and his chief protector in Moscow, but he was also unhappy about the attempt to find scapegoats in the wake of the failure of revolution in Germany and the lack of a fundamental analysis. It was clear to him that there would now be a debilitating war of succession in the Bolshevik Party.

Solidarity beyond the Soviet Union

Despite the ban on the Communist Party in Germany, imposed after the failed Hamburg uprising, the Internationale Arbeiter Hilfe (IAH) continued to expand its range of work. It had not been included in the government's ban on the Communist Party and its organisations. Münzenberg was also able to capitalise on the establishment of more friendly relations between the Soviet Union and Britain to extend its reach to the United Kingdom.

During 1924, to the consternation of many Social Democratic parties, the British Trade Union Congress (TUC) expressed interest in developing more friendly relations with Russia. The left-wing trade unionists in the TUC were hoping to be able to bring Russian trade unionists back into the European fold; on the other hand, the Soviet Union hoped to bring the British trade union movement under its own influence.

The TUC had already, during May and June of 1920, sent a delegation to visit the young Soviet Union in response to a resolution passed at the special Trades Union Congress in December 1919 calling for 'an independent and impartial inquiry into the industrial, political and economic conditions in Russia'.[1]

The second TUC visit in 1924 was prompted by an invitation from the All Russian Council of Trade Unions for a TUC delegation to 'obtain first-hand knowledge of the position in Russia'. The delegation visited during November and December. While in Moscow, it also looked at internal documents of the Comintern in an attempt to collect evidence on the authenticity (or otherwise) of the damaging 'Zinoviev Letter', which had been published by the *Daily Mail* shortly before the 1924 British general election and which was widely believed to be a forgery, but it probably played a significant role in securing Labour's electoral defeat.[2]

The Dutch trade unionist, Edo Fimmen, who was also a Christian and Social Democrat, ensured that Münzenberg's publishing house, the *Neuer Deutscher Verlag*, was given the opportunity of publishing the official report of the British delegation's visit. This detailed and illustrated report came out in 1925 under Münzenberg's imprint, but under TUC copyright.

The delegation had been given unprecedented access to life in the Soviet Union, including visits to factories and prisons, where delegates were allowed to interview imprisoned Social revolutionaries, and they were given permission to visit Georgia, where the Bolsheviks had suppressed a nationalist rebellion in the year of their visit. In May of the following year, their visit was reciprocated by a Soviet delegation visiting the TUC congress in Hull.

The first German trade union delegation visited the Soviet Union in the summer of 1925. The report of its visit titled 'What did 58 German workers see in Russia?' was also published by Münzenberg in an edition of 100,000 and sold out immediately.

In other parts of the world, those leading strikes and liberation struggles were calling on the *IAH* for help and support. Its reputation had spread. In China, in May 1925, a large strike of textile workers against the Japanese factory owners erupted and was accompanied by an upsurge of nationalist fervour. The Soviet Union offered its help to General Chiang Kai-Shek and his nationalist Kuomintang forces in their struggle against the Japanese occupiers and British colonialists. Münzenberg was tasked with coordinating the establishment of a committee to support the Chinese national liberation struggle. He set up the 'Hands Off China' campaign and persuaded leading figures in Britain from the Labour Party to sign a worldwide appeal to support the Chinese workers in their struggle.

This was followed by a second campaign, 'Against the Cruelties in Syria' in support of a renewed liberation struggle that had broken out in Syria and Libya against the French mandatory occupation. It had taken off in the wake of a revolt instigated by the Druze minority in 1925. That same year, the *IAH* launched its 'Help for the Starving of Ireland' campaign (see below).

Alongside the central role of the *IAH* in rallying support and providing aid for the Soviet Union, as well as organising solidarity on behalf of China, Syria, and Ireland, Münzenberg and the *IAH* also waged many other seemingly minor campaigns of solidarity and support for those struggling in other parts of the world.

The Irish potato harvests in 1923 and 1924 had been disastrous. An internal British government memo in November 1924 painted a grim picture of the level of deprivation in the country: 'In Industrial and Commercial occupations some 47,000 are unemployed, In Agriculture probably 40,000. Business is languishing; bank deposits are diminishing...'[3] Towards the close of 1924, hundreds of thousands in the most congested districts of the country were in dire need. 75 per cent of the people had had no potatoes – their chief diet – for the previous two months, and there were no jobs for those seeking work. The famine was said to be as bad as the devastating one of 1847.

In 1925, the *IAH* launched its 'Help for the Starving of Ireland' campaign, which was organised by its British section. On this campaign, Münzenberg, through his liaison officer, Louis Gibarti, co-operated closely with Ellen Wilkinson MP, and the British section of the *IAH* organised a massive rally in Battersea Town Hall in support of Ireland and was able to raise considerable amounts of money. The Soviet Communist Party newspaper, *Pravda*, also gave the famine prominent coverage. It was as if Münzenberg were continuously scanning the globe for situations where he could become involved and offer help.

Only a year later, in 1926, the organisation became involved in providing support for the striking workers during Britain's General Strike. On this occasion, Russian trade unions offered the TUC £72,000 as a gesture of 'fraternal solidarity', but the offer was rejected. After the TUC called off the strike, leaving the miners to fight on alone, Münzenberg set up a temporary office in Paris to help raise the political profile of the strike and provide much needed support for the miners.

In Germany, too, rallies in solidarity with the striking British miners were held and several were addressed by Münzenberg together with the legendary miners' leader, A.J. Cook. The *IAH*, in co-operation with the British Communist Party, was able to collect a substantial sum in aid of the striking miners, as well as funnel Soviet financial aid to them. All this infuriated the Labour Party's right-wing leadership who called it 'blatant interference in the internal affairs' of the country.

In September 1931, following the Japanese invasion of Manchuria, Chinese Communists declared the establishment of a Soviet state covering the areas under their control, and Münzenberg immediately set up a new international 'Help China Committee' with support from leading European political and cultural figures.

Edo Fimmen also played a key role in assisting Münzenberg in his work on behalf of the Soviet Union and in cementing contacts with trade unions in other countries through his many connections. He was very sympathetic to the Soviet Union, believing that it would eventually become a genuine Socialist democracy. He and Münzenberg had very early on developed an intimate friendship, and when Fimmen visited Berlin, the two would retire alone to a small restaurant and wine bar in the *Dorotheen Strasse* to enjoy a hearty meal and animated conversation.

Such fruitful collaboration between Communists and Social Democrats was not viewed positively by the more sectarian elements in the Comintern and the German Party, and it came in for some sharp criticism. Ruth Fischer, whose leadership tenure in the Communist Party was by 1926 drawing to a close, called it an attempt to cosy up to the Ramsay MacDonald government.

Many writers on the subject have attempted to portray the solidarity work carried out by the Soviet Union, largely through Münzenberg's *IAH* organisation, as a cynical ploy to promote the Communist cause and the profile of the Soviet Union itself.

In his seminal book, *The International Workers' Relief, Communism, and Transnational Solidarity: Willi Münzenberg in Weimar Germany*, Kasper Braskén argues, however, that the Communist movement of the interwar period, on the contrary, 'extensively articulated solidarity as a means of uniting everyone who supported the struggle of the working class in the spirit of classic Marxist workers' solidarity, and as part of a German counter-cultural workers movement'.[4] He maintains that the work carried out by Münzenberg through the *Arbeiterhilfe (IAH)* was much more than simply a cover for propping up the Soviet Union.

According to the Norwegian academic Steinar Stjernø,[5] who has written extensively about the history of European solidarity movements, the main difference between the Leninist and Social Democratic interpretation of solidarity at the time was that the latter strove to broaden the concept, to make it more inclusive, while Lenin and his followers stressed the importance of a purely working-class solidarity, which made it restrictive. He also stated that the term 'solidarity' was not used at all by the Comintern at the time, and that, although it embraced the notion of 'proletarian internationalism', it was difficult, if not impossible, to distinguish this from loyalty to the Soviet Union. He adds that the Comintern did not employ the language of solidarity even within the context of anti-colonialism and anti-imperialism.

One of the central aims of Braskén's study, was to 'reveal Münzenberg's, often forgotten, but influential role in the shaping of transnational solidarity movements during the inter-war years', through the *IAH*. In many ways, Münzenberg was indeed a pioneer and forerunner of future solidarity organisations and NGOs. He actively encouraged workers to think in global terms rather than in purely national ones and, in this way, gave expression to the Marxist concept of workers united beyond national borders. He says that with the death of Münzenberg and the demise of his organisations, international solidarity on such a scale ceased. In this, he is probably correct.

In 1925, a large campaign was launched in Germany to break the power of the Prussian landed aristocracy (the *Junkers*), who had played such a dominant role in Germany's politics and provided the manpower for the powerful military officer caste. Although the campaign had widespread support in the country to begin with, neither the Communist Party nor the Social Democratic Party would give it their official backing. Münzenberg, though, threw his weight behind it immediately. The campaign called for a referendum on the expropriation without compensation of the Prussian aristocracy. It was a popular attempt to complete the unfinished business of the 1918 revolution and rid the country of the remnants of its anachronistic feudal and military elite who were still dominant.

The campaign was led by the German section of the League for Human Rights. The renowned statistician Robert René Kuczynski was a prominent member of the league and won Münzenberg's collaboration in helping to make the campaign a highly effective one.

Münzenberg had already worked closely with Kuczynski in 1923. The latter was a keen supporter of *IAH* and had been sent by Münzenberg to France where his task had been to collect money for those starving in Germany in the immediate aftermath of the war and as a result of the hyperinflation the country had been suffering. It was Kuczynski's idea to do this, as he felt it would have great propaganda value, and Münzenberg was grateful to him for the tip.

The campaign in 1925 to expropriate the Junkers soon had widespread support among humanist, left-wing, and liberal organisations, even though the *KPD* remained equivocal. It was, though, with Münzenberg's urging, eventually persuaded to support the campaign, and once the *SPD* saw that the Communists appeared to be taking the initiative out of their hands, they also decided to pledge full support.

FIGURE 7.1 Poster for the 1925 campaign to expropriate the Prussian landed aristocracy (Image courtesy of German Federal Archives.)

FIGURE 7.2 May title page of *Der Kämpfer* newspaper Berlin. Designer anonymous

The eventual vote did not reach the required hurdle of 50 per cent of the electorate to ensure full legislative implementation, but the campaign itself was a huge success, with a majority of voters opting for expropriation. It demonstrated what support could be garnered when the two large working-class parties worked together towards a common goal. It was also the first and last time the two parties would co-operate with each other successfully.

Münzenberg played his part by publishing the brochure 'Not a Penny for the Aristocrats' and a special issue of the Workers' Illustrated Newspaper (*Arbeiter Illustrierte Zeitung* or *AIZ*) in support of the campaign. The more rational elements within the leadership of the *KPD* attempted to utilise this example of successful co-operation with the *SPD* in order to argue for a change in the party's policy, but they were unsuccessful.

One would have imagined that Münzenberg had enough on his plate with his responsibilities on behalf of the Comintern and the party, but after the national elections, he now found himself elected to the Reichstag for the constituency of Hessen-Nassau, so he had even more. These multiple responsibilities certainly left him little time for himself.

As a member of the German Parliament, in 1926, Münzenberg was appointed to sit on a government committee to investigate several particularly barbaric lynch-mob killings carried out by right-wing thugs, members of the *Blücherbund*. Although one of the gang had been sentenced and imprisoned, he was then helped by insiders to escape. The investigation had been obstructed by the military elite in the country and the Bavarian government, which clearly sympathised with the perpetrators. In his report on the case, Münzenberg argued that such right-wing groups were actively conspiring to undermine the republic and restore the monarchy in Germany and called for measures to be taken against them. Unsurprisingly, no action was taken. In that same year, 1925, he also spent time in Budapest to give support to the Communist leader Matyas Rakosi who was on trial for his life. He helped wage the successful campaign for his release from jail.

With the implementation of the Soviet Union's first five-year plan, between 1928 and 1933, a momentous industrialisation of the country was set in motion, and it still desperately needed foreign imports of machine tools and industrial plant. Germany had traditionally been one of Russia's main trading partners for the supply of such goods, but since the establishment of the Soviet Union, the country's former suppliers now got cold feet. They worried that the Soviet Union would be unable to pay for such imports.

The Soviet Union, from the outset, had been boycotted by many nations in terms of trade, and its currency was considered unstable or worthless, so in order to obtain the much needed imports from abroad, it was forced to pay for virtually everything upfront in valuta (hard currency) or gold.

Münzenberg became a key figure in helping the Soviet Union facilitate better trading relations. And he was not averse to using capitalist methods to achieve his aims in this sphere.

To make it possible for the Soviet Union to pay for the goods it needed, a consortium of banks had to be persuaded to underwrite the sums involved by issuing trade bills or *Russenwechsel* as collateral. Once this system was established, the bills became objects of much speculation and were traded at a discount of up to 30 per cent, as potential punters felt the stability and longevity of the Soviet Union was precarious and did not trust their paper value.

Münzenberg laughed about the 'timidity of the bourgeoisie' and bought up quantities of such bonds with the ready cash he had available in *IAH* coffers. However, because the Soviet Union did not have enough hard currency at the time to support the bond issue, it had to fly-in gold bullion to Berlin.

With the numerous business interests Münzenberg had been setting up under the umbrella of the *IAH*, and his readiness to take on new challenges, he had developed a reputation as someone one could go to for financial help. Friends and acquaintances were regularly trying to win his support for their own various pet projects and business ideas. If he thought they were sound and potentially ideologically useful, he would rarely turn them away. He clearly had ready access to financial resources, not only from the Comintern itself, but also from those *IAH* businesses that were successful and were showing good returns.

Already during 1924 and 1925, he ensured the financial means to establish a 'Red' co-operative association in Freiburg and a stocking-making company in Apolda; he supported a comrade in Braunschweig who was developing a new accounting machine, and in Ruhla, the local party group was given support to build a children's home, which remained only half built as a result of the economic depression and inner-party problems.

In 1932, one of the last business projects in which he became directly involved was the takeover of a Berlin cigarette factory whose owner sympathised with the *KPD*. Only a short time previously, the Nazis had persuaded a Dresden cigarette company to produce a cigarette brand called 'The Drummer' and to include cigarette cards in the packets featuring portraits of Nazi bigwigs. Münzenberg felt he could go one better and produce more attractive cards.

Despite the enormous contribution he and the *IAH* had made in the period between 1921 and 1928 in terms of gathering worldwide support for the Soviet Union in both material and propaganda terms and in supporting various other struggles, the political winds were about to veer in another direction. The policy of collaborating with other left-wing and progressive forces, of establishing broad alliances, would now, once again, be viewed as compromising with the enemy.

At the sixth World Congress of the Comintern in July/August 1928, Münzenberg and the *IAH* came under fire from a strong faction within the Comintern leadership for the first time. In the language of the time, such 'bipartisan' organisations as his were deemed opportunistic, reformist, and aberrantly quasi-Menshevik. In German Communist Party circles there was also a strong faction with an aversion to Münzenberg's role. In his defence, he argued that his aim was, '... to interest those millions of apathetic and indifferent workers, who take no part in political life, who are not interested in the economic and cultural struggle of the proletariat, who simply have no ear for the propaganda of the Communist Party'. Early on he had realised only too well that it was pointless preaching solely to the converted.

At that sixth congress, it was declared unequivocally, for the first time, that Social Democracy was the main enemy of the Communist movement. Until the foundation of Communist parties, the Social Democratic parties had been the sole political representatives of the working class. Since that time, they had become the chief competitor in the struggle for the allegiance of working people. The fact that the leaderships of most Social Democratic parties had also revealed a visceral hatred of the Communists and were not averse to collaboration with the capitalist class to block revolutionary change certainly did not help surmount the mutual mistrust and hatred.

With the change in the Comintern's political line of attack and its labelling of Social Democrats as 'Social Fascists', Münzenberg's freedom of manoeuvre from then on would become severely restricted, particularly in those areas of work, which of necessity, involved collaboration with Social Democrats and others outside the Communist orbit. However, he refused to let this new policy and any personal criticism trammel him, but instead came up with ever more creative initiatives.

From 1930 onwards, he had found himself increasingly forced to adopt a defensive position vis à vis the party leadership, particularly in connection with the editorial line of his paper *Welt am Abend* (World in the Evening). As a result of the new Comintern line, the party leadership had demanded that the editor go on the attack against the Social Democrats, but Münzenberg was unwilling to go down that road. He and his editorial team were more concerned with informing readers of the dangers posed by the rise of the Nazis. They also, quite rightly, viewed the paper as one addressed to the broader left and not as an organ of the party.

When there were arguments in the editorial office over the paper's headlines, Münzenberg would be called by telephone and asked to act as mediator. In the end, though, he did capitulate to the party's demand for a new editor and sacked the incumbent, Otto Heller, but tried to soften the blow by organising a tour of the Soviet Union for him and later publishing the fascinating book he wrote about his experiences.

Following the success of the *SPD* in the 1928 elections to the Reichstag, an amnesty for political prisoners was declared. Among those released was the maverick Communist Max Hölz, who had been given a life sentence in May 1921. He was a militant who had organised a band of around 50 men equipped with arms and bicycles to try and free those detained as a result of the Kapp Putsch. His case became a cause célèbre, and Münzenberg conducted a long campaign for his release.

In 1925, Münzenberg had also been asked for his help in connection with the so-called Cheka Trial that took place during February and April at the supreme court in Leipzig. The accused comprised a group of German Communists and the Soviet General Peter Alexander Skoblewsky (real name, Woldemar Rose) who, together with other Soviet officers, had been charged with helping to establish an illegal paramilitary organisation of the Communist Party in Germany. This illegal organisation had, it appeared, executed one of its own collaborators who had been informing the police about the Communist Party's secret plans. To compound the situation, another leading member of this paramilitary organisation decided to spill the beans to the police. The evidence appeared incontrovertible. They all faced the death penalty for high treason.

During the trial, Münzenberg published an exposé written by one of the defence lawyers which alleged legal inconsistencies and technical errors in the conduct of the trial. Nevertheless, three of the accused were condemned to death, 13 others were sentenced to imprisonment for terms varying between six months and 15 years for murder and conspiracy to overthrow the German Republic.

Once the death sentences had been announced, Münzenberg published a brochure, 'Stop a Triple Judicial Murder', in which he mentioned the many solidarity rallies he had been able to organise, as well as the support he had garnered from leading public figures. He hoped to initiate a wave of mass protests by working-class organisations against the imposition of the death penalty.

By this time, the inflationary chaos in the country had receded and, with the return of stability, many were more prepared to accept the arguments put forward by Münzenberg. On top of that, the German government was not particularly interested in seeing this 'show trial' inflated into an incendiary diplomatic incident. The death sentences were not carried out and Skoblevski was later exchanged for a number of imprisoned students in Russia. The other accused were amnestied several years later.

Willi and Babette – more than a couple

Babette Gross was first introduced to the *IAH* and to Willi Münzenberg in 1922 by her then husband, the Austrian writer Fritz Gross, who also worked for the *IAH* between the years 1922–1923. Her marriage to Fritz Gross was at this time breaking down, and it was not very long after their first meeting that Babette and Willi Münzenberg began establishing a relationship that would become unbreakable and last until his death. She, though, would become more than a loyal companion for him, she became a mainstay of his organisation and a creative spirit in her own right.

Arthur Koestler described Babette, in the 1930s, as 'tall and distinguished-looking, with a still beautiful face, and efficient in a quiet, polite way … they [she and Münzenberg] gave the impression of a perfectly matched couple'.[6] She met Willi while working in the Berlin offices of the *IAH*, and although they never married, became inseparable.

In the biography she wrote of Münzenberg, she places herself very much in the background, and the reader could think she was merely his companion. There is little doubt, however, that she became an important figure, particularly in Münzenberg's publishing world.

FIGURE 7.3 Willi Münzenberg and Babette Gross, his common-law wife, comrade, and business colleague (By kind permission of the Gross family.)

After she had moved to Berlin with her sister, she very soon found work with the Münzenberg concern. She was bright and capable and soon rose to become co-director of Münzenberg's *Neuer Deutscher Verlag* publishing house, which he had taken over in 1923. She also ran the *Universum Bücherei* (a book publishing and trading arm of the *IAH*) in Switzerland from 1933, and later, in Paris, she would become director of his publishing company *Éditions du Carrefour*. She acted not simply as his loyal lieutenant, but was an active and influential force in her own right.

Babette's son Peter, in his childhood reminiscences, writes that 'Willi and my mother were co-directors of *Neuer Deutscher Verlag*. As commercial manager, she controlled the finances, including money, often in US dollars, which passed between the Comintern and the *Neuer Deutscher Verlag*. Münzenberg's newspapers and illustrated weeklies mostly lost money and were subsidised by the Russians. But other activities like the Universum Library and Metropol, the distributors of Russian films, did make money'.[7] After the war, she was a co-founder of the well-known (West-) German newspaper, the *Frankfurter Allgemeine Zeitung*.

Babette Gross, née Thüring, was the eldest daughter of a lower middle-class Potsdam family. She was born in 1898 and had two sisters, Margarete (known as Grete) and Gertrude (known as Trude), as well as two brothers, Heinrich and Hans. Her mother, Else Merten, married Heinrich Thüring in 1898. He was a master brewer devoted to all things Prussian and was a rather authoritarian figure. He broke off relations with Babette and Margarete in 1920 after they both took Communists as partners.

Both Babette and Margarete experienced the turmoil of the First World War, the November Revolution, and the bloody birth of the Weimar Republic. After taking her school certificate, her headmistress recommended her to the Kaiser's family as governess to one of the Kaiser's grandchildren. She later, in 1919, became a qualified teacher, but in 1920, she and her sister moved to Berlin where both their lives would change radically.

At this time, they were still only in their early twenties and were captivated by the radical and Bohemian atmosphere of the pulsating city of Berlin. There, they both joined the Communist Party and became partners of leading Communists. Margarete, who was three years younger, started working in the *KPD* headquarters, where in 1929, she met Heinz Neumann, a leading and charismatic figure in the party, who was also only in his twenties. They fell in love and became inseparable from then on, until he was executed in 1938 following one of Joseph Stalin's purges. After his death, Margarete was also imprisoned in the Soviet Union for three years, before being handed over to Hitler's Gestapo by the Soviet authorities and incarcerated during the war years in Ravensbrück, a Nazi concentration camp for women. She survived both these ordeals and the war, living until 1989 in West Germany.[8]

With the rise in the number of employees, it became impossible for Münzenberg to forge a special relationship with every single employee, but Gross in her biography writes that he was, nevertheless, able to inspire almost everyone to devote their full energy and commitment to the undertaking without his having to play the boss. They invariably felt they were part of something special and belonged to a kind of family firm. There is little doubt that she felt the same.

According to her, while many of the younger employees tended to worship him as the 'great leader', older colleagues took a more sober attitude. One of them she quotes said that he felt Münzenberg had a strong inferiority complex and that was why he needed to seek continuous reassurance, and it was this that drove him to work as hard as he did and to achieve what he did. Another felt that he had something of that old Lutheran reformatory zeal about him. It was also said of him that he never felt at ease in bourgeois or intellectual circles, preferring working-class surroundings, where he could relax and unwind. But in general, he maintained a certain distance from people and few were able to get really close to him. In her biography, Gross makes no comment about the truth or otherwise of these observations.[9] Even with her, though, he appeared to have kept many of his inner thoughts and some of his activities hidden or tightly guarded.

Peter Gross wrote that, 'The higher-up comrades in the German Communist Party did not trust each other. But those in the inner circle around Münzenberg did, addressed each other and Münzenberg using the *du* form instead of the formal *Sie*, and most stayed with him through his rise and fall'.[10]

As a result of his Comintern responsibilities, necessitating a considerable amount of travelling and networking, Münzenberg had indeed developed a different lifestyle from many of his comrades. And, unlike several of those in the party leadership, he refused to make concessions in his personal life simply to placate such critics. He refused to change his behaviour in order to 'prove' his proletarian credentials. Previous biographers, like Koch and McMeekin, portray him unfairly as a vain hypocrite and as someone who hungered after a luxurious life. In fact, he, as well as those of his employees who were party members, were remunerated according to party salary scales. Only non-party employees were paid according to market norms. Münzenberg never had his own bank account nor did he personally possess stocks and shares. His lifestyle was hardly that of a millionaire, even if his expenses were generous.

He could, though, hardly be accused of living a life of leisure or of excess. He worked exceedingly long and uncertain hours; almost every minute of the day was devoted to the political struggle. His purchase, at the height of his career, of an open-topped Chevrolet car for the office and later a large Lincoln sedan, so that he could move around the country more easily and quickly, was, unsurprisingly, seen by some of his enemies as a sign of decadence and unnecessary luxury. Peter Gross, in his reminiscences, refers significantly to the Lincoln as 'the office car'.

Münzenberg himself never learnt to drive, so he was totally reliant on his chauffeur Emil Berger[11] to ferry him about. He also thought nothing of taking taxis or horse-drawn cabs. Such overt examples of a 'bourgeois' lifestyle would have played into the hands of his puritanical critics. Gross, in her reminiscences, gives no indication that he or indeed she herself had a hankering after 'bourgeois' luxury. Like so many of those at the time who devoted their lives to the Communist movement, their chief pleasure and satisfaction no doubt came out of the struggle and from the success of their campaigns.

Neither Münzenberg nor Gross owned luxurious mansions nor did they accumulate personal wealth or spend lavishly on personal items. He continued to live modestly, and the little pure leisure time he managed to steal for himself was spent with books or visiting the theatre or cinema. He could also spend time convivially with friends and hanging out with left-wing artists in their Bohemian cafes. He loved Berlin's cultural life during those hectic 1920s – the theatres performed radical plays, the artists satirised the decadence, and the cabarets lampooned the rigidly conservative social forces.

Münzenberg was one of those obsessional workers who found it almost impossible to switch off and relax. In her biography, Gross relates how she had to virtually force him to take a holiday. Although he had never expressed a desire to holiday in the USSR, Babette managed to persuade him in the autumn of 1929 to take a short holiday with other members of the IAH in the south of the country, on the Black Sea, organised by their Moscow office. It was billed as a lecture tour.

The climax of the trip, she relates, was an excursion which took in Tiflis, across the Caucasus to Vladikavkaz. The countryside was of an unapproachable beauty. The Terek, whose praises were sung by Pushkin, forged its foamy course through the bizarre gorges.

'Whenever we went downhill, the Georgian driver turned off his engine to save petrol, and we proceeded at breakneck speed into the valley. We stopped at an old inn and roasted our shashliks over a wood fire.

Münzenberg was relaxed and cheerful. For the duration of this journey, Moscow Berlin and the rest of the world with their conflicts and complications had disappeared for us'.[12]

Münzenberg's great love, though, was wandering in the countryside, where he could really unwind. Whenever he could grab a day or two, he would return to his beloved Thuringia for a few days, wandering through the forests and in the mountains, where he was as happy as a sand-boy, the world's cares falling from his shoulders for a few days.

Peter Gross describes one of these trips: 'We arrived in the mountains, the Brocken road was closed by snow. Over supper in a pub in Wernegerode, Emil and Willi told me wonderful stories about fairies, witches, dwarfs, monks, princesses and strange creatures. When I fell asleep they played Skat. Emil appears in Münzenberg biographies as both chauffeur and bodyguard. To my mother and Münzenberg he was more like a younger brother—and an uncle to me and later to my own family'.[13]

His big weakness – or was it his strength? – was that he was unable to really switch off; he braced himself to push to the limit. Was he vain? Well, he probably had a streak of vanity as many of us do, but he was able to channel that to greater purpose. He and Babette devoted their lives to communism and the Soviet Union, which they saw as representing a utopia under construction, until their growing disillusion with and eventual rejection of Stalin's distortion and betrayal of that ideal. Although, as Babette says in the prologue to her biography, because of her middle-class background and temperament, she always felt something of an outsider and was unable to accept the idea of total self-sacrifice for the cause as Münzenberg appeared to do.

Animosity towards Münzenberg by individuals within the Communist Party had tended to increase as the success of the IAH venture became ever more apparent. Such attitudes were not based on ideological differences alone, though, but also on his perceived 'non-proletarian' lifestyle and his autonomous role in a quasi-parallel political organisation. He appeared to have the enviable freedom from party discipline and could afford to remain somewhat aloof when it came to party squabbles.

Münzenberg was able to pack more into his own life than several average individuals together could achieve. His interests, activities, and energies appeared to be inexhaustible. He was not only running the *IAH* and its associated businesses, but had Comintern and party responsibilities, as well as his work as a member of the Reichstag to carry out. The incredible expansion of his undertakings during the 1920s meant that he required a growing number of staff. He did not preoccupy himself with technical details and avoided becoming involved in day-to-day decision-making on the ground, preferring a more strategic role. Fortunately, he did have the vital ability of being able to delegate responsibility, but he expected results; laziness and inertia were anathema to him.

Münzenberg's 'inner circle' of close collaborators was small and, apart from his partner Babette Gross, consisted essentially of Otto Katz, Louis Gibarti, Emil, his driver, and Jupp, his bodyguard and odd-job man. Katz, his right-hand man, and Münzenberg complemented each other perfectly: Münzenberg was the doer, the man with ideas, while Katz was the cultured and capable journalist who could speak four languages and was able to establish and nurture the necessary international contacts. He was invariably elegantly dressed and had a genuine charm which undoubtedly helped him move easily in sophisticated circles. He also appeared to have had a ready supply of cash to finance his many trips abroad on behalf of the *IAH*. Münzenberg was monolingual, speaking only German, and his writing ability was commensurate with the less than basic education he had received; Koestler maintained, rather patronisingly and exaggeratingly, that he 'couldn't write a single coherent paragraph'.

Katz and Gibarti became Münzenberg's invisible 'roving ambassadors'. When Arthur Koestler was arrested by Franco forces in Spain while reporting on the civil war, Katz unleashed a vigorous campaign for his release. Alongside Katz, Gibarti was Münzenberg's most trusted comrade. He was a very capable organiser and, like Katz, spoke several European languages, but inexplicably is not mentioned by Koestler as a close collaborator.[14]

The few descriptions and comments we have been bequeathed by Münzenberg's contemporaries provide us with only a sketchy portrait of the individual behind the political figure. One of these is a short, but graphic account given by Arthur Koestler in the first volume of his own biography:[15]

> My first meeting with Willy Münzenberg made a strong impression on me. I became deeply attached to him – an attachment which lasted until he was assassinated in 1940... When I met him he was forty-four – a shortish, squat, heavy-boned man with powerful shoulders, who gave the impression that bumping against him would be like colliding with a steam-roller. His face had the forceful simplicity of a wood-cut, but there was a basic friendliness about it. His broad, cosy Thuringian dialect, and his simple, direct manner

further softened the powerful impact of his personality. He was a fiery, demagogical and irresistible public speaker, and a born leader of men. Though without a trace of pompousness or arrogance, his person emanated such authority that I have seen socialist Cabinet Ministers, hard-boiled bankers, and Austrian dukes behave like schoolboys in his presence ... his collaborators were devoted to him, the girl comrades worshipped him ...'. Koestler goes on to describe his having a 'fertile mind, brimming with ideas'. 'Everyone called him "Willi" and spoke to him using the intimate address of "Du", rarely formerly, by his surname.

This assessment of Münzenberg was written by Koestler after he had become disillusioned with communism, so it cannot be suggested that he was still mesmerised by all things Communist and naively gave Münzenberg a halo. He resigned from his job with the Münzenberg organisation shortly after the Spanish Civil War, before drifting rapidly away from his erstwhile Communist beliefs.

The widow of the executed leader of the Munich Soviet, Meyer-Leviné, also penned a succinct description of Münzenberg in her own reminiscences:[16]

> 'I first met Münzenberg in the summer of 1919', she writes, 'while recuperating in a Black Forest spa from an illness after Munich. He came to hold a meeting in the nearby industrial town (Schwenningen) embracing some 10,000 well organised workers, chiefly members of the SPD and USPD.
>
> Münzenberg was short, slender and boyish looking, but bristling with energy and the self confidence of a man who knows his own powers. He considered me first of all for my publicity value. We had hardly exchanged a few words before he exclaimed excitedly: "I will announce on the posters that the widow of Leviné will be in the audience."
>
> "Don't, I warned, or I shall not come at all". ...
>
> His brilliant speech erased the unpleasant interludes. He became for me the man with the power to carry on the great work. To him I was a useful propaganda object – sufficient grounds for a good friendship.
>
> The great publicity genius was not discouraged by my refusal to play my part in the small town. He would make more tempting offers. He planned a tour all over the country, which he believed could be extended outside Germany, with me as the star attraction. He thought it all out: "What a sensation! We might even be invited to America – we would become world famous celebrities." Of course, the great orator did not need my help. My presence was only to serve as a living monument to a tragic event. We were to cash in on my grief. But he knew no limits and it took him quite a while to become reconciled to my refusal. He meant so well, and perhaps also expected a prize for himself.'

Ruth Fischer, one of his most vehement critics, said of him:[17]

> Already in this early period (1914 to the early twenties) could be seen
> something of his extraordinary talent for mass propaganda which would
> later come to full fruition. Already before the war, even if still clumsily, he
> made political theatre in the service of propaganda, his "proletarian the-
> atre" was, with all its drama, in which it transformed the editorials and dry
> lectures, no less unyieldingly class conscious. In order to win over young
> girls to the movement, he organised, for instance, a meeting with the
> topic: "Who should a working-class girl marry?" Many came to hear the
> talk, but as he spoke only about socialist principles, half the audience fled.
> Still, in a period when girls joining political organisations was unusual,
> Münzenberg managed to persuade more girls to join the youth movement
> than any other organiser.

In a short prologue to her biography of Münzenberg, Babette Gross explains why
she was motivated to write about this man she fell in love with and to whom she
remained true and loyal until they were forced to part by the Nazi invasion of
France, a parting that became a final leave-taking with Münzenberg's death in 1940:

> Among the many actors on the political stage during the twenties and
> thirties … Münzenberg was undoubtedly one of the most controversial.
> Who was this rather unremarkable man of medium height, nervy and
> with untameable energy, a man possessed, with his dark – at first glance
> gentle but then powerfully captivating – eyes and thick mop of perma-
> nently unruly, dark-brown hair? Was he an adventurer for whom the ends
> justified any means in order to satisfy his own lust for power, or a political
> leader whose fate denied him the fulfilment of his hopes and dreams?

She goes on to say that at some time or other all these contradictory judgements
have been made about Münzenberg and that both his enemies as well as his comrades have puzzled over what sort of man he really was.

In February 1933, the year she and Münzenberg were forced to flee the country,
the Nazi Brown Shirts raided their flat in Berlin and all their private letters and
photo albums were taken and have to date not been recovered, so we are unlikely
to gain more insight into the personal relationship between the two of them.

Notes

1 https://warwick.ac.uk/services/library/mrc/explorefurther/digital/russia/tuc/.
   Accessed date: July 2019.
2 Ibid.
3 An internal Irish government memo of November1924.

4 Braskén, Kaspar, *The International Workers' Relief, Communism, and Transnational Solidarity – Willi Münzenberg in Weimar Germany*, Palgrave Macmillan, 2015. pp. 233/234.

5 Stjernø, Steinar, *Solidarity in Europe – The History of an Idea*, Cambridge University Press, 2005.

6 Koestler, Arthur, *The Invisible Writing: The Second Volume of an Autobiography, 1932– 1940*, Collins with Hamish Hamilton, London, 1954.

7 Gross, Peter, 'Memories of Willi Münzenberg,' *Quadrant* 54, no. 4 (2010), pp. 83–87.

8 Margarete Buber-Neumann, *Under Two Dictators – Prisoner of Stalin and Hitler*, Pimlico Press, 2009.

9 Gross, Babette, *Willi Münzenberg – Eine Politische Biografie*, Forum Verlag Leipzig, 1991, p. 262.

10 Gross, Peter, 'Memoirs of Willi Münzenberg', *Quadrant Magazine* 54, No. 4, 2010, opus cit. p. 83.

'Emil Berger came to work for the *IAH* after living in Britain for three years as a prisoner-of-war. Following three happy years on a farm in Essex, he came back to finish his training as a mechanic in Berlin. He joined the Communist Party and Münzenberg's *IAH* in 1924. In 1928, he met "Hannchen" (Johanna Engel), who had just started as telephonist in the *IAH* office in 48 Wilhelmstrasse. She was 18.

After fleeing the Nazis together with Münzenberg and Babette, and living in Paris, in 1936, he volunteered to fight in Spain and, after undergoing training in the Soviet Union in 1935, he went to Barcelona and fought as a driver-commander of a Russian tank. He was injured and lost an eye in the only tank battle of that war. In the normal course of events, he would have been repatriated back to the Soviet Union with the other Russian ex-international-brigadiers, but Münzenberg, though his contacts with the Republican Spanish government managed to get him repatriated to France. Emil left Marseilles in July 1940 for Algiers and joined by Babette Gross and Else Lange in Mexico in 1942. He returned to West Germany in 1954 and finally married his girlfriend Hannchen after she left East Berlin. If Willi had been interned with Emil and Hans Schulz, he probably would have survived the war'.

11 Gross, Babette, *Willi Münzenberg*, Forum Verlag Leipzig, 1991, pp. 312–314.

12 Gross, Peter, opus cit. p. 83.

13 Münzenberg's chauffeur, Emil Berger, was much more than an employee as revealed by Babettte's son Peter Gross in his '*Memories of Willi Münzenberg*' 'Münzenberg's chauffeur, Emil Berger (1897–1973) came from a Berlin working-class family, served in the First World War, and was taken prisoner by the British in 1916.'

14 The Hungarian Laszlo or Ladislas Dobos, better known as Louis Giberti or Gibarti was viewed as 'a smooth operator' and was intimately connected to Münzenberg.

In 1913, he studied political science in Oxford for three months. In 1919, he went to Vienna and opened the *Neue Europa* press office there. While in Vienna, he met the Norwegian Fridtjof Nansen (In 1922 Nansen was awarded the Nobel Peace Prize for his work on behalf of the displaced victims of the First World War and related conflicts), who was working for famine relief in Russia. He invited Gibarti to take part in the founding conference of the IAH. As he spoke a number of languages, in 1921, he was made international secretary of the IAH, a post he held until 1927. In this capacity, Münzenberg sent him as a liaison person to many other countries. Münzenberg also tasked him with setting up the League against Imperialism and Colonial Oppression. At its Brussels congress, he was elected as international secretary. He resigned from the league in 1929 to take up work with the IAH in the USA and helped establish the US branch. In 1933, he was active in the organisation of the League against War and Fascism and was elected general secretary. In 1933, he fled to France and joined Münzenberg there and continued collaborating with him on writing and publishing anti-Fascist materials. He was a key figure helping set up the Marley Committee against the Hitler terror and the subsequent counter Reichstag

Trial, held in London. In this connection, he travelled to the USA and was able to enlist the help of the renowned US barrister Clarence Darrow, among other lawyers. During this period, he was editor of the *Volksecho*, the successor of *Der Arbeiter*, a Communist newspaper. He also represented Münzenberg's Weltfilm GmbH in the USA. In 1936, he also helped set up the Medical Bureau of American Friends of Spanish Democracy. When Münzenberg was expelled from the KPD in 1938, Gibarti also left the party after composing a letter protesting about Münzenberg's expulsion.

While some of the active individuals in the Comintern left a trail of documents, compiled and categorised in personal files, Gibarti's file consists only of half a page (RGASPI 495/205/6048: Louis Gibarti (LUIZ GIBARTI), which fails to give any substantial evidence or clue about his role or the contributions he made in various Communist movements or activities during the 1920s–1930s. Ironically, the sparse content in Gibarti's personal file in the Comintern archive stands in stark contrast with his personal file, located in the British National Archives at Kew.

Gibarti played a significant role in shaping the outcome of the League against Imperialism and the anti-war movement (the Amsterdam Congress in August, 1932), to mention just two examples. In 1941, the political police in Madrid arrested Gibarti 'while trying to cross illegally to Spain', and he spent 27 months in Spanish prisons and camps. After the Second World War, Gibarti held a position in UNESCO in Paris, contributing articles to the *Tribune des Nations*. After his break with the Comintern and once the war was over, he became an informant for the FBI in connection with the 'Communist spectre' beginning to haunt the USA as the Cold War unfolded, and he was almost certainly the informant (Newark Confidential Informant cited in the FBI's Einstein file). In 1955, Gibarti re-established some of his contacts from the 1920s, and he interviewed the Indian Prime Minister Jawaharlal Nehru for *Le Monde Diplomatique* in connection with the Bandung Conference of 1955. This is one of several historical threads which link together the Bandung Conference in 1955 with the first International Congress against Colonialism and Imperialism in Brussels in 1927.

Gibarti's "total" personal file in the Comintern Archive can be found at: RGASPI 495/205/6048: Louis Gibarti (LUIZ GIBARTI). A secret CIA memorandum dated 1/8/49, Central Intelligence Agency (US) details Gibarti's (here he is named as Ladislas Dobos) association with Münzenberg. https://www.cia.gov/library/readingroom/docs/DOC_0005632259.pdf

http://theeinsteinfile.com/.

The FBI's Summary Report, written by agent Vincent Murphy (his name remains blacked out in the FBI's file) is based partially on testimony from an FBI Informant named Louis Gibarti who was later disowned by J. Edgar Hoover. The Einstein file includes a note about a letter (dated 20 January 1933) from Münzenberg in Paris to Einstein with information about the International Committee for the Defence of Paul and Gertrude Ruegg. Einstein was a member of this and various other relief and aid committees, including the League against War and Fascism. The Rueggs were a couple of uncertain nationality working in China for the Comintern. They had been arrested in China, and Münzenberg was instrumental in setting up a defence committee campaigning for their release (see *Policing Shanghai 1927–1937* by Frederic Wakeman for more detail). And see: https://vault.fbi.gov/Albert%20Einstein.

15 Koestler, Arthur, *The Invisible Writing: The Second Volume of an Autobiography, 1932–40*, 1954, p. 250, Chapter XVII titled Red Eminence.

16 Meyer-Leviné, Rosa. *Im Inneren Kreis: Erinnerungen einer Kommunistin in Deutschland 1920–1933* (published in English translation as *Inside German Communism: Memoirs of Party Life in the Weimar Republic*, Pluto Press, 1977). p. 238.

Rosa Meyer-Leviné was a very perceptive and intelligent observer of the left-wing political scene, as well as many of its leading figures in Germany and the Soviet Union during the 1920s. However, her views were strongly coloured by her second marriage to the leading German Communist Ernst Meyer, who would fall out of favour and suffer severe ill-health and an early death probably as a result of the way he was treated by the KPD and his comrades.

Through him, Rosa Meyer-Leviné was able to move in top party circles and gain insights that other less illustrious members could not.

She was born in Tsarist Russia, and spoke fluent Russian, giving her access to leading Soviet political figures too. Her descriptions of the inner-party workings, intrigues, and backstabbing as well as her thumbnail sketches of leading revolutionary figures in Germany and the Soviet Union are, no doubt, largely true and accurate, but she could be highly acerbic and sharply critical in her judgements, as she herself attests, and hardly anyone comes away unsullied when seen through her lens. Her description of Münzenberg is certainly illuminating and sums up the man very succinctly.

17 Fischer, Ruth, *Stalin under deutsche Kommunismus*, Dietz Verlag, Berlin, pp. 275–281.

8

PUBLISHING MOGUL

From his early days as a political activist, Münzenberg became aware that if he were to persuade others to join him in the struggle for socialism and against militarism, then effective communication was the key. Already in Switzerland, from 1912 onwards, he had become actively involved in publishing the young socialists' paper, *Jugend Internationale* (Youth International), and for even younger members, the *Junge Saat* (Young Seedcorn). Then, in 1918, back in Germany, he launched a new version of *Jugend Internationale*. In 1921, after he was given the task of mounting an international campaign to help the famine-afflicted Soviet Union, he realised more than ever that an effective information and propaganda campaign on behalf of the Soviet Union was vital if he were to be successful. He would need access to printing and publishing facilities. In this way, his involvement in publishing and propaganda became central to his campaigning work. He was able to embark on his ambitious publishing ventures largely because of financial support from the Comintern and was able to create what would become, at the time, the largest left-wing media consortium of any state outside the Soviet Union. The historian, Carter-Hett, in a back-handed complimentary way, says that 'today we might think of Münzenberg as a Marxist Rupert Murdoch'.

Once the Communist Party and its publications had been banned in the wake of the abortive Hamburg uprising in 1923, the need to circumvent this ban became crucial. Münzenberg and his organisations were not included in the ban, so he began looking around for a publishing house he could use as a cover to continue producing Communist literature, but one that would not be accused right from the start of being Communist.

With his purchase of the *Neuer Deutscher Verlag* publishing house in 1924, Münzenberg began to build up a huge print and media network; the *Arbeiter Illustrierte Zeitung (AIZ)* itself was born out of the small paper, *Soviet Russland im Bild*

(Soviet Russia in Pictures), later *Sichel und Hammer* (Sickle and Hammer), and would be turned into the most successful left-wing weekly at the time in the world. By the imaginative use of montages, polemical cartoons, and eye-catching headlines, the *Arbeiter Illustrierte Zeitung* (Workers Illustrated Newspaper) attracted a wide readership. It focussed on photography as a creative tool in the class struggle. Münzenberg was a mobile, diligent, and flexible businessman with an unbelievable inventiveness; he knew instinctively how to make use of modern media, whether print, theatre, or film.

His venture into book production at the *Neuer Deutscher Verlag* came about more by accident than design. Apart from anything else, the party had several of its own publishing houses and potential competition from Münzenberg was, to begin with, not viewed sympathetically. However, as a result of his political connections, he slowly collected around him a whole stable of authors who were willing to write for him, but who might not have been prepared to commit wholeheartedly to the *KPD*.

He was lucky that Felix Halle, a sympathetic solicitor, who had bought the deeds to a publishing house, the *Neuer Deutscher Verlag* (New German Publishing House), already before the First World War, now offered it to Münzenberg for nothing. He grasped the opportunity without hesitation and placed the undertaking in the capable hands of Babette Gross who became its managing director. In the coming years, he would go on to amass a whole stable of publications, from the daily newspaper, *Welt am Abend* (The World in the Evening), the illustrated magazine, *AIZ*, the Kosmos publishing house, the Universum book club, and many more.

In the first years, not entirely surprisingly, Münzenberg's publishing enterprises faced continuous financial problems. Babette Gross related that she often had to go to the treasurer of the party with a begging bowl, asking him to help them out, something he was, she says, always willing to do, even though the hard-left leadership group around Fischer and Maslow viewed Münzenberg and his organisation with unease. His enterprises were tolerated, though, because he still had strong support in Moscow and, they had to grudgingly concede, that he was indirectly supporting the party and its work.

This new publishing venture would turn out to be successful. It enabled him to bring a number of leading writers under his wing. Its first publication would be a popular illustrated brochure, *Lenin*, which came out in a large print run only two weeks after Vladimir Lenin's death.

Münzenberg had returned from Moscow with a sheaf of photos and took them into the office, telling his staff that the brochure had to be out within a week. At that time, they had no publishing experts, few contacts, no capital, and no distribution system to supply bookshops or newsagents. However, with massive enthusiasm and energy, the staff went about the task and managed to get it out on time.

Most of the publishing enterprises associated with Münzenberg were not ones that he actually set up, but ones he took over and transformed into effective means of communication and propaganda. He did this by using innovative layouts, reporting sensational stories of high-level corruption, and devising new ways of using pictures as integral parts of the story rather than add-ons. The media empire he would build up was, as he saw it, one devoted wholeheartedly to the working-class movement.

For left-wing journals, particularly Communist ones, attracting advertising was nigh on impossible – no self-respecting capitalist business would want to be associated with an organisation or paper that threatened its very existence – so Münzenberg's journals had to be heavily subsidised and self financing; many were not profitable. Large circulations would be essential if they were not to become financial liabilities.

In August 1922, he took the opportunity of purchasing the newspaper title, *Die Welt am Abend* (The World in the Evening), a left-leaning paper that had been losing circulation and the owners wanted to offload it, so Münzenberg was able to obtain it cheaply. He knew that in order to turn it into a success, he would need a well-established network of distributors, so he appointed Hans Schüler,

FIGURE 8.1 Berlin working-class family in the 1920s (Image taken from *Deutschland Deutschland über Alles* by Kurt Tucholsky, published by Universum Bücherei, Berlin, Germany.)

a former Independent Social Democratic Party of Germany (USP) man who had been responsible for distributing that party's paper. Together, they managed to turn a falling circulation of around 3,000 into one of 100,000 and rising in a short space of time. *Die Welt am Abend* would go on to become the most widely read working-class evening paper in Berlin, and by 1928, its circulation had reached around 175,000 copies.

Die Welt am Abend's circulation figures were also boosted by such sensational reports as the coverage of a large corruption scandal involving the Kutisker Company, which sold surplus German army uniforms and had been falsifying invoices to gain massive credit from the state bank. However, its increased circulation was also very much due to the network of 'newspaper boys' who sold it on the streets, 'the party's gold' as Münzenberg called them.

The paper also took on the sponsorship of a number of monthly events and mass rallies, which had the support and participation of leading artists, a factor that also helped gain readership and brought in vital advertising.

Although the party, to begin with, welcomed an additional left-leaning evening newspaper and was even more pleased when its circulation increased, the leadership put pressure on Münzenberg to appoint a 'reliable' party member as editor.

When Ernst Meyer, a founder member of the *KPD* and later de facto chair of the party, was removed from the party leadership during the 1920s, Münzenberg gave him a job as one of the editors at the paper.[1] He offered similar help to the very capable young journalist Rudolf Herrnstadt who, in 1930, had applied to join the Communist Party, but been continually fobbed off by the bureaucrats. Tired of not getting anywhere, Herrnstadt went to Berlin and visited Münzenberg in his flat, and the latter promised to help him speed up his membership application and, at the same time, gave him a job as an editor on one of his journals. These are just two of the many examples, where Münzenberg offered help and support to those considered personae non grata by the party gatekeepers. He was clearly unfazed by potential criticism or censure from the party leadership for employing such 'dissidents' or individuals who were 'out of favour' if he felt they were capable workers. Herrnstadt would later become the editor of the Socialist Unity Party's newspaper, *Neues Deutschland* in post-war East Germany, before also falling foul of Stalinist machinations later.[2]

In view of the success of the *Welt am Abend* evening paper, it seemed logical to Münzenberg that he should launch a daily too, so he established a new company, *Wilhelmstadt GmbH* for this purpose. Thus, *Berlin am Morgen* (Berlin in the Morning) was born. It was similar to its sister paper, *Die Welt am Abend*, and although editorially committed to a left-wing position, it was not tied to a party line. Münzenberg appointed the Austrian journalist Bruno Frei as managing editor. Under Frei, the paper concentrated on local reporting, revealing the small and larger stories of sleaze behind the bourgeois facades, as the hook on which to hang a broader social critique. In 1932, according to its own figures, it had a circulation of around 80,000. It also provided a platform for a number of leading writers of the political left and continued to be published until banned in 1933.

In 1932, the paper created a sensation by carrying a series of exclusives about the intrigues of a clairvoyant performer and charlatan called Erik Hanussen. The series revealed the man's secret relationships with Nazi leaders.

It was rumoured that it was he who gave Hitler lessons on how to perform in front of an audience, an episode captured in bitingly satirical form by Bertolt Brecht in his play *The Resistible Rise of Arturo Ui*. After Hitler came to power, Hanussen was murdered in March 1933, probably by a gang of SA men, but the actual circumstances were never clarified.

Not surprisingly, Münzenberg and his newspapers became vocal adversaries of Josef Goebbels, Hitler's propaganda supremo, and of Alfred Hugenberg, the big newspaper proprietor and leading supporter of the Nazi Party. But despite the Nazi wrath and the high level of unemployment and poverty in the country, the paper managed to ratchet up a substantial circulation.

Not content with his success with *Berlin am Morgen*, Münzenberg then took up a suggestion made by the well-known Berlin painter, Otto Nagel, to publish a satirical paper. *Der Eulenspiegel* (named after Till Eulenspiegel, the apocryphal German iconoclastic figure from the Middle Ages) became one of the country's best loved satirical magazines – and its successor is still going strong today. The inimitable Berlin comic artist of working-class life, Wilhelm Zille, was also one of its founders, and many of those artists who already supported the *IAH* provided illustrations for it. By 1931, it had a circulation of 50,000.

A later journal to be set up by Münzenberg was the illustrated women's magazine, *Der Weg der Frau* (Women's Way). Based on his experience in the Swiss youth movement, he made sure that while it treated women as intelligent and socially aware beings, it carried less heavy political content, but plenty on fashion, household questions, sport, and hygiene, which its readers clearly wanted. It was folksy without being patronising and cleverly edited.

As its editor, Münzenberg appointed Marianne Gundermann,[3] a party member who only shortly beforehand had been severely criticised by the party leadership for 'conciliatory right-wing deviation'. She was also a supporter and advocate of women's reproductive rights. Here, again, Münzenberg was prepared to risk irritating the leadership by appointing a 'dissident', but capable individual against their wishes.

Despite the fact that the magazine was launched in July 1931, in the middle of a depression that saw almost 6 million unemployed in the country, it also became a runaway success, with a circulation reaching 100,000.

The former *IAH* publication, *Sowjetrussland im Bild* (Soviet Russia in Pictures), later re-named *Sichel und Hammer* (Sickle and Hammer) was also taken in-house by Münzenberg and, in 1924, would be reborn as a magazine of modern design and renamed, the *Arbeiter Illustrierte Zeitung* (Workers' Illustrated Newspaper), published weekly from 1925 onwards. The two forerunners were characterised by page after page of dense text and when photos were used, they were technically of poor quality.

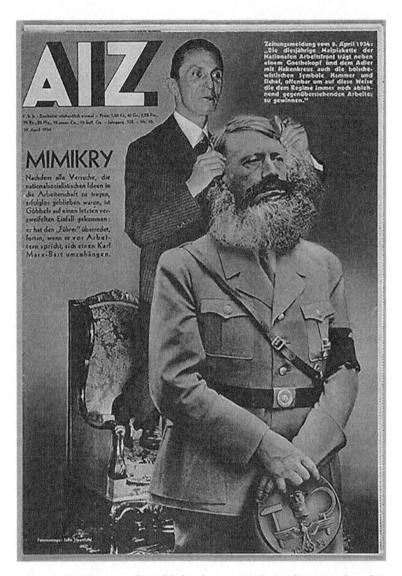

FIGURE 8.2 AIZ title page of Goebbels adorning Hitler with a Marx beard (Image taken from the book *Deutschland Deutschland über Alles* by Kurt Tucholsky, published by Universum Bücherei, Berlin, Germany.)

As an example of the triumph of the 'new human being' in the Soviet Union, an article in the magazine *Sichel und Hammer* in early 1924 depicted how women in Turkmenistan, in the Soviet Far East, were being liberated from backwardness. Campaigns had been unleashed to free them from having to wear the burka and against the powerful wealthy landowners, combatting Islamic ideology, and thus allowing them to become fully participating Soviet citizens.

With the launch of this new journal Münzenberg hit the jackpot. The first issue was published on 7 November 1921, under the motto: Soviet Russia in Word and Picture. His aim was to sear into people's consciousness the dire humanitarian situation pertaining to the Soviet Union as a result of the famine. It would be an informative and educational journal.

Münzenberg again managed to bring on board leading journalists, photographers, and artists, like John Heartfield, to work for it. It became a huge success and would be published also in Austria and Czechoslovakia.

Being published by an ostensibly privately owned company, without overt connections to the Communist Party, meant that the ban on Communist publications could be, at least partially, circumvented.

Babette Gross relates how she and Münzenberg undertook a tour of Germany in 1923, meeting party district leaders, to try and persuade them to take on responsibility for distributing their publications, particularly the *AIZ*. In a short space of time, they were able to establish a whole network of distributors throughout the country made up mainly of unemployed party workers. This network would eventually also cover the German-speaking areas outside Germany, including Austria, Czechoslovakia, and Switzerland. By 1925, the *AIZ* had become a weekly with a rising circulation. By the 1930s, it would attain a circulation of 420,000, a phenomenal figure in those days, thus securing the publication's financial viability.

The *AIZ* was a genuinely working-class counterpart in Germany to the American magazine *Life* (founded in 1883). It promoted international solidarity and gave space to radical artists and writers. With the input of John Heartfield, it also pioneered a modern use of images. Alongside global news reports, it had reportage, a poetry column, and short stories. For the first time, here was a magazine devoted to the real lives of working people and their struggles, with photographs illustrating the news stories, reports on strikes, and demonstrations, as well as on social problems. And, because of its focus on working-class life in different countries, it was able to convey a sense of trans-national working-class unity to its readership.

The use of photography in European journals at this time was still the exception, and certainly the power of the photographic image was scarcely recognised at the time. Victor Gollancz's Left Book Club in Britain, for instance, totally ignored photography, despite the club being a propaganda undertaking, and *Picture Post*, Britain's first illustrated magazine, was first published only in 1938.

AIZ was edited, to begin with, by the Austrian journalist, Franz Höllering, who had worked earlier with Bertolt Brecht and John Heartfield, and who was introduced to Münzenberg by the 'flying reporter' Egon Erwin Kisch. Höllering would remain chief editor of the *AIZ* from 1925 until 1928. Münzenberg was very pleased with the rapid success of his weekly, which became the jewel in the crown of his publishing ventures.

The radical left party leader, Ruth Fischer, wrote with grudging admiration that, 'In order to support his campaign [for international solidarity], Münzenberg began to supplement the official communist press with lively and well-written magazines. *The Red Flag* and other Party newspapers were written in a jargon that non-communists found objectionable and difficult to comprehend and their pages were full of endless resolutions and manifestos … In the crisis years of 1929–1933, the Münzenberg concern developed every form of antifascist propaganda utilising the whole Russian cultural merry-go-round, with films, literature, science and theatre. Progressives and liberals throughout the world who wanted to join the anti-fascist struggle found a refuge in one of the numerous Münzenberg organisations'.[4]

Höllering, as editor-in-chief of the *AIZ*, was largely responsible for producing such a well-designed and pioneering magazine. Münzenberg described it in the following way, 'The *AIZ* differs fundamentally from all other illustrated newspapers. It focuses unflinchingly on life and struggling workers in all areas of work. It brings pictures from factories, strikes, job centres and demonstrations, from rallies and famine areas …'. The magazine clearly addressed a need among large sections of the working class to see their own lives portrayed realistically in a newspaper and also reflected a desire to see a united working-class movement once more. An important aspect of the magazine's role was also to report regularly on the Soviet Union.

Münzenberg encouraged a number of worker photographers to supply the *AIZ* with picture stories. One of them was the young working-class German Communist Willi Jungmittag who married the budding Irish artist, Brigid Macnaghten after they met in Berlin during the 1920s. Brigid's father was a judge, privy councillor, and unionist MP for Londonderry and her mother the daughter of Social reformer Charles Booth. So, unsurprisingly, her parents viewed her relationship with the Communist Jungmittag with dismay. The young Willi Jungmittag had studied photography at the Bauhaus and was commissioned by the *AIZ* to undertake a photo reportage in London. The photos were published by the *AIZ* and some in the British *Daily Worker*. From London, he and Brigid travelled to the South Wales coalfield, where they made another photo reportage on the living conditions of the miners, and walked all the way back to London with one of the unemployed hunger marches. Willi Jungmittag would be executed in November 1944 by the Nazis, while Brigid survived the allied bombing of Berlin together with their two children and returned to live in Britain.[5]

The *AIZ* became such a runaway success that the French Communist Party was keen to emulate it, and Münzenberg readily offered his help. On 1 May 1928, the first copies of *Nos Regards, Illustré Mondial du Travail* hit the streets.

In the late 1920s, Kurt Tucholsky, one of Germany's foremost radical satirists, expressed a desire to work for Münzenberg's *AIZ* for an appropriate salary and, after making an approach in 1928, was snapped up by Gross and Lilly Becher, the *AIZ*'s chief editor. Tucholsky was impressed with the magazine's political argumentation, and its educational role, using photography, documentary reporting, and picture stories. From the early 1920s on, he had been fascinated by the role he felt photography could play in communicating ideas. Becher would send him photos to which he would pen witty verses.[6] The collaboration became an incredibly fruitful one for both parties.

In 1929, although Tucholsky was already living in exile, Babette Gross and John Heartfield managed to persuade him at last to collaborate with the *Neuer Deutscher Verlag* in publishing a book of political reportage. It would be his first solo work for this publisher. The book, *Deutschland, Deutschland über alles*, a satirical review of capitalist Germany in text and picture, with an eye-catching cover by Heartfield, would become a sensational success.

Tucholsky demanded total autonomy in choosing text and images, and this was granted. He was clear that this hard-hitting, satirical text combined with powerful images would stir up a storm once published. Wieland Herzfelde commented that it mercilessly pilloried 'the pitiful cultural philistinism of the leading German industrial barons and landed aristocracy, their militarism and chauvinism'.[7] Its initial print-run of 15,000 was immediately sold out, and it had to be reprinted.

FIGURE 8.3 Namibian woman in the 1920s (Image taken from *Deutschland, Deutschland über Alles* by Kurt Tucholsky, published by Universum Bücherei, Berlin, Germany.)

The *Neuer Deutscher Verlag* publishing house produced a number of excellent volumes for a readership keen on expanding its horizons, including a monograph on the Mexican Muralist, Diego Rivera, 'Diego Rivera and his work' and a political travelogue by the American journalist, Anna Louise Strong, 'China Journey', among others.

In its 1931 edition, the *AIZ* magazine included a series on the daily life of a Russian working-class family, 'The Filipovs', which became very popular, even though it did convey a rosy view of life in the Soviet Union. During this time, the country was still experiencing serious food shortages as a result of the forced collectivisation of agriculture, so life for ordinary citizens was far from rosy. It also featured a number of informative articles on the Red Army. And on its 10th anniversary, the *AIZ* published a special commemorative issue, with the motto: 'Defend the Soviet Union'. The weekly, unlike many radical journals of the time – which contained one turgid political or philosophical article after another – was lively, attractively designed and an enjoyable read.

In 1932, the magazine despatched a large delegation, over 2,000 strong, of employees and supporters to the May Day parade that year in Leningrad, as well as a group of reporters to cover the parade in Moscow. Münzenberg wanted his colleagues and supporters to see the Soviet Union for themselves and enjoy a trip which many of them could otherwise have hardly dreamed of.

A group of the delegates marched in the Leningrad parade, carrying a banner proclaiming themselves the '*Stossbrigade der AIZ*' (the shock brigade of the *AIZ*). Many of the *IAH* employees on that delegation had been chosen from among the around 2,000 distributors of the paper. These 'newspaper boys' were the backbone of the paper's success and every week cycled or walked considerable distances to ensure the weekly reached even the most isolated areas.

At around the same time, Münzenberg helped to arrange another delegation to the Soviet Union of managers and representatives of big German brand names, such as the owner of the massive Reemtsma cigarette company. He was fully aware of the vital importance of promoting trade between the two nations and the need to win over the business community and not just the support of working people.

The *AIZ*, from 1921 until it was banned by the Nazis in 1933, provided a narrative arc, depicting a Soviet Union undergoing profound change. From a country on its knees and in need of aid, to the implementation of the first five-year plans, and the gradual industrialisation and mechanisation of a previously backward country. The reports and articles were largely uncritical and dominated by photographic images as evidence of progress. They were unashamedly propaganda for the Soviet Union, but the coverage had a diversity and persuasiveness that ensured the magazine maintained a wide readership.

Münzenberg undoubtedly saw himself and his web of publishing businesses as the de facto and sole representative of the Soviet Union in Germany. This hubris would lead to a damaging spat between him and another leading Communist, the renowned writer and publicist, Eduard Fuchs. Unlike his convivial working relationship with Tucholsky, with Fuchs it was more an adversarial than comradely one.

Fuchs was born almost 20 years before Münzenberg, in 1870, but would die in the same year, also in French exile. He became a Doctor of Law and practiced as a lawyer. He was also a founder member of the *KPD*, a friend and supporter of Rosa Luxemburg and Karl Liebknecht, as well as of Lenin. He became a German Marxist scholar, writer, art collector, and political activist. The sales from his books made him a relatively wealthy man. The first of these was *Karikatur der europäischen Völker* (Caricatures of European Peoples), published in 1902 and his magnum opus, an examination of moral practice, *Sittengeschichte*, which, by 1912, had run to six volumes. In 1892, he became editor-in-chief of the satiric weekly *Süddeutscher Postillon* and later co-editor of the *Leipziger Volkszeitung*. His inflammatory articles in newspapers – one accusing the Kaiser of being a mass murderer – resulted in periodic jail sentences.

He had been, like Münzenberg, a pacifist during the war. Lenin's government put him in charge of the prisoner exchange with Germany after the war; and he was among the leaders of the German Comintern in Berlin in 1919.

Fuchs was one of the first to sign Münzenberg's 'Hands off China' appeal to help the starving and striking Chinese workers, which raised 250,000 US dollars. He was also one of the key members of the Association of Friends of the New Russia, and became close friends with Trotsky's sister, Olga Kameneva, who worked in the Peoples Commissariat for Culture and Theatre.

He visited the Soviet Union in November 1927 for the celebrations commemorating the 10th anniversary of the revolution and for the World Congress of Friends of the Soviet Union. The German delegation that year was the largest from any country, comprising 173 delegates, among them, Käthe Kollwitz, Robert René Kuczynski, Helene Stöcker, and Münzenberg.[8] Fuchs would resign from the party in 1929, to join the small *KPD(O)* (Communist Party of Germany in Opposition, the so-called 'right-wing' opposition).

Fuchs had already come into bitter conflict with Münzenberg in early 1927, after the latter had just founded the New German Publishing House, publishing 'Soviet Russia in Pictures'.

Like Fuchs, Münzenberg had recognised early on the power of images, particularly photography and film. Fuchs's biographer, Ulrich Weitz writes, 'In a sense, Willi Münzenberg and Eduard Fuchs would have formed the dream team of Communist publishing, but jealousies, hurt, and a solid narcissism on the part of both protagonists led to conflict instead of collaboration'.[9]

Münzenberg attempted to isolate the group around Fuchs, Felix José Weil, and the Malik Verlag, and sought to obtain a monopoly for his own publishing group in terms of carrying out publicity and solidarity work on behalf of the Soviet Union.

Already in January 1927, the central committee of the *KPD*, with the agreement of the Comintern, had taken the decision that the magazine, '*New Russia*', would be published by Malik. Münzenberg was livid at this decision; he wanted to keep all German-Soviet friendship matters under his aegis. According to a report from Fuchs to Clara Zetkin, he told Baron, the business manager of the friendship society, 'Certainly, I'm the loser this time, but when in a few weeks my new magazine, "Soviet Russia in Pictures", comes out, you with your miniscule literary club and your meshuge [Yiddish: crazy] Olga will be forced to the wall'.[10] Such comments certainly reveal a vainer and less friendly side of Münzenberg's character.

Fuchs tried to mobilise leading figures like Nicolai Bucharin, Olga Kameneva, and Clara Zetkin against Münzenberg. He called for a meeting of the party's Central Committee to discuss Münzenberg's attempt to sideline his Society of Friends of the New Russia with his own Club of Friends of Soviet Russia. Ironically, Fuchs argued that Münzenberg's approach was sectarian, whereas he wished to broaden the appeal, taking it beyond party ranks, but that was exactly what Münzenberg was also doing successfully.

At the meeting of the Central Committee where the issue was discussed, Fuchs reported that Clara Zetkin mounted a vehement defence of his position and accused the party leadership of turning the 'KPD into WMD' [the Willi Münzenberg Party] and betraying the revolutionary legacy of Luxemburg and Liebknecht. In the end, the leadership came down on the side of Münzenberg, which led to Fuchs leaving the party and joining the small *KPD(O)*.

After this setback, Fuchs managed to obtain sole rights to the collected works of Franz Mehring (the first Marx biographer) from his widow, Eva Mehring. But it would appear that, in the meantime, he had come to some form of reconciliation with Münzenberg, because all six volumes of Mehring's works were, in the end, published simultaneously by Fuchs's publishing house and Münzenberg's *Universum Bücherei*.

Tragically, Münzenberg and Fuchs were never fully reconciled and even in their Paris exile, later, would have little to do with each other, although by this time Fuchs's health was rapidly failing.

In 1924, he set up an in-house book publishing section, not connected directly with the *IAH*, and coincidentally, in the autumn of that year, Radek visited him in Berlin and introduced his friend Larissa Reissner. She had been to Hamburg the year before and interviewed those who had taken part in the 1923 abortive uprising. She had compiled her interviews and observations into a dramatic and moving manuscript, titled 'Hamburg on the Barricades' and the two of them persuaded Münzenberg to publish it. Shortly after its publication, though, it was banned by the government censors and copies confiscated, as it was deemed to be 'an incitement to civil unrest'.

In 1926, he had set up his own book club, *Universum-Bücherei für Alle* – a forerunner of Victor Gollancz's Left Book Club in Britain – and by 1931, it had published its hundredth book. This was a pioneering attempt to provide cheap, but good literature and educational reading to working-class families.

That same year, his *Internationaler Arbeiter Verlag* published a large-format *Illustrierte Geschichte der deutschen Revolution* (Illustrated History of the German Revolution), celebrating the 1918 November Revolution and, for its time, employing pioneering typography and illustration.

'Hello, hello, here speaks Willi Münzenberg, representing the International Workers' Relief (*IAH*)': his voice boomed out to the tens of thousands gathered in Berlin's huge Sports Palace to celebrate the 10th anniversary of the *IAH*, and it carried weight.

In the autumn of 1931, he had organised a fittingly celebratory congress in Berlin, which was also attended by hundreds of delegates from other parts of the world. At this congress, delegates discussed what sort of road the *IAH* should take in the future, in terms of its solidarity work and how that should be defined in the context of a deepening global crisis. To commemorate its own 10th anniversary, the *AIZ* published a book of 23 poems by Tucholsky with a powerful cover illustration by Käthe Kollwitz.

Despite Münzenberg's successes on the political as well as on the business front, Babette Gross, wrote that 'politically he fell more and more into a lethargy, that seemed almost like cynicism'. He was depressed about what he saw looming on the horizon. Support for the Nazis in Germany was growing significantly, making the Soviet Union increasingly fearful of encirclement and attack by the capitalist powers. The disturbing and confusing state of affairs in Germany, as a result of the party's own mistakes, together with the rapid rise of the Nazis, also led to increasingly heated debates within the *KPD* itself. It had become a victim of its own myopia as far as the Fascist threat was concerned and of sectarian Comintern dictates: the chickens were coming home to roost.

Many working-class people who had suffered months and even years of unemployment and poverty were now saying, 'You Communists are OK, but Adolf will get the job done quicker and we can't wait any longer'. They had run out of patience and weren't prepared to wait for pie in the sky. Such attitudes were reflected in the increased vote for the Nazis in the most recent elections and in the very near future would help propel Hitler to power.

However, such a shift in political allegiance was hardly reflected in Münzenberg's activities at the time: despite the seemingly inexorable rise of the Nazis, the years between 1930 and 1932 were exceedingly busy and successful for him in terms of establishing new undertakings and organising rallies and conferences.

The last newspaper he founded in 1932, the *Neue Montagszeitung* (New Monday newspaper), was, however, not such a success. Unlike his other newspapers, this one was not well run editorially, and with Hitler's accession in 1933, its future was in any case sealed.

Notes

1 During the German Revolution of 1918–1919, Meyer emerged to serve on the editorial board of *Die Rote Fahne* (The Red Flag), the official organ of the Communist Party. He was a founding member of the Communist Party of Germany in December 1918 and was elected onto the Central Committee.

In 1921, Meyer was elected as a Communist to the Prussian Landtag (parliament). He returned to Moscow in 1922 as a delegate to the fourth World Congress of the Comintern. After his return, he became one of the main architects of a united front policy in Germany. This policy was developed in reaction to the failed March 1921 uprising, Instead of insurrection, the KPD now sought to build a mass base. With the rise in strength of the ultra-left faction around Fischer and Maslow, his 'conciliatory' position was strongly criticised and he was not re-elected to the Central Committee. He nevertheless remained an important member of the party, returning to the top echelon after another factional shift in 1925.

As one of the leaders of the *Versöhnler* (conciliatory) group in the party and an opponent of the Fischer-Maslow-Thälmann faction, he was removed from all party functions at the *KPD*'s 12th Congress in June 1929.

2 Liebmann, Irene, *Wäre es schön? Es ware schön – Mein Vater Rudolf Herrnstadt*, Berliner Taschenbuch Verlag 2009.

3 Born into a German-Jewish family, Marianne Gundermann went on to work for various Berlin publishers in the thirties. She was delegated to the party school in Moscow in 1936. After her return to Germany, in 1938, she was sent by the party to undertake clandestine work in the Netherlands. In 1943, she was arrested by the Gestapo and under torture and after several suicide attempts was interned in Auschwitz and Ravensbruck, but survived and, after the war, settled in the Soviet Zone, later GDR, where she won various awards for her literary work.

4 Fischer, Ruth, *Stalin und der deutsche Kommunismus*, Dietz Verlag, 1991.

5 Youngday, Biddy, *Flags in Berlin*, self-published by her daughters, 2012.

6 Bemman, Helga, *Kurt Tucholsky – ein Lebensbild*, Ullstein Verlag, 1994. p. 395.

7 Bemman, Helga, *Kurt Tucholsky – ein Lebensbild*, Ullstein Verlag, 1994. p. 417.

8 Weitz, Ulrich, *Der Mann im Schatten Eduard Fuchs*, Karl Dietz Verlag, Berlin, 2014 (p. 268).

9 Ibid. p. 304.

10 Ibid. (Letter from Fuchs to Clara Zetkin from 27 January 1927) (p. 305).

9

THE INFLUENCE OF THE KPD AND MÜNZENBERG'S ORGANISATION ON WORKING-CLASS CULTURE IN GERMANY

By the latter half of 1922, the German Communist Party had gained many new members and influence, and this was primarily at the cost of the Social Democrats. It had absolute majorities on 80 city councils and had the largest party representation in a further 170; it could count more than 6,000 councillors in total and was the dominant force in almost 1,000 trade union branches, with 400 members in leading positions. Its strength and influence was, unsurprisingly, strongest in the large conurbations of Berlin, Hamburg, and the Ruhr. The party's influence, though, could be felt far beyond the narrow political and into the wider cultural and social fields.

Münzenberg's *IAH* and the activities it promoted, alongside, but also separately from the party, played a key role in developing and maintaining a lively and alternative proletarian culture. This important aspect of his influence has been ignored in most accounts of his life and work.

The party, together with the *IAH*, were not merely political organisations as such, but catered to the widest of interests, from sport to theatre, choral singing to photography and, whatever your special interest, Münzenberg published journals to cater to you. This flourishing sphere of alternative working-class culture played a key role in giving thousands of young working-class boys and girls a social and political education not provided by their basic state schooling and opportunities for physical activity, country pursuits, as well as, importantly, reinforcing a sense of working-class cohesion and solidarity.

The *IAH* itself was, in some ways, almost like a parallel political party: 'it developed separate sections for women and youth, it was engaged in organising summer camps and orphanages for workers' children ... it provided strike support and education during work time ... it was involved in family affairs, child nurturing, sexual enlightenment and became engaged in issues such as fighting the notorious Paragraph 218 which criminalised abortion … it was in fact involved in forming a whole new solidarity experience, which included all aspects of life'.[1]

Underlying so many of his endeavours in the publishing, film, and propaganda worlds, Münzenberg was keenly aware that 'man does not live by bread alone', and even though changing the economic system was central to bettering working people's lives, the cultural sphere could not be ignored. He was very conscious of his own culturally deprived upbringing, so was acutely aware of the nourishing role culture could and should play in working people's lives.

Throughout the 1920s, the *IAH* became deeply involved in promoting cultural activity as an essential element of its solidarity work, from organising large entertainment events, supporting amateur dramatics, putting on art exhibitions, and encouraging worker photographers. It became extremely successful in providing workers with a cultural world outside their homes and workplaces and very different to the largely escapist ones offered by the establishment.

Access to cultural activities that helped transport them beyond their own otherwise circumscribed lives played a key role in the development of many working-class boys and girls. The *IAH* offered them film showings, organised public meetings and seminars on current affairs, and, from 1929 onwards, organised an annual international day of solidarity. The impact on working-class culture by such organisations is well described by the actor and friend of Bertolt Brecht's, Erwin Geschonneck, in his own reminiscences.[2]

Born in Berlin in 1906, Geschonneck was Münzenberg's junior by 17 years, but the harshness and poverty of his upbringing during the 1920s, his political awakening and early membership of the Communist Party, were very similar to Münzenberg's own, and he was unemployed for a lengthy period in his younger years.

Berlin at this time, in the so-called 'golden twenties', was a cosmopolitan hot spot, subjected to continuous social, political, and technological upheavals; its post-war society marked by crises, utopian dreams, misery and decadence, hope, and despair. Not an easy city to grow up in if you were young, poor, and probably unemployed. For many working-class youngsters living in this helter-skelter world, the Communist Party gave meaning to lives that would otherwise have been aimless.

Geschonneck writes, 'Of course I joined one of the clubs. That could, of course, only be a workers' sports club'. He joined the *Fichte Verein* and takes up boxing and wrestling, boating, cycling, and rambling, then joins an amateur dramatic troupe, performing agitprop pieces, a workers' choir, and a political discussion group, which met in a local pub. Geschonneck's own group, *Sturmtrupp links* (Stormtroop Left), performed political agitation on behalf of the *IAH*. He also joined Erwin Piscator's red cabaret group at the *Junge Volksbühne*, where they were always applauded for their performance of Kurt Tucholsky's 'An elderly, drunk Gentleman' in which Geschonneck played a drunk in the audience who attempts to mount the stage despite the director's objection. The audience, of course, thinks at first that this is for real and becomes involved in the fracas. They are then thoroughly amused at the drunk's inability to choose which party to vote for.

These performances were in aid of the Communist Party's campaign for the upcoming Reichstag elections. Geschonneck also took part, as an extra – one of the hundreds of young working-class sportsmen and women who did so – in the classic film, *Kuhle Wampe* (1932), directed by Slatan Dudov with Bertolt Brecht, which celebrates this working-class culture and the emergence of a 'new type of individual'. It was produced by Prometheus, another Münzenberg enterprise.

As Geschonneck writes, 'what a contrast to the stifling and dreary petit-bourgeois lifestyle ... because it is to them – those combative boys and girls – to whom the world really belongs and they will change it'. Not surprisingly, the official censor banned the film, *Kuhle Wampe*, demanding significant cuts and changes; the Nazis would also ban it. The film reflected that short period, before the Nazis came to power, of working-class comradeship, the joy, strength, commitment, and optimism so many felt and expressed through these Communist and Socialist mass organisations.

In class and political terms, this rather close-knit web of cultural activity meant that Communists and their sympathisers, due largely to their social circumstances, tended to move in a ghetto-like cultural context and remained largely unconnected with what was happening outside their own circles. This strong working-class movement was, by its very nature, also largely confined to urban areas, with the result that those living and working in rural communities were neglected and would, in a few years hence, become a bastion for Nazi ideology.

It is difficult to establish when exactly Münzenberg became fascinated by film and photography, but from very early on he demonstrated an awareness of the power of visual imagery and the impact it could have on people.

Promoting interest in photography and encouraging young working-class photographers was one of his key achievements. His interest in this field may have been sparked by the well-known German satirist, Kurt Tucholsky in 1925, although the *AIZ* had already been using photography in a creative way from 1924 onwards.

In a key article in the political magazine, *Die Weltbühne*, Tucholsky had complained of the feebleness of the old-style satirical papers compared with the power of photography, and it was perhaps this article that helped ignite the development of the worker photographer movement.

One of the best-known Soviet journalists, Mikhail Koltsov, became the first editor of the Soviet journal *Sovietskoe Foto* (Soviet Photography) in April 1926, and the magazine was devoted especially to the encouragement of 'worker photographers' both in Russia and Germany. A similar awareness of the essential subversiveness of this medium encouraged Münzenberg to use the growing funds of the *IAH* to found a *Vereinigung der Arbeiterphotographen* (an Association of Worker Photographers) and to support it by publishing the journal *Der Arbeiterphotograph* (The Worker Photographer), which was founded in Erfurt in that same year.

Münzenberg's *AIZ* had already demonstrated that the standard of professional and press photography was higher in Germany than in any other European country at the time.

As a result, Soviet Photography magazine, together with the Association of Worker Photographers itself, became one of Münzenberg's favourite projects. He had helped found the organisation and gave it vital support. His aim was that the association would provide further education and training, in an ideological sense as well as technically, for budding photographers and could promote talented workers from the movement. *The Worker Photographer* magazine was envisaged as the 'eye of the worker' – the world seen through a working-class lens.

Münzenberg had been incredibly successful in reaching out to wide sections of the working-class movement and beyond, as well as cementing broad alliances and eliciting support across political, social, and national boundaries. But despite the work he was doing to promote Communist ideas – as so often, particularly in political organisations – his popularity, effectiveness, and creative flair meant that a number of top party officials envied him and cast suspicion on his integrity and his motives. His imperviousness to flattery, lack of interest in material reward, and his hatred of toadying undoubtedly compounded that animosity. They labelled his collaborators belittlingly as 'Münzenberg men'.

The *IAH* became a powerful political solidarity organisation for the left during the 1920s and 1930s, but it had been largely ignored by historians before Kasper Braskén's work brought it to light and had been, like the figure of Münzenberg himself, almost completely erased from those official histories of Germany published in the GDR, as well as ignored by writers and publishers in the West.

Christopher Isherwood, in his novel *Mr. Norris Changes Trains*, was one of the few who pays a small tribute to the significance of the *IAH*. His character, Mr. Norris, based on the real-life Gerald Hamilton who worked for Münzenberg's organisation, addresses an *IAH* meeting in the novel on the subject of the exploitation of Chinese peasants.[3] Indeed, Isherwood himself, through his acquaintance with Otto Katz, undertook some translation work for Münzenberg's *IAH* in Berlin and wanted to join the organisation.[4]

German-Soviet cultural collaboration

Beyond the work Münzenberg was doing in promoting German working-class culture, the *IAH* also played an instrumental role in promoting Russian-German co-operation in the wider cultural field.

After the establishment of the *IAH*, he, along with leading artists who were sympathetic to the Soviet Union, set about establishing an international committee of intellectuals interested in strengthening relations with the new Russia. In 1922, Georg Grosz and the Danish novelist, Martin Anderson Nexö, went to Russia to join a mixed delegation led by the writer, Arthur Holitscher, which helped pave the way for the establishment in Berlin of a Society of Friends of the New Russia the following June, especially among intellectuals and artists.

The pioneering and experimental theatre director and producer, Erwin Piscator, already an avid supporter of the *IAH*, became secretary of its *Kunstlerhilfe* (Artists' Aid) section. At the time, he was working with Walter Gropius from the Bauhaus on a new *Totaltheater*, which would democratise all seating categories, making it feasible for workers to buy tickets. But after a visit to Berlin by the influential Soviet 'Blue Blouse' agitprop theatrical group in the autumn of 1927, he devised his own *Revue Roter Rummel* (Red Hurly-burly Revue), which became a model for the new agitprop theatre in Germany.

Following Piscator's example, Berlin's young Communists went on to develop their own form of militant theatre and managed to persuade Maxim Valentin of the *Deutsches Theater* to become their artistic director. Münzenberg's *IAH* had not only invited the Soviet group to Berlin, but gave publicity to their first performance at Piscator's theatre. The *IAH* went on to sponsor a group of its own, *Kolonne Links* (Column Left). The young Communist group became *Das rote Sprachrohr* (The Red Megaphone) – the name adopted by Ewan McColl in 1940s Manchester for his workers' agitprop theatre group – and very soon there was a whole network of such agitprop theatre groups throughout Germany. This new and vibrant theatrical movement would also have a considerable influence on Brecht's work.

In 1925, the *IAH*, under the able direction of the painter, Otto Nagel, was able to bring together 126 German artists of all schools, including Bauhaus artists, to participate in a large exhibition of German modern art to be shown in the Soviet Union. 'Its impact', John Willett notes, 'can be compared with the large Berlin Soviet exhibition of 1922. Far the strongest impression was made by the Verists of the Red Group', he says, 'among them, Grosz, Dix, Schlichter, Griebel, and Davringhausen'. It was these who led Lunacharsky, the Soviet Commissar for Education, to comment that the Germans had 'surpassed nearly all other artists in the degree of their mental assimilation of the revolution and their creation of revolutionary art'.[5]

In order to distribute Soviet films in Germany effectively, it was necessary to have a radical company that could compete with established commercial distributors, but run on a commercial basis. In 1929, when one of Münzenberg's old friends from his Spartacus days, Emil Unfried, told him that the *KPD* wanted to offload a small, insignificant firm called Prometheus, which had just produced a propaganda film, *Nameless Heroes* (1925 silent film made in 1925 and directed by Kurt Bernhardt), he grasped the opportunity with both hands and appointed Unfried and another comrade as its managers. He would also set up a similar distribution company, Spartacus, in France.

To begin with, the Soviet film distribution representatives in Berlin were not keen to offer their films to Prometheus, a new, untried company; they preferred to deal with the mainstream, commercial distributors. In the end, though, Münzenberg managed to persuade them to give Prometheus a go, and it obtained the distribution rights to the first Russian–German co-production, *Superfluous People* (1926), directed by Alexander Rzumny, in which Werner

Kraus and other leading German actors took part, but the film was not the financial success its makers had hoped, that would come later.

It was Prometheus that would give the majority of Soviet exported films the titles by which they became known abroad, like *Storm over Asia, Bed and Sofa*, etc. In the period up to 1927, more Soviet films were being exported to Germany than to any other country, according to the US film historian, Jay Leyda.

In January 1926, the Russian trade representative invited Prometheus managers to view a new Soviet film at a private showing in the Soviet embassy. That film was *Battleship Potemkin,* and what they saw blew their minds. They knew this film would become a roaring success if only they could get it past the censor.

The Soviet trade delegation probably gave the film to Prometheus this time, rather than one of the big capitalist distributors, as they felt certain the German censors would ban it anyway. Prometheus managers convinced Piel Jutzi to edit a German version and commissioned a musical score from Edmund Meisel who had worked with Piscator. Eisenstein himself came to Berlin to discuss the music with him and the result was a powerful musical score. The censors by then having seen the film did promptly ban it. The film company managers appealed against the decision, and with the help of Erwin Piscator, they managed to persuade the renowned theatre critic Alfred Kerr, affectionately known as the 'Cultural Pope', to watch a repeat showing of the film in the censor's office and to lend his support for its release, which he did. At this showing, Prometheus's lawyer, Paul Levi, also delivered a scintillating defence of the film, and as a result, with a few minor cuts, it was given a certificate for public showing.

As so often, attempts to ban works of art often end up giving them the publicity which the ban intended to deny them. Münzenberg, wily publicist that he was, capitalised on the resulting furore, promoting *Potemkin* extensively through a poster and press campaign.

The actor, Erwin Geschonneck, was one of the thousands who saw this and other Soviet films in Berlin and was stunned by their powerful messages, as he describes in his reminiscences.[6]

Cinema owners who were shown the film were impressed, but refused to show it because they feared demonstrations and uproar, resulting in possible damage to their cinemas. The right-wing press, which had caught wind of the film's revolutionary content, did everything it could to get its release revoked. The resulting furore only increased people's curiosity, and they queued in the thousands to see it. For Prometheus, it became a resounding success. However, the right wing continued its campaign against the film and, as a result, it was once again banned in a number of regions.

During this period, 1925–1929, the great foreign films shown in Germany were, for critics and public alike, those of Pudovkin, Eisenstein, and Chaplin. *Potemkin*, though, had the greatest impact when it was premiered in Berlin in 1926, only a month after its first showing in Moscow.

Berlin at this time was an international cultural centre, a magnet for artists, cultural voyeurs, and Bohemian adventurers. There was a permanent coming and going of Russian actors, theatre people, and directors who did much to promote the Soviet Union among the Berlin public, and Soviet films, with their often revolutionary content and innovative styles, attracted large and curious audiences.

Prometheus would go on to produce a number of its own films, but few, if any, made significant amounts of money. Among the better ones were *Jenseits der Strasse* (Beyond the Street, 1929), directed by Leo Mittler, the first time the subject of unemployment had been taken on as a film subject and was a success.

The film *Salamander* (also 1929) that portrays the Soviet Union as the only guarantor of scientific freedom was immediately banned by the German film censor. But one of them, which did go on to become a classic, was *Mutter Krausen's Fahrt ins Glück* (Mother Kraus's Journey to Happiness), directed by Phil Jutzi in 1929. It was based on images and stories from that quintessential recorder of Berlin working-class life, Heinrich Zille. The film reveals the abject misery of working-class life in Berlin's tenements, and how a mother, driven by poverty and despair, resorts to suicide.

Jutzi also made a documentary reportage on the starving mine workers in Silesia, called *Hunger in Waldenburg*, but the last film to be made by Prometheus in 1931 was the Brecht film, *Kuhle Wampe* (Whither Germany), which was banned in 1932.

Gross says that Prometheus, 'in contrast to other firms belonging to the "Münzenberg concern" had continual financial problems'. On the plus side, the party, curiously, showed little interest in film at this time, so gave only meagre support to Prometheus's endeavours, but, as a result, the company was subject to less political interference than other Münzenberg undertakings.

By 1928, the *IAH* had become seriously involved in the film world. That year, Münzenberg set up a company, *Weltfilm*, to distribute 16 mm copies of Soviet films to working-class organisations in Germany, but in 1929, it went on to produce more films itself. Already by the early 1920s, he had seen how documentary films and newsreels made in the famine areas of the Soviet Union had had an enormous impact in terms of bringing the facts to a global audience. He was also keenly aware of the need to produce films in order to effectively promote the international working-class movement.

This first real contact with the medium undoubtedly laid the seeds for his interest now in developing this aspect of his campaigning work. The company made a short and effective Movietone–news–style advert for his weekly *AIZ*.

In a very short space of time, the director of *Weltfilm* established an efficient film distribution network, supplying films to working-class organisations, cultural, and sport associations. It had in effect a distribution monopoly on what was then a new technical innovation, making it possible to show films copied from 35 mm stock onto 16 mm (the amateur standard), thus making it much easier to show them in small venues, using less cumbersome equipment. Later Weltfilm was also managed by Emil Unfried. Soon, under his management, a whole number of workers' film groups sprang up in those European countries where the

IAH had a presence, in order to show the new Soviet films, boycotted or banned by the commercial cinemas, and to promote 'proletarian art'.

The story of Münzenberg's involvement with film-making in the Soviet Union really began by accident when the Rus co-operative film studio in Moscow fell into financial difficulties as a result of Vladimir Lenin's New Economic Policy, introduced in 1921 as a short-term expedient. This policy had been introduced in an effort to overcome chronic lethargy in the Soviet economy by introducing what, it was hoped, would be temporary capitalist stimuli. To this end, a stock exchange was established in Moscow, and the *IAH* came to the Rus studio's aid, reorganising it as a joint project under the name of Mezhrabpom-Rus, later to be called Mezhrabpomfilm (Mezhrabpom is the Russian acronym for *IAH*). Although a stock-holding company, it was not listed on the Moscow exchange; shares were held by the workers. The Rus company already owned cinemas and later acquired its own film-stock producing factory. It employed hundreds of workers and owned two large film studios and its own sound film production unit.

This German-Russian company would be involved in film production from 1922 until 1936. The production studios were set up in Moscow, with company headquarters in Berlin. Münzenberg put the Italian, Francesco Misiano, in charge of the Moscow operation.[7] Like Münzenberg, he was also a cinephile.

By 1928, Meschrabpom had become a commercial success, registering a turnover in the millions. Between 1924 and 1931 it produced 241 films, mainly for the Soviet market, generating considerable income. It was responsible for such early classics as the science fiction *Aelita* and *Cigarette Girl from Mosselprom* (both 1924) and was able to bring together a strong team of directors. *Aelita* was a silent feature directed by Yakov Protazanov and based on the eponymous novel by Alexei Tolstoy. It was a science fiction film representing the dreams, hopes, and desires for a new utopian society

Some of the films made by the company were not only successful within the Soviet Union, but also abroad. The director, Pudovkin, was one of those who joined the company, and in 1926, made his classic films, *The Mother* and *The End of St. Petersburg* and, in 1927, *Storm over Asia*.

Pudovkin travelled to Berlin for the premiere of *Storm over Asia* and was able to witness its success, with audiences rising to their feet and giving it rapturous applause. He stayed on in the city to work as the lead actor in the film *The Living Corpse* (1929), adapted from Leo Tolstoy's play of the same name, in a Prometheus-Mezhrabpomfilm collaboration.

With the emergence of the sound film, the company was presented with new challenges, not the least, the need to import expensive sound and camera equipment from the West. Although at the time, many saw sound as a hindrance to genuine visual creativity, as an unnecessary addition, it became unstoppable.

The company was certainly not averse to experimentation and helped the Russian engineer, Pavel Tager, who was already working on an optical sound system in 1926, develop a sound-film projector that used optical analogue transference technology. The first Russian sound film, *Road to Life*, based on Makarenko's pioneering educational work with street children, was made in 1931 and was directed and written by Nikolai Ekk. It became one of its most successful films.

In graphic and realistic imagery, *Road to Life* portrayed the dire circumstances of orphan street children of whom there were thousands roaming the country after the war, often in gangs and surviving as best they could. The film won an award at the 1932 Venice International Film Festival, and it holds the distinction of being the very first film to be awarded the best director award at any film festival.

The Mezhrabpom studios would later also produce the first sound film for children, *The Torn Shoes* (1933), directed by Margarita Barskaya, which told the story of children helping their parents deal with the rise of Fascism.

Mezhrabpom would become one of the fundamental pillars of *IAH* work in the Soviet Union, and film specialists from abroad were brought in to help develop this still young mass medium. Very soon a number of leading actors and directors from the Soviet Union and Germany were working for the company.

The German director, Hans Rodenberg, became deputy director of Meschrabpom during the early 1930s after being forced to flee Germany following Hitler's rise to power, and Piscator made several films for it.

In 1931, after the collapse of the third *Piscator-Bühne* due to financial problems, Piscator took himself off to Moscow to make his experimental film *Revolt of the Fishermen*, based on the Anna Seghers' novel of the same name, for Mezhrabpom.

John Willett noted that throughout the pre-Hitler years, Piscator's 'commitment to the Russian Revolution was a decisive factor in all his work'.[8] With Hitler's rise to power in 1933, Piscator's sojourn in the Soviet Union became an involuntary exile, but, in 1936, he would leave the Soviet Union for France.

Jay Leyda himself was sponsored by Mezhrabpom to study at VGIK (the Gerasimov Institute of Cinematography), the renowned Russian film school in Moscow. He writes that there were as many foreign directors, mainly German refugees, at the company as Russian ones. At the time, Gustav von Wangenheim was beginning to make a film about the resistance to Hitler, and the Belgian documentarist, Joris Ivens, was planning a film about the miners in the Borinage, but shot in the Soviet Union.[9] German actors, like Paul Wegener, Lotte Lenya, and others, took roles in Russian-made films.

It is hardly surprising that the passionate propagandist Münzenberg very early on saw the potential of cinema, which was still a relatively young mass medium. In *Film und Volk* (Film and People),[10] a magazine in his portfolio of publications, he commented that it would be 'demagogic' to view film as a 'neutral art form', because 'all bourgeois and socialist parties and the church have their own film organisations and productions ... One should invest the same effort in it as for newspapers and publishing. Film is the most progressive means of propaganda'.

He wrote those words in 1929, the year that the sound film was born, marking the beginning of film as a true mass medium. Already in 1922, the company

Aufbau, Industrie und Handelsgesellschaft, founded by the *IAH*, had been buying up German film licences and distributing the films in the Soviet Union.

From 1925 onwards, Münzenberg's partner, Babette Gross, accompanied him on many of his trips to Moscow. There, they usually stayed in the comfortable Hotel Metropol near the Grand Opera, preferring to avoid Hotel Lux, where most of the Comintern leaders and foreign comrades stayed, not wishing to become entangled in the intrigues and rumour-mongering that went on there.

At this time, life in Moscow reflected the years of peace and the positive repercussions of the New Economic Policy, Babette Gross writes, 'Food was plentiful' and 'for a few Roubles you could buy a good midday meal', although life was still rather Spartan. At this time, party members and officials had not yet become a separate caste and officials earned the party-stipulated maximum salary that was equivalent to that of a skilled toolmaker. Their visits were organised by the employees of Mezhrabpom and its 'temperamentful' director, the Italian Communist, Francesco Misiano, a friend of Münzenberg's from his early days in Switzerland.

On her first visit to Moscow with Münzenberg in 1923, Babette accompanied him to visit Clara Zetkin, the iconic German Communist leader, who was living there at the time, in an annexe of the Kremlin, in 'whitewashed rooms, that in their sobriety gave the impression of being like cells of a religious order ... it was amusing for me to see how suddenly shy the normally very self-possessed Münzenberg became in her presence. He had enormous respect for Clara Zetkin and knew her severe attitudes to marriage and family – and how he breathed more easily once he saw that I had won her grace'. She also accompanied him to visit other friends, like Karl Radek, although in the meantime he had lost his post as Comintern advisor to the German section. They also visited Leon Trotsky who 'sat in his office like a reining aristocrat. In a light grey civilian suit, he presented a distinguished and very un-Russian appearance. He was very polite, but reserved and somewhat arrogant', she writes.

Trotsky tried to win Münzenberg's support in the murderous factional battle that was then taking place within the Soviet Party leadership. But, although Münzenberg respected and admired his achievement as the creator of the Red Army and, alongside Lenin, as a figurehead of the October Revolution, and co-founder of the Soviet state, he remained cautious about taking sides. In his talks with Münzenberg, Trotsky tried to persuade him that Comintern policy towards the British trade unions and by implication Münzenberg's own activities in this field, were incompatible with a genuine Bolshevik position. Trotsky viewed such collaboration with 'reformist' organisations as wrong-headed. Münzenberg, however, was of the view that to adopt Trotsky's line would be to align oneself with the ultra-leftists in the German Party and would make any broader alliances impossible. These differences with Trotsky, though, did not hinder the two from maintaining cordial relations. Münzenberg would later publish Trotsky's works in Germany and help popularise his reputation abroad.

In 1926, when Trotsky spent several weeks in a Berlin sanatorium, Münzenberg visited him regularly and was given the German rights to his *The United States of Europe*, in which Trotsky argues against Münzenberg's old friend, the Dutch trade unionist, Edo Fimmen, who had written a booklet with the same title. Trotsky argued that his ideas were 'reformist illusions', and that a united Europe could only come about once a world revolution had become victorious.

Around this time, Münzenberg also signed a contract with 'Comrade Thomas' (born Jakov Reich and known, amongst other aliases as Arnold Rubinstein), who was also an admirer of Trotsky, to publish two comprehensive volumes: an illustrated history of the Russian Revolution and an illustrated history of the Russian Civil War.

For his publishing house, Münzenberg also bought the rights to a travel guide of the Soviet Union put together by the Society for Cultural Relations with Countries Abroad and edited by the Hungarian-born geographer, Alexander Rado (a world renowned geographer who later achieved a different renown as a top Soviet secret agent during the war and, as a reward for his efforts, was imprisoned by the Joseph Stalin regime).

The guide was a comprehensive work, quite unprecedented at the time, containing many regional maps and street guides to the big cities. It was published at a time when factional infighting was intensifying within the Soviet Communist Party. Later, when war fever and the fear of spies gripped the country, it was deemed to be a dangerous publication, and the state began buying up all copies to remove them from circulation.

In Berlin, Rado would soon work on another similar publication: In 1928, the Soviet civil airline company Aeroflot had signed an agreement with Lufthansa covering flights between Moscow and Berlin. Rado designed maps of the air routes, which were handed out to passengers free of charge. They were printed by Münzenberg's *Neuer Deutscher Verlag* and, as a result, he and Babette were able to fly all over Germany and to Moscow at highly discounted rates. This guide also would later be subject to much criticism in the paranoid atmosphere engendered under Stalin's leadership.

By 1926, the ideological battles in the Soviet Union had become much sharper, centred around the question of whether it was indeed possible to build Socialism in one country.

While Trotsky, at this time, had been maintaining a low profile, Zinoviev and Kamenev openly opposed Stalin's policy of attempting to build Socialism in one country as 'opportunist and un-Marxist'. But, by the next plenary meeting of the Comintern in May 1927, Stalin had consolidated his control of the party apparatus and eradicated any opposition to his policies in the Comintern, expelling Trotsky and his supporters.

The tenth anniversary of the Russian Revolution in 1927 was to be celebrated in grand style. The idea of internationalising the commemorations had come from Münzenberg, who presented his proposals to the agitprop department of the Communist International already in 1925.[11]

Matters related to the composition, invitation, and funding of the delegations were officially entrusted to a special international commission made up of representatives of various Soviet institutions and the Comintern. However, Alfred Kurella, of the Comintern's agitation and propaganda section, *Agitpropotdel*, advocated that 'a large part of the campaign should be left up to the initiative of Münzenberg and organisations influenced by him'.[12]

Münzenberg knew that sending only delegations of already convinced Communists would hardly help broadcast the ideas embodied by the Soviet Union. His idea was to make the delegations as broad as possible. In a circular he issued, he wrote: 'To give this campaign for the sending of delegations to the USSR the broadest possible dimension, it is advisable for the first calls, the first manifestations to come from organisations, groups, people and newspapers located as far as possible from the communist movement'.[13] He ensured that this was done when composing delegations from Germany.

Publicity surrounding the tenth October Revolution festivities echoed around the world, through newspapers, special publications, radio, and newsreels, followed by documentary and fiction films. Just as during the 1921–1923 campaign to alleviate the famine in Russia, it was Münzenberg who set the tone of the international publicity.

The most famous film commissioned by the Soviet government in honour of the tenth anniversary was Eisenstein's *October*, based on the book, *Ten Days That Shook the World* by John Reed and Pudovkin's *End of St. Petersburg*.

Münzenberg also mobilised his company, *Aufbau, Industrie und Handel*, to produce memorabilia which could be sold: posters, commemorative postcards, slides for slideshow evenings, and also flags, ribbons, and other trinkets, busts, porcelain, and badges. This marked the beginning of revolutionary merchandising. The revolution had become a festival, indeed a succession of commemorative festivals.

The success of the 10th anniversary of the October Revolution allowed Münzenberg to expand his International Workers' Relief organisation and his own influence in Moscow and Berlin.

The clamour and the glitter of these celebrations made it possible to hide the repression of the Left Opposition by Stalin. Excluded from the Central Committee of the party, the leaders of the Opposition decided to come out publicly on 7 November by joining the demonstrations in Moscow. On that day of the traditional parade in Red Square, a group of them had occupied a balcony of the Hotel Paris, in which a number of Münzenberg's delegates were also staying. The Opposition shouted slogans at the marchers below, displayed banners with their own slogans, like 'Long live the leaders of the revolution, Zinoviev and Trotsky' and 'Maintain Bolshevik Unity' and held up photos of Lenin, Trotsky, and Zinoviev. This demonstration was rapidly broken up by the state militia and GPU men searched the hotel rooms. These events, unsurprisingly, caused consternation among those few delegates who witnessed them, but it was explained to them that the demonstrators were 'traitors, Whites and counter-revolutionaries'. It also provided Stalin with a suitable justification for the later widespread purge of hundreds of 'oppositional elements' within the party. Like the majority of other foreign Communists present, Gross and Münzenberg were possibly not even aware of these discordant notes.

In 1928, Stalin's 50th birthday year, large celebrations were again organised throughout the Soviet Union, but, according to Babette Gross, Stalin was very much against such personal adulation and only went along with it for tactical reasons; the masses, it was said, yearned for a great leader. It is, though, difficult to accept such a simple explanation for the cult of the personality around Stalin. After the death of Lenin and the internal struggles over the leadership of the Communist Party, the 'cult of personality', the projection of Stalin as Lenin's legitimate heir and as the new 'father' of the republic became an oppressive and ubiquitous factor.

Only a year later, in Germany, the economic miracle that had been brought about by the injection of dollars as a result of the Dawes Plan vanished like a mirage as a consequence of the crash of the stock exchange in New York in October 1929. The oxygen of foreign investments that Germany needed for its continued economic expansion was suddenly withdrawn. The number of unemployed in the country rose from around 7 per cent to 31 per cent between 1928 and 1932. As a result, the country was once again thrown into political turmoil and provided a fertile breeding ground for the virus of Fascism. By February 1932, there were 6.2 million unemployed in the country, unemployment benefits and invalidity pensions were cut, incomes fell, and suicides reached a European record level. In the streets civil war unfolded once more, with Fascist storm troops battling the Communist Red Front units. Bloodshed becomes the norm again, while the Social Democrats still put their faith in government to overcome the crisis and desperately hope to reverse their recent electoral losses.

The elections in July 1932 demonstrate the realities: votes for Hitler's NSDAP rise from 18.3 to 37.3 per cent and, with 250 members in the Reichstag, is now the largest faction. However, in the November elections that same year, the Nazi votes fall to 33.1 per cent, a loss of 2 million voters.

FIGURE 9.1 Willi Münzenberg addressing one of the last legal communist rallies 1933

Münzenberg would visit Moscow again in 1935 for the seventh World Congress of the Comintern and, as usual, met Radek who still lived close to the Kremlin and had now become a close adviser to Stalin. But when they met, Radek made no mention of any inner-party conflicts, according to Gross's report, but merely spoke of improvements in the economy and in living standards.

Gross herself asked rhetorically how it was possible that Münzenberg apparently accepted the ousting of so many leading figures of the revolution. He had never had a close friendship with Zinoviev, finding him 'too hysterical and exalted, too far removed from the realities in post-war Europe', but he took Trotsky seriously, as well as others around Stalin like Bucharin, Tomski, and Rykov. It was, though, now clear to anyone with any sense of reality that Stalin would stop at nothing to eradicate those he considered an enemy; but Münzenberg, like so many others, was still reluctant to recognise this.

Over the years, Münzenberg had very few direct contacts with Stalin and, as he spoke no Russian, the two could only converse through interpreters (unlike many of his other close contacts who were fluent in German). Also, to speak to Stalin, Münzenberg, like everyone else, had to go through the time-consuming and formal bureaucratic process of arranging a meeting; he couldn't just knock on the door as he did with his other Russian contacts. Such formality was against his nature. His real doubts about Stalin's leadership, though, surfaced sometime later when it was impossible to ignore the fact that Stalin was systematically removing all his competitors – the majority of whom had been Lenin's close comrades and installed an 'unrestrained Byzantine structure'. This, though, didn't stop him publishing in the *AIZ* a several-page long homage to Stalin on his 50th birthday, together with a 'man of steel' image on the cover.

Münzenberg's role in promoting inter-cultural exchange between Germany and Russia and in deepening understanding between the two peoples was immeasurable. And it has not been given the recognition it deserves. It cannot be simply dismissed as a cynical attempt on his part to whitewash the Soviet Union and to present a picture of a utopian workers' paradise to a gullible German working class. I would argue strongly that Münzenberg was motivated in the main – of course also by a deep attachment to and love for the Soviet Union – by a profound sense of international solidarity.

Notes

1 Braskén, Kasper, 'The International Workers' Relief and Willi Münzenberg, a paper delivered at the 2015 Willi Münzenberg Forum in Berlin.
2 Geschonneck, Erwin, *Meine Unruhigen Jahre*, Aufbau Taschenbuch Verlag, 1993.
3 John Willett, *The New Sobriety: Art and Politics in the Weimar Period 1917–1933*, Da Capo Press, London, 1996. p. 224.
4 Fryer, Jonathan, *Isherwood: A Biography of Christopher Isherwood*, Hodder & Stoughton Ltd, London, 1977.
5 John Willett, *The New Sobriety: Art and Politics in the Weimar Period 1917–1933*, Da Capo Press, London, 1996. p. 114.

6 Geschonneck, Erwin, *Meine Unruhigen Jahre*, Das Neue, Berlin, Germany, 2009. p. 45.

7 Misiano, Francesco.

Born 1884, in Ardore, Calabria, Misiano died in 1936, in Moscow.

He joined the Italian Socialist Party in 1907. From 1908 to 1914, he was secretary of the Socialist Federation and the railway men's union in Naples.

Drafted into the army in 1916, he refused to take part in an imperialist war.

Misiano emigrated to Switzerland, where he became editor of the newspaper *L'Avvenire del Lavatore*, the organ of the Italian Socialists in Switzerland.

In 1918, he went to the Soviet Union to carry out propaganda among the Italian units of the interventionist corps on the Murmansk front. During his stopover in Berlin, he took part in the January Uprising of 1919; after the defeat of the uprising, he was sentenced by the German authorities to ten years in prison.

But through a protest campaign by Italian workers who had elected him to parliament and with the help of German left-wing Social Democrats, Misiano was freed and returned to Italy. He fought for the revolutionary rejuvenation of the Italian Socialist Party; in 1921, he was among the founders of the Communist Party and became a member of its Central Committee. He was re-elected to parliament that same year, but under attack from the forces of extreme reaction, was deprived of his parliamentary mandate and sentenced to ten years imprisonment. By a decision of the Central Committee of the Communist Party, Misiano emigrated.

In Germany and later in the USSR, he became first a member of the Executive Committee of Profintern (Red Trade Union International), and then a member of the Executive Committee of Mezhrabpom (Workers' International Relief), becoming its representative in the USSR.

8 Willett, John, *The New Sobriety*, Thames and Hudson, 1978.

9 Leyda, Jay, *Kino – A History of the Russian and Soviet Film*, Princeton University Press, 1960. p. 310.

10 *Film Und Volk* (Film and People) was the journal Münzenberg set up for the Volksverbandes für Filmkunst (Popular Association for Film Art), which was under the chairmanship of the writer, Heinrich Mann.

11 Quoted by Bela Kun, secretary of ECCI, 30.11.1925, F.495/30/141, doc.159, RGASPI and F.495/60/117, doc.43-49, RGASPI

12 See Jean-François Fayet: "'Hands off the USSR": *Münzenberg and the Internationalisation of the Commemorations of the 10th Anniversary of the October Revolution*' (Beiträge zum Ersten Internationalen Willi-Münzenberg-Kongress 2015 in Berlin).

13 Münzenberg's proposition to the tenth anniversary of October Revolution, 14.11.1926, F.495/30/264, doc.132–135, RGASPI.

10

LEAGUE AGAINST IMPERIALISM

After the subsidence of revolutionary activity in Germany, the Comintern, from 1924/1925 onwards, had come to the realisation that there would be no revolutionary upsurge in Europe for the foreseeable future. As a result, it began devoting more attention to potential allies outside Europe and particularly those struggling for liberation in the colonial countries. It felt that it could play a key role in not only mobilising anti-colonial forces, but also in helping direct them towards Communist goals. It realised that the *IAH* would be the ideal vehicle for mounting such a campaign. It clearly saw the potential of such a worldwide anti-colonial movement, but wanted to ensure that it would develop a clear Marxist perspective and, from the outset, rejected what it viewed as 'liberal and pacifist' approaches. This could be interpreted as a criticism of Münzenberg's attempt to establish a movement that was more than just a Communist one; it also put him under pressure, but he could to a large extent ignore it, which he did.

In its solidarity campaigns, the *IAH* had· already been focussing attention on questions related to the political and social development in colonial and semi-colonial countries, but up until now, this had been more of a philanthropic exercise and with a case-by-case approach. However, the consolidation of a real anti-colonialist campaign in Europe required, according to Münzenberg, the establishment of an effective organisation. The Comintern therefore gave him the green light in 1926 to go ahead to set up a new organisation, the League against Colonial Oppression, as a connective and organising force to accomplish a twofold objective, one of convening a representative gathering against colonialism, and two establishing a League against Imperialism. This organisation would become one of the most globally significant and influential in terms of promoting colonial liberation.

The early post-war period coincided with an upsurge of struggle against the colonial occupying forces in a number of countries outside Europe. Already in 1925, the *IAH* had waged a campaign to aid Arab rebels in Syria and Morocco who were at war with the colonial powers, France and Spain. It also mounted a broad campaign to denounce French massacres in Syria, where 10,000 Arabs had been slaughtered during the French bombardment of Damascus in that same year.

The Berber rising in the Rif mountains in Morocco, under Abd el-Krim, led to the establishment of a short-lived republic there. It was suppressed by a joint French-Spanish force, and the Spanish lost over 13,000 soldiers in the fighting.

In Algeria, Ahmed Ben Messali Hadj, the 'father of Algerian nationalism', after serving in the French army during the First World War, led an armed struggle against the French occupation of his country and set up the Étoile nord-Africaine national liberation movement in 1926.

Similar rebellions were taking place in North Africa and on the Indian sub-continent and Indo-China. In Latin America, also, the subject peoples were stirring. Nicaragua had been occupied by the United States marines in 1912, but they had to face a drawn-out guerrilla struggle led by Augusto Sandino from 1927 onwards. In response to the invasion of Nicaragua, Münzenberg initiated a 'Hands off Nicaragua' campaign too. These events and others elsewhere revealed the stirring of a new consciousness in the colonial countries, which was in many cases given impetus by the 1917 Russian Revolution.

Based in Berlin, the League against Colonialism was established in 1926 and placed in the capable organisational hands of Louis Gibarti and Lucie Peters. It won ready support among refugees from colonial countries already living in European exile, not only in Germany, but others living in Paris, London, and elsewhere: Chinese, Indo-Chinese, Indonesians, Indians, Africans, and Arabs.

A short time later, the name of the League was changed into League Against Imperialism and for National Independence, which was felt to be a more appropriate title. Once established, it soon developed strong links with young nationalists from many of the colonised countries, a number of whom were studying in Europe at the time. Münzenberg, and the Indian revolutionary Virendranath Chattopadhyaya, then based in Berlin, became the League's first secretaries.

With Germany's economic revival from 1924 onwards, the Aid for Germany programme had become redundant, so Münzenberg began focussing the organisation's energies elsewhere. He was able to capitalise on the many contacts he had already built up through the *IAH*'s previous work to do this.

The Weimar Republic had given asylum to a number of political refugees from the colonial world. As an example, at Berlin's university at the time there were more than a hundred Chinese students, and the Chinese Kuomintang nationalist movement had its own office in the city and its young secretary was a friend of Münzenberg's. The Vietnamese nationalist leader, Ho Chi Minh, who was residing in Paris at the time, would drop into Berlin regularly to see Münzenberg on his way to and from Moscow.

The Polish-born, founding member and secretary of the Communist Party of Palestine, Joseph Berger-Barzilai, after he joined the Comintern, was sent in

1932 to work for the League in Berlin, alongside Münzenberg. There, together with the Indian nationalist, Clemens Dutt, he edited several of the League's publications.[1]

The Indian Communist, Manabendranath Roy, had been in Berlin since 1922 and published his radical paper, the *Vanguard*, there. The Indian revolutionary journalist, Virendranath Chattopadhyaya, who also became a friend of Münzenberg's (Chattopadhyaya became the partner of the North American journalist and great friend of China, Agnes Smedley) was also living in the city.

In 1937, in Moscow, Chattopadhyaya would meet Babette Gross's sister, Margarete Buber-Neumann, and confided to her at the time that he feared for his life. He was not mistaken and became one of Joseph Stalin's many victims during the first great purge of the late 1930s and was executed in Moscow that same year, 1937.

In 1925, a large strike had erupted among Chinese workers in the Japanese-owned textile industry and, in response to the intervention of British troops, it became a general strike soon affecting the whole of China, and then morphed into a national rebellion against all foreign capitalists amid calls for national liberation. Moscow gave its support to a young military commander, Chiang Kai-Shek and the founding father of the Republic of China, Sun Yat-Sen.

Münzenberg made use of his trade union contacts in Britain first of all to drum up support for his campaign of solidarity with the striking Chinese workers and for the newly founded League. A whole number of leading figures, like George Lansbury, Arthur Cooke, Alex Gossip, George Hicks, Tom Mann, Ellen Wilkinson, James Maxton, and John MacLean soon signed his appeal. He was also able to rally support for the China campaign in Austria and Norway.

On 16 August 1925, Münzenberg organised an international congress in Berlin's *Herrenhaus* – the banqueting hall of the Prussian parliament building – under the motto, 'Hands Off China', in order to 'unite the Western with the eastern proletariat'. During this campaign, he developed a close and life-long relationship with Soong Ching-Ling, the recently widowed partner of Sun Yat-Sen. She would become a strong supporter of many of Münzenberg's other campaigns.

The British government was particularly nervous and alarmed about Münzenberg's campaign on behalf of Chinese liberation (see Chapter 14, Münzenberg as seen by the secret services) and began keeping a very close eye on the activities of both Münzenberg and later the League against Imperialism.

Under Münzenberg's direction, the League's campaigns developed into something much more than charitable aid programmes and would impact on future solidarity campaigns in terms of their political, cultural, and moral ramifications.

There was already increased awareness among many liberally minded people in Western countries of the fact that colonial oppression was a moral abomination, and many were more than ready to give their support to campaigns for the liberation of the colonies, and Münzenberg was able to capitalise on this.

In August 1926, he penned an article in which he attempted to drum up support for the holding of an international conference on the subject of colonialism. While the Comintern gave its support to this initiative, it also made it clear to Münzenberg that he should connect such anti-colonialist and anti-Fascist campaigns with raising an awareness of the continued risk of war against the Soviet Union. The connection between these two issues would not be immediately obvious to most people, but Münzenberg agreed to do what he could.

FIGURE 10.1 Willi Münzenberg with Vallabhbhai Patel (later to become deputy prime minister of India) at a conference of the League against Imperialism c. 1929 (Courtesy of Deutsche Bundesarchiv.)

In January 1927, he staged a large event in Berlin's *Festsaal des Herrenhaus*, in which anti-Fascist and anti-colonial positions were given a full airing. There were speeches by the Italian trade unionist, Guido Migliolo, by the Afro-American William Pickens for the National Association for the Advancement of Coloured Peoples, and by the Chinese Ch' ao-Ting Chi, who represented the Association for Spreading Sun-Yat-Senism in America.

The League's first international congress in 1927 was to be held in Paris, but the draconian response of the French government to League representatives there made it impossible, so the venue was moved to Brussels. There, only recently the Social Democrat leader Emile Vanderfelde had taken over as secretary of the Second International and he could hardly be seen to be opposing the holding of such a congress.

Before the Brussels conference in February, Münzenberg approached the Comintern with a proposal of organising an international congress against Fascism, but the Comintern told him that he should abandon this idea as that was a campaign to be waged by the Comintern itself and the individual national parties.[2]

Münzenberg sent Gibarti to Brussels to negotiate with Vanderfelde, who declared that he would be prepared to lend his support to the congress as long as the Belgian Congo was kept off the agenda and a list of delegates was submitted in advance to the Belgian Sûreté. Münzenberg agreed to these demands – he had little option if the congress were to go ahead. Through his friend, Professor Alfons Goldschmidt, working in Mexico, he also managed to persuade the Mexican government to provide funding for the event.

The congress was duly held in the prestigious Egmont Palace in Brussels in February of that year. It would be the first and last of its kind. Albert Einstein was the honorary chairman and, in his letter of greetings to the congress, expressed the hope that 'through your congress the efforts of the oppressed to win independence will take tangible form'.[3]

There had never been such a representative gathering of delegates from countries around the world struggling for national liberation, bringing together black and white and those from very different cultural and political backgrounds, on an equal basis, to discuss colonialism. There were 174 delegates attending, representing 134 organisations from 37 countries; 104 came from the colonies or from areas suffering imperialist domination.

The Indian National Congress sent its young general secretary, Jawaharlal Nehru and Virendranath Chattopadhyaya ('Chatto'), Mohammed Hatta, and Ahmed Sukarno and Mohammad Hatta came from Indonesia, Manuel Gomez from the USA, Augusto Sandino and Julio Antonio Mella from Latin America, and Tiémenko Garan Kouyaté (Kujaté) from West Africa, among others. There were 'Indian princes, Kuomintang generals and trade union leaders' among the delegates. It was a huge success, not the least because of the capable input of Münzenberg's friend, the Dutch trade unionist, Edo Fimmen.

FIGURE 10.2 At a conference of the League against Imperialism. From left to right: John W. Ford (USA), Willi Münzenberg (Germany), and Garan Tiemoko Kuoyaté (French Sudan, now Mali) in 1936 (Courtesy of Deutsche Bundesarchiv.)

Münzenberg was in his element at the congress, moving easily among the delegates, and meeting old friends and acquaintances. In his concluding speech, he said: 'We … believe today that we are able to recognise the outline of a development for the coming decades that, in our opinion, will bring about the liberation of the colonial and semi-colonial countries … We want to try, by mobilising the human willpower, to accelerate these developments in order to bring about freedom more quickly for the peoples.'

This 1927 congress sent tremors of perturbation through the corridors of power in the colonial countries, particularly France and Britain, as the since released MI5 files reveal. For that reason, the organisation was kept under permanent surveillance by the British secret services, and its post, including letters from Münzenberg to British members of its Executive, was intercepted. The imperialist nations feared its potentially explosive impact in their colonies. Münzenberg, who had applied for a visa to enter Britain to win support for the League's work, was refused, so had to liaise with his British supporters by post and courier.

The leaderships of the Social Democratic parties in Europe had been adamantly opposed to the League from the outset, characterising it as a Communist front organisation, manipulated from Moscow, but that in itself by no means rendered the League ineffective. Even those who might have had reservations about the League's Communist links could not avoid recognising that it was the only organisation of its kind actively promoting colonial liberation, as opposed to charitable aid and honeyed words of sympathy. It was, though, an attitude that certainly hampered Münzenberg's aim of bringing together all Socialist and progressive forces into the struggle against imperialism.

This lack of co-operation was then made worse by the Comintern's new 'class against class' policy, formulated at its 1928 congress, and the labelling of Social Democrats as 'Social Fascists'. This misguided and catastrophic policy played into the hands of the right-wing leaders of the Social Democratic parties and appeared to confirm their allegations that the League was merely a Communist front. However, it would have been reasonably clear to most interested parties who were behind the League right from the outset; its establishment and deliberations were hardly secret, hidden, or camouflaged.

The League's second congress was again planned for Paris in July 1929, but was banned by the French government, again out of fear of repercussions on its own colonies. The British government, too, was concerned about the influence of the League and potential repercussions in its own empire. It was particularly worried that the already volatile situation in India could be further exacerbated.

As a result, the venue was switched from Paris to Frankfurt am Main. By this time, sections had already been established in Central and South America and elsewhere; 16 in all, of which four were in Europe and one in the United States. However, of the 200 delegates from 50 odd countries attending the congress in Frankfurt, only about 15 had travelled directly from the colonies.

Among those who began playing an active role in the League were several future leaders of so-called Third World countries, like Nehru in India, Kenyatta in Kenya, Sukarno in Indonesia, and Lamine Senghor in Senegal.

Shortly after the congress concluded, Edo Fimmen and the US civil rights activist, Roger Baldwin, met in Amsterdam in an attempt to construct and unite a bloc of anti-imperialists within the League who supported the spirit of the Brussels Congress. In letters from Baldwin and Fimmen to Nehru, both noted the troubles in the Berlin secretariat and the unenviable pressure placed on Münzenberg and Chatto [Virendranath Chattopadhyaya] by Moscow. 'Baldwin wrote that he knew 'from an authoritative source that there [was] great tension existing between Moscow and Münzenberg.' Baldwin added that 'Münzenberg knew very well it would be "stupid" to make the League a tool of the Comintern, but that the "eye of Moscow" had been in Frankfurt and reported on him "in a very unfavourable manner"'.[4]

Particularly because of its well co-ordinated global web of prominent figures in the liberation struggles and the key role played by Communists, the League was seen as a significant threat by the colonial and imperialist countries and every effort was made to counter its work.

One of its chief enemies became the Secretariat of the Second (Socialist) International, and even though it had originally been involved in setting up the founding conference its animosity remained. It was particularly concerned that Münzenberg's name was too closely associated with it. When it came to the crunch, the leaderships of all Social Democratic parties in Europe invariably joined arm-in-arm with their country's conservative and pro-empire forces.

Although the leadership of the British Labour Party was, from the very beginning, suspicious of the League and certainly gave no support to the anti-imperialist struggle, Münzenberg was able to bring on board progressive and more enlightened Labour Party figures such as Reginald Bridgeman, the MPs Fenner Brockway and George Lansbury, as well as Arthur MacManus, together with intellectuals from other countries like the writers, Henri Barbusse and Romain Rolland, from France, the writer, Upton Sinclair, from the USA, and Albert Einstein from Germany. Einstein, Barbusse, and Mrs. Sun Yat Sen, the widow of China's great nationalist leader, were the organisation's three honorary presidents. Reginald Bridgeman became the British section's very capable secretary, and it had the support of the Independent Labour Party's James Maxton, the Labour MP Ellen Wilkinson, together with Communists Shapurji Saklatvala MP, Harry Pollitt, and former suffragette Helen Crawfurd. The revered British Labour Party MP, George Lansbury, was unanimously elected chair of the League's Executive Committee and another Labour MP, Fenner Brockway, was elected chair of its British section.

There is no doubt, that the organisational drive which brought the League into being and gave it impetus as a functioning international organisation was down to Münzenberg above all others and demonstrated why he was so feared and demonised by his opponents. The League became very effective worldwide with a network that was unsurpassed during the interwar period.

Already during the early 1930s, following Hitler's accession to power, the Soviet Union had become particularly keen on raising European awareness of the impending danger of war, but the League against Imperialism was hardly the right vehicle for mounting what was a separate campaign. Münzenberg was persuaded to begin a new one.

The World Congress, 'Against Imperialist War', was held in Amsterdam on 27–29 August 1932. Although Münzenberg organised it, he clearly had the full support and backing of the Soviet Union. He was, though, careful to avoid giving the impression that it was just another Soviet initiative because, in terms of gaining broad support, it would have been stillborn.

Even though it was advertised as the World Congress Against Imperialist War in Communist publications, it was called the World Congress Against War elsewhere. The French writers, Romain Rolland and Henri Barbusse, issued the invitations in order to give it a semblance of independence from Moscow.

The congress was attended by more than 2,000 delegates from 27 countries, and the majority of them were non-Communists. However, many did belong to organisations associated with the Communist Party or were known to be sympathetic to the Soviet Union.

At this congress, the World Committee against Imperialist War was founded and was, to begin with, based in Berlin. Münzenberg had managed to convince many prominent pacifists to join the committee. In addition to Barbusse, Rolland, and Gorky, other members included Albert Einstein, Heinrich Mann, Bertrand Russell, Havelock Ellis, Theodore Dreiser, John Dos Passos, Upton Sinclair, and Sherwood Anderson. Most of the discussion at the congress focussed on the need to protect the Soviet Union.

Later that same year, Dimitrov was appointed secretary general of the World Committee against War and Fascism, replacing Münzenberg. This organisation would take on added importance as the clouds of war gathered over Europe during the 1930s.

The role played by the *IAH* in the interwar years, in the sphere of international solidarity and in giving a voice to the burgeoning anti-colonial struggle, had been largely ignored by historians. Kasper Braskén, in his book, *The International Workers' Relief, Communism, and Transnational Solidarity. Willi Münzenberg in Weimar Germany*, has gone a long way in remedying that fact.

He argues, convincingly in my view, that the *IAH* was a genuine solidarity organisation albeit with unabashed links to the Communist movement and the Soviet Union. Certainly, the many leaders from colonial nations who joined the organisation, and who were not Communists, would have been very much aware of its ties and its role, but this did not appear to perturb them unduly.

The central campaigning issue of fighting oppression which the *IAH* had championed tied in with the call for the liberation of all colonial countries and for the defeat of imperialism; no other organisation at the time was making such demands. In conceptualising this global task, Münzenberg reached beyond party and class and, on that basis, was able to build up widespread support for the struggles against colonialism, imperialism, Fascism, and the continued threat of war.

This situation would change once the Comintern's sectarian 'class against class' policy came into force, together with the stricture that Communists should not collaborate with 'Social Fascists' (i.e. Social Democrats). The policy had serious repercussions within the League, much to Münzenberg's dismay; he realised that one could not force an organisation like this to adopt narrow Comintern positions if one wanted it to remain broad and effective.

An example of this retrograde policy was the vehement criticism made of James Maxton of the British ILP in 1929 at its Frankfurt congress for not sufficiently condemning the British Labour government's policy towards India. The Labour government, the congress stated, had become 'the caretaker of capitalism and continues the policy of British Imperialism'.

In July 1931, at a meeting of the League's leadership in Hamburg, James Maxton was expelled and the British Communist Party's newspaper, the *Sunday Worker* parroted the Comintern line, that his connection with the League was 'maintained for the purpose of sabotaging its activities'. This was a grossly unfair charge. It would be more accurate to describe Maxton's position as not sufficiently subscribing to the League's full Socialist and anti-imperialist policy, as determined by the League's leadership. The progressive British miners' leader, Arthur Cook, also resigned in solidarity with Maxton.

In 1931, the League's international office in Berlin's Friedrichstrasse would be raided by the Berlin police. Of the documents seized in that raid, several were in due course passed on to the British security services.

In 1933, after the Nazis came to power, the League's office was moved to Ahrweiler Strasse, as a letter addressed to Bridgeman, intercepted by Britain's secret services reveals. Later in that year, the international office was relocated to Paris and a short time afterwards to London.[5]

Notes

1 Only a year later, in 1932, he was again summoned back to Moscow and became a Soviet citizen. In 1934, he became a victim of Stalin's purges, but amazingly survived, after being condemned to death twice and spending years in various Gulags. In 1956, he was rehabilitated and lived for a while in Poland, before leaving for Israel. In the later 1960s, he dictated his reminiscences to friends, and they were published in 1971 in Britain with the title *Shipwreck of a Generation* and in the United States as *Nothing But the Truth: Joseph Stalin's Prison Camps: A Survivor's Account of the Victim's He Knew*. From: Kessler, Mario Die 'Ulbricht-Verschwörung' gegen Münzenberg (1936–1938)/The 'Ulbricht conspiracy' against Münzenberg (1936–1938).

2 See Petersson, Fredrik. 'Willi Münzenberg: A Propagandist Reaching Beyond the Party and Class' in *Weimar Communism as Mass Movement*, Lawrence and Wishart, London, 2017. p. 244.

3 Gross, Babette, *Willi Münzenberg*, Forum Verlag, Leipzig ,1991.

4 Petersson, Fredrik cited in *Comrades against Imperialism: Nehru, India, and Interwar Internationalism*, by Michele L. Louro, Cambridge University Press, 2018, p. 166.

5 Ellison, John, 'The League against Imperialism – the hidden history of the British section' (The Communist Party's Our History series), 2018.

11

FLEEING THE NAZIS TO FRANCE

Münzenberg's last appearance on a political stage in Germany was on 27 February 1933, when he spoke at an election hustings in the small town of Langenselbold in Hesse. Several comrades had warned him not to do it, given that Nazi attacks on Communist meetings had already become commonplace. This had led him to take security measures; he did not stay in a hotel as usual, and he had already called his driver, Emil, to come to Frankfurt early to pick him up.

The meeting went well and his passionate speech, in which he pilloried the Nazis, received an enthusiastic response from his audience. Then, only ten minutes after he had left the meeting by a side door, an SA commando squad forced its way into the hall to arrest him. At this time, he had no idea what was taking place in Berlin at that very moment and returned to the flat of the local *IAH* secretary, where, totally relaxed, the two played cards until late into the evening. It was almost midnight before this comrade's wife returned home and told them that the Reichstag had been set on fire, but she did not know the exact details.

In the meantime, Münzenberg's partner Babette Gross had arrived back in Germany from Switzerland, taking the train to Frankfurt, where she was met by Emil. They conferred about how to prevent Münzenberg coming to meet them at the station café as had been agreed, but where he could easily be picked up by the Gestapo. They decided to stand at either end of the station square to keep an eye out for him and warn him of the danger. Emil spotted him first and took him immediately to the car before collecting Babette Gross and speeding off towards Darmstadt. But what now? They could not return to Berlin, and attempting to go underground where they were was also rather pointless, as they had few contacts in the area and the party groups were themselves already going into hiding.

When they saw the next day's midday editions of the papers, they read Münzenberg's name high on the list of the most 'wanted' fugitives, alongside the writers, Lion Feuchtwanger and Heinrich Mann, the theatre critic, Alfred Kerr, and the Communist leader, Wilhelm Pieck, along with seven others. Driving back to Berlin and going underground was no longer a viable option. Their only way of avoiding almost certain arrest would be to flee over the border to France, but Münzenberg needed a passport in a different name.

It suddenly occurred to Babette Gross that her sister's father-in-law, the Jewish philosopher Martin Buber, lived not far from Darmstadt. Surely, he could help. Although he was alarmed to see them, he gave them a letter of recommendation to a university colleague of his who lived in Saarbrücken and with whom Münzenberg could perhaps stay until they were able to make firm plans. Saarbrücken, in the Saar region, was still under French control as a consequence of a League of Nations mandate in 1920, and they would be safer there.

Once again, the comrade in Frankfurt came to their aid and offered to help obtain a passport.

The three then drove to Mainz where the annual carnival was still in full swing, its citizens in a carefree mood and seemingly oblivious of the incipient terror. Emil and Babette Gross left Münzenberg there, reasonably safe, inconspicuous among the hundreds of revellers, while the two drove back to Frankfurt and to the *Neuer Deutscher Verlag* and *AIZ* offices. There, a young comrade, called Studzinski, ran home and returned to give Babette Gross his own pass for Münzenberg to use, even though the passport photo showed a man who was 14 years younger and had little resemblance to him. (In the post-war period, Studzinski would become mayor of the small Thuringian town of Sonneberg, representing the *SED*.)

In the centre of Frankfurt, carnival was also in full swing and in the festive crowds she and Emil temporarily lost sight of Münzenberg. They went to look for him in a nearby café where they hoped he might be waiting for them, but one of the waiters told her not to go inside, as the police had just been there and had been looking for Münzenberg. In the end, they managed to locate him wandering along the banks of the Rhine, enveloped in snow flurries. He clambered into the car, and they then drove along unfrequented country roads into the evening dusk.

All the border crossing points already had 'Wanted' posters displayed prominently with the names and pictures of those high on the Nazis' wanted list. Their hearts were in their mouths as they pulled to a halt at the Saarland checkpoint. Luckily the border guard on duty that evening, probably thinking they were revellers returning from the carnival celebrations, just took a peek into the car and waved them over the border.

That night, safely in Saarbrücken, Münzenberg said to Babette Gross: 'Hitler now sits firmly in the saddle. His regime will last for a long time; we'll probably have to reckon with 8 or 10 years. Who knows whether he can be toppled without a war?' He then added, 'Once again we've escaped with our lives, but who knows if we'll ever see Germany again?' How prescient his comment was.

Unlike many of his comrades in the party leadership who thought Hitler and Fascism would be a fleeting phenomenon, his perception of reality proved to be the more accurate.

Münzenberg and Emil soon discovered that it was quite easy to obtain a French visa, which they needed to enter France proper. Any tourist office simply sent the passports to the French consulate in Mainz, where they were stamped. But even at this late stage, things almost went pear-shaped when the professor, who had agreed to give Münzenberg shelter for a few days, turned out to be a Nazi sympathiser. All of a sudden he was keen to get rid of him, once he realised who he had under his roof.

Once the passports had been returned to the tourist agency, Emil collected them and took them to their temporary hideout. Wasting no time, on a bright and sunny spring day, Emil drove Münzenberg to the border. Much relieved, they drove on via Metz towards Paris. Babette Gross returned to Berlin and would follow them later. She was not on the Nazis' wanted list at this time, so was not under immediate threat of arrest. She does not say why she returned to Berlin, but she probably wanted to rescue personal documents and belongings from their flat.

Not long after Babette Gross joined him in Paris, they managed quite easily to find a temporary place to live. They began renting a small, newly built flat in the working-class suburb of Issy-les-Moulineux, in the southwest of the city, and from there they would travel to the office in the centre.

As a high profile and internationally known Communist, Münzenberg was not exactly welcome in Paris any more than he had been in Germany, but here at least he would have a breathing space.

In addition to his close collaboration with the Bolsheviks during the First World War, his work in the League against Imperialism had hardly endeared him to the French establishment. Despite his reputation, however, and with the help of his many French friends, he was able to procure temporary political asylum, along with a number of his comrades. As long as they refrained from involvement in French internal affairs, they were told, they could do very much as they wanted in terms of fighting Fascism.

The Comintern now appointed him their new Paris-based West European head of 'Agitation', i.e. responsible for information and propaganda.

German citizens opposed to the Nazis had been fleeing the country in increasing numbers, Communists, Social Democrats, conservatives, Protestants, Catholics, Jews, scientists, and artists. They fled to many countries, but to begin with, those close to or bordering Germany: Czechoslovakia, Switzerland, Scandinavia, and France. Many would be forced to move countries several times before finding a safe refuge. Brecht, for instance, went first to Czechoslovakia, then Austria, to Switzerland, Scandinavia, and via the Soviet Union to California.

At the time they arrived in Paris, there were already around 4,000 refugees from Germany living in the city. It was the first haven to which many of those fleeing intensified persecution came, and it became the centre for anti-Fascist activity in Western Europe until the Nazis occupied France. The German Communist Party also had its Western headquarters there, and Gestapo agents were increasingly active, keeping tabs on their opponents.

With the help of his French friends, Münzenberg set up a *Welthilfskomitee* (World Aid Committee) to provide support for the victims of German Fascism whose situation was, in many cases, dire. Its office in Paris soon became a meeting place for a steady stream of German artists and intellectuals, politicians, and journalists fleeing Hitler, among them also former employees of Münzenberg's *IAH* organisation in Berlin.

Although Paris had rapidly become a sanctuary for tens of thousands of refugees fleeing Fascism, it did not embrace these interlopers with open arms. Many French citizens resented their presence, and they were daily made aware that they were there on tolerance. In sections of French society, there were also strong Fascist sympathies.

Refugees were, in most cases, not allowed to take paid employment, so lived hand-to-mouth, and every day they feared being deported if some gendarme in a bad mood decided to arrest them for a minor infringement or their identity papers were deemed to be not in order. They were deracinated and often treated little better than feral dogs. A number of them felt that their lives had become meaningless and, losing hope, committed suicide. The Parisians, though, went about their business in their usual carefree manner, as if this flood of refugees and the massive build-up of weaponry on their eastern border had no bearing at all on their own lives.

Many of the refugees still clung to the belief that the Hitler regime would last no more than a few months before it was overthrown, but Münzenberg was not one of them; his view was more realistic and thus pessimistic.

From May 1933, several of Münzenberg's friends began publishing a newspaper called *Unsere Zeit* (Our Time), which was printed in Strasburg and could easily be smuggled into Germany. Münzenberg, together with his comrade, Alexander Abusch (who would become minister of culture in the first GDR post-war government) and Bruno Frei, also began publishing the fortnightly, *Gegenangriff* (Counterattack), which would later come out weekly. It was given this title with the deliberate intention of echoing Goebbels' own paper, *Der Angriff* (The Attack). He would go on to publish other journals and numerous books during his involuntary sojourn in Paris.

Despite being the Comintern's most talented anti-Fascist propagandist, he had been given only limited leeway in the *KPD*; his abilities in this area were not as recognised as they should have been and his ideas not always adopted. This attitude he found increasingly frustrating and infuriating and led him, in July 1933, to write to Stalin telling him that, 'If there hadn't been so many obstructions, if I could have had as much freedom as the Nazi propagandists had, I would have given them a run for their money every day'.[1]

The situation was not helped by the fact that Stalin and the Soviet Party leadership themselves had an equivocal attitude to the rise of Fascism in Germany. On the one hand, they appeared to see it as a nationalist anti-capitalist movement and even one that could speed the process of social revolution in the country, despite Hitler's avowed anti-Communism. On the other hand, they could not entirely dismiss Hitler's clear intention of confrontation with the Soviet Union and to 'smash Bolshevism'. During this period, the Soviet Union took no anti-Nazi measures and continued to maintain normal diplomatic relations with Germany. During the early 1930s, while Communists were being rounded up, incarcerated, and killed in Germany, Stalin was carrying out a similar purge of German Communist refugees in the Soviet Union, albeit on a smaller scale.

Not very long after settling in Paris and gearing up to re-establish his anti-Fascist campaigning work in this new environment, Münzenberg was able to persuade Lord Marley, the Labour Chief Whip in the British House of Lords, to become president of his Relief Committee for the Victims of German Fascism, which soon had an active section in Britain. Isobel Brown, a longstanding Communist Party activist, was the secretary of the Workers International Relief, and she became joint-secretary of the Committee, alongside Dorothy Woodman, an intimate friend of Kingsley Martin, editor of the *New Statesman*. The Independent Labour Party appointed Jennie Lee, later to become the wife of Aneurin Bevan, as its representative on the Committee. Ellen Wilkinson MP, later a minister in the 1945 Labour government, became its treasurer. The anti-Fascist campaign began to gain considerable momentum, not only in the labour movement, but among sections of the leisured, literary, professional, and cultured middle classes. Before the end of 1933, the Relief Committee was able to muster on its platforms, alongside such Communist Party professionals as Ted Bramley and Isobel Brown, figures such as the Labour MP Sir Stafford Cripps, the scientist Lancelot Hogben, and the leader of the Independent Labour Party, James Maxton. By May 1934, the coverage had extended to include Aneurin Bevan, the Grand Rabbi Fraenkel, J.B.S. Haldane, Naomi Mitchison, and Lord Marley, the under-secretary of State for War in the second Labour government and others.

The Relief Committee for the Victims of German Fascism was an effective means of mobilising hitherto unattached individuals, the Reichstag Trial Defence Committee (see next chapter) was to prove another. In this latter endeavour, Dorothy Woodman was again involved, on this occasion accompanied by Kingsley Martin in person to the hearings, along with Harold Laski. After Dimitrov's acquittal in Leipzig, Dorothy Woodman and Ivor Montagu would fly to Leipzig to make arrangements for his release.

In March 1934, Lord Marley would undertake a 20-day tour of the USA to publicise and raise support for the defence of the German Communist leader, Ernst Thälmann, who had been imprisoned by the Nazis. After Marley's return, Aneurin Bevan MP, Münzenberg, and a former Weimar Social Democrat minister, set out to tour North America in Marley's place. By the summer of 1935, the Relief Committee also had at its disposal a sound film *Free Thälmann*, made by Ivor Montagu, which was shown at meetings around the country.

Towards the end of 1934, the young British Communist, James Klugmann travelled to Brussels to attend the first World Student Congress against War and Fascism, which grew out of the World Committee against War and Fascism that had been set up by Münzenberg. The theme of the congress was opposition to the militarisation of young people, and it would showcase the role students could play in the anti-Fascist movement. The congress had made clear that a potential now existed for the building of alliances between Christians, liberals, and Social Democrats. Out of this congress emerged the *Rassemblement Mundial des Étudiants* (World Student Association) in which Klugmann would play a leading role. He was excited by being part of the upsurge in international solidarity and sharing a world view that was capturing the imagination of a whole generation of young people.

The Cambridge Communist lecturer Maurice Dobb had sent his student Klugmann to Paris to work in the *Rassemblement Mundial des Étudiants* offices in 1936 and would give up a promising academic career for full-time politics. Only the previous year Dobb had sent Philby there with a letter of introduction to Münzenberg's organisation.

In his biography of Klugmann, Geoff Andrews writes that, 'Paris had become the "Mecca for political exiles", a city of émigrés, where left intellectuals, workers' movements and anti-fascist activists converged at a time when the French left were gaining support ... The *Rassemblement Mundial des Étudiants* shared an office with another of Münzenberg's organisations at 1 Cité Paradis, a five storey building built in 1910 and which had also been identified by MI5 as one of Otto Katz's private addresses'.[2] The Marxist historian Eric Hobsbawm also visited Klugmann at the Communist Youth International headquarters there, which 'operated out of one of those small, dusty Balzacian backstairs offices so characteristic of unofficial pre-war politics, in the ill-named Cité Paradis, a gloomy, dead-end in the 10th *arrondissment* ...'[3]

The World Aid Committee had its headquarters first in Rue Mondetour near Les Halles and later at 83 Boulevard Montparnasse. Once established in the new offices, Münzenberg and Babette Gross also began setting up their own publishing house *Éditions du Carrefour*, which Babette Gross would manage. The two secretaries there were Hans Schulz and Jopp Füllenberg, who were responsible for implementing his stream of ideas. Schulz would remain in France during the war and join the underground resistance.

At *Carrefour* they began compiling what would become the most effective instrument for propagating details of Nazi oppression, *Das Braunbuch* (The Brown Book). The first of the two volumes, *Brown Book of the Hitler Terror and the Burning of the Reichstag*, was published in August 1933. Münzenberg and comrades made every effort to ensure that all quoted facts in the book were based on meticulous research, had been corroborated, and were accurate. They could not afford to lay themselves open to accusations of falsifying or exaggerating, so every little detail had to be evidence-based if it were to hold up against Nazi attempts to discredit it. This book would become 'the Bible' of the anti-Fascist campaign worldwide. Almost all of the documentation in it was compiled from firsthand reports made by German political refugees, many of whom were also Jewish arriving or passing through Paris.

The first *Brown Book* came out in a rapid sequence of several editions and was soon published in Britain, the USA, France, and elsewhere. 25,000 copies alone were printed in French and German by Münzenberg's *Éditions du Carrefour*. It was eventually translated into 17 languages, and all in all, at least 70,000 must have been printed worldwide. Its cover incorporated a caustic caricature by John Heartfield of Goering as a bull-necked butcher, wearing a blood-stained apron and wielding a meat cleaver, in the background is the burning Reichstag. Two editions were distributed clandestinely in Germany, but camouflaged under innocuous covers. As Arthur Koestler put it, even if somewhat hyperbolically, the booklet 'probably had the strongest political impact of any pamphlet since Tom Paine's *Common Sense'*. Or as another historian recently put it, 'the *Brown Book* was the prism through which most of the world saw Nazism for more than a generation'.[4]

It contained the first comprehensive reports on the concentration camps, including statistics, lists of victims, and details of the institutionalised persecution of the Jews. It also included a detailed investigation into the background of van der Lubbe, the man accused of setting fire to the Reichstag.

Among its various acts of support for Hitler's victims, the World Aid Committee set up a home specifically for the children of German refugees, who found themselves suspended in a precarious limbo and particularly vulnerable. In his autobiographical sketch, *The Invisible Writing*, Arthur Koestler provides a short, but accurate description of the turbulent life in this home.[5]

The Nazis labelled the World Aid Committee office in Paris a 'witches kitchen of communist agit-prop specialists'. By 1933, reports of the brown terror in Germany were beginning to filter through to the world at large, and Münzenberg played an active role in making sure the reports on the terror were given a higher profile and achieved a wider circulation.

Another major step in pushing forward the anti-Fascist struggle was the organising of a European-wide Anti-Fascist Congress. Originally planned for Prague, the congress was later scheduled for Copenhagen, but was eventually held in Paris over the two days of 4 and 5 June 1933 at the Salle Pleyel, a concert hall not far from the Arc de Triomphe.

The congress, like its predecessor in Amsterdam, was extremely well attended. The speeches of participants were translated into seven languages. Those attending from Germany wore masks, to hide their identity from the Gestapo, which helped heighten the dramatic effect.

In the course of the proceedings, a World Committee Against War and Fascism was elected, and the so-called Amsterdam-Pleyel movement was launched, and proposals were adopted to establish League Against War and Fascism branches around the world. Thereafter, little by little, the anti-Fascist committees which resulted were fused with the anti-war committees formed as a result of the Amsterdam congress that had been held the previous year. The organisation was co-chaired by Henri Barbusse, André Gide, and André Malraux. The German Communist exiles, Alfred Kurella and Albert Norden, were responsible for routine organisational issues.

After helping to organise the conference in Paris under the auspices of the *Comité contre la Guerre et le Fascisme*, Münzenberg flew to Moscow once more. Only shortly before his arrival, Clara Zetkin, who had been living in exile there, had died. She could perhaps count herself among the fortunate ones, as a whole number of other leading comrades, who were exiled in the Soviet Union, did not have the luxury of a natural death, but had already or would be eliminated by Stalin's *NKVD*.

It was not an auspicious time. According to Babette Gross, Münzenberg found his patience tried to the limits during this visit. He had continuous problems with the Moscow section of the *IAH*, whose work was being made increasingly difficult by the Soviet bureaucracy.

Münzenberg had come to Moscow to appeal to the Comintern for help in organising a more effective anti-Fascist propaganda campaign to be launched from Paris. His appeal was largely in vain. He and German Party leaders like Heinz Neumann and Hermann Remmele had consistently pushed for a more consistent anti-Fascist engagement and, albeit belatedly, a united front policy, but encountered unexpected resistance. Both Neumann and Remmele would soon be executed in the Soviet Union and, although Münzenberg escaped Stalin's clutches in Moscow, he would die in mysterious circumstances a short time later while still in French exile.

While he was in Moscow, among other things, he cited a letter that the writer and Communist sympathiser, Bernhard von Brentano, had written to Bertolt Brecht on 18 July 1933 as evidence of both the 'monstrous acrimony' of the struggle within the German opposition for a coherent anti-Fascist policy and the reasons why 'this work must be done over the official party's objections and resistance'. Brentano was horrified by the *KPD*'s attitude and even claimed that regional *KPD* branches were co-operating with Nazi Stormtroopers and denouncing Trotskyists and members of the non-communist Left to the police. Brentano appealed to Münzenberg to do something.[6]

In August 1933, the Nazi *Reichsanzeiger* newspaper issued the first list of individuals who were to be expatriated and their assets confiscated even though most of them had already left Germany. The list of 33 included the cream of German writers, artists, and left-wing political activists, including Willi Münzenberg, Kurt Tucholsky, Heinrich Mann, and Lion Feuchtwanger.

The renowned German historical novelist Lion Feuchtwanger would also spend several years in exile in Paris and was very active within the exile community, particularly among the writers, in an attempt to promote the formation of a united front, make appeals, and call for global solidarity. He was a co-founder of the German Writers' Defence Association, which was established in response to the Nazi book burnings in Germany. He met regularly with Münzenberg to discuss the difficulties in achieving effective unity among the exiles and ways of overcoming these. They would also quite often go for a meal, along with other artist and writer friends, to the same restaurant on Boulevard Hausmann. Münzenberg loved French food, but at this time he was already suffering from increasingly irksome stomach ulcers, probably as a result not only of his hectic lifestyle, but the increasing stresses caused by events taking place in Moscow and Berlin, so he had to be careful with his diet.

In May 1934, with the support of the then PEN president, H.G. Wells, Heinrich Mann, and other prominent writers, Münzenberg set up the German Freedom Library in Paris. Apart from collecting books by writers banned by the Nazis and anti-Fascist literature in general, the Library organised poetry readings, published a newsletter, and put together illegal pamphlets to be smuggled into Germany.

Feuchtwanger went to Moscow in November 1936 to seek financial support for the German exile literary magazine, *Das Wort* (The Word) that he, together with Willi Bredel and Bertolt Brecht, had begun to publish in support of exiled writers. He had a high standing in the Soviet Union, where his novels were widely read. The magazine would be published monthly from July 1936 until March 1939, when it closed after its 30th issue.

While in Moscow, Feuchtwanger had a two-hour conversation with Stalin and confronted him with what he saw as the unnecessary political trials taking place at the time, and even praised Trotsky to his face, which couldn't have endeared him to his interlocutor. His wife, Marta relates that Stalin rejected Trotsky's insistence on world revolution as the only way forward, and told him: 'We first have to bring our own house in order, first the life of our people has to be improved, first we have to feed the people before we embark on a world revolution'. He also confided that he was, 'convinced that Hitler will one day attack me'.[7] When, in early 1940, the Nazi invasion of France became imminent, Feuchtwanger would be interned, along with his compatriots in exile, but the personal intervention of Eleanor Roosevelt would secure his release and visas would be issued for him and his wife to travel to the USA.

From his office near Les Halles, Münzenberg had led the worldwide protests against the Reichstag fire show trial (see Chapter 12) the Nazis were organising in Leipzig, and it was around this time that the young Hungarian born journalist and Communist, Arthur Koestler, began working for him. He says that he first met Münzenberg in Paris in 1933 'and like so many others, immediately came under his spell'.

Ruth Fischer also notes his influence in France at the time:

> In 1935, when in France and then throughout the whole world Peoples' Fronts were being established, Münzenberg was in Paris; together with him thousands of other German refugees. The success with which the Communist Party line was propagated among Social Democrats and liberals, the publishing of *Ce Soir* in Paris and *PM* in New York, the thousands of artists and writers, medics and lawyers, actors and singers who intoned a potpourri of the general line – all this had its origin in Willi Münzenberg's Workers' Aid.[8]

It was not until long after the end of the war, in 1954, that Münzenberg's name resurfaced in any meaningful way again since his death, when Koestler wrote about him in the second volume of his autobiography.

He had known of Münzenberg when he was a young newspaperman in Berlin during the early 1930s, before he began working for him in Paris for a period of almost seven years (1933–1940). Koestler was deeply impressed by Münzenberg's talents as an organiser, publisher, and propagandist, by his ability to generate a seemingly endless stream of newspapers, magazines, and books to support the Communist cause, and by the apparently magical ease with which he set up his various 'front committees', while keeping the Communist role in them largely in the background.

In his foreword to the Babette Gross biography, Koestler gives a vivid description of the atmosphere in Münzenberg's Paris office:

> His comrades in the office worshipped him and his private secretary the tall, but crippled, Hans Schulz would often remain in the office until three or four in the morning in order to write down in a readable and implementable form all the ideas that flowed unceasingly from Münzenberg's fertile brain. Münzenberg dictated to him in the form of what he called 'theses' or 'little ideas', that went somewhat like this: 'Write to Feuchtwanger. Tell him article received with thanks and so forth, Tell him we need a brochure by him, 16 sides, we'll smuggle 10,000 into Germany; he should write about the cultural legacy. Old man Goethe and so forth let him decide the rest. Greetings and a hug. Then, buy a meteorological guide. Hans, check out the highs and lows and so forth, how the wind will be blowing over the Rhine; how many leaflets in octavo format can an air balloon carry, where the balloons are likely to land and so forth. Then, Hans, get in touch with a couple of balloon manufacturers and tell them we're looking at exporting to Venezuela, ask for a quote for 10,000, wholesale price. Then, Hans …'.

The new Paris headquarters had become a hive of activity, and as one can imagine, the Nazi secret services were not letting this 'witches kitchen' of Communists in Paris continue its work without monitoring it closely. Berlin's Gestapo HQ was sent regular reports on Münzenberg's activities in the city. Their agents reported that, as in the past, Münzenberg was attempting to establish a non-partisan means of propaganda against the National Socialist regime. The Gestapo was, understandably, particularly interested in discovering exact details of his publishing undertakings.

In May 1935, the Austrian Communist journalist, Kurt Neumann, fled Vienna for Paris, where he adopted the pseudonym 'Harry Olten'. He became involved in Münzenberg's *Comité Mondial contre la Guerre et le Fascisme*, as well as in associated organisations whose aims were to increase awareness in the world of the crimes committed by the Nazi regime.

Neumann wrote that, 'In France I worked with the *Rote Hilfe* (Red Aid) and other communist organisations as well as with French radical socialist and other anti-fascist groups in a people's front against Hitler and Mussolini. It was my task to establish committees of prominent individuals against Hitler and Mussolini.

In Paris I set up a committee with well-known writers. I was also sent to London where I attempted to form a committee there with leading members of the House of Lords and the House of Commons. I was received by Attlee and a whole number of others. All of them agreed that we had to undertake action against Hitler … I made similar trips to the Scandinavian countries.' (For additional details about how the Labour Party officially reacted to Neumann's attempts, see Chapter 13: Münzenberg as seen by the secret services). According to correspondence in the Labour Party archive, Neumann was also organising support for aid to the victims of the Italian–Abyssinian War, in the wake of the Italian invasion of Abyssinia (today Ethiopia) by Mussolini's Fascist troops and their brutal suppression of the determined resistance. That war would last from 1935 to 1939.

In Paris, Münzenberg became close friends with another renowned German writer, Rudolph Leonhard, who, after fleeing Hitler, founded the *Schutzverband Deutscher Schriftsteller im Ausland* (The Association for the Defence of German Writers Abroad). Leonhard would return to East Germany after the war and died in 1953. Curiously, in his papers, researchers found references in his unpublished notes to dreams he had had concerning Münzenberg and his death, referring to 'murder', but these dream notes can hardly be classified as evidence of the latter's supposed murder by the *NKVD* in 1940 (see Chapter 14).

The situation for German refugees in France, particularly those who had entered the country illegally, was made very difficult by the French authorities and deportations were taking place often based on the whim of individual officials. As a result, in November 1935, numerous organisations came together to form an umbrella group, the *Féderation des Emigrés d'Allemagne en France*. The *Féderation* sent a delegation of four under the leadership of Heinrich Mann to the League of Nations in Geneva, where they handed over a memorandum on the situation of emigrants in France requesting urgent action. An International Conference for the Right of Asylum was organised in Paris in June 1936, which brought together numerous aid organisations. As a result of this conference, a brochure was published under the name of Harry Olten, *'Weltappell für Asylrecht. Zur Pariser Internationalen Asylrechtskonferenz vom 20. und 21. Juni 1936'* (World Appeal for the Right of Asylum),[9] which documented the appalling situation of many refugees and, on the basis of the enumerated facts, called for a 'genuine right of asylum'. Neumann/Olten also self-published a book, *Kirche, Volksfront, Bolschewismus* (The Church, People's Front and Bolshevism).[10]

In the summer of 1936, the German dictator presided over a meticulously organised Olympic Games, which was turned into a grand theatrical event extolling German Fascism, and it would lift his prestige in the world immensely. The world flocked to Berlin and was duly impressed by German efficiency and organisational panache. Hitler could bask in the glory and the widespread admiration expressed by participating countries. For those who had been forced to flee the regime's brutality, though, this expression of support for German fascism was another cruel blow and was viewed with foreboding. The German exile community was plunged into deeper depression.

Münzenberg, though, did not let such events dent his determination.

He had been immersed in a frenetic round of activity during his first three years in Paris. There, he had managed to establish a variety of organisations and committees to confront the Fascist threat and to publish reams of material in support of the campaign. He was instrumental in alerting people to the real dangers of Fascism on a global scale. With his comrades and friends, he made Paris the Western hub of anti-Fascist activity. But from 1936 onwards, following the outbreak of the Spanish Civil War, the Comintern and the German Communist Party began to pull the rug from underneath him. The final three years before his death in 1940 would see his star slowly wane. Once the *KPD* and the Comintern withdrew their support from him, many of his erstwhile comrades also abandoned him, and he became very much an isolated figure, which seriously undermined and hampered his campaigning work.

Why did the Comintern do this at a time when Münzenberg's anti-Fascist campaign was becoming ever more effective? There is no easy answer, but Münzenberg was already being undermined by some in the leadership of the German Communist Party who disagreed with his political stance. A key factor would also have been Stalin's realisation that it was increasingly unlikely that the Soviet Union would achieve an alliance with the Western powers to counter Hitler and would sooner or later be obliged to enter a pact on its own 'with the devil himself'. A continuation of Münzenberg's vehement and effective anti-Nazi propaganda would then not be helpful. However, the petty jealousies and animosities expressed by key figures in the German Party leadership would also have played their part. Such personal factors invariably take on an exaggerated importance within exile communities and organisations. With the German Communist Party inside Germany itself virtually eradicated by Hitler, the leadership scattered and ineffective in opposing Hitler, Münzenberg's autonomy and his key role in the exile community, functioning largely outside direct party control, provoked a vindictive response.

Notes

1 Bayerlein, Bernhard H., 'The Entangled Catastrophe: Hitler's 1933, "Seizure of Power" and the Power Triangle – New Evidence on the Historic Failure of the KPD, Comintern, and the Soviet Union' in *Weimar Communism*, ed. Hoffrogge and Laporte. (Bayerlein et al. (eds.) p. 265.)
   DRK Doc 330.
2 Andrews, Geoff, *The Shadow Man*, I.B. Tauris, 2015. p. 77.
3 Hobsbawm, E, *Interesting Times*, Abacus, 2002. p. 123.
4 While right-wing German historian Fritz Tobias and others have subsequently dubbed the *Brown Book* a 'fabrication' or 'full of half-truths', much of it has been historically substantiated by mainstream historians.
5 Koestler, Arthur, *The Invisible Writing*, Vintage, 1984.
6 Bayerlein, Bernhard H., 'The Entangled Catastrophe: Hitler's 1933, opus cit.
7 Hermann, Ingo, *Marta Feuchtwanger Leben mit Lion*, Lamuv Verlag, 1991, p. 61.
8 Fischer, Ruth, *Stalin und der Deutsche Kommunismus*, Vol. 2, p. 280.
9 This brochure was published by Éditions Universelles in 1936.
10 This book was published in Prague in 1938.

12

REICHSTAG FIRE AND COUNTER TRIAL

Germany, by 1929, had been experiencing a period of relative stability; the economy had been growing and there was a widespread air of optimism in the country. The Wall Street crash of late October 1929 destroyed all that. From New York, it reverberated around the world, but its impact was particularly devastating in Germany. Many German banks had invested heavily in shares, and a significant number of German companies were dependent on US loans. They collapsed almost overnight, causing a run on the banks and creating mass unemployment. Towards the end of 1930, German industry had ground to a virtual halt, millions were unemployed, and millions of others worked only a few days a week. Families lost all hope and were prepared to grab at any life jacket thrown to them. The Nazi party offered them that life jacket, and its membership grew exponentially. The mass of the people had become tired of the eternally squabbling mainstream parties and their ineffectiveness, and many workers had given up hope of the Communists achieving anything, so looked elsewhere for a solution.

The rapidity with which the economic downturn had happened took everyone by surprise, not the least the Communist Party. Despite the party's strength and its large following, it was unable to grasp the initiative. The financial backing that Hitler was now getting from conservative forces and big business tipped the balance.

As a result of the rapid rise of the Nazis, there were increasingly heated debates within the *KPD* as to how to respond. It had also become a victim of its own myopia and of sectarian Comintern dictates: the chickens were coming home to roost.

Many working-class people who had suffered months and months of unemployment and poverty were now saying, 'You Communists are OK, but Adolf will get the job done quicker, and we can't wait any longer'. They had run out of patience and weren't prepared to wait for pie in the sky. Such attitudes were reflected in the increased vote for the Nazis in the 1930 elections and helped propel Hitler to power. But Hitler was not content with the chancellorship, and the fact that his party was the largest in the Reichstag, he wanted total hegemony. He was not prepared to risk that goal by allowing free and fair elections, scheduled for 5 March 1933. Extreme measures were required to ensure Nazi dominance. These would be the last national elections in which more than one party was on the ballot, even though the Communist and Social Democratic parties had been effectively outlawed.

On 27 February 1933, while Münzenberg had been speaking at an election rally in a small town near Frankfurt, more dramatic events had been taking place in Berlin: the Reichstag had been set aflame. This event was utilised by the Nazis to unleash a wave of terror and mass arrests in which thousands of Communists and Socialists were rounded up and interned. Münzenberg was one of those at the top of the Nazis most-wanted list and someone who the Nazis accused (in their paper, *Der Völkische Beobachter*), of being a 'spiritual leader' behind the arson attack on the Reichstag; all the *IAH* offices and publishing houses were immediately occupied and taken over by the Nazis.

Late that evening as the fire crackled through the Reichstag, the citizens of Berlin living near the iconic building were drawn out of their houses and onto their balconies to see orange flames shooting from its domed roof. The snow-covered streets were turned red in the flames' reflection. Several fires had been set within the building deliberately and simultaneously. The exact circumstances surrounding the fire have been disputed, but in his recent book *Burning the Reichstag*, Professor Benjamin Carter Hett, cites considerable documentary evidence that the Nazis were responsible.[1]

The Reichstag fire was undoubtedly a key moment in Hitler's bid for total power. It was the tool he desperately needed in order to persecute the Communists, Social Democrats, and other non-Nazi parties and to destroy liberty throughout Germany.

Before the fire, Hitler had headed nothing more than a shaky coalition in which the Nazis had only 3 out of 13 cabinet seats. The fire marked the real beginning of what was arguably the most violently destructive regime in human history.

Its historical significance is underlined by Carter Hett, when he says that by firmly establishing the truth around the Reichstag fire and controlling the narrative of how it happened means to control the narrative of everything that followed.[2]

There is little doubt that Nazis committed this criminal act of arson, entering through secret tunnels that led from Marshal Hermann Göring's nearby residence, but they immediately placed the blame on the Communists in a well-prepared propaganda coup. It was only one month since Hitler became chancellor.[3]

National elections were due to be held in a few days' time on 5 March, and although the Nazis were already the largest party in the Reichstag, they needed total control to achieve their goals. Over the next days, following the fire, the police, supported by Nazi Stormtroops swooped on all known Communist and Social Democratic offices, as well as their homes, ransacking the buildings, beating and arresting anyone they suspected of being either a Communist, a Social Democrat, or trade unionist. These will be followed by radical Christians and Jews. No one would ever be punished for these acts of terror. The prisons are stuffed with these 'enemies of the state', and the first provisional concentration camps are established. The Nazis achieved their aim, and although the Communist and Social Democratic parties were nominally still allowed to contest the elections, they were in effect outlawed, giving the Nazis a free path to total power. Despite the manipulation, however, the Nazis only managed to win 43.9 per cent of the votes, but that did not hold Hitler back. In June, he simply banned the formation of new parties and declared the NSDAP as the only legal party in the country.

On 23 March, Hitler's dictatorship is formally entrenched through his *Ermächtigungsgesetz* (Enabling law), then, on 10 May, public book burnings take place in many cities, organised by the Nazis, on which the works of the cream of Germany's writers will be incinerated. Despite this rapidly deteriorating situation, leading Communists like Walter Ulbricht are arguing that the Social Democrats are still the main enemy because 'they are diverting vital sections of the proletariat from taking revolutionary action'. Even among many left-wing intellectuals, Hitler and the National Socialists are still being under-estimated, and their reign seen as a fleeting abnormality.

The historical novelist and Münzenberg friend, Lion Feuchtwanger, was one of those who saw the dangers much more clearly. In an article he wrote for Münzenberg's *Welt am Abend* as early as January 1931, he said: 'War has released the barbaric instincts of the individual and society as a whole to such an extent that was previously unimaginable. National Socialism has artfully organised this barbarism. Among intellectuals it is called OBD: German Organised Barbarity'.[4]

By the summer of that fatal year of 1933, Münzenberg was again in Moscow conferring with the Comintern on what measures could be taken to campaign effectively against the forthcoming Reichstag fire show trial due to take place in Leipzig. The Nazis envisaged this trial as a grand demonstration to the world at large of how perfidious and ruthless the Communists were. Münzenberg alone seems to have realised the potential international significance of this trial and how vital it was to counter its propaganda impact.

When Marshal Hermann Göring began preparing this show trial, Münzenberg decided to seize the initiative and organise an effective pre-emptive counter trial in order to counter its purpose. But he knew that he would have to have the Comintern on board if he were to pull it off.

Despite Stalin's equivocation towards the German Fascist regime, the Comintern agreed with Münzenberg's genial suggestion to organise a counter trial in a Western country and persuade internationally known lawyers to participate, in order to undermine the Nazis' case. This was the first time in history that anyone had hit on such an idea. A public shadow trial or 'counter trial' like this was a novelty in the West. In a twist of irony, Münzenberg had hit on the idea when he recalled the secret courts that were held in Russia by the Tsar's secret police before the Bolshevik Revolution.

The Comintern gave him the necessary authority and financial means to organise it. The counter trial would be officially titled, the Reichstag Fire Enquiry, and London was chosen as the venue.

A key collaborator in this Enquiry was the distinguished British lawyer and Labour Party member, D.N. Pritt. In the latter's biography, he relates what an impact this undertaking had on him. It was, he wrote, 'A landmark not only historically but personally for me – for it was my first active clash with Fascism, and a milestone in my political development – came with the Reichstag Fire'.[5]

The Reichstag Fire Enquiry was, Pritt writes, 'designed to "head off" the trial at Leipzig in the eyes of world public opinion by ascertaining and publishing the true facts, but still more to bring the direct pressure of public opinion on the trial court by making public its own fully-reasoned conclusions, based on evidence, before the hearings in Leipzig began'.[6] He notes that the Labour Party frowned on his collaboration with this Enquiry and, 'conveyed to me their disapproval of my "unwisdom" in doing anything that might be helpful to the Communists'.[7] Nevertheless, he was able to call upon the support of a number of leading Labour Party figures.

Very soon, a group of seven renowned lawyers were brought together for the Enquiry, from Holland, France, Sweden, the USA, Denmark, Belgium, and the UK; lawyers from Switzerland and Italy were 'kept away by official pressure', Pritt said.

The Committee of Enquiry began its deliberations on 14 September 1933, and the first public session was opened in the courtroom of the Law Society of London by Sir Stafford Cripps. It was cleverly scheduled to take place only a few days before the actual trial in Leipzig. Its conclusions would be announced to the world press a day before the trial in Germany began.

The hearings were attended by many prominent figures, including H.G. Wells, but its instigator, Willi Münzenberg, would not be among those attending as the British government had continually rejected his requests for an entry visa.

Its 'verdict' – announced at Caxton Hall, London on 20 September – was that the accused Communists were innocent of all charges and that it was the Nazis who were the guilty ones. The verdict was published in 15 languages.

The Nazis had already reacted with nervousness when they heard about the establishment of an international counter trial in London, but they were livid after it announced the conclusions of its deliberations on the eve of their own trial. In Berlin, they knew full well who was the string-puller behind this counter trial initiative. The Nazi paper, *Völkischer Beobachter*, devoted a whole number of column inches to attacking 'the man behind the Reichstag Fire, the communist grand capitalist Münzenberg'. His ability to win the support of leading European statesmen and cultural figures time and time again for his campaigns continued to infuriate the Nazis.

The counter trial had been able to present anti-Fascist propaganda to a mass audience and deliver a massive psychological blow to the Nazis. It was a tremendous propaganda victory and pre-empted any verdict that would be made in Leipzig. It also obliged the Nazis to conduct the trial in a blaze of international publicity and to issue subpoenas to their own top officials to take the witness stand. Also, in an unprecedented moment of criminal trial history, the *Brown Book*[8] was cited at the trial as the 'sixth defendant'. The Reichstag fire trial in Leipzig, in which five Communist Party members were charged with committing arson and high treason, turned into a fiasco for the Nazi regime.

A key factor in the success of the counter trial had been the access participating lawyers had to the indictment brief prepared by the Nazis. This was down to an unusual constellation of personal relationships. The Communist, Leo Roth, trained in Moscow at the secret *KPD* military school, had won the affection of Helga, the third child of Kurt von Hammerstein, commander in chief of the German army from 1930 to 1933, who was party to the trial documents.

During the preparation of the show trial, copies of the secret bill of indictment had been given to only a small circle of top officials, but one of them was von Hammerstein. Helga and her sister managed to purloin the document from their father's study for two hours, sufficient time to allow the 235 pages to be photocopied by *KPD* security personnel and for Leo Roth to then smuggle the film out of the country and send it to Münzenberg in Paris. This vital piece of documentation enabled the lawyers to carefully counter every accusation contained in it and use this to great effect in the pre-emptive counter trial.

The award-winning author, Hans Magnus Enzensberger, wrote later: 'For this victory of the defence, the *Braunbuch über Reichstagsbrand und Hitlerterror* (Brown Book of the Hitler Terror and the Burning of the Reichstag) played a key role, already published by the agit-prop genius of the Party, Willi Münzenberg, and already published that summer in Paris, it led to an unparalleled international campaign. It was translated into 17 languages and printed in editions of millions'.[9]

The *Brown Book* was published in dedicated editions to be smuggled into Germany, and these books were printed on especially thin paper and with fictitious covers. Enzensberger says, 'I still have a copy, which is made to look like a *Reklam* booklet and has the title: Goethe, *Hermann and Dorothea* ... another edition came into the country under the cover of Schiller's *Wallenstein*'.[10] The comrades knew their classical literature!

Concerning the Reichstag fire trial in Leipzig, Stephen Koch, in his Münzenberg biography, states that Georgi Dimitrov, who was the main accused, 'was one of the most famous leaders of the entire Communist International; a man known to be one of Stalin's closest advisers'.[11] However, Professor Benjamin Carter Hett, the US specialist on German history, writes of Dimitrov in his book *Burning the Reichstag* as 'an obscure figure in early 1933, marginalised within his own party by factional disputes, the Reichstag

Fire trial rocketed Dimitrov to political stardom'. It was indeed the Reichstag fire trial that brought him to world prominence, and he only became general secretary of the Comintern in 1935.

Koch also asserts that, 'Once Dimitrov was arrested, for example, it was plain that Münzenberg's agents had been placed throughout the prison where the Comintern official was being held'.[12] This is pure fantasy. Münzenberg did not have 'agents' as such and certainly in Hitler's Germany when virtually all Communists and certainly anyone with links to Münzenberg had already either fled the country or were in a concentration camp. To establish such agents there would have been impossible and in any case ineffective.

FIGURE 12.1 John Heartfield poster: Dimitrov facing Goering at the Reichstag Trial in 1933

The Nazis could hardly have envisaged that this trial would make them a subject of ridicule throughout the world. Dimitrov, the Bulgarian Communist and chief accused, was able to turn the tables on his accusers, particularly the pompous Göring, who completely lost his cool in front of the world's media. In the face of incontrovertible evidence, the Nazis had little option but to acquit the accused, apart from the hapless van der Lubbe who was found guilty and executed. With Georgi Dimitrov's unexpected acquittal, Münzenberg's victory was complete. As a result, he became even more of a hated figure for the Nazis than he already was.

Despite the resounding success of the counter trial and Münzenberg's ongoing anti-Fascist propaganda work, the internal reports he made at this time reveal that neither the Comintern nor the *KPD* were providing much support to his efforts. Despite his latest visit to Moscow in that summer of 1933, his appeal for more support appeared to fall on deaf ears. But on his return to Paris, he shook off his worries and any doubts he may have had and continued campaigning as before.

Only in retrospect and as a result of more contemporary research do we now know what a strange double role Stalin played at the time, and how he was prepared to sacrifice many leading Communists for the sake of maintaining stable relations with Germany, even a Fascist led one. But this was slowly dawning on Münzenberg himself, and his doubts would be confirmed with the signing of the Hitler-Stalin Pact of August 1939.

Between 1933 and 1937, under Münzenberg's leadership, his publishing house in Paris brought out around 50 German language brochures and books, a number of which were also translated into French and English. Many of these leaflets and brochures were distributed by the anti-Fascist movement around the world and were also smuggled into Germany, but they could all be easily traced back to Münzenberg and his organisation by the German secret services. He was a veritable gadfly to the Nazi regime. His name and his operations were often cited in Gestapo files, and these are held today in the German State Archives in Berlin.

Not surprisingly, his exertions as well as his frustrations had already by the year 1933 left him exhausted and with a desperate need for a break. He and Babette Gross decided to take a fortnight's holiday on the Côte d'Azur to get away from it all. They headed south by car, taking their first tour through France and then staying for a few days in Roquebrune on the Riviera to enjoy the early spring. However, the daily news from Germany allowed the couple no rest. Gross relates that they heard that the Nazis had shot a number of leading Communist officials, including a friend and former colleague of his from his Stuttgart days. Thälmann had also been arrested. Then they heard that pro-Fascist demonstrators in Paris had gone on the rampage. Münzenberg decided to curtail the holiday and head back to Paris.[13] Almost immediately, he began organising the international campaign to obtain Thälmann's release and that of those, including Dimitrov, who had been acquitted at the Reichstag fire trial in Leipzig, but were still in custody.

In June 1934, the couple undertook their first journey overseas. Louis Gibarti had arranged for Münzenberg and several other supporters to make a tour of the

USA to address meetings there about what was taking place in Germany and to raise money for the Committee for the Relief of the Victims of German Fascism.

Through the efforts of his deputy, Otto Katz, and other intermediaries like Helen Wilkinson, Münzenberg was able to persuade the British Labour MP Aneurin Bevan to travel with him and Babette on their tour of the USA, where they hoped to raise awareness to the Fascist threat. They were accompanied by the Social Democratic Berlin lawyer, Kurt Rosenfeld.

At this time in Britain, many at the grassroots level in both the Labour and Communist parties were increasingly forming loose collaborative links with the realisation that the Fascist threat could only be defeated by such unity. However, the Labour Party leadership appeared to be more alarmed by this collaboration than by the Fascist threat. It issued a decree announcing that, 'United Action with the Communist Party or organisations ancillary or subsidiary thereto without the sanction of the National Executive Committee is incompatible with membership of the Labour Party'.

Aneurin Bevan had already become more and more implicated in such joint activities and ignored his party's strictures. His wife, Jennie Lee, who was a member of the Committee for the Relief of the Victims of German Fascism, had urged Bevan to join Münzenberg on that trip. Bevan was no doubt fully aware of the role played by Communists in the organisation, but it did not seem to bother him.[14] As Michael Foot noted in his biography of Bevan, 'in July [1936], French Socialists and Communists agreed to establish a United Front, with the Spanish Socialists and Communists following suit in September. The mood was changing on the Continent and might do so here ... In any case, what Bevan was looking for was not so much a formal unity with the Communists but the new upsurge of fighting spirit which might come from an unqualified recognition that the only real enemy was on the Right ...'[15] The Labour Party leadership saw things differently, still viewing the Communists as equally as dangerous as the Fascists.

The small group travelled across the country from coast to coast, and both in terms of money collected and in its propaganda value, their trip to the USA turned out to be a huge success.

The well-known Hollywood character actor, Lionel Stander, was active in the US anti-Fascist movement during the 1930. He was a Communist and trade union activist and would become a victim of the McCarthy witch hunts in the 1940s. He describes how he and others 'saw a lot of what was happening [in Europe] through the eyes of the German refugees – actors, writers, directors, – who came here through the activity of mass organisations like the Hollywood Anti-Nazi League, et cetera. ... I threw a party at my house,' he said, 'and the people who were there included Prince [Hubertus zu] Loewenstein from Germany – anti-Hitler, naturally; Otto Katz, who was the number three man in the German Communist Party (sic) and everyone in Hollywood you could think of technicians, and artists ...'[16]

Katz would have been there on behalf of Münzenberg, raising funds for the World Committee for the Relief of the Victims of German Fascism. Interestingly, according to Katz's biographer, he became the model for Victor Lazlow in the classic film *Casablanca* as well as the anti-Fascist Kurt Müller in Lillian Hellman's play (also a film), *Watch on the Rhine*.[17]

While Münzenberg and Bevan were on the boat steaming towards New York, they were informed of the 'Night of the Long Knives' on 30 June – the brutal bloodletting between Hitler's supporters and Röhm's Brownshirts. Hitler and his big business supporters were determined to eradicate Ernst Röhm and his powerful, largely working-class street army, many of whom still had the illusion that National Socialism did mean Socialism in one country. This infighting and brutal suppression of the Brownshirts showed, the group felt, that the Nazi regime was vulnerable, and it gave them a glimmer of hope that it might even tear itself apart.

In July 1934, a memorandum had been put together by top military figures in the Wehrmacht who opposed Hitler, addressed to Hindenburg, suggesting that he replace Hitler with a new government. It comprised only a few pages and was published under the cover title, *Englische Grammatik* (English Grammar) with a fictitious Leipzig imprint. This camouflaged brochure also contained, in miniature form, and printed on special paper, the *Weissbuch über Erschiessungen des 30. Juni* (White Book on the executions of 30 June), on the elimination of Ernst Röhm and the Brownshirts. The unnamed publisher was the *KPD* and the original was published beforehand by Münzenberg's Paris publishing house.

The Spanish civil war

In October 1934, the Asturian miners in northern Spain had gone on strike and risen up against the right-wing central government, following a call from the Socialist Party's national leadership. Their resistance was rapidly suppressed with extreme brutality by the government. This failed uprising drove the first wave of Spanish refugees to France, particularly Paris. Münzenberg immediately sprang to their aid and got to know many of the leaders personally.

One of the miners' leaders, Gonzalez Pena, was captured and sentenced to death. There was outrage throughout the world at this draconian sentence and Münzenberg, too, campaigned for his release. An English commission of investigation including Ellen Wilkinson and the Earl of Listowel was hastily put together and sent to Madrid. The vehement international protest succeeded in getting the death sentence commuted to life imprisonment. In the 1936 elections, he would be chosen as a candidate for the Socialist Party and was duly elected and thus obtained his release from prison.

The bloody suppression of the miners' strike in Spain had helped put the country in the world spotlight. At the 1934 anniversary of the October Revolution, the Soviet Union invited a large delegation of miners to Moscow to demonstrate the Soviet government's solidarity. At this time, the Socialist journalist and politician, Alvarez del Vayo, contacted Münzenberg and invited him to Spain to get to know the country.

During the Christmas of 1934, Münzenberg and Babette Gross travelled to Madrid and made a tour of the country to assess the situation. In the early summer of 1935, he would make a second journey to Madrid accompanied by a colleague from the International Red Aid organisation, Maike Schorr. This time, they held meetings with Communist Party officials and with Socialists who were friendly towards the Soviet Union. In the early summer of 1935, Münzenberg returned again to Spain with Maike Schorr, a colleague working for the Rote Hilfe (Red Aid). They were to meet Communist organisations, Socialists, and anyone sympathetic to the Soviet Union.

In new elections held in Spain in January 1936, a new 'Popular Front' government in Spain was elected, which included Socialists and Communists. This horrified the country's conservative élite and the Catholic Church, and they began plotting the new Republican government's downfall.

On 17 July 1936, General Franco, a right-wing Spanish general, ignited a military rebellion in Spanish-occupied Morocco, with the eventual aim of toppling Spain's new progressive, Republican government. The rebellion soon fanned out to mainland Spain, but Franco's forces encountered strong resistance there. The support of the conservative Catholic Church, but, above all, military assistance from Mussolini and Hitler, would give Franco's forces a strong boost. The avowed 'non-intervention' stance maintained by other Western European powers hampered the republic's ability to defend itself and counter the Fascists.

It was not only in Spain that Fascists would attempt to overthrow a democratically elected government. Already in February 1934, French paramilitary Fascist groups had held a large rally in the Place de la Concorde with the aim of provoking an uprising and a coup against France's Social Democratic government. This attempt by the right wing in France to take power failed, but nevertheless precipitated a belated rapprochement between the Socialists and Communists in the country, and it would at last lead to the establishment of a 'Popular Front' to confront the fascist threat.

Unlike the Comintern itself, Münzenberg immediately recognised the significance of the Franco-led military uprising in Spain. On 5 October, he delivered a report to the Comintern on the work of the Committee against War and Fascism, and in it, he raised the issue of solidarity with Spain.

With regard to Spain, Münzenberg, it would appear, had up until then operated off his own bat, using *IAH* finances, and not on instructions from the Comintern. He also utilised his publishing house, *Éditions du Carrefour*, to aid the Spanish Republic with publicity and give it a voice.

Werner Abel, who with Esther Winkelmann, has compiled a bibliography of Münzenberg's *Édition du Carrefour*, says, 'Examining the meetings of the Presidium of the Comintern during the second half of 1936, i.e. after the Generals' putsch in Spain on 18/19 July 1936, one can see that the event itself and the situation that arose out of it was, at least to begin with, given no more attention than other international problems and those concerning the other parties that belonged to the Comintern.'[18]

Münzenberg visited Spain once again towards the end of May/beginning of June 1936 to reassess the situation. He had, in the meantime, established good relations with a number of leading Spanish politicians like Luis Araquistáin, who became Spanish ambassador to France, Julio Álvarez del Vayo, who would become Minister for Foreign Affairs, and Fernando de los Rios, among others. De los Rios and del Vayo would be instrumental in collaborating with Münzenberg in establishing the *Comité France-Espagnol* and the press agency *Agence Espagne*, of which Otto Katz became director. From Spain's Minister of Finances, Juan Negrin, Münzenberg would be given adequate sums of money to help finance these projects. The *Agence Espagne*, based in Paris, would provide the French press with news and commentary on the Civil War from a Republican perspective.

Very early on, he also raised the question of sending volunteers to fight in Spain to help save the republic, and collaborated with his friend, the French writer, André Malraux, who managed to persuade the French government to donate several planes to Spain, although these were obsolete at the time. Malraux would also go to Spain himself to help organise a modest international air force unit there.

Münzenberg's earlier report to the Comintern was followed up in October by one given by the French Comintern member, André Marty, on the Spanish situation, and this appeared to give the Comintern the impetus it needed: resolutions were agreed to expand the Spanish aid campaign. Responsibility for this work was given to Maurice Thorez of the French Communist Party, Harry Pollitt of the British Party, and Willi Münzenberg.

'What Münzenberg clearly did not know at this time,' Abel reveals, 'was that hardly three weeks after this meeting, the Comintern Secretariat would give instructions to investigate Münzenberg's Apparatus and its members in Paris'.[19]

Once news of the military coup in Spain had reached the rest of the world, Communists, Socialists, and Democrats everywhere became alarmed and began taking action. It was realised that the so-called civil war taking place in Spain could be the overture to a Fascist takeover in Europe. For these individuals, it was clear that if Franco and his forces were not stopped, Europe would be plunged into a devastating war. Tens of thousands of volunteers, from many countries, joined the International Brigades to fight alongside Republican forces against Franco. The Soviet Union gave military and logistical support, as well as sending volunteers, who joined the thousands of others from around the world who were determined to defend democracy and halt the Fascist threat.

The Spanish Civil War would rage over three years and provided the world's anti-Fascist movements with an opportunity to demonstrate that they were the true defenders of freedom and democracy; it was seen by all on the left as a key struggle.

On the initiative of Swedish trade unions and with the full support of the Spanish embassy in France, hundreds of child refugees from Spain were accommodated in children's homes in France. Münzenberg was actively involved in securing financial support for the running of these homes. In Britain, too, the National Joint Committee for Spanish Relief, an offshoot of Münzenberg's Spanish Relief organisation, under its president, the Duchess of Atholl, successfully pressured the UK government to allow several thousand Basque children to come to Britain.

Among those who came to Münzenberg and expressed the wish to volunteer for Spain was the young Communist, Arthur Koestler. Münzenberg and Otto Katz persuaded him, instead, to report from the Franco side as a journalist and send reports which would reveal how the Italians and Germans were aiding Franco. They gave him money to ensure he could operate easily. Koestler used this experience to write his first book on the Spanish Civil War, *Menschenopfer Unerhört, ein Schwarzbuch über Spanien* (Human victims innumerable, a Black Book on Spain. It was published in German, in 1937, by Münzenberg's *Carrefour* publishing house and shortly afterwards in English as *Spanish Testament*).

Notes

1 Hett, Carter, Benjamin, *Burning the Reichstag*, Oxford University Press, 2014.
2 Ibid. p. 25.
3 Ibid. Professor Benjamin Carter Hett, in his recent book, *Burning the Reichstag*, has undertaken a detailed investigation and examination of the available Reichstag fire documentation.

   He quotes witness statements from the time. One fire officer at the scene relates how he encountered 'police officers in brand new uniforms suddenly appearing from the cellars of the Reichstag building and how he was forced to retreat when threatened by them with being shot. (The cellar was connected by a tunnel to Göring's residence). There should have been only one policeman on duty in the cellar. Where did the others come from? From witness reports about the fire itself indicated that the rapid spread of the fire, which seemed to be burning in a number of locations, could only have been lit by several people. The Nazis placed the blame on one individual, the hapless Marinus van der Lubbe.

   The fire began around 9.00 p.m. in the evening, but already by 9.45 both Hitler and Göring had arrived by car to see firsthand what was happening. Sefton Delmer, the Berlin correspondent of the *Daily Express* had also been tipped off and was recognised by Hitler who said to him: "God grant that this be the work of the Communists. You are now witnessing the beginning of a great new epoch in German history, Herr Delmer. This fire is just the beginning." Göring then chipped in and said, "Without a doubt this is the work of the Communists, Herr Chancellor'".

   Rudolf Diels, the commander of the Department IA of the Berlin police (German equivalent of the FBI or Britain's MI5) was also on the spot soon after the fire began. He recalls Hitler in a violent rage, ranting, 'Now every Communist official will be shot where he is found. The Communist deputies will be hanged this night. Everybody in league with the Communists must be arrested. There will no longer be any leniency for Social Democrats either.' By the time Diels had returned to Berlin's central square, the Alexanderplatz, he saw 'astonished arrestees, dragged out of their sleep', being hauled into the square in droves.
4 von Sternberg, Wilhelm, *Lion Feuchtwanger, ein deutches Schriftsteller Leben*, Aufbau Taschenbuch Verlag, Berlin, 1919.
5 Pritt, D.N., *The Autobiography of D.N. Pritt, Part I, From Right to Left*, Lawrence and Wishart, 1965. p. 42.
6 Ibid. p. 51.
7 Ibid. p. 53.
8 Münzenberg, Willi et al., *Brown Book of the Hitler Terror and the Burning of the Reichstag*, Victor Gollancz, 1933.

9 Enzensberger, Hans Magnus, *Hammerstein oder Der Eigensinn*, Suhrkamp, 2008. p. 126.
10 Ibid. p. 127.
11 Koch, Stephen, *Double Lives: Stalin, Willi Münzenberg and the Seduction of the Intellectuals*, HarperCollins, 1996. pp. 97/98.
12 Ibid. p. 63.
13 Gross, Babette, *Willi Münzenberg*, Forum Verlag Leipzig, 1991, p. 409.
14 Michael Foot, *Aneurin Bevan, a Biography Vol. 1, 1897–1945*, Four Square Books, 1966. pp. 148–149.
15 Ibid. pp. 148–149.
16 McGilligan, Patrick and Buhle, Paul, *Tender Comrades: A Backstory of the Hollywood Blacklist*, St. Martin's Press, 1999. p. 613.
17 Miles, Jonathan, *The Nine Lives of Otto Katz*, Bantam Books. 2010. p. 227, 279.
18 Abel, Werner, 'Die versuchte Neutralisierung der "Münzenberg-Kreise" durch die KPD-Abwehr im republikanischen Spanien', https://www.muenzenbergforum.de/wp-content/uploads/2018/07/IWMF_V15.pdf.
19 Abel, Werner, opus cit.

13

BATTLES WITH THE KPD LEADERSHIP

From his earliest days in politics, Münzenberg took on leadership roles, particularly in the burgeoning Socialist youth movement just before and during the First World War. But he was always a 'doer' rather than a theoretician or bureaucrat.

Although he became a founding member of the German Communist Party, he was never offered, or appeared interested in taking on, a leadership role within it. He was though elected as a Communist Party candidate to the Reichstag in 1924 and to the Party's Central Committee in 1927.

To begin with, he was happy having a leading role in the Young Socialist International and then the Young Communist International, after the split between the Communist and Social Democratic wings of the movement in the wake of the Russian Revolution.

When Lenin persuaded the Comintern to make him their European emissary, he found himself with considerable powers as well as financial support and was able to operate virtually as a one man show. Ironically, his talent for organisation, for by-passing bureaucracy and getting things done, together with his ability to forge cross-party collaborative action also made him enemies, not only on the right, but within his own camp and among leading Social Democrats.

In the early years after the end of the war, he was firmly on the far left wing of the Communist Party and believed armed revolution was necessary to bring about Socialism in Germany. With the defeat of the 1918 November Revolution and successive, but unsuccessful attempts to win power through armed struggle, he moderated his position and became a strong opponent of armed struggle in Germany. This stance made him more enemies among the powerful, far left faction within the *KPD* during the early 1920s.

The International Workers Relief organisation that Münzenberg established in 1921 became international in a real sense and developed considerable clout on the international stage. It was seen by many as a parallel or front organisation of the Comintern and the various National Communist parties. Its office in Berlin became a hub through which travelling Communist officials and sympathisers from around the world passed through, including numbers of political refugees.

At the sixth World Congress of the Comintern in July/August 1928, Münzenberg and the *IAH* had come under fire for the first time from a strong faction within the Comintern leadership. In the language of the time, such 'bipartisan' organisations like his were characterised as being opportunistic, reformist, and aberrantly quasi-Menshevik. It was at this congress that the catastrophic 'class against class' policy was formulated, characterising the Social Democrats as 'Social Fascists' and as much the enemy as the real Fascists. This went counter to everything Münzenberg believed in and had worked towards. But it is difficult to determine how far such policies and the impact of Stalinisation within the German Party affected Münzenberg's thinking at that time.

At its sixth World Congress, the Comintern had declared that Social democracy was now the main enemy of the Communists movement. With that change in its political line, Münzenberg's freedom of manoeuvre from then on became severely restricted, particularly in those areas of work which very much involved a collaboration with Social Democrats and others outside the Communist orbit. However, he refused to let the new policy and any personal criticism trammel him, but instead came up with ever more new initiatives to broaden the movement.

Since taking on his role as Comintern emissary, a strong faction within the German Communist Party had developed an aversion to what Münzenberg was attempting to do. But the aim of his organisation was, as he put it: '... to interest those millions of apathetic and indifferent workers, who take no part in political life, who are not interested in the economic and cultural struggle of the proletariat, who simply have no ear for the propaganda of the Communist Party'. He realised only too well that it was pointless preaching solely to the converted. He had been able to successfully cultivate sympathisers from outside Communist Party circles to support his many campaigns and these would later be termed 'fellow travellers'. Such independent thinking and conciliatory attitudes were not to the liking of the sectarian leadership of the *KPD* and Comintern.

The expulsion of Trotsky from the Soviet Union in February 1929 and Stalin's determination to root out Trotsky's influence in the World Communist movement polarised loyalties even further and fomented acrimonious division on the left. Trotsky became the bogeyman, and anyone who attempted to challenge Comintern policy or question Soviet strategy and tactics could be accused of being a Trotskyist. It became not only a term of abuse and a means of avoiding genuine debate, but for many of those so accused and who found themselves in the Soviet Union, it could also mean imprisonment and even death.

His star wanes

In the years following Münzenberg's arrival in Paris, in March 1933, after escaping Nazi Germany, differences between him and the party leadership had become acute.

Only three months after his arrival, he sent a long letter to Stalin in Moscow. He says in this letter that he 'doesn't have much faith in letter writing' and very few of the letters he wrote during his lifetime have been preserved.

This one is a special and moving testament to Münzenberg's struggle against the bureaucrats and intriguers within the movement. In it, we have the evidence for his anger and frustration that had been built up over many years. He writes that he found his work continuously sabotaged by the German Party leadership, who have put obstacles in his path throughout his political career. He also bemoans the way the vibrant Socialist youth organisation he built up was incorporated and emasculated, and how the Fascists were helped to power by the incompetence and inaction of the party leadership.

It is tragic that, in this letter, he addresses Stalin, without irony, as 'perhaps the most objective and upright friend'. This blind trust in Stalin as omnipotent leader and righteous figure reveals a surprising naivety and blindness to the real truth. But he was of course not the only one with such blind faith.

His letter, with its severe criticism of the German and international Communist leaderships, could only be interpreted by any perceptive reader as a de facto critique of Stalin himself, but Münzenberg does not appear to appreciate this. It seems very likely that this letter represents one of the key moments that turned Stalin against Münzenberg and began, or accelerated, the process of his demonisation and eventual exclusion from the party.

Below is a slightly shortened version of the full text, as the original is long and at times repetitious.

> 20 July 1933.
>
> Dear Comrade!
> I wanted to write this letter two years ago, then certainly three months ago. I have always put it off, because I don't have much faith in letter-writing. But now because of my lengthy absence from there [Moscow], various issues have piled up, and as a friend is travelling there, I can give him my letter – I recall Lenin's reproach to me at the 3rd congress, [asking me] why I hadn't written to him earlier – so I have decided to send you this letter.
>
> I know of no one apart from you to whom I would send such a letter and about whom I am certain that it will be received in the way it is meant. There must be someone in this world to whom one can express one's views without reservation and hesitation. And for me, that can only be you. …
>
> Today, I am more deeply convinced than ever of the correctness of my understanding of the youth issue in 1921. I am certain that the … rejection

of my concept at that time – not by the youth congress because, as is well known, I enjoyed a majority there, but in the Political Commission – and particularly in the following years the extraordinarily extreme, doctrinaire, dogmatic, stiff and inflexible, formal propaganda was largely to blame for the fact that the broad masses of young people that we had rallied around our flag during the war, were lost to the communist movement and fell easy prey to national socialism and chauvinism.

It is symptomatic that in Germany, those who are most often ignored and have been swept up in the chauvinist wave are young people, when it was the reverse situation during the war, when it was the youth who were first to mobilise against war and were able to organise really large mass demonstrations like the ones on International Youth Day...

That was for me the most bitter disappointment of my life, but Lenin attempted to mitigate things by intervening personally and ensuring that I remained on the youth executive and was entrusted with the *IAH* ... Also in recent years, on tactical issues, I have made repeated attempts to take clearly differentiated positions... 'I warned about the fascist developments in Germany. You will recall that already in 1923, I set up a special office with a designated newspaper devoted to the study of national socialist issues and raised this question. ... And particularly towards the end of 1933, when it was announced that the national socialist danger in Germany had been overcome.

Differences arose, particularly, as you know, on the question of mass propaganda and the means and methods used in such propaganda. I am today even more convinced that my attitude on this was absolutely and one hundred per cent correct. The otherwise so inventive propagandists of the Third Reich took over the *Welt am Abend* (World in the Evening) newspaper and the *AIZ* (Workers Illustrated Newspaper), and imitate our exemplary films, and the methods and ways we have organised our celebrations and mass campaigns which, in official Party circles, led to my being dubbed an American rabble-rouser.

I recall with especial gratitude that it was you, with a few friends there who made this work possible for me, but in the place where I had to carry out this work [in Germany] I was confronted with resistance and difficulties put in my way by the official Party and its apparatus. I can tell you that in the first hours after the Reichstag fire events, but especially after hymns of praise had been heaped on Goebbels and his allies for their inimitable propaganda activities, I experienced a veritable visceral fury. I felt that if I hadn't had rocks strewn in my path and if there had been the freedom in my ranks that the national socialist propagandists had in their ranks, I could have matched them daily and I am prepared to match them tomorrow.

Despite all these tactical differences, that have existed since 1921, I have always accepted the Party line. I know only too well that I have made mistakes on various issues but on other questions such as, for instance, that concerning young people, the assessment of German fascism, the question of the means and methods of mass work, I have been right. But for me, on all these issues, both then and now and always will be the unbridled determination to work in the movement. And today I'm writing this letter to you, dear comrade, not in order to inform you of some misgivings or belly aches about political or tactical issues, but I am turning to you today as a friend, perhaps the most objective and most upright friend since Lenin's death, because the present circumstances, irrespective of tactical considerations, are threatening to rip us apart and make the straightforward, practical work for the movement impossible. ...

I can't help recognise that we – and especially in recent years – have not developed any strong personalities from among the young members and allowed them to rise in the movement, neither on the theoretical nor on the political level, nor in the field of education (agitation), the organisation of propaganda ...

I'm writing to you because I hope that this account will assist in undertaking an examination of the working methodology of our movement and give hundreds of comrades who are raring to get down to work a certain space to manoeuvre and to develop their own initiatives.

I won't list all the cases and all the experiences that I've made in order to prove my thesis that the lethargy of the apparatus and the way it works does not help promote initiative, but cripples and kills it, thus damaging the movement. They are unhealthy methods that inhibit and destroy the development of our working practice.

Another chapter: the anti-fascist congress. Towards the end of March I received news, the first letter letting me know about the organising of the anti-fascist congress, a foul, outrageously unqualified and insulting letter, such as I've never received in all my life. Several weeks later, I had a heated argument with those responsible for organising the conference and with the comrades tasked with doing so, with the result that not only was I, but a large international organisation, been barred from taking part in the congress. It is a real scandal that on the basis of an argument the most bitter injustice for years has been committed. Of that I am still today profoundly convinced. I, as one of the most widely known anti-fascists and seen by the German bourgeoisie, and in the press, correctly or incorrectly, as one of the staunchest promoters of the anti-fascist struggle and as an active fighter against fascism, have been completely excluded, from any discussion and even of taking part in the congress. This is an inexcusable political scandal, that an organisation like the *IAH* is excluded simply because I'm its secretary and had an argument with the organisers of the anti-fascist congress, and am treated like dirt at the congress. ...

There is no one here apart from me. I am trying to set up committees, secure financial support, because no one is making the effort and it is indeed happening, to create the first waves [of support] from elsewhere. Then, after several weeks, the commissions come, the under-commissions, the sub-commissions, the mandated representatives, the sub-representatives, and find that the initiative is of course a good one, but one is not allowed to implement it. Initiative will be called for in resolutions, but one is not allowed to develop them. In response to the first real upsurge of the movement, they interfere and destroy hundreds of connections, ban further initiatives, complain about them, threaten disciplinary action, send letters there, send couriers there, send telegrams every day, about a man who is sitting here, who works too much and has too much initiative...

Another question: the counter trial. In March I will be meeting our friend M. [Dmitri Manuilsky] who you had sent and who had, among other things, informed me about your personal wish to organise a counter trial with the help of Romain Rolland. I have eagerly taken up the issue. It has been possible to gain the support of ten of the world's most renowned jurists. The counter trial has now shifted to become a focus of public interest. ...

Then the *Rote Hilfe* (Red Aid) suddenly receives a telegram requesting the organisation of similar trials in the Hague and in Paris. These people will have to turn to the same jurists and those jurists will be convinced we are either crazy or confidence tricksters. And it carries on like this.

In England, in Spain, in Holland, we've managed to win over thousands of leading intellectuals who until now had distanced themselves from us. For the first time they have been persuaded to take action, and every day one has nothing better to do than ward off attacks so that the committees aren't driven apart and destroyed. 90 per cent of all one's energies are needed to ward off the interference and only 10 per cent remains to carry on the real work. That can break the strongest horse. ...

I want to achieve one thing, so that I and hundreds of others who want to work can work and are given the opportunity of working. That everyone, with all their energies and strength, are permitted to work for our movement and for the proletarian revolution without the daily threats of having their bones broken.

Herewith I express my confirmation that I am and remain the most stalwart and unbreakable comrade-in-arms

signed, Willi Münzenberg[1]

We do not know what Stalin's response was to this letter, and there appear to have been no immediate repercussions. Münzenberg continued his anti-Fascist campaigning and would become heavily involved in the defence of republican Spain.

Georgi Dimitrov had been released by the Nazis towards the end of February 1934 and allowed to travel to Moscow after the show trial debacle. There he was given a hero's welcome and was made head of the Comintern. A year later he presided over the last world congress of that organisation in Moscow in 1935, which Münzenberg attended as a delegate after an absence of over a year.

Behind the façade at that congress, there was, Babette Gross says in her Münzenberg biography, a strange disquiet or unease. In December of the previous year Kirov, the Leningrad party secretary, had been assassinated and Stalin utilised this murder, which he probably instigated, to carry out a purge of all so-called oppositional elements. This had serious repercussions on the *IAH* also.

Caught up in the persecution mania and reacting to Stalin's continued warnings of the danger of a coming war, all foreigners and foreign-influenced organisations came under increased suspicion. The *IAH*, too, was to be caught up in this web of suspicion, and its days would be numbered from then on. This general atmosphere was accompanied by a fear of spies around every corner and an upsurge in xenophobia. The *IAH* offices in the Soviet Union were staffed largely by foreigners, many of them exiles from Germany, so on that basis, the Soviet secret services now viewed the organisation with increased suspicion.

Although Münzenberg had, since 1933, become less involved directly in the *IAH*'s work there, the decision by the Soviet Central Committee to close it down came as a personal blow to him and represented a loss of prestige. Nevertheless, he took it on the chin.

The seventh World Congress of the Comintern took place against that backdrop. However, Dimitrov, as its head, announced a new political line, an about-turn: a Popular Front policy. Communist parties would now be expected to work together with Social Democrats, their erstwhile 'enemies', to build a broad alliance against the Fascists.

This new policy shift was viewed by Münzenberg with the bitter satisfaction of someone who had been pushing at a closed door without success for ages; he'd been advocating Communist-Socialist collaboration for years as the only way to halt the rise of Fascism. Now it came, as history has since demonstrated, too late.

After leaving Moscow, he attended the special so-called 'Brussels Conference' of the German Communist Party and, despite his clear differences with the party leadership, he was elected onto its 15 strong central committee. Returning from there to Paris, he began to help put the new political line into operation, bringing Socialists and Communists together in a united front.

Very soon he was able to cobble together a *Komitee zur Schaffung der Deutschen Volksfront* (Committee for the Establishment of a German People's Front), which was officially set up in February 1936.

At this time, a statement issued by Münzenberg and addressed to exiled German Social Democrats in Prague was welcomed warmly. In that statement, he said that he envisaged a People's Front based on freedom of conscience and went on to say that the previous policy of the German Communist Party had been wrong, and that in the future, a genuinely German policy should be pursued. His words were taken by the recipients to be ones endorsed by the Comintern.

It was perhaps symptomatic that Münzenberg's own efforts to set the stage for the creation of a Popular Front were successful because he had already had years of experience working with others of different political persuasions, of building bridges, and gaining trust. In France, one of the biggest successes of the new

Popular Front policy was the coming together of the two big trade union organisations: the Socialist CGT and the Communist CGTU in 1936.

That same year, Münzenberg was the driving force in Europe promoting the 'peace offensive' launched by the Russians in a last ditch attempt to prevent a new world war. He helped bring together as broad a constellation of forces as possible to campaign for measures to prevent the outbreak of war in Europe. This time the initiative had come from the Soviet trade unions rather than the Comintern itself.

A headquarters was set up in Paris with the title of *Rassemblement Universel pour la Paix/Weltfriedensbewegung* (Universal Assembly for Peace/World Peace Movement), and its secretary was Louis Dolivet (Dolivet is mentioned in Soviet secret service files – Vassiliev *White Notebooks* – as a Romanian-born Jew of German background who obtained French naturalisation under unusually easy circumstances and was suspected by the Soviet secret services of being an enemy agent), although there is no available evidence for that accusation. He was a close collaborator of Münzenberg's.

The Universal Assembly for Peace held its first congress in Brussels in September 1936. Its aim was to promote the forces for peace in the world and to strengthen the League of Nations. In order to counter the argument that it was 'just another communist front', the Communists had beforehand agreed not to discuss the issue of Fascism and anti-Fascism.

In July 1935 the German Communist Party itself had been making efforts to organise a broad-based peace conference and set up an anti-fascist German People's Front in order to better co-ordinate the anti-Fascist struggle. It issued a statement calling for broad co-operation to bring down the Hitler dictatorship. In this statement it said: 'The Central Committee of the *KPD*, in the name of all communists in Germany, declares that: The *KPD* is prepared to struggle together with every organisation that is willing to fight for the maintenance of peace and contribute to the bringing down of the Hitler dictatorship'. It continued: 'The Central Committee of the *KPD*, by foregoing the issuing of statements of principle, declares itself prepared to table acceptable proposals to this conference, which would make possible the creation of a united antifascist peoples' front, in which all organisations could take part. An appeal is to go to all organisations of the Social Democratic Party, the Centre Party and other groups abroad.' This appeal by the Communist Party came too late for it to have any chance of being effective; Hitler had already fully consolidated his power and had successfully suppressed all meaningful opposition.

Willi Münzenberg (nominally representing the *Comité contre la Guerre et le Fascisme*) became a member of the Committee for the Establishment of a German Peoples' Front (there were nine representatives in total).

In response to the party's proposal, a statement drafted by Münzenberg (*KPD*) and Viktor Schiff (*SPD*) was submitted to the Central Committee of the *KPD* and Executive of the *SPD*, towards the end of September, in which it stated that, 'The *SPD* and *KPD* (or the signatories on behalf of the two parties) have established that – irrespective of what judgements on any specific past events are made – any continuation of the factual and personal conflict between Social Democrats and Communists can only be viewed as an objective support for Hitler fascism. It is therefore in the interests of our joint struggle, whose basis and aim is to topple the barbaric Hitler regime and to reinstall a democratic people's justice, that the last symptoms of the fratricidal struggle between Social Democrats and Communists are finally put aside. The question of any future structure of the German working class movement must, though, in the first instance be decided by those waging the heroic, illegal struggle themselves …' This represented belated, but promising progress. All parties recognised the increasing danger of Hitler's drive to war and the urgent need to overcome old hostilities and co-operate with each other, as well as to look how to form a new German government to replace Hitler when the time came.

As part of this attempt to set up a People's Front, a Committee for a Free Germany was established and convened its first meeting on 26 September 1935. It was convened in the Hotel Lutetia, in Paris, thus acquiring the sobriquet, 'Lutetia Group'. In a historical irony, this same hotel would become the SS head-quarters during the subsequent Nazi occupation. The purpose of the group was to explore the feasibility of establishing a German Popular Front. It brought exiled Communists and Social Democrats together in a structured way for the first time. Münzenberg's idea was also to bring together leading political fig-ures, artists, and intellectuals who had already stamped their mark on Germany's cultural world. It was hoped, that by elaborating a unifying programme, to influence and win over those independent-minded, non-Fascist individuals and groups in Germany. Further meetings were held during the autumn and winter of 1935–1936.

Most of those Münzenberg had invited did turn up for the meetings. Without Münzenberg's high standing in the anti-Fascist movement and his initiative in creating a climate for the creation of a People's Front, such meetings would not have taken place. The other Communist Party leaders themselves were not capable of doing such work effectively.

The first Lutetia Executive Committee included Leopold Schwarzschild, edi-tor of the successful German émigré weekly, *Das Neue Tagebuch*, the writer, Heinrich Mann, who chaired, Max Braun, Otto Klepper, a former German minister of finance, Viktor Schiff (formerly the editor of the *SPD* newspaper *Vorwärts* and since working for the *Daily Herald*, for whom he had reported from Spain), Georg Bernhard, publisher of the *Pariser Tageblatt*, Hans Erich Kaminski, Dr Hallgarten, Prof. Gumbel, Wilhelm Kiefer (from the Christian trade union organisation of the Saar region), Otto Lehmann-Russbueldt, Dr Bach, Rudolf Leonhardt, Reissner (representing the League for Human Rights), Ernst Toller, Lion Feuchtwanger, and Prof. Robert Kuczynski (the last two on the list were designated, as 'coming from the bourgeois-democratic sector'). There were four representatives from Communist parties, Münzenberg, Wilhelm Koennen, André R. (France?), and H. Belfort (UK), 22 in total. All in all, a very represen-tative cross-section of the émigré community.

The group's manifesto, published in February, reflected the preparedness to create a truly broad front, calling on 'all groups and all individuals who follow this appeal to unite'. This new committee proclaimed to the German émigré community everywhere that there was a need to preserve the German nation and other peoples from the ravages of a new world war. Münzenberg later gave a report to the *KPD* Central Committee on this meeting.

In October 1936, in the wake of the declaration of the new Popular Front policy, Münzenberg again travelled to Moscow. Arising out of the Lutetia meeting, he took his report that gave an analysis of the current situation in Germany and made suggestions about what needed to be done in terms of countering Nazi propaganda. He was, however, very disappointed at not being given the opportunity of presenting his report to the Comintern.

If he had also hoped that the purges and the tidal wave of persecution would be over, he was sorely disappointed. The purging of most of the founding members of the Bolshevik Revolution and numerous foreign Communists had really only just begun. People in Moscow were disorientated, they were at a loss to understand what was happening. When Münzenberg tried to arrange a meeting with his old friend Radek, he learned that he had been arrested shortly beforehand, alongside other leading figures who, until very recently, had been among Stalin's most loyal followers and propagandists.

When he eventually managed to arrange a meeting with Comintern leaders, he was told to immediately hand over his Paris operations to the Czech Communist Bohumír Šmeral and begin work in the agitprop department of the Comintern in Moscow, where they clearly felt he could be more easily controlled. He did not reject this proposal, but was able to procrastinate and countered by demonstrating to them how important his activities in Paris were at this key moment and, at the same time, urged the Soviet Union to provide the Spanish Republican government with much-needed weaponry.

Despite the fact that the Soviet Union was a co-signatory to the League of Nations' non-intervention agreement, intended to prevent the supply of arms to both sides in the Spanish Civil War, the Soviet leadership was made aware of how vital it would be to provide aid for Spain at this critical juncture. As everyone was aware, the agreement was already being blatantly flouted by Nazi Germany and Mussolini's Italy. If the Spanish Republic were to survive, support from the Soviet Union would be vital and also help shore-up public support for the Soviet Union.

Parallel to the discussions Münzenberg was holding in Moscow, he was also called before the 'Control Commission' of the Comintern (the body set up to review and monitor the loyalty and reliability of members; it was also a means of purging dissident individuals from the party). He was grilled about his 'lack of revolutionary vigilance' and asked to explain why he had employed a certain Liane Klein whose father had been a spy for Franco. She had been a typist in the League against Imperialism's office in Berlin and had then moved to Paris of her own accord to again work in one of Münzenberg's offices.

Münzenberg dismissed the accusation as a bagatelle and told his interrogators that she had never worked on any sensitive or secretive documents. He managed to ride out this concerted attempt to relieve him of his present Comintern responsibilities and keep him in Moscow under the watchful eye of Stalin's security services. But the die was now cast for his subsequent demise.

His central involvement in the organising of solidarity with the Spanish Republic gave him the opportunity of convincingly arguing with the Comintern's representative, Palmiro Togliatti, leader of the Italian Communist Party, that he had to return to Paris to tie up loose ends before handing over to Šmeral. This was agreed.

Before leaving, he and Babette had an emotional leave-taking from her sister and partner Heinz Neumann, who had been relieved of all his previous responsibilities and had been under continual interrogation by the Comintern's Control Commission. He and Margarete were in a state of utter hopelessness. Before they had decided to return to Moscow in that fateful summer of 1935, Münzenberg had pleaded with them to remain in Paris where he felt they would be safe, but they had disregarded his advice with tragic consequences.

The situation with her sister and Heinz Neumann undoubtedly made Münzenberg and Babette even more nervous and keen to leave that Kafkaesque place. The evening before their planned departure, they were to meet Soviet officials at the railway station to receive their passports and exit visas, but they waited in vain. With a sense of dread, they returned to their hotel.

In her biography of Münzenberg, Gross writes, that 'during that night in the hotel we were unable to close our eyes and waited for the knock on the door of the *NKVD*'. But the night went by without that ominous visit. In the morning, Münzenberg went straight to see Togliatti and made quite a scene, which clearly had its effect. In Münzenberg's presence, he phoned the police, and they received their papers the same day. No doubt, when their train eventually crossed the border, they both heaved a deep sigh of relief, but remained concerned about Babette's sister and the comrades they had left behind with the daily nightmares of arrests and disappearances.

Heinz Neumann would be executed in November 1937, and shortly afterwards Margarete would also be arrested and despatched to various labour camps, before being handed over to the Nazis in 1940, and she would spend the rest of the war years in Ravensbrück concentration camp.

After arriving back in France that autumn in 1936, Münzenberg began compiling final reports and accounts of all the committees and publishing ventures under his control in order to hand them over to Šmeral as the Comintern's appointee to replace him. However, instead of preparing to return to Moscow, Münzenberg placed himself in the hands of Dr Le Savouret, a Socialist who happened to be married to Plekhanov's daughter and, as a result of the extreme stress to which Munzenberg had been subjected, he would spend several weeks in his sanatorium. There it was established that he had a light 'cardiac neurosis'. Münzenberg justified his delaying tactics to Moscow by underlining once again how he is being undermined and slandered by perfidious rumours that were circulating. At this same time, the second big show trial was taking place in Moscow, and he must have been very relieved that he was not one of those on trial.

Only a short time beforehand, Le Savouret had told Munzenberg that he had been together with Nikolai Bukharin who had come to Paris to deliver a lecture, but when he met Bukharin, he found him in a very confused and nervous state, he said. Bukharin had apparently just received a telegram from Moscow recalling him immediately. Although Le Savouret tried to dissuade him, Bukharin felt he had no option but to return even though knowing what fate awaited him. He would be executed in Moscow in March 1938.

In the meantime, on 10 October 1937, Dimitrov had sent another urgent and threatening letter to Münzenberg in Paris, demanding his return to Moscow.

Not two weeks after the letter had been despatched, Dimitrov was called to a private meeting with Stalin on 11 November 1937.[2] In Dimitrov's secret diaries, he wrote about this meeting and noted the following oral exchange: Stalin: 'We'll probably arrest Stassova. She's revealed herself to be a scoundrel ... Münzenberg is a Trotskyist. When he arrives here, we'll arrest him immediately – make every effort to entice him back here.' Dimitrov goes on to note that, 'Münzenberg's arrival in Moscow would have meant his certain death'.[3] Luckily, Münzenberg's sixth sense saved him and he never returned to Moscow after his last visit.

Hardly had Münzenberg returned to Paris from Moscow – the last visit he would make – than the first ugly rumours about him began to circulate, Gross tells us in her biography. In one or two of the leading mainstream newspapers, stories of his arrest in Moscow had already been circulating. They labelled him 'Moscow's paymaster for Western Europe', and that because he couldn't keep his mouth shut about his clandestine financial dealings, he had been arrested. A Russian émigré journal said he had been accused of siphoning off large sums from the Comintern for his own personal use. Clearly, the scene of his demise was being set. However, his return to Paris, served to rebut such rumours.

Gross writes that these rumours did not overly trouble him, but he withdrew from public activities and began writing a book that he had been planning for some time, his classic, *Propaganda als Waffe* (Propaganda as Weapon). He saw propaganda as a means of achieving political goals. In its narrowest sense, the book is an analysis of Nazi propaganda methods and about his own views on the role of propaganda. In it, he implicitly criticised the usual way National Socialism had been characterised by the *KPD* and the latter's inability to recognise how effective the Nazis' propaganda was, and how they had been able to utilise suggestibility for their cause (i.e. how they had been able to home in on, and latch onto, deeply felt nationalistic and cultural traditions). He also detailed how agitation and propaganda could be used creatively to mobilise people.

The book was strongly criticised by the *KPD*. Münzenberg was accused of exaggerating the power of Nazi propaganda and of severely underestimating the effectiveness of Communist propaganda, and by doing so, had knifed the anti-Fascist movement in the back.

In his review of Münzenberg's book, Wilhelm Pieck is highly critical in his lengthy review:

> 'The content of the book, *Propaganda als Waffe,* is not Marxist. Throughout, the writer makes no use of Marxist but rather an idealistic-psychologising methodology'. He concludes, 'Details of Nazi propaganda will find revulsion among antifascists … in this sense, Münzenberg's book is commendable, but in a book with this title', Pieck writes, 'the aim should have been to provide a route map for the anti-fascist or People's Front movements in terms of what their counter propaganda should look like. This task has not been achieved by Münzenberg's book'.[4]

The rumours and stories in the press were the first public expressions of a rift between the *KPD* and Münzenberg; the real attacks, though, would begin in the autumn of 1937. His continued roles in the People's Front committee and in Spanish support committees were now being undermined by the party apparatus. In the Comintern, though, 'The Münzenberg Case' appeared to have been temporarily shelved; the recent waves of arrests in Moscow had apparently paralysed its normal functioning. Gross relates that Dimitrov and Gibarti were tasked with trying to persuade him to return to Moscow 'for talks', but Münzenberg declined: 'No' he said, 'they'll shoot me as they have the others, then 10 years later, they'll say they have made a big mistake'. Laughing, he responded that he would prefer to remain in Paris. Several of his friends attempted to moderate between him and Moscow, but to no avail. On 23 June 1937, his friend, Lion Feuchtwanger noted in his diary, 'Münzenberg here. He has been called to Moscow and is in dreadful fear that he will be held there or arrested'.[5]

He was fully aware that with his refusal to return to Moscow and the increasingly hostile attitude towards him by the German Communist Party leadership, that his bridges had been burnt.

A Novosti report from 27 July 1937 refers to 'The general delegate of the Comintern in Western Europe – on his refusal to come to Moscow – there was a letter from Münzenberg printed in *Humanité* and the *Pariser Tageszeitung* in which he defends himself vis à vis the rumours of his differences with the Party'.

On 28th July, in *Sozialdemokrat,* the central organ of the German *SPD* in the Czechoslovakian Republic, it stated that, 'From reliable sources in Paris we gather that Willi Münzenberg has fallen into disfavour'. And further: 'Münzenberg was the greatest propagandist of the Comintern. Most of its slogans were created by and popularised by him …' Other Western papers also covered his break with the Comintern.

In October, in a final desperate attempt to clear his name, Münzenberg wrote once more to Dimitrov in Moscow:

Paris 29.10.1937

Perhaps everything is an awful misunderstanding, perhaps all this wouldn't have happened if I had met you in October 1936 and if I'd discussed and clarified with you a number of things that worried me in the summer of 1936. But that was, sadly, not the case.

Allow me, today, to speak openly and without holding back, when for me it concerns everything in life that's dear to me and of value and has been the core of my life for more than 30 years, and when all that is threatened with being lost.

There are two questions that occupy me, torture me and that have prevented me from otherwise immediately following the instructions of your invitation. It is a question of our tactics in the German united and people's front (as the whole organisation of the German revolution against Hitler) and a personal, humanitarian question. I have, since Walter's [Ulbricht] return [to Moscow] raised the alarm, I am tired of warning about the politics he is promoting, which signify an abandonment of the motions carried at the Brussels conference and of the 7th world congress and will (as I predicted in April) lead us to the breaking up of the foundations of a People's Front, to a new, more total isolation than in 1931–1932, to a breaking of all bridges to allies and …

You've been informed about the accusations in the press from Doriot, Goebbels etc. about Münzenberg, the 'Comintern treasurer with funds of millions' etc. (I was never, even in the smallest group, the treasurer). I have already signalled to you where these rumours originate, who is fabricating them, who is promoting them. I had hoped that you [plural] would have intervened, believed that you would at least have prevented these perfidious rumours from circulating in the future. …

What I simply do not understand and about which I've been pondering, but without finding an explanation, is the enormous contradiction that exists between [on the one hand] your invitation, the tolerance you have shown at my postponing the journey [to Moscow], and in offering me another responsible task abroad and [on the other hand] the malicious witch-hunt against me as a political activist, as a communist, as a socialist revolutionary and human being by Walter Ulbricht.

He goes on to relate how a Fascist agent, who had been arrested in Madrid, told a party group: 'If Münzenberg had travelled [to Moscow] he would already have been shot'.

This monstrous witch-hunt which is now being conducted by especially crazy individuals has taken on the character of an incitement to murder … yesterday the police here came to me and told me that they had heard from immigrant circles that communist 'friends' were planning to attack me.

I have never felt so ashamed in all my life. I put it down to malicious lies spread by the Gestapo …

Other stories, that I have been wandering around with a revolver in order to murder comrade Stalin. What crime, in god's name have I committed that after a lifetime of hard and successful Party work people are allowed to hound me and subject me to such despicable slanders? When once again, another of the craziest lies comes to my ears I am close to screaming and exposing this whole poisonous kitchen of the most infamous lies and rumours to the whole world. Only my trust in you and comrade Stalin, to the friends there, to the cause of communism holds me back, and your letter of 10 October proves to me that I was justified.

signed, Willi Münzenberg[6]

In her biography, Gross says that, 'As the year 1937 progressed, it became clear that Münzenberg had distanced himself from the communists'. This changing attitude would, no doubt, also have been influenced by the personal news from Moscow. In May, Babette's sister, Margarete, sent her a postcard in which she informed her of the arrest of her partner, Heinz Neumann; the two continued to correspond throughout the year until Margarete herself was arrested.

In her own reminiscences, Margarete Buber-Neumann writes that 'Between unimportant observations, I slipped in everything of importance, and so my sister was kept informed of my desperate situation and able to take steps on my behalf'.[7]

Gross, though, gives no indication of the sort of conversations she must have had with Münzenberg during this critical period and gives hardly any indication of what must have been going through his head. It can be imagined, however, despite his strong sense of party discipline and loyalty to the cause of Communism and the Soviet Union, that he must have felt a deep trepidation about the way history was unfolding. Gross does write that, 'In a deeply depressed spirit, which he knew how to conceal, he opened the first – and what would be the only – German People's Front conference in Paris on 10 April 1937'. Münzenberg probably sensed that a genuine collaboration between Social Democrats and Communists was not going to work and took a back seat from then on. On his last visit to Moscow, he had warned of the dangers of pursuing narrow policies that would repel other members in a Popular Front, but his warnings were not listened to.

Lion Feuchtwanger had met Münzenberg in Paris in 1936, where he was awaiting a visa for the USA. That may have been the first meeting between the two men, as it is the first time Münzenberg's name appears in Feuchtwanger's diaries.[8] While in Paris, until he left for the USA, Feuchtwanger would become very involved in trying to set up a broad political-cultural front of anti-Fascists in exile and would work closely with Münzenberg on this task.

During the autumn of 1937, Feuchtwanger had become deeply involved in the attempt to establish a People's Front against the Nazis. He had been urged to do this by Heinrich Mann, who was keen to get him on board. Up until then, he had been very much an outside observer of the process. The reason he did eventually become involved seems to have been as a result of the squabbling between the group around Mann and Münzenberg versus the group around Schwarzschild and his newly established 'Association for a Free Press and Literature'.

It was becoming increasingly difficult to achieve consensus and a unity of purpose among the anti-Fascist exiles in France. There is no doubt that old allegiances and loyalties, mistrust, and suspicion fuelled this lack of unity.

Schwarzschild had felt unable to continue co-operating with Münzenberg and had set up his own association. In a letter Heinrich Mann wrote to Feuchtwanger at the time (29 October 1937), he said: 'The most urgent task is to get rid of Ulbricht. He is the second, alongside Schwarzschild, who is determined to destroy the People's Front'. This situation was temporarily resolved when Ulbricht was shortly thereafter called to Moscow.[9]

Undoubtedly what was happening in the Soviet Union was not helping to heal differences in the émigré community. Feuchtwanger met many other intellectual émigrés gathered in Paris at that time in an attempt to bang heads together. One of those with whom he held talks was the theatre director, Erwin Piscator, who was 'very embittered about his time in Russia'. The two spoke about the arrest of the actress Carola Neher in Moscow and the show trials taking place there. Neher was the actress for whom Brecht wrote the role of Polly Peachum in the *Threepenny Opera,* which Piscator directed. During the Great Purge, her colleague, the renowned actor Gustav von Wangenheim, was accused of denouncing her and Becker as Trotskyites.

These show trials, wrote Feuchtwanger, had shocked Europe and lost the Soviet Union two thirds of its supporters. He decided, though, despite being attacked for doing so, to travel to Moscow himself to find out firsthand what was happening and to see if he could help build bridges. There, in 1837, he had meetings with Dimitrov twice and also met Stalin, Litvinov, and other party leaders. He also actually witnessed the trial of Karl Radek, Georgi Pyatakov, and others.

After meeting Stalin, Feuchtwanger appeared to have been taken in by his arguments, and the report he wrote about his time in the Soviet Union, *Moskau 1937. Ein Reisebericht für meine* Freund (Moscow 1937 - a travelogue for my Friends) was praised at the time by Brecht and Heinrich Mann, but criticised by others who could see more clearly Stalin's machinations.[10]

Feuchtwanger advised moderation in dealing with the different factions and in the exile community and saw himself as a successful political moderator between the fronts. 'Münzenberg rang and told me that on the basis of my advice he had been able to prevent the falling apart of the People's Front', he noted on 9 November 1937.

Together with Heinrich Mann, Feuchtwanger pleaded with Dimitrov to intervene in support of the People's Front. On 18 November, Münzenberg thanked Feuchtwanger: 'good news that your assessment and your advice were correct', and added that 'Ulbricht should be relieved of the post he has at present', as this would pave the way for a more positive approach, so 'do your best to ensure that the contradictions do not become sharper, but help smooth them over. The more the alternatives are posited, either U[Ulbricht] goes or we are leaving the People's Front, the more difficult it becomes for Moscow to mediate'. But this hope that, 'in the end everything will work itself out' turned out to be a false one.

On 25 March 1937, Feuchtwanger told the writer, Maria Osten, 'The Münzenberg case is indeed serious, and clearing it up in the best way possible is in the interest of all of us'. 'But from this point onwards,' Anne Hartmann writes, 'his[Feuchtwanger's] interest in the people's front had long been extinguished and he deserted practical politics, turning to his literary work once again. His contact to Münzenberg also cooled. The window of opportunity for a new awakening and for feasible alternatives had been closed for some time'.[11]

Wilhelm Pieck was in Paris when Münzenberg first arrived and, as the party's chief representative there, the two met fairly regularly. Here, the detailed notes and correspondence kept by Pieck are illuminating. His personal notes give an insightful glimpse into the increasing animosity between the party leadership and Münzenberg. These documents are now held in the Bundesarchiv in Berlin. Below are short extracts from the voluminous documentation which give an inkling of the increasing alienation of Münzenberg from the party during this period, and that would lead eventually to his resignation and his treatment as an apostate.

On 29 October 1935, in a letter to the Comintern general secretary, Dimitrov, Pieck had confirmed that the present Central Committee [of the *KPD*] made up of 15 members included Münzenberg. And, in June 1936, in a note, he wrote that as long as the Political Bureau is [still] in Prague, the 'Paris representation [of the Party] consists of Herbert and Münzenberg. But the latter is already under suspicion'.

'I am worried about taking responsibility'[for Münzenberg], Pieck notes, helplessly. Then, on 22 April 1936, he writes: 'It must be dealt with quickly – in order to free the Party from Münzenberg'. Then again in a letter to Comintern secretary Dimitrov, he suggests what measures should be taken:

1. A strong reprimand for Münzenberg
2. A new party representative instead of Dengel, suggest Rädel.
3. Münzenberg [should no longer] act independently in the name of the party as far as discussions on the People's Front are concerned and should speak only in agreement with Rädel.

On 28 October 1936, at a meeting of the Presidium of the Executive Committee of the Comintern, it was agreed to 'investigate' the 'Münzenberg Apparatus'. This recommendation was acted upon immediately, and in December, detailed instructions were issued to remove anyone connected with the so-called 'Münzenberg Apparatus'.

On 29 January and 16 February 1937, the 'Münzenberg case' was discussed in the Control Commission of the Comintern and a recommendation was made to the *KPD* that Münzenberg should be expelled from the party. This was made on the basis that Münzenberg had not followed party instructions to 'publicly dis-avow the Trotskyist spies and the POUM crimes'[in Spain]. In fact, it alleged, he had done the opposite and actively 'associated with Trotskyist elements'. He was, though, removed from the Central Committee of the party on 14 May 1938.

In his personal notes for 1938, Pieck mentions investigatory proceedings into 'the case of Willi Münzenberg' and the latter's appeal against his removal from the Central Committee. Pieck wrote to the Central Committee in response to Münzenberg's non-appearance at his appeal against his removal from the Central Committee: 'Non-appearance has to be viewed as contempt for the most ele-mentary forms of revolutionary discipline in the working class movement and in the Party … but even in his absence the issue should be dealt with and resolved'. He went on to say that, 'People who have worked closely with Münzenberg should also be interviewed'.

In a later letter (probably to the Central Committee or to Ulbricht) from 21 September 1938, Pieck writes, 'Issue of Willi Münzenberg. What should be done with him? – resolution – a decision by the IKK (Comintern) urgent'. Here, he also mentions problems with Münzenberg concerning the newspaper, *Die Zukunft* (The Future), and that Münzenberg has installed a new manager with-out informing the party. 'Münzenberg – has for a long time been against the Party and the Comintern … only attempts to manoeuvre. Social Democrats and Bourgeois elements have been mobilised against the Party and Comintern – sus-pect close relations with Trotskyists and Trotsky' and 'supported financially and contacts with Neumann'.

This accusation surfaces on several occasions, one alleging that Münzenberg 'has links with the Trotskyist, Liesel Cornills'. He is also accused of belonging to a group of 'conciliators'. Even Otto Katz, his close collaborator and the Director of *Agence Espagne* was suspected of 'Trotskyist' associations. Efforts were also made by representatives of the *KPD*'s 'counter intelligence' section to 'neutralise the Münzenberg group' in republican Spain itself.

'The inner Münzenberg group' was listed as being composed of Münzenberg himself, his partner, Babette, Walther Schulz, [Peter] Maslowski, Höft, Pritzel, Off, Heil, Hahnen, Artur(?), Fritz Granzow, Gentner, Köstler (this probably refers to Arthur Koestler), Marta Rup, and two former employees. Pieck describes them as, 'an inner party group of moaners, without a specific political line'.

On the critical situation, Pieck in his personal diary notes: 'Münzenberg has informed [Paul] Bernhard before his journey to Moscow about differences between him and the PB [Political Bureau]. A. Becker attacked Münzenberg also for his vanity – expressed in a speech that he gave in Paris to a preparatory meet-ing on the German Peoples' Front'.

The pettiness, but increasing irritation with Münzenberg, reflects the widen-ing gap between his views and those of the party leadership on how best to deal with the rise of Fascism and the building of broad alliances.

A letter (dated 6 July 1937) is included in the Pieck archive from the secre-tariat of the Central Committee of the *KPD*, at the time temporarily located in

Prague, in which it requests Münzenberg's attendance at a leadership meeting in Moscow re. 'the resolution of political differences'. The letter expresses Pieck's disappointment that Münzenberg appears unwilling to travel to Moscow for such talks (He was at the time 'on holiday' in the countryside).

Wilhelm Pieck, by this time in Moscow, wrote in his private notes during that autumn of 1938, that 'The main threat is not Trotskyism but Münzenberg'.[12] Münzenberg, along with Heinz Neumann and Hermann Remmele, was accused of forming a Trotskyist splinter group.

In the autumn of that same year, undoubtedly with a heavy heart, Münzenberg circulated a statement to his friends in which he explained why he was leaving the Communist Party: '... Because of the situation in Germany and the escalation of the international crisis which demands the commitment of everyone, my political past, my socialist sense of responsibility and my temperament force me to leave an organisation that has made further political action impossible for me'.

In his statement, he avoided any expression of bitterness or of making accusations aimed at his former comrades; he confined himself to drawing up a reasoned balance sheet on policies he deemed to be wrong-headed and not compatible with his own aims and goals. In conclusion, he said that his attitude towards the Soviet Union remained unchanged.

It is perhaps also surprising that even here, he said not a word about Stalin's purges. Perhaps he felt that, as an isolated individual, to take on Stalin would demand too much of him or that it would have been pointless and even counterproductive.

He wrote a lengthier statement to the party on his reasons for resigning and would publish it in his paper, *Die Zukunft* (The Future), on 10 March 1939. His statement ended with the words: 'And so I retain the place I chose and which I've occupied since 1906, alongside Karl Liebknecht, later alongside Rosa Luxemburg, Clara Zetkin and, in 1915, alongside Lenin, my place in the battle ranks of revolutionary socialism'.

The party and the Comintern's response was to accuse him of being responsible for the failure of the People's Front movement and of being a member of the now reviled, so-called 'Neumann Group' in the *KPD*.

On 15 December 1938, in a desperate attempt to clear his name, Münzenberg again wrote to Dimitrov in Moscow, demanding a full explanation of what he was being accused and of what was in the defamatory statements that were being circulated. In this letter, he argues that his closest colleagues should be asked to comment on the accusations and lists them as, Louis Dolivet, Martha Staschek, Hans Schulz, Fritz Granzow, and Else Lange, as well as his friends Rudolf Breitscheid, Heinrich Mann, Lion Feuchtwanger, Professor Marek, Emil Gumbel, George Bernhard, and Max Braun. In addition, Münzenberg demands to have access to the dossier that has been compiled on him and, in a poignant addendum, adds: 'I don't doubt that you will help me, at least to make it possible for me to mount a defence, as I did for you through my actions in setting up the counter trial in the autumn of 1933 in the face of your Leipzig trial'. Dimitrov did not respond.

In August 1939, in desperate need of a break, Münzenberg and some members of his inner circle left for the Normandy coast, to a holiday house between Étretat and Fécamp, which Babette rented every summer.

There they would celebrate Münzenberg's 50th birthday on 14th August, but the celebrations would have been muted, given the dire political climate. At this time, the Germans and Russians were drawing up their non-aggression pact in Moscow, which was signed on 23rd.

Peter Gross describes the atmosphere: 'For Willi it was the end of his nearly twenty-year relationship with Russian Bolshevism. But on his birthday, we all went down to the beach, my mother and I swam out to the "Needle" and la Porte d'Aval and the men sat on the sand with their trousers rolled up. Not one of them could swim. After lunch we stood round a small fire in the garden and sang – not communist *Kampflieder* this time but old sentimental German songs about the rosy past'.[13]

In November 1939, in his paper, *Die Zukunft*, Münzenberg would write publicly for the first time that he felt the Comintern had not implemented the resolutions carried at the seventh congress, and he also criticised Stalin's emphasis on the 'class question' which, he felt, automatically meant that the Communists would attempt to dominate any broad front, and that they would only go through the motions of being equal partners in a genuine People's Front. This article set out his profound differences with the Comintern and KPD leaderships.

Unrelated to Münzenberg's situation, but indicative of the lengths Stalin would go to eliminate all and any perceived Trotskyist opposition, is the case of Ignaz Reiss. A year earlier, on 4 September 1938, the Austro-Hungarian-born Communist and early Bolshevik, Reiss, was assassinated near Lausanne by agents of the Soviet secret service, after he had written a letter to Stalin announcing his defection and in which at the same time he denounced the latter's bloody annihilation of leading Bolsheviks. 'I am joining Trotsky and the Fourth International', he said.

He had been a full-time agent of first *GRU* and then the *NKVD*. Others who renounced Communism in response to Stalin's purges were harassed and denounced. Münzenberg, himself, was sent a number of threatening messages and, because of his intimate knowledge of the workings of the Comintern and the Soviet state, he would certainly have felt very vulnerable.

In her biography, Gross writes that towards the end of 1938, Münzenberg was sitting with his friend and comrade Kurt Kersten in an inn in Strasburg, 'reminiscing about his time with the old Bolsheviks in Switzerland and he concluded the conversation depressingly by saying: "Now I must be one of the last among the living of those Zimmerwald Leftists who met together in Kienthal"'. She goes on to say, that he didn't let such melancholic thoughts dominate his life, but sought to overcome them through a concentrated and intense activity.

This meeting took place shortly after he had set up his journal, *Die Zukunft*, in 1938 – the final ambitious undertaking of his last years. It represented his last endeavour to unite the German anti-Fascist opposition in exile and stave off the war, even though time had already run out.

He envisaged his weekly, *Die Zukunft*, as a mouthpiece for a non-sectarian, politically non-aligned approach to promote unity in the German émigré community. His old friend, the Swedish banker, Olof Aschberg, then also living in France, was prepared to finance the new paper. It lasted until Jan 1940.[14]

Given the historical and political context, Münzenberg's goal of creating unity, overriding party allegiances, was also doomed. He was, though, probably one of the very few leading political figures of the time who had the potential of being able to unite the left. He was prepared to go beyond Socialist and Communist circles, to work with progressive liberals and Christians of all shades. He also realised that narrow nationalism was inimical to a wider peace and unity between the separate European states, and that an internationalist perspective was essential if war were to be avoided and Fascism defeated.

In the meantime, *Die Zukunft*, had become the mouthpiece of 'Friends of Socialist Unity' or the group around Münzenberg. He had begun thinking about establishing a new International, to unite left-wing Socialists, but separate from the Communist Party and the mainstream Social Democratic parties. In a long article in the paper, he proposed a programme for a future, reformed German united party of the working class. Central to those discussions, as he formulated it in the columns of the paper, was the issue of a future German constitution, and in an editorial, Münzenberg demanded a rethink on questions of dictatorship and democracy. He also attempted to extend the reach of his paper beyond the confines of German émigré circles by publishing a German-English special issue, edited by Arthur Koestler.

A Gestapo report from July 1939, by an agent in or close to his organisation, noted that the Münzenberg group was making every effort to turn the paper into the mouthpiece of the whole [anti-Fascist] opposition, saying that, 'Thanks to Münzenberg's skill, this journal, despite the short period of its existence, has become the leading paper of the emigrant community and also of the general German opposition'.

During that depressing period and in the immediate wake of the Chamberlain-Hitler Agreement of September 1938, Münzenberg held a meeting with Jawaharlal Nehru who had been visiting his fatally ill wife in a Black Forest clinic. They were both clear that the Munich Agreement meant that war was now inevitable.

Stalin could only draw one conclusion from this last ditch attempt by the British and French governments to appease Hitler: they were not prepared to enter into a pact with the Soviet Union to oppose him, but instead were hoping to encourage him to move east. So, on 19 August 1939, the Soviet Union signed a trade deal with the Hitler regime and on the 23rd a non-aggression pact. This apparent about-turn by the Soviet Union left anti-Fascists everywhere in a state of profound shock.

Gross, in her Münzenberg biography, says this crucial event 'caused the dams to burst in Münzenberg and everything that he'd suppressed flowed out of him with caustic bite in the pages of *Die Zukunft*'.

He characterised the Stalin-Hitler Agreement as a 'Russian stab in the back'. He wrote that 'Peace and freedom have to be defended against Hitler and Stalin, victory must be fought for against both of them, and the new, united party of German workers needs to be forged in the struggle against Hitler as well as Stalin ...'

He followed up this appeal with articles condemning the 'great purges' that had decimated the Soviet Bolshevik Party and given the Comintern the coup de grâce. His article, 'The traitor, Stalin, is you', set out cogently the reasons for his break with Stalin's domination of the international Communist movement and the consequent undermining of the anti-Fascist struggle. As a last effort, Münzenberg, as a publisher and a man of renown, attempted to gather together a significant section of the non-Communist German and European anti-Hitler opposition under his wing, but this time independently of the party.

One of Münzenberg's closest comrades had been Otto Katz with whom he had begun working in 1924 in Berlin. Katz had earlier been a close associate of the great left-wing theatre director and Brecht collaborator, Erwin Piscator, but when the latter's theatre project folded, Katz was given work by Münzenberg in one of his publishing houses. When Katz later and unwittingly found himself being chased for unpaid taxes in connection with Piscator's failed theatre project, Münzenberg managed to find both of them work in Moscow in the film department of Meschrabpom. Then, in 1933, he had asked for Katz to be sent to Paris to join him there.

As secretary of the Marley Committee, Katz would travel to Britain and the USA to raise money for the committee. With the outbreak of the Spanish Civil War, he was put in charge of Münzenberg's *Agence Espagne*. Much later, after Münzenberg had severed all links to the Comintern, all Communist German refugees in Paris who had worked with him were told to sever their own links with him. Katz, probably reluctantly, followed Comintern instructions. This, however, didn't save him from Stalin's ire. He would be convicted in Prague as part of the Stalin-instigated Slansky show trials of 1952 and hanged. At his trial, he 'confessed' that he 'was a member of a Trotskyist group centred around Münzenberg'.

Münzenberg's gradual alienation from the Communist Party over the years and the party leadership's distancing itself from him undoubtedly had a variety of reasons, but one of the most significant ones was his adamant defence of his independence. From the very beginning of his involvement in the Socialist movement, he demonstrated a strong independent streak. He was not someone who was prepared to subject himself totally to an iron party discipline, but remained determined to sail his own course.

There were those in the Communist movement, Like Ulbricht and Pieck, who had a rather narrow view of what a classless and Socialist utopia would look like. They saw the process more in terms of achieving necessary change through the concerted and disciplined action of a vanguard party, character-ised by a quasi-militarised, well-ordered, and regulated imposition. And, on the other hand, those like Münzenberg or Luxemburg, who had a more generous vision and imagination, seeing a new society as a blossoming of opportunity and creativity, embracing a freedom to build from below, and with a more pluralistic society as the final goal.

A number of those who met Münzenberg commented on the fact that he gave the impression of someone who was an independent operator, as the father of the narrator in Peter Weiss's docu-novel, *Aesthetics of Resistance*, put it: 'He was the last of those who stayed true to Luxemburg's maxim, stressing the need for open debate within the party'.[15] And it was that attitude which made him mortal enemies in the increasingly narrow-minded and Stalinist leadership of the party from the 1930s onwards.

Notes

1 Comintern Document Archive RGASPI 495/205/7000; pp. 115–141.
2 Bayerlein, Bernhard H. ed. *Tagebücher Georgi Dimitrov 1933–1943*, Aufbau Verlag, Berlin, 2002.
3 Weber, Hermann, Drabkin, Yakov, Bayerlein, Bernhard H. (Eds.), *Deutschland, Russland, Komintern - Dokumente (1918–1943)*, opus cit. Dimitrov Diaries, De Gruyter, Oldenbourg, 2014, p. 165.
4 Notizen über Leitungsitzungen der KPD vom 21.09.1938 in Paris, SAPMO Bach NY4036/495.
5 von Sternburg, Wilhelm *Lion Feuchtwanger, ein deutsches Schriftstellerleben*, Aufbau Taschenbuch Verlag, 1999. p. 39.
6 Comintern Document Archive RGASPI 495/74/127.
7 Margarete Buber-Neumann, *Under Two Dictators – Prisoner of Stalin and Hitler*, Pimlico Press, 2009.
8 Hartmann, Anne 'Willi Münzenberg, Lion Feuchtwanger und die Frage einer "Ästhetik des Widerstand,"' Willi Münzenburg Forum, 2014.
9 Janka, Walter, *Spuren des Lebens*, Rowohlt, 1991. p. 228, also: von Sternburg, Wilhelm, *Lion Feuchtwanger – ein deutsches Schriftsteller leben*, Aufbau Taschenbuch Verlag, 1999. pp. 394–5.
10 Ibid. p. 426.
11 Hartmann, Anne, Anne 'Ich kam, ich sah, ich werde schreiben'. Lion Feuchtwanger in Moskau 1937. Eine Dokumentation. Wallstein Verlag, Göttingen 2017.
12 Notizen über Leitungsitzungen der KPD vom 21.09.1938 in Paris, SAPMO Bach NY4036/495. opus cit.
13 Gross, Peter, '*Memories of Willi Münzenberg*', Quadrant April 2010. p. 87.
14 At the end of the 1920s, Aschberg moved to France, where he bought Château du Bois du Rocher at Jouy-en-Josas. He helped finance the Popular Front during the Spanish Civil War. Münzenberg was often invited to Aschberg's Paris townhouse on the place Casimir-Périer and received the funds for launching *Die Zukunft* (The Future), a weekly political broadsheet. This townhouse was gradually transformed into a kind of all-purpose Münzenberg salon, which did attract the attention of the Gestapo, spying on the meetings taking place there.
15 Weiss, Peter, *Die Ästheitk des Widerstandes*, Suhrkamp Verlag, 1981.

14

FRENCH INTERNMENT AND MYSTERIOUS DEATH

On a crisp autumn day on 17 October 1940, two local men from the village of Montagne – M. Gobertier and M. Argout – were out hunting with their dogs and on the lookout for game in the Le Cougnet forest, not far from the village of Montagne in the Vichy-administered part of southern France. With food strictly rationed in wartime France, what you were able to shoot yourself for the pot was a valuable supplement to an otherwise restricted diet. But these two men came across something they had not expected. One of the dogs nosed it out first. Propped up against the foot of a large oak tree, obscured in a drift of fallen leaves, was the half-putrefied and still clothed body of a human being. They didn't linger, but hurried back immediately to inform local gendarmerie, and two officers from St. Marcellin then undertook an on-site investigation. Although the ravages of time and the attention of wild animals had made visual identification problematic, the man still had his few belongings and the all-important ID in his jacket pockets. They identified him as Willi Münzenberg, a German refugee. The conclusion drawn by the investigating authorities was that this death was the result of suicide and no foul play was suggested. Their transcript lies in the archives of Grenoble.[1]

FIGURE 14.1   Willi Münzenberg portrait c. 1930

The gendarmes also drew a sketch and recorded that the corpse was found under an oak tree, six metres from a path, lying on its back with its legs bent underneath, the left arm at the side of the body, and the right one on the chest. The body was desiccated and the flesh from the skull had rotted away. A three-ply twine was still around the corpse's neck and another piece of around 1.5 metres long was strung over a branch of the oak tree above it at a height of 3.30 metres. In the inside pocket of the jacket on the corpse, the police found a leather wallet containing several documents, including a French ID issued to foreign residents, in the name of none other than Willi Münzenberg. There was also a postcard sent on 18 June 1940 to Münzenberg in Chambaran from Babette Gross from here own internment camp in Gurs. In a side pocket they found a pair of spectacles.

FIGURE 14.2 Babette Gross in 1939, photo taken in the year before Münzenberg's death (Courtesy of Gross family.)

The unusual circumstances surrounding the death of a leading anti-Fascist, high on the wanted list of the Gestapo, but also very much out of favour with Joseph Stalin, has led conspiracy theorists to wild speculation as to the real cause of death, invariably suggesting it was Stalin's doing. Most writers on this subject since have accepted this suggestion, and it does fit perfectly the established narrative patterns that depict an all-powerful, unscrupulous and omnipotent Soviet security services. There is, though, no solid evidence for such a conjecture.

Already in 1939, with the German army massing on France's border, the Daladier-led government immediately began interring all German and Austrian citizens, irrespective of whether they were anti-Fascists or not. Most of the refugees, men and women – at least those under 50 to begin with – were transported to concentration camps in various parts of the country where they were held in often primitive conditions under armed guard. Few were able to escape the net. Willi Münzenberg was among those to be interned before he had time to organise an escape.

In only six weeks from the start of their invasion on 10 May 1940 the Nazis had conquered France. In the wake of their invasion, two months later, a proxy French government, the so-called Vichy regime, was established under Marshal Pétain, and it collaborated fully with the Nazis. It was given administrative control of the southern part of France, but was beholden to Nazi occupational forces.

The novelist Leonard Frank was also one of those interned. He described his experience in his autobiographical novel, *Heart on the Left.* Only a few years previously, in 1930, his play, *Carl and Anna,* had been performed in Paris, and he had been warmly received by French government ministers, he was also a well-known anti-Nazi, but all this would make no difference to how he was now treated. He, along with 1,400 others, was herded onto lorries and transported to a temporary camp on a deserted farm. They – many of them Jewish – had to sleep on the cold concrete floor of the barn, strewn with stinking straw and had only one water tap between them. The farm was guarded day and night by armed soldiers, with orders to shoot anyone who tried to flee.[2] Despite the danger, he did though, with two other internees, decide to flee and after a gruelling trek, and then by ship, he would find refuge in the USA.

Münzenberg who had just reached 50 remained free to begin with and undertook every effort to lobby the French authorities in an attempt to obtain the freedom of his older colleagues who had been interned.

On 10 May 1940, Hitler's 'Blitzkrieg' began and France would rapidly be overrun. As a result of the invasion, the French government demanded that all foreigners, even those over 50, would now have to report to collection points and be interned immediately. Münzenberg was among those to be rounded up.

His partner, Babette Gross, would be interned in a women's camp in the Pyrenees. But with the approach of the Nazi troops, the commandant allowed all those women who felt politically threatened by the Nazi advance to leave the camp and make their escape as best they could. After she had tried to locate Münzenberg, but without success, she made her way via Portugal to safety in Mexico.

In mid-May 1940, Münzenberg was taken from Paris to the military internment camp of Chambaran, 70 km southwest of Lyon, which was under the control of the 143rd French infantry regiment. Here, several hundred Germans and Austrians were interned. Other refugees were taken from Paris to various camps dispersed around the country.

Chambaran camp was in the Isère Valley not far from Grenoble. He was held there alongside other German anti-Fascists.

In the camp, internees were detailed to carry out forestry work, but Münzenberg managed to procure a less arduous job in the garden of the camp commander and worked there together with the Social Democrat and trade union organiser, Valentin Hartig. They both utilised their privileged position to supply their comrades with vegetables which were otherwise in short supply.

On 14 June, Nazi troops entered Paris, and by 19 June, they were already in Lyon and pushing rapidly south. On 20 June at 3 a.m., the order did come through to decamp. However, when the camp authorities refused to hand back the prisoners' ID papers, there was open rebellion, and in the end, the internees themselves took control and handed out the papers. That same day, the French military commander took the decision to evacuate the camp and march the several hundred inmates southwest towards Rhônetal.

The column began its march south while it was still dark, but before dawn broke, Münzenberg and several other fellow internees – according to the few eyewitnesses, three or four, but there is uncertainty about how many joined him or who they were – used that opportunity to flee. They were not too far from the Swiss border or even from Marseilles and the chance of finding a ship to take them to freedom. They took their chance and ran off into the woods in an attempt to reach potential safety. From here on the facts become blurred and have left the field open for conspiracy theorists and wild speculation from all sides.

The French investigating authorities were convinced that in the case of Münzenberg's death, it was a straightforward case of suicide. They discovered nothing that would persuade them otherwise. And if true, he would sadly not be the only one to have taken this route. The writer, Walter Hasenclever did so after being interned like Münzenberg, Walther Benjamin took his own life just over the French-Spanish border, Stefan Zweig, after he had found refuge in Brazil, as did the great satirist, Kurt Tucholsky, in Sweden, and the playwright Ernst Toller in New York, to name but a few.

The first independently written report of Münzenberg's death was compiled by the writer/journalist and old friend of Münzenberg's, Kurt Kersten. Most of the information he gleaned was from an interview granted him by Hans Siemsen who had been in Chambaran with Münzenberg.[3]

Siemsen told him that after they took a rest during the march south, Münzenberg, sitting on a tree-stump, spoke with his companions, Leopold Schwarzschild, Hans Siemsen, Kurt Wolf, Paul Westheim, and Clément Korth about making a break for it. He tried to persuade them to join him, to leave the column and take their chances alone; only in this way could they be sure of escaping the rapidly approaching Nazis, he felt. They should try and make their way to Switzerland which was not too distant, he told them. His companions, however, decided to stay with the main body of internees.

Münzenberg confided to Siemsen that he had 2,000 Francs and with it hoped to buy a car to aid his escape. (There is no mention of this money being found on the body or of the map he apparently possessed when he fled. Did he perhaps give the money to one of his companions to buy a car, together with the map, or was he robbed?)

From examining a map of the area, it seems that Münzenberg and several companions had been heading east, probably towards the Isère Valley and from there aimed to reach to Geneva. He clearly hoped to find refuge in Switzerland, where he still had friends, as well as his teenage son, Uli.[4] However, he must also have been conscious of the fact that since he had been expelled from that country in 1918, he would not find it easy to regain legal entry.

The last section of the terrain he and his compatriots had to cross was a rugged one, hilly and covered in woodland and scrub – for those unfamiliar with the area, very challenging and difficult to find one's way.

When villagers in Montagne were asked some years later about a group of Germans appearing in the village at that time, they recalled encountering four such individuals. They saw them sitting in a café, and they had, according to the villagers, attempted to buy a car.

According to Siemsen, Münzenberg fled together with Hartig and two others, including a mysterious red-haired young man who had been with them in the camp. No one knew who he was and he later disappeared into thin air. He had, according to witnesses, latched onto Münzenberg and avidly supported Münzenberg's plans to make a break for it. Münzenberg, though, was also well versed in how to survive in exile and in dangerous situations and would, one supposes, have chosen any comrades accompanying him very carefully. It is doubtful that he would have put his trust in an unknown individual.

Another eyewitness said that after the four had entered the woods, only three came back to the village and tried to hire or buy a horse and cart as 'one of their companions was unable to walk any further as his feet were hurting'.

A document that may throw additional light on Münzenberg's death was only discovered many years later.[5] It is a report given by Heinz Hirth, a German Communist who joined the resistance, staying on in France during the war. In his report, he says that he was an eyewitness to Münzenberg's suicide. His report differs in detail significantly from those given by other eyewitnesses and commentators. It was found in the archive of the exile organisation of the German Communist Party in France.

The undated report was made sometime in 1945 and signed by Hirth personally. In it, he gives information about his internment with Münzenberg and their joint flight in 1940. He said that he and Münzenberg were with a group of around 20 others, but after discovering that 'we were completely surrounded' [presumably by German troops], 'we split up into four smaller groups'. He goes on to relate that Münzenberg was in a demoralised state at this time and one night, while they were sleeping in the woods, managed to slink away and was found the next day hanging from a tree. This story may have reached Wilhelm Leo and through him his son, Gerhard, to give rise to his own version of Münzenberg's death by suicide. Hirth's report, while interesting, hardly provides confirmation of how Münzenberg died, but merely adds to the confusion and mystery.

Stephen Koch, in his Münzenberg biography, writes that his flight [from French internment and the Nazi advance in France] 'was being tracked by the secret services of at least three different nations'. He provides no evidence for this, however, and, under the difficult and chaotic circumstances pertaining at the time, it is very doubtful if his movements could be tracked at all.[6]

Babette Gross, who looked closely into the circumstances surrounding his death, doubts that he committed suicide. She quotes contemporary witnesses who maintained that he had not been depressed at the time and was in otherwise good spirits. He had sent a telegram to Babette while still in the camp at Chambaran in which he expressed his hope that they would soon be reunited and told her she should have courage.

In her investigations, she also relied on information given to her by Valentin Hartwig who had worked alongside Münzenberg in the garden at the Chambaran camp.

Another of his fellow internees, Hans Siemsen, wrote in 1940 to tell her that Münzenberg had been 'active and full of energy and had withstood the rigours of the march better than I had'. This would seem to imply that Münzenberg had completed the march from Chambaran to the south, but that would contradict the fact that he escaped shortly after the march set out, as indicated by the place, not far away from the route, where his body was found. His close companion and fellow internee, Valentin Hartig, also wrote to Gross in 1963, and said, 'I would rule out suicide'.

Siemsen also said that he saw Münzenberg with several other companions making their way across fields and waving to the remaining internees as the latter proceeded on their march south. But, Gross writes that, 'no other witnesses confirm this sighting and there remains a lack of clarity about the place [where he made his break] and about how many others were with him'.

In 1947, Gross herself was able to make detailed enquiries in St. Marcellin where the Gendarmerie held the papers concerning the Münzenberg case, and she also spoke to M. Georges Argoud, a woodsman from St. Antoine and one of the two hunters who discovered Münzenberg's body, but she was unable to discover anything more than was already known.

Interestingly, only Koch of Münzenberg's three biographers mentions Gerhard Leo's story concerning Münzenberg's death, as told in Leo's autobiographical reminiscences. Rather predictably, he dismisses it as mere disinformation.

Leo was a young German Communist who fought heroically in the French Resistance during the war. His father, Wilhelm, was a German-Jewish lawyer (not a member of the Communist Party) who had also fled Hitler's persecution to France. Wilhelm, like Münzenberg, was interned in France.

Gerhard Leo, a journalist working for the GDR press, returned in 1984 to the village of Montagne, where Münzenberg had died, in an attempt, he says, to discover the truth. In the first edition of his reminiscences, *Frühzug nach Toulouse* (Early Train to Toulouse) he writes that his father, Wilhelm, spent the last hours with Münzenberg and told his son at length about what had happened.

According to Leo, his father was actually interned in Chambaran together with Münzenberg and was one of two internees who escaped with him. According to

Wilhelm Leo, as related by his son Gerhard, the three of them were attempting to reach the Swiss border. They tried unsuccessfully to find a Frenchman to give them a lift in a vehicle or lend them a horse and cart. Soon Münzenberg said his feet were hurting and he needed a rest, telling them to go on and he would catch up. When he didn't arrive, they retraced their tracks and found Münzenberg hanging from a tree.

Leo dismisses the conspiracy theories of his being murdered by Stalin. In his own investigations in 1984, he said that he spoke to several local people who experienced the Nazi occupation. One, Fernand Germain, said he remembered clearly the tragic circumstances surrounding Münzenberg's death. Nazi troops, he related, were only 20 km distant, when three German refugees came from L'Herbassse and sought out the village innkeeper, as they had heard he owned a horse and cart which they wished to hire or buy from him. One of the three, he said, had difficulty walking – Leo assumes that would have been Münzenberg.

The innkeeper refused to give them his horse and cart, and they were obliged to continue on foot. Germain had this story from the innkeeper himself and the two hunters who found Münzenberg's corpse.

Gross herself, according to Koch, dismissed Leo's version of events, because he was working as a journalist for the GDR state and therefore, in her view, not to be trusted. Leo's daughter, the historian Annette Leo, believes her father may have conflated what his own father told him and what the latter probably picked up from a statement given by Heinz Hirth, who reported that he had been with Münzenberg during the last days of his life.

Interestingly, Gerhard Leo removed the Münzenberg episode from the second edition of his book. His daughter says that he refused to discuss the issue with her, despite her asking for an explanation.[7]

After the police investigation into his death was completed, Münzenberg was buried in the small cemetery of Montagne, near St. Marcellin, in the Isère region, not far from where his corpse was found. He was interred on around 20 October 1940 in the presence of around 20 villagers, but none of his former friends or comrades. Surprisingly, perhaps, there is no death certificate in Münzenberg's name in the archives of the council offices of Montagne.

There is no doubt that both the Nazi regime and Stalin would have been more than happy to be rid of the irritant Willi Münzenberg, but whatever the exact circumstances of his death, assassination by either would seem unlikely on the basis of the hard evidence we have.

If he were murdered, why were his personal documents left in his jacket pocket? Both the Nazis and the Soviet secret services were not known for their reticence or squeamishness about how they disposed of their opponents, and if they had wished to cover their spoor, they would surely have removed any identifying documents from the body; or, if they had wanted to make an example of Münzenberg as a deterrent to others, then surely they would have ensured that his body was left in a place where it would be discovered more easily. Why go to the trouble of making a killing look like suicide when it was extremely unlikely that the body would be found anyway – certainly not in the short term – and in such an out of the way place?

For one or even two men to be able to overpower a fit and strong man and then hang him from a tree is certainly questionable. If there was a determination to murder him, it would have been so much easier, as in other cases where deemed enemies were assassinated by the secret services, to have shot or poisoned him.

Another question that would come to mind if he had been in fact murdered by either Stalin or Hitler is why he was not assassinated earlier when doing so would have been much more straightforward. There was ample opportunity to do this during his years of exile in Paris, despite the fact that, aware of the danger he was in, he would have become increasingly circumspect about his movements and more cautious in everything he did. The US author, Sean McMeekin, asserts that 'NKVD agents tracked Münzenberg's every move in exile in Paris from 1938', and we know the Gestapo kept him under close surveillance too.

In the spring of 1940, once the French government began interning all Germans and Austrians, mainly anti-Nazis, and transporting them under armed guard to various concentration camps, tracking Münzenberg's movements would have become much more difficult for his enemies.

For Soviet agents to have been able to follow their man during the chaos and uncertainty of the internment process and count on persuading him to make an escape attempt in order to kill him by hanging, with the German army only a few miles away, seems rather too outlandish to be true.

For more detail about the French investigation and the conflicting witness statements surrounding Münzenberg's death, see the paper, 'Die Rätsel um Münzenbergs Tod – Eine lokale Perspektive' (The puzzle of Münzenberg's death – a local perspective) by Micheline Revet und Michel Jolland.[8]

Despite the fact that Münzenberg was a figure deeply hated by the Nazis, was on top on their 'Most Wanted' list and his every move in Paris was being monitored by them, the possibility of their being involved in his murder is rarely mentioned by writers on the subject. The ready acceptance of his being murdered by the *NKVD* fits only too comfortably into the mainstream narrative. Most authors on the subject have simply taken the murder by the *NKVD* theory as the most credible. The historian, Geoff Andrews, certainly does. He writes: 'Münzenberg left Paris in 1940; he was briefly interned by the Daladier government and then murdered – presumably by Comintern agents ...'[9] [Author's note: Daladier was no longer in power at the time Münzenberg was interned. He had resigned on 21 March 1940.]

It is a conundrum. None of the above provides firm proof for any of the possible scenarios of how he met his death, but there are pertinent questions that cannot be easily brushed aside in the desire to paint his death as yet one more to be laid at Stalin's door or indeed at the Nazis' either, even though both regimes were certainly responsible indirectly, if not directly, for his untimely death.

Certainly, despite circumstantial evidence that Münzenberg was in no way depressed or demoralised at the time, his position was objectively dire. The prospect of his being captured by the Nazis or surviving to experience what appeared likely to be a post-war Europe very much dominated by Stalin's Soviet Union was hardly an enviable choice, and this might have been what he feared he was facing and affected his mental state, but this can only remain speculation. It was, in a sense, a death foretold, whatever the exact circumstances.

The whole story surrounding Münzenberg's escape and subsequent death is very muddled, with conflicting and, now, unverifiable detail. All we know for certain is that at some stage during his attempt to flee, he became separated from his companion/s and ended up beneath a tree, with twine around his neck beneath an oak tree from which he appeared to have hanged himself in the forest. Now with no eyewitnesses still alive, it will be virtually impossible to establish the full truth, but speculation surrounding his mysterious death will no doubt continue and provide a lucrative field for those with their own axes to grind.

Notes

1 Revet, Micheline and Jolland, Michel, 'Die Rätsel um Münzenbergs Mord. Eine locale Perspektive', Global Spaces for Radical Transnational Solidarity. Contributions to the First International Willi Münzenberg Congress 2015 in Berlin, ed. by Bernhard H. Bayerlein, Kasper Braskén and Uwe Sonnenberg, International Willi Münzenberg Forum, Berlin, 2018.

2 Frank, Leonhard, *Heart on the Left*, Arthur Barker Ltd., 1954. p. 504.

3 Revet, Micheline and Jolland, Michel, opus cit. p. 505.

4 Research carried out by Ursula Langkau-Alex and revealed in a paper she gave to the first International Willi Münzenberg Congress: 'Die Frau im Hintergrund. Babette Gross und die anderen in Münzenbergs Netzwerken der 1930er Jahre' (The woman in the background. Babette Gross and the others in Münzenberg's networks of the 1930 years) have revealed for the first time that Willi Münzenberg had an illegitimate son in Switzerland, called Uli. One of Uli's daughters was, at the time the paper was delivered, still alive and spoke to the author. Ursula Langkau-Alex came across a photo of Uli. The original, as a postcard, is to be found among the 1938 letters of Babette Gross in the IISH Fritz Brupbacher Papers, file 147. On the back, Babette has written: 'This is Willi's sprig. Many thanks for all! Yours Babett'. https://www.muenzenbergforum.de/wp-content/uploads/2018/07/IWMF_V15.pdf

5 Pech, Karlheinz, Ein neuer Zeuge im Todesfall Willi Münzenberg, *Beiträge zur Geschichte der Arbeiterbewegung* 37, no. 1 1995: 65–71.

6 Koch, Stephen *Stalin, Double Lives: Stalin, Willi Münzenber and the Seduction of the Intellectuals*, Enigma Books, 2004. p. 4.

7 Leo, Annette 'Selbst Mord oder Mord? Der Umgang mit Leben und Tod von Willi Münzenberg in der DDR der achtziger Jahren', a paper delivered at the First International Willi-Münzenberg-Congress, held between 17 and 20 September 2015 in Berlin. Also, personal correspondence between the author and Annette Leo.

8 Revet, Micheline and Jolland, Michel, 'Die Rätsel um Münzenbergs Tod. Eine lokale Perspektive'. Their paper provides the most up-to-date factual detail about Münzenberg mysterious death. Based on the researches of Michel Jolland who became preoccupied with Münzenberg's death. He has been researching the circumstances surrounding his death since 2007, seeking evidence that could help throw light on it. Solid evidence remains elusive. If he was indeed murdered by Stalin's NKVD, then evidence should be somewhere in a Moscow archive, but up until now, nothing has been found. See: First Willi Münzenberg Congress, https://www.muenzenbergforum.de/ebook/.
9 Andrews, Geoff, *The Shadow Man*, I.B. Tauris. 2015. p. 91.

15

MÜNZENBERG'S BRITISH
SECRET SERVICE FILES

FIGURE 15.1   Drawing of Willi Münzenberg in 1920 by Isaac Brodsky

Münzenberg and his activities were not only of interest to the German authorities. He was already on Britain's Secret Intelligence Service radar in September 1919, when he began rebuilding the 'German Young Socialists' organisation. From that time onwards, his movements were continually monitored by SIS/MI6, and their agents in various European countries sent regular reports to London. As the global ramifications of his organisations grew, and particularly with the impact of the Workers' International Relief and the League against Imperialism, the interest of Western secret services increased accordingly. There are substantial files on him compiled by the French, Swiss, United Kingdom (UK), and US secret services.

The UK government archive contains a whole swathe of documents that relate directly to Münzenberg and his activities. Two comprehensive files are dedicated to Münzenberg alone, but those on his close colleagues, Otto Katz and Louis Gibarti, as well as Harry Pollitt, the then general secretary of the Communist Party of Great Britain, also cover Münzenberg's activities.

While these files don't throw a great deal of light on Münzenberg as an individual, they do reveal how seriously he and his activities were viewed by the British Secret Intelligence Services and indeed governments and the Labour Party. Below are a number of examples taken from the files, which give a sense of what the authorities were particularly concerned about, and about what measures they, as well as the Labour Party, took to counter Münzenberg's work.[1]

The files concerned solely with Willi Münzenberg are titled MUNZENBERG, WILHELM and the documents are filed under: COUNTER-BOLSHEVISM.[2] There are also three large files devoted to Münzenberg's close comrade and collaborator, Otto Katz. From these, it is clear that from 1919 onwards, Münzenberg was a priority target for investigation and monitoring, and for this purpose, MI5/MI6 had agents in Berlin and other European cities who spied on him and monitored his activities. All correspondence between him and addressees in Britain was intercepted and copied. The government and secret services were particularly interested in his involvement with the League against Imperialism, but also in the International Workers' Relief (*IAH*).

In trying to keep tabs on Münzenberg and his organisations, the secret services did not recoil from spying on Britain's members of Parliament. They routinely intercepted letters from Lord Marley and the MP Ellen Wilkinson. SIS also asked its spies to keep tabs on Lord Marley when he sailed to Shanghai for a world anti-war conference in 1933. A letter from the novelist, Christopher Isherwood, to Gerald Hamilton in Paris was also intercepted by MI5 and is included in the files.[3]

Otto Katz was a high profile figure in Münzenberg's organisation, and it is difficult to believe that the Germans could not 'identify him positively' (as noted in a British Intelligence Service file) or that anyone with good contacts to the British Communist Party leadership would be unaware of who he was. He was a regular visitor to Britain and was in touch with the leading Communist and secretary of the British section of the Workers' International Relief (WIR)/*IAH*, Isabel Brown, as well as with the Labour MP, Ellen Wilkinson, and with the publisher, Victor Gollancz, among many others.

In the Otto Katz files,[4] there is a note that says: re. 'Otto Katz, alias "Rudolph". There is the strongest reason for supposing that this individual is in close and constant touch with WILLI MUNZENBERG (sic) of the Central Committee (sic) of the League Against Imperialism and W.I.R. "Rudolph" is also of great importance in the organisation...'

MI5's response to one request by Otto Katz for an entry visa for the UK was rather predictable: 'Otto Katz was about as bad a case as could be found. He was closely associated with Willi MUNZENBERG and in fact was being used as a cover for MUNZENBERG's correspondence, sent by Lord MARLEY and others from this country.'

The first two documents in Münzenberg's file, dated 14 September 1919, are copies of letters to the 'Representative de la Seine of the French Socialist Organisations of Young Men' concerning a possible invitation to an illegal congress of the International Socialist Youth Movement to take place in October. The letters are signed by Heilmann, Lazar Schatzkin, and W. Münzenberg.[5] There is also a report dated 31 December 1919 of the arrest of Willi Münzenberg in Stockholm.

The 1924/1925 files are made up largely of a chain of correspondence between departments of the security services dealing with the probability that Willi Münzenberg was planning to visit the United Kingdom for a conference. There is also correspondence between government departments about other attempts by Münzenberg to obtain a visa. The secret services recommended that 'he should not be granted an entry visa'. And this recommendation was clearly accepted by the governments of the day, as he was never granted a visa. In the 1930s, he was again trying to obtain a visa to enter Britain and a note in the file records his 'impending arrival in the UK', but whether he ever managed to set foot in Britain, perhaps using false documents, has never been ascertained.

Ironically, Münzenberg's closest collaborator, Otto Katz, was able to visit London regularly between 1933 and 1936, even though the secret services undertook concerted efforts to persuade the Home Office to deny him a visa. His excellent contacts with leading Labour Party figures like Lord Marley and Ellen Wilkinson MP ensured that enough pressure was brought to bear and he was allowed in time and again. His every visit, though, was closely monitored by Special Branch and MI5. He was granted a visa on the understanding that he would visit the country solely to raise funds for the Relief Committee for the Victims of German Fascism or, as a journalist, for work purposes.

MI5 followed closely the progress and expansion of the International League of Young Socialists, led by Münzenberg. In the files, there is a report of Münzenberg's arrest in Stockholm in December 1919. There are details of meetings of the 'Friends of Soviet Russia', with correspondence, reports, etc. Also, in the files, is a photo of his delegate's ID with a photo of 'Reichstag Abgeordnete Munzenberg' when he attended the second anti-imperialist world congress in Frankfurt (20 August 1929).

On 2 September 1929, an unnamed operative in MI5 wrote the following letter to the head of counter espionage, Valentine Vivian:

Dear V.V.

Willy Munzenberg, the well known Communist General Secretary of the Workers International Relief in Central Office, Berlin, and also prominent in the League against Imperialism, etc., etc., is to be in Berlin from the 5th to 12th September, during which period he will probably be visited by a British representative of the Workers International Relief. After that Munzenberg is going off on a journey which has been planned for some time, but the direction and purpose of which are not known to us. Do you think anything could be done to find out his movements?

This letter again reveals the lengths to which MI5 was prepared to go to keep him under close surveillance.

There is also a report marked SECRET and dated 2 March 1930

'Dear Robinson

I gather that the recent discussion to admit Willy MUNZENBERG, the well known German Communist, to this country, was given on the understanding that he would refrain from political activities while here ...

There is, further, definite proof of Münzenberg's intention to confer with Jack Leckie of the Workers International Relief organisation here regarding the latter's work, which will of course include the Atlas Film Company and the Federation of Workers Film Societies.'

The report also notes a recent circular from the Labour Party forbidding its members from belonging to the Workers International Relief organisation on the grounds that it is a subsidiary of the Communist Party.

This is followed by a lengthy report from Scotland Yard, dated 20 September 1929, on the 'Willy Münzenberg Concern' and includes diagrams (drawn like a web) with the names of all his political, businesses, and media organisations. It notes: 'There is no doubt that Münzenberg is at the centre of a spider's web of Communist activity in Germany.'

MI5 characterises him as a 'kind of Bottomley of the KPD'. (Horatio William Bottomley (1860–1933) was an English financier, journalist, editor, newspaper proprietor, swindler, and member of Parliament. He was editor of the popular magazine, *John Bull*. His career came to a sudden end in 1922, when he was convicted of fraud and sentenced to seven years imprisonment.)

According to the former Soviet intelligence advisor, Oleg Tsarev, and John Costello, MI6 reports obtained via the British-born Soviet agent, Donald Mclean, alerted the NKVD to the fact that by March 1937, British intelligence had succeeded in penetrating the entourage of Willi Münzenberg. 'This expatriate German Comintern leader was the architect of many of the

Communist "front" organisation including the League Against Imperialism, The Workers' International Trust [sic] and the World Committee for the Relief of the Victims of Fascism. Among the most successful "fronts" was the League Against Imperialism which, like others Münzenberg created, was part propaganda and part intelligence gathering. Such operations sprang up like red mushrooms after Münzenberg had been forced to leave Berlin in 1933'.[6]

Many of the photocopied letters and documents are concerned with the League against Imperialism and for National Liberation and Münzenberg's role within it. MI5 was clearly very worried about the role the League would/could play in undermining the British Empire. However, they were also concerned about the role of the *IAH* in carrying out solidarity and anti-war campaigns. The correspondence also tracks Katz's and Münzenberg's movements throughout Europe and contains potted biographies of the two as well as several photos.

MI5's concern about the role the League against Imperialism could play in fomenting unrest in the UK is particularly revealing. The letter below was sent to Sir E.W.E. Holderness at the Home Office:

> Evidence of the proposed transference of the International Secretariat of the League against Imperialism to London has been accumulating… We should view with apprehension the admission of this body of individuals, perhaps the most important, active and able group of Third International propagandists outside Russia. Its presence in London could not fail not only to stimulate the workings of communist united front organisations such as the Workers' International Relief, League against Imperialism and the Seamen's Minority Movement, but would also tend to the encouragement and improved organisation of the movement as a whole.

What is of particular concern is the evidence, as revealed in these files, that Britain's Secret Intelligence Services saw nothing ethically dubious in liaising with the Gestapo when seeking information about suspected Communists and Münzenberg collaborators. It also becomes apparent that they were more concerned with Comintern activities than the threat of Fascism even after Hitler came to power.[7] They also have little sympathy for German refugees from Hitler's Germany as revealed in a note from 25 September 1933, in which they deprecate the fact that the 'radical Socialist' Home Secretary in France is affording German refugees like Münzenberg 'a measure of protection on the plea that they are political refugees, and certainly with a desire to annoy Hitler'.

Even the mounting of the Legal Commission of Inquiry into the burning of the Reichstag in London alarms the secret services, despite the fact that such an inquiry could only help undermine the Nazi regime. In discussing the Inquiry, MI5 inexplicably suggests that 'it has done the communists more harm than good'. It would have liked to have prevented the legal inquiry taking place at all and would have preferred it if witnesses had been banned from attending, but this was a delicate issue for the government of the day.

MI5 was also preoccupied with the Brown Book, which detailed Nazi crimes, as if this were a dangerous and subversive publication! A Special Branch/MI5 report from 7 January 1933 is also of interest, in view of the various statements that have been made by British establishment figures that they had not been aware of Nazi atrocities at the time and given as a reason for government inaction. This report mentions 'gruesome tales coming out of the concentration camps' as detailed by Otto Katz when speaking at a German Relief meeting at Essex Hall in London.

As justification for the secret services attempts to keep any and all organisations and individuals connected with Münzenberg out of the UK, a note in the files mentions that Münzenberg's organisations have also been banned by the Labour Party and 'branded' as belonging to the 'Communist Solar System'.

Below are sample letters from the files to give an idea of the British government's/ Secret Intelligence Services concerns and attitudes:

No. 1

'19 Sept 1924

My Dear Pedder,
With reference to Home Office file 34647/2 in which the application is made by Mrs. Helen Crawford for the notorious Willy Munzenberg to visit this country, I attach information regarding the latter. You will see that he is particularly undesirable from every point of view. Even more so is the organisation which he represents [Workers International Relief]. ...
signed B.E.W.C.'

It was not only Münzenberg's organisations that gave the secret services a headache, but even his 'Worker Photographer' magazine was viewed as dangerous and subversive:

No. 2

'21 February 1930
From J.R. Clynes at the Home Office to the Foreign Secretary [Arthur Henderson].

Dear Foreign Secretary,
I have received a letter, of which I enclose a copy, from Mr. W.J. Brown, M.P., about Willi Muenzenberg, one of the Communist members of the Reichstag, who wishes to come to this country for a visit at the end of March or the beginning of April.

I enclose a secret memorandum ... setting out recent information about Muenzenberg's activities. He is without doubt one of the cleverest and most active of the Continental Communists and his position in the League against Imperialism gives him a particular interest now in view of events in India. It would save risk of embarrassment to the Government if this rather notorious character were not allowed to come to this country ...'[8]

In another letter (20 January 1930) from W.J. Brown to Clynes, he writes that Münzenberg had offered to give 'an undertaking to abstain from any kind of political propaganda while in Europe, if that is necessary'. He wished to visit Britain for 'business purposes'. Henderson responds that he has no view one way or the other re. Muenzenberg's proposed visit. In response Clynes writes, that 'I am satisfied, on the information he has afforded me, that Muenzenberg's contemplated visit would be used for political purposes (in connection with Colonial students at present in this country) contrary to the public interest'.[9]

No. 3

'From: Captain Miller
Scotland Yard
(marked "secret")

20 August 1930

I hereby authorize you to detain, open and produce for my inspection all postal packets and telegrams addressed to: – MUNZENBERG, Willi, Twerakaia Jemskaia 3, Moscow or to that name at any other address if there is reasonable ground to believe that they are intended for the said MUNZENBERG, Willi and for so doing this shall be sufficient warrant.
signed J. R. Clynes
One of His Majesty's Principal Secretaries of State.'

No. 4

letter from MI5, dated 19 July 1930

'...I attach for your information, a copy of a letter from Modern Books Limited to Nuer Deutcher Verlag (sic), Berlin. The Berlin firm, under the direction of Willi MUNZENBERG, was responsible for the issue of the special Indian number of "A.I.Z." You will see that unfortunately 3960 copies have succeeded in getting through. It is hoped, however, that some of them at any rate may be caught in the course of distribution here.
Yours sincerely,'

[This letter is followed by a copy of a letter from the Modern Bookshop complaining of problems with distribution of the magazine (probably as a result of MI5 interference) and various others about stopping distribution in India and elsewhere and detaining and destroying all possible copies.]

The publishing of the special *AIZ* magazine edition on India clearly exercised the British Secret Intelligence Services and government enormously, as evidenced from the numerous references to this in the Münzenberg files.

In another letter from an MI5 officer in the above connection it says:

> We understand that there is to be another special issue of A.I.Z. dealing with the life and struggles of the black race (sic). Copies are likely to be sent to King Street[Communist Party headquarters] and other addresses in this country. We should be glad if any of these could be held pending examination.

No. 5

> 'date: 15 August 1930
>
> Herewith, as received from our representative in Germany, two copies of "Der Arbeiter Fotograf" of which Willi MUNZENBERG is the responsible editor.
>
> For V.V.
> [copies of the *AIZ* are included in this file and an invoice for ordered copies from The Workers' Bookshop, CP HQ, King Street, London]

Who, one may wonder, was/were "our representative/s in Germany". Were they German police officers, anti-communist activists or even perhaps Nazis?'

No. 6

> 'Movements of Willi Munzenberg (sic)
>
> From:
> Captain Miller
> Scotland Yard
>
> date: 21 April 1931
>
> Reference your SZ/1918, dated 6.3.31. enclosing a letter from MUNZENBERG to BELLAMY of the W.I.R. [Workers' International Relief] in which he stated he would be absent from the Bureau from February 29th – March 20th:
>
> Our new source in Berlin reports that, on the 26th February MUNZENBERG presided over a public meeting in Berlin, which

protested against the arrest for illegal practices of Dr. Friedrich Wolf [the well-known German playwright]. During the first part of March, MUNZENBERG was in Breslau and, from there, went to Vienna and Munich. On the 13th March he was back in Berlin and met the Italian MIGIOLI … etc.

"for V.V." [Valentine Vivian, vice-chief of SIS or MI6 and first head of its counter-espionage unit]'

There is also a single reference to a former Austrian, with the name of Ernst Adam (aliases Mikulas BEDVEA, Mikulas BEDAM, Nickolas ADAM, Nickolas BEDAM), who apparently worked for Münzenberg in Paris:

Ernst Adam
'From 1933, Adam's political views caused him to leave Germany. He went to Paris where he worked as a journalist until 1936, when he went to Spain. During the Civil War he served first as a captain in the Republican Army and later became adjutant to General Kleber …
From 1938 to 1940 he was again in Paris as a journalist and working for Willy MUENZENBERG's Freedom Station [this probably refers to the German Communist Party's *Freiheitsender 29.8*] which broadcast from there …'[10]

The files also contain copies of correspondence between Harry Pollitt, General Secretary of the CPGB, and Münzenberg. They demonstrate that Münzenberg and Pollitt were in regular communication.

They reveal that Pollitt was in Brussels, on 9 February 1927, for a 'League of Oppressed Peoples' conference. This refers undoubtedly to the founding congress of the League against Imperialism (referred to above), which was established on Münzenberg's initiative and of which he became its general secretary. Pollitt became a member of the British section of the League. He was also a delegate to the League's congress in Berlin (30 May–2 June 1931). In October 1931, he was again in Berlin for the world congress of Münzenberg's Workers' International Relief and was elected chair of its international committee. So he would have met and held conversations with Münzenberg on each of such occasions.

One document in the files refers to Münzenberg wiring £150 to cover Harry Pollitt's deposit when standing as a parliamentary candidate. Pollitt wired back to Münzenberg on 13 October 1932 as follows: 'Reply your wire election deposit £150 is serious difficulty stop Can you help'. [It was undoubtedly illegal to accept monies from foreign sources during elections and if such a donation were to be made public, it would have been seriously embarrassing to the British Communist Party].

Münzenberg also offered his support when a campaign was being organised to obtain the release of Pollitt and Tom Mann after they had been arrested in 1932 for holding 'seditious' meetings attacking the national government and in support of the hunger marches.

A letter from Louis Giberti,[11] secretary of the League against Imperialism from Berlin, dated 16 December 1931, also offers *IAH/*WIR support for a large textile strike taking place in Lancashire in 1932:

> Dear Cde Pollitt
> From the British press we learn that the situation in connection with the Lancashire conflict is getting sharper daily. We would like to bring in the W.I.R. [Workers' International Relief i.e. *IAH*] from the very beginning into the preparation of this very important mass struggle in which the minority movement[12] will again have to perform the function of a revolutionary leadership in the masses of the textile proletariat ...This activity would immediately activate the W.I.R. in this region and the propaganda for this coming strike could be raised first nationally and internationally...

These and other documents intercepted and filed by MI5 do reveal a very close relationship, not only between Pollitt and Münzenberg, but between national Communist parties, like the CPGB and the Comintern, but it is difficult to see these links as posing a serious threat to national security in the UK.

With the suppression and collapse of the revolutionary movement in Germany in the latter half of the 1920s and little prospect of Socialist revolutions elsewhere in the immediate future, Stalin had rejected Trotsky's concept of world revolution and decided to attempt to build Socialism in one country. The result of this changed policy was that the world Communist movement became very much a means of defending the Soviet Union rather than for fomenting world revolution. Virtually all Stalin's activities on the global stage were focussed on that aim. Thus, clandestine activity, including espionage and intelligence gathering were not, in the first instance, aimed at undermining the countries targeted, but in protecting Soviet interests. However, this policy change appeared to have little influence on the activities of the British Secret Intelligence Services or on the attitude of the Labour Party leadership.

While Münzenberg made no secret of the fact that he was working on behalf of the Comintern – and this was common knowledge in political circles, he was still treated as a dangerous agent.

So much about his activities and those of his organisations could have been gleaned by straightforward monitoring and by collecting publicly available information. However, espionage organisations have to justify their budgets and staffing levels, and thus the importance/danger of enemies and supposed enemies have to be inflated and their 'clandestine' activities investigated. So much of the information collected by spies and undercover agents could be obtained by any curious outsider or good journalist.

From examining the voluminous documentation amassed by the secret services on Münzenberg and Katz during the 1920s and 1930s, it appears that the security services were unable to find a shred of evidence that either of them undertook any espionage work against the UK or damaged the country in any way. The activity of both men seems to have been solely concerned with liaising with supporters of the Workers' Relief organisation, the League against Imperialism, the World Committee Against War and Fascism, and the World Committee for the Victims of German Fascism, all laudable undertakings one would have assumed. But the association of these organisations with the Comintern was enough to make them toxic and have them placed on the 'most dangerous' list.

The many hours and the costs involved in tracking Münzenberg's and Katz's every move and the opening of all their correspondence to and from the UK, certainly had little or no impact on their activities or their effectiveness. Ironically, despite MI5's rigorous efforts, the real Soviet agents operating in Britain were, with one or two minor exceptions, never brought to book.

It was not, though, only MI5 that was interested in Münzenberg and Communist organisations. The Labour Party also showed an obsessional interest. In a file relating to the Austrian, Kurt Neumann, who had been sent by the *Comité mondial contre la guerre et le fascism* (World Committee against War and Fascism) to London to win Labour Party support, there is a comprehensive list of suspected Communist-dominated organisations.

William Gillies, the first international secretary of the Labour Party, compiled a comprehensive list of what he viewed as Communist or Communist 'ancillary' organisations, and the Labour Party published a booklet on them, called '*The Communist Solar System*'.

This booklet was published by the Labour Party in September 1933 and includes a comprehensive attack on the Communist International, whose aim is, it says in its opening chapter, 'to organise an armed struggle for the overthrow of the international bourgeoisie and the establishment of an international Soviet Republic as a transition to the complete abolition of the Capitalist State' (quoted, it states, from the Statutes and Constitution of the Communist International, although the constitution does not say anything about an armed struggle[13]).

It aims its heavy guns, though, at Münzenberg, and his various organisations in particular, presenting him as the demonic *deus ex machina* of international Communism. 'The true inventor of the "sympathising mass organisations"', the booklet says, 'is the German Communist, Mr. Willi Muenzenberg, formerly of Berlin, now Paris. In Berlin, they were known as "Muenzenberg Shows". He is the versatile author and producer of every piece. He chooses the titles. He is the unseen prompter, stage manager and scene shifter. The Workers' International Relief was his first and greatest success ...'.

The author goes on again to misquote the German Federation of Trade Unions' report which alleged that it was Münzenberg who coined the term 'Innocents' Clubs', set up to entrap the unwary (quoted from Dr F. Adler and supposedly taken from Workers' International Relief minutes). The term in the original German refers to the 'Harmlosen', which translates as the harmless, not the 'innocents'.

There are separate sections dealing with the Workers' International Relief, the League against Imperialism, and the Relief Committee for the Victims of German Fascism, among other prominent organisations, together with the names of their chief organisers in Britain.

The brochure concludes with words that could have been taken from a cheap spy novel: 'But the influences of the Communist Party are not radiated by the light of day or through the illuminated obscurity of the night (sic). With the exception of a few leaders, it is not known who are the members of the Communist Party of Great Britain. It is a secret society'.

Appended is a long list of organisations that are ineligible for affiliation to the Labour Party [also applying to individual members].

A note to these files on the government archive website says:

> re. '"Ancillary Organisations of the Communist International".
> This collection should be called "alleged ancillary organisations of the Communist International", since many (if not most) of the organisations concerned in this collection had little, if any, contact with the Communist party, let alone the Kremlin. William Gillies (1885–1958), the Labour Party International Secretary from 1920 to 1944, set about finding out which political organisations had Communist financial backing or Communist members and any one which did (and Communist member meant any known Communist who had attended a meeting) immediately came under suspicion (sic). It did not only include British organisations, but International ones, where Gillies suspected the hand of Wilhelm Munzenberg (sic) starting the World revolution through anti-Fascist movements. The result was that virtually all the anti-Fascist and many Peace and Unemployment movements were made ineligible (sic) for affiliation to the Labour Party and Party members were discouraged from associating with them.
>
> The accumulation of Gillies' labours was a booklet published called "*The Communist Solar System*" – describing in his view–the infiltration by the Communist International into radical organisations. Although it was published in 1933 – the year the Labour Party's proscribed (sic) list was first brought out, Gillies continued his ferreting until the Second World War and even then did not stop it.'[14]

In the Labour Party archive, there is a letter dated 9 January 1936, from William Gillies, its international secretary, to James Middleton, the Labour Party general secretary that refers to Dr Kurt Neumann. It is in response to a meeting that Neumann had with Clement Attlee about the idea 'of constituting a Committee for dealing with the suffering through the Italo-Abyssinian War'. Gillies goes on to say that any action should be taken through the League of Nations Union.

He undertook further investigations into the person of Kurt Neumann, along with the Paris-based Association of International Jurists, which provided expenses for his trip to London. This Association is also, 'I am certain, a well-known Muenzenberg organisation', Gillies writes. He goes on, 'Neumann is a penniless Austrian Social Democrat who has, therefore, appeared in London on three different mission (sic): to organise the British representation to an Inter-Parliamentary Conference in Brussels; to arrange the visit of two British MPs to Austria; and to create a Committee for dealing with the sufferers from the Italo-Abyssinian War. These are entirely unrelated matters. I am convinced that the connecting link is Muenzenberg'.

It appears from a second letter from Gillies to Middleton, dated 10 January, that Neumann attended the Labour Party conference that year in Brighton, 'when he claimed to represent the Front Populaire ... Dr. Neumann had therefore appeared in London in connection with four different missions. There is no longer any doubt in my mind,' he concludes, 'that he is a representative of the Muenzenberg organisations'.[15]

It is perhaps rather surprising in the face of Mussolini's invasion of Abyssinia and his brutal subjugation of its people, and the inexorable rise of Hitler Fascism in Germany, that the Labour Party's international secretary should be overly concerned about Neumann's connections with Münzenberg and his organisations. The singling out of Münzenberg by both the Labour Party and the secret services underlines the key role he played during this period.

Notes

1 KV2/772 covers the years 1924/1925; KV2–773_1 and 773_2 (titled: MUNZENBERG, WILHELM) cover the years 1930/1931.
2 KV2-773_1; 773_2; 772_2.
3 KV2 -1382 (memo dated 21 December 1933).
4 British Government Secret Services Archives, File KV2-1382.
5 KV 2 722-1.
6 Tsarev, Oleg and Costello, John Edmond, *Deadly Illusions*, Century 1993. pp. 204/205.
7 Note from the head of MI5, V. Vivian, dated 20 July 1933: 'I wonder if it has been possible to obtain anything from the Germans on the lines suggested ...' (This note was made after Hitler had become German chancellor and indicates that MI5 is co-operating with the Gestapo in asking for information on suspected communists).

    Also on 25 May 1933, a note to V.V. (head of MI5) 'as regards other people mentioned in your report, I think it would be interesting to have any information that the Germans could give us about: 8 names mentioned including Babette Grosse(sic) ... photographs and handwriting, in addition'.
8 On 26 January, the Indian National Congress had declared this day as Independence Day. On 2 March, Gandhi informed the British Viceroy of India that civil disobedience would begin. On 12 March, Gandhi set off on a 200-mile protest march to protest about the British monopoly on salt.
9 'British Government Archives. File No. FO 800.281'.
10 Government Archives KV-2-2193–12.

11 https://www.cia.gov/library/readingroom/docs/DOC_0005632259.pdf.
This is a link to a copy of a CIA memorandum, marked 'secret'. Subject: Ladislas DOBOS alias Louis GIBARTI alias Ladislas DOVOSGAS, which was approved for release on 12 April 2011. Although it concerns Gibarti, it refers on his close association with Münzenberg.

12 The National Minority Movement was set up by the CPGB in 1924 to organise a radical presence within the existing trade unions. It was headed by Tom Mann and Harry Pollitt.

13 The correct quotation from the constitution of the Communist International is: 'The ultimate aim of the Communist International is to replace world capitalist economy by a world system of Communism. Communist society, the basis for which has been prepared by the whole course of historical development, is mankind's only way out, for it alone can abolish the contradictions of the capitalist system which threaten to degrade and destroy the human race'.

14 Labour Party Archive held at People's History Museum, Manchester. File: LP/ID/CI/72/2-4 Title: Notes Gillies to Middleton re Kurt Neumann. Date 1936 January 9th and 10th.

15 Labour Party Archive held at the People's History Museum, Manchester. File: LP/ID/CI/72/2.

16

SUMMING UP MÜNZENBERG'S HISTORICAL CONTRIBUTION

Willi Münzenberg is one of those unfortunate historical figures who was not only hated by his enemies, but eventually reviled by his erstwhile friends, with the result that his name and his achievements have been largely forgotten or airbrushed from the historical record. What little has been written about him has done more to blur and distort his historical contribution than to clarify who he really was and what he actually achieved. What is undisputable is that he was a committed Socialist all his life, a vehement anti-militarist, and anti-Fascist.

More than almost anyone else in the Communist movement during the inter-war years, he embodied the principle of internationalism and inspired many others to embrace the idea of international solidarity. In terms of his global impact, Münzenberg was one of the most capable political figures to emerge from the Communist movement during the twentieth century and became one of the most effective organisers and propagandists for the cause of Communism and in defence of the Soviet Union.

Münzenberg's detractors have invariably described him as a cynical operator, a devious propagandist whose strings were pulled by Moscow, and as someone who lured innocents into working for the Communist cause.[1] In fact, Münzenberg made no attempt to hide who he was, who he worked for, or what he did. Those who had anything to do with him were fully cognisant of this aspect. He was also someone who continually found himself swimming against the current of official thinking, bureaucracy, and sectarianism, but this didn't break his faith in Soviet Communism.

His subsequent eclipse in the West is also undoubtedly associated with his life-long commitment to a Soviet Union that had become Stalin's plaything, and he appeared to be unshaken despite the mounting evidence of Stalin's crimes. His break with Stalin came very late in his career, only shortly before his death. Unlike a number of other former Bolsheviks and committed Communists who had become disillusioned with Stalin's Soviet Union much earlier, and expressed it clearly, Münzenberg clung to his belief until his position was made untenable by his almost total marginalisation and vilification by his erstwhile comrades. He went along with Stalin's demonisation of Trotsky, despite his friendship and respect for Trotsky, and never gave any indication of wishing to join Trotsky and his followers in exposing Stalin's crimes. Despite these shortcomings, though, his contribution in so many areas to the struggle for Socialism, against war and Fascism, should be recognised.

If we look only at the key moments of his role in the global solidarity movement of the years between the two world wars, we can see that he was inspired by a genuine internationalism. He was a key organiser of the Socialist Youth International, which became the largest European-wide anti-war movement in the run-up to and during the First World War.

He was instrumental in establishing the largest left-wing media empire outside the Soviet Union and pioneered the use of photography and photomontage in his journals, encouraging leading artists and writers to contribute. A vibrant left-wing working-class culture in Germany was promoted and boosted by his work.

As a film distributor and promoter, he brought modern Soviet films to Western Europe. As a publicist and manager, he built up the most influential left-wing media empire in the Weimar Republic, and he was a long-time member of the Reichstag. He became the most effective opponent of Hitler and Goebbels' propaganda machine, exposing the venality and brutality of the Nazi regime.

During the 1920s, he co-ordinated an international famine relief campaign to aid the struggling young Soviet Union, and out of that was born the International Workers Relief organisation which had branches in many countries – a forerunner of the myriad global aid organisations and NGOs, which mushroomed after the Second World War.

Arguably, the creation of the *Internationale Arbeiterhilfe* (*IAH* or International Workers Relief) became Münzenberg's greatest achievement. Although this has been stigmatised by some commentators as merely a tool of Moscow and a 'Communist front organisation', such descriptions only serve to obfuscate its real significance. Kasper Braskén, in his book on the *IAH*, argues convincingly that although Münzenberg's aim was to revolutionise society, he was also concerned about giving practical assistance to those engaged in struggle.

The initial launch of the *IAH* was not, as has often been implied, the result of a well prepared propaganda campaign, but in response to a desperate call for solidarity with a famine-hit Soviet Russia, in response to a humanitarian crisis. Münzenberg, virtually single-handedly, built it into an effective solidarity and propaganda organisation, setting the parameters for the many solidarity organisations and NGOs that were to follow. Significantly, seen from today's context, he also changed the perception of aid from a charitable one motivated largely by pity for the weak and helpless, into one of solidarity and of positive action by his skilful use of images and words. As Fredrik Petersson writes, 'Münzenberg lived in a milieu profoundly influenced by the political context of the Weimar Republic, and this shaped his development as a propagandist'.[2]

Although the *IAH* was officially blacklisted by the German Social Democratic Party, as well as the British Labour Party, both of whom forbade official affiliation or collaboration with it, Münzenberg still managed to turn it into a global organisation that bridged state and party lines.

The concluding words in Braskén's study of the *IAH* are a fitting comment on its significance: 'The often still hidden history of international organisations such as the *Arbeiterhilfe* and their radical articulations and counter-cultures of transnational communities and solidarities need to be reintroduced into history to understand the development and formation of the entangled, interconnected and globalised world of today'.[3]

Münzenberg was the initiator of the League against Colonialism and for National Independence, which represented the first attempt to create a united global response to colonial and national liberation. The establishment of the League is arguably his second most significant achievement.

Einstein, in his greetings to the first congress of the League in Brussels in 1927, wrote to say that the historical dominance of those few white nations over the much more numerous non-white ones had to be ended. He told Münzenberg, 'I am convinced that the success of the task you have taken up will be for the good of all those who take human dignity to heart'.

Describing Münzenberg's League against Colonialism simply as 'a tool of Moscow', as many writers have done, is to be blind to its genuine and effective role in rallying anti-colonial and anti-imperialist forces and accelerating the eventual liberation of oppressed nations worldwide in the wake of the Second World War.

In 1955, at the first Bandung conference, held to establish a stronger voice for the Asian and African peoples, President Sukarno of Indonesia, in his opening address, paid tribute to Münzenberg's League, saying: 'I recall in this connection the Conference of the "League Against Imperialism and Colonialism" which was held in Brussels almost thirty years ago. At that Conference many distinguished delegates who are present here today met each other and found new strength in their fight for independence'.[4]

Münzenberg, through his key operations in Paris during the 1930s, became one of the most prominent and effective opponents of the Nazis, exposing their brutality, racism, and aggressive warrior mentality. He was indefatigable in his desperate attempts to hinder the relentless drive to war in Europe. And even if his efforts were, in the end, unsuccessful, his courageous attempt to halt the rise of Fascism and the outbreak of war deserves recognition.

Towards the end of his life, he broke with Stalin's hegemonic hijacking of the world Communist movement, only to pay the price. He has been air-brushed out of official Communist histories and largely ignored by Western historians.

He had been a personal friend and student of Lenin's and experienced first-hand the Bolshevik Revolution and its repercussions throughout Europe. During the inter-war years, his name was known to everyone on the political left. He was a founding member of the German Communist Party and remained a member until his break with Stalin shortly before his mysterious death in 1940.

His devotion to that cause did not prevent the movement and the comrades to whom he had felt absolute loyalty dropping him like a scalding pan once he fell out of favour with those in power, and they vilified him shamelessly, even blaming him for their own mistakes and incompetence.

His life story is one of devotion, idealism, and heroism that, in the end, was shattered on the reefs thrown up by the cynics, the opportunists, the wilfully blind, the self-righteous, envious, and devout adherents of the same cause that he espoused, as well on the formidable crags thrown up by those he saw as his chief enemy: the Fascists.

It is a life that reflected the hopes of the world's oppressed at the time and how they were given a new impetus by the Bolshevik Revolution, only for those aspirations to become distorted and manipulated, engendering a dystopian form of Socialism in the Soviet Union and, post-war, in Eastern Europe. The Soviet Union was allowed to impose a centralised control over the international Communist movement with fatal consequences.

That era, from the beginning of the twentieth century until almost its close, was characterised by extreme polarisation: capitalism felt mortally threatened by the rise of Communism and the world became divided between two opposing and implacable camps: you were either 'with us or against us'. On the Communist side there was much idealism, but also fanaticism. Those actively involved in fighting the cause of Communism felt that the world was on the cusp of a profound revolution that would bring about justice, an end to capitalist exploitation, racism, and colonial oppression, and they invariably felt that with only a little more effort they would help bring about the yearned for revolution. Thus, any criticism of the party or expression of difference was seen as hindering that revolution.

There was also little tolerance of those with divergent views or for those seen as renegades or apostates. Münzenberg lived through those times and actively participated, he experienced the turbulence, flux, and euphoria, the sectarianism, intolerance, and the blinkered visions, but he never lost his integrity or his vision of a better world.

Many ask, though, how it was possible for an individual like Münzenberg to continue to support the Soviet Union in the face of Stalin's crimes. The context of the times goes someway to help explain this phenomenon. The very survival of the Soviet Union and its fate was seen by all Communists as indissolubly linked with the struggle and eventual success of Socialism globally. That is largely why Communists felt such loyalty and devotion to the Soviet Union even when it was becoming increasingly clear that under Stalin's leadership, the dream was being transformed for many into a nightmare. They were reluctant to accept that everything they had fought for was being corroded from inside.

The overwhelming number of people who became Communists, particularly during the 1920s and 1930s, were motivated primarily by a profound belief in the betterment of humanity and particularly by the perceived need to confront Fascism in Europe. Most were, like Münzenberg, enthused with the idea of changing society for the better, imbued with a strong sense of solidarity and justice, not unlike the many Christians who have been similarly motivated throughout history.

These individuals had an implicit belief in the individual as an integral part of society and believed that we should not stand outside or on the margins doing little or nothing to help our fellow human beings. For those not part of the movement, such motivations and actions consequent upon them may be considered naïve or inane, but that is hardly a useful basis for evaluating the lives of those who became Communists.

Most of those who joined the Communist movement in that period did so for one of two reasons or a combination of both, even if those reasons were often complex and individually diverse. There were those who were attracted primarily by the concept of an all-encompassing ideology which, together with the necessary discipline and loyalty that being a member of a Communist party demanded, provided them with a philosophical framework for their lives, and secondly, those who were enthused primarily by the utopian idea of a universal Socialist fraternity. All those who became Communists found their raison d'être and fulfilment in the struggle itself. And Willi Münzenberg's life has to be seen in that light.

As Uwe Sonnenberg writes of Münzenberg and his generation:

> ...from their example we are able to experience the continuity: the ideas, ideals and hopes, that were born with the Second International, and which were firstly picked up again in the Youth International and, in a certain sense, represented there in their most sincere form. In full sympathy with these, they took them further, through and beyond the epochal rupture. In this way, the Youth International bridged the eras. This is the impression left in those who read *Die Dritte Front* (The Third Front).[5]

Münzenberg was a recognised expert in the field of propaganda, not as may be assumed, as a cynical manipulator of opinion, but as someone who fully understood that while propaganda can be misused by the unscrupulous, it can also be employed in a positive way, in helping people become aware of issues that have been hidden or ignored by mainstream communications. His seminal book, *Propaganda as Weapon*, is a scalpel-like dissection of Hitler's use of propaganda in the service of an inhuman ideology.

He was very aware of how propaganda could be misused; he was no cynic. As he writes in his book on the subject, anyone who uses propaganda for nefarious purposes will find themselves scoring an 'own goal'. He argued, in 1937, that Hitler's propaganda must, with time, become a weapon against National Socialism itself. The incessant repetition of lies, he argued, will be turned against them as soon as the truth breaks through.

He has been called a 'genius of political warfare',[6] and many, particularly US scholars, have seen his role in a similar light. Called by Sean McMeekin the 'Godfather' of 'front organisations' and 'Moscow's secret propaganda Tsar in the West'.

However, the propaganda he carried out is worlds apart from that perfected and misused by Hitler. He may have seen the Soviet Union at times through rose-coloured spectacles, but his aim in promoting the Soviet Union was not to disseminate lies or to deliberately distort, unlike Hitler's conscious manipulation of truth and reality.

The tendentiousness of both Stephen Koch's and McMeekin's biographies is underlined by Babette Gross's son Peter in his own booklet of reminiscences about Willi Münzenberg.[7]

Historically, the German Communist Party was born from the womb of the Bolshevik Revolution in Russia. The links that Lenin and other early Bolsheviks forged with German Socialism, from the early theoreticians, Marx and Engels, through August Bebel and Karl Kautsky to Rosa Luxemburg and Karl Liebknecht, helped cement a strong relationship between the two countries – Russia and Germany – as well as between individuals in the Communist movement of both countries. Not only had Lenin and his comrades engineered a successful revolution, by bringing about the collapse of a feudal empire and creating the foundations for a Socialist industrial state, but many of those early Russian Bolsheviks also had profound knowledge and experience of the struggle in a number of European countries. The young German Communist Party looked to them as their gurus and leaders. And, despite Rosa Luxemburg's warnings, followed their example almost to the letter.

Despite the fact that during the early part of the twentieth century the German Communist Party would become the largest and most influential in the world behind the Soviet Party, it behaved and was treated by the Soviet leaders as an offshoot of their own party. This state of affairs would have disastrous consequences, particularly once Stalin had taken full control of the Soviet Party. His paranoid and suspicious nature, his conspiratorial mindset and extreme parochialism – for him, the first objective of the world Communist movement was to defend the Soviet Union, above all else – would infect the German Communist Party disastrously.

Münzenberg, for all his idealism and the excellent work he carried out on the international stage, cannot be wholly excused from culpability. He was, after all, a willing participant over many years in that all-encompassing apparatus, with its network of spies, its clandestine working methods, its military-style organisational structures, and its ruthlessness.

He had devoted his whole life to defending the Soviet Union, campaigning on behalf of the Communist Party and in fighting Fascism. To cut the umbilical cord binding him to that tradition, to the comrades who had stood alongside him, and to the ideas that motivated him was traumatic.

It is pointless now to speculate what role the German Communist Party could have played on the world stage had Rosa Luxemburg's warnings about the dangers of a party dictatorship been heeded and if the German Party had taken a more autonomous road. It would, however, almost certainly have had positive resonances and history may well have turned out very differently.

Today, we face different demons to those that Willi Münzenberg had to face, but there are parallels. Right-wing and racist groups are again rising from the swamps and, like the Pied Piper of Hamelin, seducing a new generation of gullible followers. We still have wars, dictators, political assassinations, and nefarious propaganda conducted by cynical politicians. In facing such challenges, Münzenberg's life story can offer inspiration.

For many, though, the life and work of Willi Münzenberg can still offer inspiration and historical insight, but also salutary reminders of how idealism can easily become a dogma and how sectarianism can undermine unity and effectiveness. Faced with a world in which an elite comprising 1 per cent of the global population owns more wealth than the other 99 per cent, and with a rise in right-wing autocracies, intolerance, and discrimination, the ideas and organisations that Münzenberg pioneered are as relevant now as they were in his own day, just as the lessons are that we need to learn from his life.

Notes

1 Among his chief detractors are Sean McMeekin and Stephen Koch, who have both written biographies of him: *The Red Millionaire: A Political Biography of Willi Münzenberg*, and *Double Lives: Stalin, Willi Münzenberg and the Seduction of the Intellectuals*, respectively. Both are too marred by Cold War prejudice and their authors' visceral hatred of communism to be considered definitive accounts.

The biographies written by these two US authors depict the Bolshevik Revolution and the whole Communist project as inherently inimical to Western democracy, and the actions of Communists themselves, it is implied, could only have been motivated by cynicism, callousness, and deviousness. Such a simplistic portrayal makes their narratives suspect and certainly tendentious.

The biography by Münzenberg's widow, Babette Gross, is probably the most accurate and credible biography to date – after all she was at his side for much of his adult life – and it is not distorted by such deep-seated Cold War ideology, although her version also has to be seen in the light of her own disillusionment with Communism and her conviction that Münzenberg was betrayed by the movement to which he devoted his life.

Unfortunately, her biography tends to very much adhere to the chronology of events that shaped his life and, despite her intimate relationship with him, she reveals very little of conversations she or others had with him, of what must have been going through his mind at various junctures, or about his most intimate friends. Above all, she was intent on rehabilitating his reputation and her biography has to be seen in that light.

The British writer, Jonathan Miles, has written a biography of Otto Katz, Münzenberg's long-time comrade and collaborator, *The Nine Lives of Otto Katz*, which also includes much on Münzenberg, and his biography is well-researched and informative. He places the various stages of Katz's life in their historical context. But while the narrative skeleton is there, Miles chooses to embellish his text, by using a thriller writer's vivid imagination, thus mixing fact with wild speculation and spurious psychological insights. His biography is a thrilling, page-turner, but he forgets that he's not supposed to be writing a novel.

He, like McMeekin and Koch before him, can't envisage Communists as individuals genuinely motivated by idealism and a desire for a more just world, even if, like anyone else, they have their failings and weaknesses. Katz and Münzenberg are here again portrayed as cold and cynical, unscrupulously manipulative, incorporating the most fiendish attitudes. Despite the numerous individuals who admired and were captivated by them, and the fact that they had highly cultured backgrounds, with a keen interest in literature, theatre, and music, they are portrayed as robotic and blinkered servants of Stalin, concerned only to ensnare as many unsuspecting individuals as they could to spy for the Soviet Union.

2 Petersson, Fredrik: 'In Control of Solidarity? Willi Münzenberg, the Workers' International Relief and League against Imperialism, 1921–1935,' Comintern Working Paper 8, Åbo Akademy University, 2007.
3 Braskén, Kasper, *The International Workers' Relief, Communism, and Transnational Solidarity: Willi Münzenberg in Weimar Germany*, Palgrave MacMillan, UK. 2015. p. 240.
4 https://www.cvce.eu/en/obj/opening_address_given_by_sukarno_bandung_18_april_1955-en-88d3f71c-c9f9-415a-b397-b27b8581a4f5.html.
5 'Die dritte Front. Willi Münzenberg und die Jugendinternationale', a written version of the paper presented to the Linke Party executive and the Historical Commission, 'Epochenbruch 1914–1923. Krieg, Frieden, soziale Revolution' on 24. February 2018.
6 Morris, Bernard S. Communist International Front Organisations. *Their Nature and Function; World Politics* 9:11, Cambridge University Press: 18 July 2011.
7 Gross, Peter, *Willi Münzenberg – A Memory*, Catherine Gross, Kendal NSW, Australia, 2007.

SELECT BIBLIOGRAPHY

Badia, Gilbert, 'Vom orthodoxen Kommunisten zu Rebellen. Ein Abriss der politischen Laufbahn Willi Münzenbergs' in Schlie, Tania, Roche, Simone (eds.): *Willi Münzenberg. 1889–1940. Ein deutscher Kommunist im Spannungsfeld zwischen Stalinismus und Antifaschismus*, Frankfurt am Main, Peter Lang, 1995.

Bayerlein, Bernard H., 'The Entangled Catastrophe: Hitler's 1933 "Seizure of Power" and the Power Triangle – New Evidence on the Historic Failure of the KPD, the Comintern and the Soviet Union,' in *Weimar Communism as a Mass Movement 1918–1933* eds. Ralf Hoffrogge and Norman Laporte, Lawrence and Wishart 2017.

Bollinger, Stefan, *November'18 – als die revolution nach Deutschland kam*, ed. ost, Berlin, Germany, 2018.

Braskén, Kasper, *The International Workers' Relief, Communism, and Transnational Solidarity. Willi Münzenberg in Weimar Germany*, Palgrave Macmillan, 2015.

Buber-Neumann, Margarete, *Under Two Dictators – Prisoner of Stalin and Hitler, the Reminiscences of Margarete Buber-Neumann*, Pimlico Press, London, 2009.

Carter Hett, Benjamin, *Burning the Reichstag: An Investigation into the Third Reich's Enduring Mystery*, Berlin, Germany, 2014.

Dugrand, Alain and Laurent, Frédéric, *Willi Münzenberg: Artiste en révolution (1889–1940)*, Fayard, London, 2008.

Christopher, Andrew and Gordievsky, Oleg, *KGB: The Inside Story of Its Foreign Operations from Lenin to Gorbachev*, London: Hodder & Stoughton, 1990.

Ellison, John, 'The League Against Imperialism – The Hidden History of the British Section' (The Communist Party's Our History series), Berlin, Germany, 2018.

Fischer, Ruth, *Stalin und die Deutsche Kommunismus* (2 volumes), Dietz Verlag, London, 1991.

Fischer, Ruth, *Stalin and German Communism: A Study in the Origins of the State Party* (Social Science Classics), Routledge, London, 2017.

Geschonneck, Erwin, *Meine Unruhigen Jahre*, Aufbau Taschenbuch Verlag, London, 1993.

Gibarti, Luis (reminiscences, published in 1971 in Britain under the title) *Shipwreck of a Generation* and in the United States as *Nothing but the Truth: Joseph Stalin's Prison Camps: A Survivor's Account of the Victim's He Knew.*

Green, John, *A Political Family; The Kuczynskis, Fascism, Espionage and the Cold War*, Routledge, London, 2017.

Gross, Babette, (translated by Marian Jackson), *Willi Münzenberg: A Political Biography*, Michigan State University Press, 1974.

Gross, Peter, *Willi Münzenberg – A Memory*, Catherine Gross, NSW, Australia, 2007.

Haffner, Sebastian, *Die verratene Revolution, Deutschland 1918/1919*, Berne, Munich and Vienna, 1969.

Halbrainer, Heimo, '*Von Judenburg nach Hollywood Kurt Neumann (1902–1984)*', Gratz, Austria, 2012.

Hartmann, Anne '*Willi Münzenberg, Lion Feuchtwanger und die Frage einer "Ästhetik des Widerstand"*' (Willi Münzenberg Striftung).

Hobsbawm, Eric, *The Age of Extremes: The Short Twentieth Century, 1914–1991*, Michael Joseph, London, 1994.

Janka, Walter, *Spuren eines Lebens*, Rowohlt, Berlin, Germany, 1991.

Kersten, Kurt, '*Das Ende WM. Ein Opfer Stalin's und Ulbrichts*'. In *Deutsche Rundschau* No. 5, 1957, pp. 488–499.

Kessler, Mario 'Die "Ulbricht-Verschwörung" gegen Münzenberg (1936–1938)'/'The "Ulbricht conspiracy" against Münzenberg (1936–1938)'.

Koch, Stephen, *Double Lives: Stalin, Willi Munzenberg and the Seduction of the Intellectuals*, Enigma Books, USA, 2004.

Koestler, Arthur, *The Invisible Writing. The Second Volume of an Autobiography: 1932–1940*. (1954) London: Vintage, 2005, pp. 250–259, 381–386.

Leo, Annette, '*Selbst Mord oder Mord? Der Umgang mit Leben und Tod von Willi Münzenberg in der DDR der achtziger Jahren*' (Willi Münzenberg Stiftung, Berllin).

Leonhard, Rudolf. '*In derselben Nacht: Das Traumbuch des Exils.*' (Steffen Mensching Ed.) Berlin: Aufbau, 2001.

Leyda, Jay, *Kino – A History of the Russian and Soviet Film*. Princeton University Press, 1960, p. 310.

Liebmann, Irene, *Wäre es schön? Es ware schön – Mein Vater Rudolf Herrnstadt*, Berliner Taschenbuch Verlag, 2009.

Louro, Michelle L. *Comrades against Imperialism: Nehru, India, and Interwar Internationalism.* Cambridge University Press, 2018.

Mauthner, Martin, *German Writers in French Exile, 1933–1940*. London: Vallentine and Mitchell, 2007.

McMeekin, Sean, *The Red Millionaire: A Political Biography of Willi Münzenberg, Moscow's Secret Propaganda Tsar in the West, 1917–1940*. New Haven, CT: Yale University Press, 2003.

Meyer-Leviné, Rosa, *Inside German Communism, Memoirs of Party Life in the Weimar Republic*, London: Pluto Press, 1977.

Müller, Gerhard, '*Warum schreiben Sie eigentlich nicht?*' Bernard von Brentano in seiner Korrespondenz mit Bertolt Brecht (1933–1940) Heft 2.

Münzenberg, Willi, *Der Dritte Front*, Schriftenreihe AdV, Verein der Funke, Switzerland, 2015.

Münzenberg, Willi, *Die sozialistischen Jugendorganisation vor und während des Krieges*, Junge Garde, Berlin, 1919.

Münzenberg, Willi, *Lebenslauf. Glashütte im Taunus*: Auvermann 1972 (facsimile of a 29 p. typewritten manuscript; Staatsarchiv Canton of Zurich).

Münzenberg, Willi, *Propaganda als Waffe*, Éditions du Carrefour, Paris, 1937.

Raßloff, Steffen, "Willi Münzenberg und Erfurt: Die Anfänge des roten Propaganda-Zaren." *Vereins für die Geschichte und Altertumskunde von Erfurt, 70. Heft*, Neue Folge, Heft 17, 2009, Artikel des Historikers Dr. Steffen Raßloff.

Schlie, Tania/Roche, Simone: Willi Münzenberg (1889–1940). Ein deutscher Kommunist im Spannungsfeld zwischen Stalinismus und Antifaschismus, Frankfurt/M., Berlin, 1995.

Petersson, Fredrik: 'In Control of Solidarity? Willi Münzenberg, the Workers' International Relief and League against Imperialism, 1921–1935,' Comintern Working Paper 8, Åbo Akademy University, Sweden, 2007.

Petersson, Fredrik, Willi Münzenberg: 'A Propagandist Reaching Beyond Party and Class' in *Weimar Communism as a Mass Movement 1918–1933*. eds. Åbo Akademy University, Sweden, 2017.

Petersson, Fredrik, *Willi Münzenberg, the League against Imperialism, and the Comintern*, 1925–1933, Queenston, Edwin Mellen Press, 2013.

Podljaschuk, Pawel, *Inessa*, Dietz Verlag, Berlin, 1987.

Stadtarchiv, Erfurt, 1440/1889 Birth certificate of Wilhelm Münzenberg.

Stadtarchiv Erfurt, 'Mitteilungen des Vereins für die Geschichte und Altertumskunde von Erfurt,' No. 70. Heft, Neue Folge, Heft 17, 2009 is an article by the historian Dr. Steffen Raßloff 'Willi Münzenberg und Erfurt: Die Anfänge des roten Propaganda-Zaren'.

Sternberg, Wilhelm von, *Lion Feuchtwanger – ein deutsches Schriftstellerleben*, Aufbau Taschenbuch Verlag, Berlin, Germany, 1999.

Tobias, Fritz, *The Reichstag Fire*. Arnold J. Pomerans, trans. New York: Putnam, 1963.

Volodarsky, Boris, *The Orlov KGB File: The Most Successful Espionage Deception of All Time*. New York: Enigma Books, 2009.

Wessel, Harald, *Münzenbergs Ende: Ein deutscher Kommunist im Widerstand gegen Hitler und Stalin: Die Jahre 1933 bis 1940*, Dietz Verlag, Berlin, 1991.

'Wilhelm Munzenberg, International Secretary YPSL', *The Young Socialists' Magazine*, vol. 12, No. 4, April 1918.

Willett, John, *The New Sobriety: Art and politics in the Weimar Period 1917–1933*, Da Capo Press, Boston, USA, 1996.

TV Programmes on Willi Münzenberg

Willi Münzenberg oder Die Kunst der Propaganda. Dokumentation, 62 Minuten, Germany, 1995, Dir: Alexander Bohr, Production: ZDF/ARTE; Shown on 26. September 1995 in ARTE.

Münzenberg – Der letzte Gang. Documentary film, 45 minutes, Germany, 1992, Dir: Hans-Dieter Rutsch, on behalf of WDR.

Propaganda als Waffe. Documentary, 45 minutes, Germany, 1982, Dir: Thomas Ammann, Jörg Gremmler, Matthias Lehnhardt, Gerd Roscher, Ulrike Schaz, Walter Uka, Production: WDR 1982, Producer: Ludwig Metzger.

Flucht – Der Fall Münzenberg. Drama, 90 minutes, Germany, 1971, TV-Production, Dir: Dieter Lemmel, with actors: Kurt Jaggberg, Günter Mack, Willi Semmelrogge.

INDEX

Note: Page numbers in italic refer to figures.
Page numbers followed by n refers to notes.

Printed in Great Britain
by Amazon

48076289R00170